Inflation, Disinflation, and Corporate Financial Decisions

Tamir Agmon
Tel Aviv University
University of Southern California

Reuven Horesh
The Management College, Tel Aviv

Lexington Books
D.C. Heath and Company/Lexington, Massachusetts/Toronto

1 0001 000 019 824

Library of Congress Cataloging-in-Publication Data

Agmon, Tamir.
  Inflation, disinflation, and corporate financial
decisions.

  Bibliography: p.
  Includes index.
  1. Corporations—Finance. 2. Accounting—Effect
of inflation on. 3. Industrial management—Effect
of inflation on. I. Horesh, Reuven. II. Title.
H64026.A36   1988   658.1'5   86–45062
ISBN 0–669–13060–5 (alk. paper)

Published simultaneously in Canada
Printed in the United States of America
International Standard Book Number: 0–669–13060–5

Library of Congress Catalog Card Number 86–45062

The paper used in this publication meets the minimum requirements of
American National Standard for Information Sciences—Permanence of
Paper for Printed Library Materials, ANSI Z39.48–1984. ∞™

88 89 90 91 92 8 7 6 5 4 3 2 1

To Ora and Varda

Contents

Figures and Tables

Figures

Tables

Introduction

L ike the weather, inflation has become an integral part of our life and
a force that we have to deal with. The demise of the gold system has
made money a policy variable for governments. Therefore, changes
in the prices of goods and services over time, as well as changes in prices of
similar goods in terms of different moneys (currencies) have become very
common.

The key element in understanding the effects of inflation and relative
inflation on corporate financial decisions is unanticipated changes. The
cycles of inflation/disinflation in the major countries add one more dimension of risk. As always, risk is a source of both potential loss and gain for the
business firm, but whether to prevent a loss or take advantage of an opportunity, the risk has to be estimated and managed. It follows that the understanding of the nature of the inflationary/disinflationary process at a certain
time is critical for efficient financial management of the firm. Hence, this
book.

This book grew from our experience in Israel and the United States.
Israel provides an excellent case for the research on the effects of both inflation and disinflation on corporate financial policy. The Israeli corporate and
financial sectors are very sophisticated. Their daily practices are very similar
to those in developed countries. Yet, Israel went in a relatively short period of
time from a very high rate of inflation (some say hyperinflation) to a relatively low rate of inflation. The processes of inflation and disinflation were
not fully anticipated, and both had profound effects on many corporations.
We had the opportunity to observe these developments both from the academic position and from a consultant's point of view. The rather extreme
Israeli experience was mitigated against our American experience both at the
University of Southern California and at Columbia University. We hope that
the outcome will serve as a bridge between the research and the practical
managerial aspects of this important issue.

Writing a book, even a modest one, is a complex undertaking. In doing
so, we drew on the help of many of our colleagues both in academia and in
the business world in Israel and the United States. Much of the work was

done while Tamir Agmon was at the University of Southern California, and Reuven Horesh was at Tel Aviv. We are grateful for the help we received in both places. In particular, we are grateful to Amihud Dotan for many useful ideas and to Wael Tarazi for his valuable research help.

As economists, we are great believers in the concept of opportunity cost. Our families gave up much time that we could have spent with them pursuing their interests, so that this work could be accomplished. We are thankful for their help and the understanding.

1

Inflation, Disinflation, and Financial Decisions

C hanges in the price level in most countries in the world are one of
the characteristics of our time. Changes in price levels, as well as
changes in relative prices, reflect not only changes in the physical
environment and technological changes, but most of all, these changes are
expressions of the central role of the national states in the modern world. The
processes of inflation and disinflation (in which the inflation rate is declining)
are prime examples of the interdependence between economics and politics.
Persistent changes in price levels in different countries may have several
causes. They may reflect domestic considerations or be the result of international changes. In this respect, focusing on processes of changes in prices is
similar to focusing on the symptoms, rather than the underlying reasons
which produce the symptoms. This is a proper thing to do for the purpose of
discussing financial decisions. What counts in financial decision making is
not the reason for the inflationary/disinflationary process, but the existence
of the process. The expected changes in the prices of outputs and inputs, as
well as the distribution of the actual price changes in the future, form the
environment in which financial decisions are made. An understanding of the
possible changes in the relevant prices is a necessary condition for appropriate financial decision making.

A Taxonomy of Inflation

Inflationary and disinflationary processes can be divided into two major
groups according to their effects on financial decisions: "across-the-board"
price changes and "terms-of-trade" inflation/disinflation. Across-the-board
inflation is a pure monetary phenomenon; terms-of-trade inflation, while it
may originate in monetary policy, has real effects.

A secondary taxonomy is based on the rate of inflation in the future. A
distinction is made between a known rate of inflation and an uncertain rate of
inflation. The case of an across-the-board inflation with a known rate of

inflation corresponds to the "textbook case." This is also the only case in which inflation does not matter. Once an uncertain rate of inflation is introduced, some financial decisions depend on the specific assumptions with regard to the uncertain rate of inflation.

Although it is possible to think of actual cases where across-the-board inflation with an uncertain rate of inflation is a good description of an actual situation, the general case is that of terms-of-trade inflation. The changes in relative prices may be the triggering event for the inflation/disinflation. In this case, they are not part of the inflationary process itself. A more common case is where the changes in the relative prices are the result of efforts of different groups in the population to avoid the cost of inflation and to shift it to others. In this case, the changes in the relative prices are part of the inflationary process. Understanding the process of changes in relative prices may help in predicting possible change or at least the direction of the change. As we will see later, this is an important piece of information for financial decision making.

Financial Decisions and Processes of Change in the Rate of Inflation

The term *financial decisions* is used to denote a series of business decisions that involve financial variables. We will focus on three groups of financial decisions in particular: capital budgeting, cost of funds, and costing. The first group deals with investment decisions and may be seen as the prime means by which corporations create value. The second group deals with the financing aspects of the outcomes of the first group, although there is an interdependence between the two types of decisions via the cost of capital if the latter is used as the discount factor. The costing decisions take a certain pattern of production (which is the result of prior capital budgeting decisions) as given. The costing decisions are secondary, or derivative, decisions given the investment policy and the financing decisions. Yet a valid costing procedure contributes to a proper generation of the cash flows on which the capital budgeting is based.

Financial decisions are affected by inflation/disinflation only to the extent to which they differ relative to a noninflationary situation. In the case of capital budgeting, for example, we are looking for (1) changes in the type of projects to be selected, assuming technologically mutually exclusive projects, (2) the discount rates to be used, and (3) the value of a given project.

Before we procede any further, a number of assumptions have to be made. The major assumption is that the financial decisions are of importance to management, to the existing shareholders, or to both. This assumption implies a partial equilibrium, or some version of transaction cost model, similar to bankruptcy costs. Another possible interpretation is that managers maximize their own utility rather than that of the shareholders. A well-known example of such an approach is the class of models based on agency theory. Given these assumptions, we will focus on a single firm or even a single project, and we will ignore the portfolio effect.

Most treatments of inflation and financial decisions in the literature assume, either explicitly or implicitly, across-the-board inflation, and the main problem is consistency between nominal and real terms (Brealey and Myers 1984: 88–91). On the other hand, there are a large number of studies on the effects of inflationary processes on relative prices, on the level of risk in the economy, and on the political nature of inflation. These studies for the most part look at the inflationary process per se. Their frame of reference is macroeconomic and they are not concerned with microeconomic decisions in general or with corporate financial decisions in particular. Parks (1978) and Pindyck (1984) are two examples of studies that deal with the relationship between inflation and changes in relative prices as well as the association between inflation and risk. Sargent (1986) and Agmon (1985) are two examples of studies on the political economy of the inflationary/disinflationary process. Dietrich and Heckerman (1980) have derived the demand for capital given a specific process of price changes. Their study is one of the few that relates inflation to decisions made by firms. Studies on the relationship between inflation and share prices—such as Bodie (1976), Modigliani and Cohn (1979), and Agmon and Findlay (1982)—are related to the issues discussed in this book through the valuation involved in the determination of share prices. However, they approach the issue of inflation from the point of view of the stock market, rather than focus on corporate finance. Most of the studies in the field assume a certain type of inflationary process, but the researchers are not following the taxonomy of inflation I have just suggested.

For our purposes, we will examine both the textbooklike across-the-board inflation and the more realistic terms-of-trade inflation. In the former, we make the distinction between the case where the rate of inflation is known and the case where the rate of inflation is uncertain. The first case is applicable to a situation where the rate of inflation has been very low and stable. The second case relates to periods of high and variable rates of inflation. For the purpose of most financial decisions, there is no great difference between annual rates of inflation of 2 and 3 percent, and we may assume that the rate of inflation is known. A change of similar proportion from an annual rate of inflation of 40 percent to 60 percent does make a lot of difference.

As we pointed out earlier, terms-of-trade inflation/disinflation is a more common case. To make this type of inflation operative in terms of financial decisions, we should be able to say something about the direction of the changes in the relative prices of certain outputs and inputs, given a certain rate of inflation/disinflation. As we will see later, it is possible to do so with regard to some classes of inputs and outputs.

The process by which a given change in the economic and political environments is translated into a set of financial decisions can be presented schematically as follows:

Firms are classified by their inputs and outputs as well as their technology of combining inputs. The environment can be described as a vector of price changes of different natures. Where the vector is run through the matrix of the different types of firms (classified by the responses of their inputs and outputs to different processes of price changes), the result is a matrix of financial decisions. The matrix of financial decisions includes elements such as the real cost of funds, debt/equity ratio, capital decisions, and costing of specific goods. The financial policy matrix corresponds to the firms' matrix. That is, given a certain type of inflation/disinflation—as well as a characterization of the firm by its inputs, outputs, and technology—a specific financial policy can be derived. The financial policy is expressed through a vector of financial decisions like those just described.

Another way to describe the economic nature of the firm is by the production function. The production function is a mathematical relationship which describes the way in which inputs are being transformed into outputs. In general, it can be written as:

$$F(C_i, L_i, M_i) = G_j; \quad i = 1, \ldots n; \quad j = 1, \ldots m$$

C denotes capital input; L denotes labor input, including management; M is purchased materials; i is an inputs index across all inputs; G_j is a vector of outputs. F is the functional form (for example, Cobb-Douglas). Inputs and outputs are translated into monetary values through a price vector.

The production function can be thought of as a generating process for cash flows. This is done by multiplying the various inputs and outputs by their respective prices. The cash flows for the specific projects under consideration provide the basis for the capital budgeting decisions. The distribution of the periodic cash flows for the firm as a whole provides the basis for the cost of funds, the cost of capital, and the capital structure. Taken together, the investment policy and the financial policy create the value of the firm. Another facet of this process is expressed in the financial reports. The financial reports are based on the economic process represented by the production function. The records which are the building blocks of the financial reports reflect a number of agreed-upon conventions. There is a vast literature on the interface between inflation and accounting. Financial decisions are affected by the way in which profits and losses appear in the financial reports. However, in this book, we do not deal either with the interrelationship between accounting and inflation or with the interface of accounting and financial decisions.

Different types of inflation have different impacts on relative prices. These impacts are transmitted through the system as follows: Changes in relative prices affect production. The initial change in the relative prices may have an effect on the quantities of various inputs and outputs. The primary effect may be strengthened or mitigated by higher-order effects. (In general, we will observe both income and substitution effects.) The changes in the production function affect cash flows. Different cash flows do mean different financial decisions.

Inflation/disinflation affects more than one country and more than one currency. Relative inflation is a major factor in explaining changes in the exchange rates. The unanticipated changes in the exchange rates are similar to the unanticipated changes in the rate of inflation and disinflation. The conceptual framework and the applications to be presented in this book apply to a multicurrency world as well or better than to a domestic, single-currency economy.

Changes in the Rate of Inflation and Financial Decisions: An Illustration

For example, let us examine and compare three different processes of change in the rate of inflation: a decrease in the rate of inflation as a result of a change in the economic and political regime, an increase in the rate of inflation as a result of a radical increase in the price of oil, and an increase in the rate of inflation following an exogenous increase in the variance of the rate of return of real capital.

In the first case, the market perceives a change in the economic regime which leads to a process of disinflation. The disinflation is a result of a change in policy. For example, political decision makers may feel that high inflation carries a higher political cost than unemployment which may result from a process of disinflation. If most actors in the market have similar expectations, the process of disinflation may be fast, and it will continue even in the presence of economic indicators which under a different regime would be interpreted as inflationary. For example, in such a world, it is possible to have disinflation coupled with a large and persistent federal deficit. This approach is consistent with the rational expectation view of inflation (for example, see Sargent 1986).

We will assume that such a process does not affect relative prices and that all the prices of inputs and outputs are decreasing at the same rate. An alternative assumption is that the rate of the change in the prices (or the change in the rate of change of the prices) will vary among the various inputs and outputs, but that price changes are randomly distributed among the different outputs and inputs. Such a distribution is described by a trend plus a random error term. The trend is the expected rate of inflation, and the uncertainty about the rate of change is expressed by an error term with a zero mean and a given standard deviation.

In the second case, the change in the rate of inflation is caused by a change in the relative price of one major commodity or a major industry. Given both substitution and income effects, the original change in the prices of a single industry or major commodity has developed into a change in the general price level and detectable changes in the relative prices. The radical increase in the price of oil brought about both an increase in the price level and a change in oil's relative price. But the changes in both the price level and relative prices did not stop at that. After the change in the price of oil, those products and services with strong relative demand in the net oil-exporting countries exhibited an increase in their relative prices. The same was true for close substitutes for crude oil. The end result has been a process of price increases coupled with changes in the relative prices over an extended period of time. The important aspect of such a process from the point of view of corporate financial decisions is that the direction of changes in the relative prices is detectable.

The change in the volatility of the expected return on real capital, or an increase in the general "riskiness" of the world, is a more subtle process. Such a process may be related to the nature of the current political and economic regime as well as the expectations with regard to its stability. In this case, one can talk about an association between the increase in the riskiness and an increase in the volatility in the changes in the rate of inflation. Causality is hard to detect. It is also hard to talk about the direction of changes in the relative prices beyond broad generalities.

The three different processes of price changes just described can be applied to specific types of firms. Given the type of the firm as expressed by its production function, we can assess the effect of a given process of inflation on the cash flows and derive a vector of specific financial decisions. This is the core of this analysis. A conceptual framework is derived and applied to actual cases in the following chapters. However, to get a glimpse of what is involved in the interface between the processes of changes in the rates of inflation/disinflation and financial decision making, let us examine a few cases. In the matrix terminology used before, we are looking for the effect of a given element in the inflation vector on a given corporation. The effect is expressed in terms of changes in a specific financial decision.

For the first example, let us assume an investment project in a production facility. There is one input and one output. The input is imported from another country, the output is sold in the domestic market. The output has to compete with similar products which are produced domestically. Suppose that we are making an investment decision late in 1974. The decision horizon for the project under consideration is five years. A feasibility study (based on 1974 prices and assuming constant prices) recommended acceptance of the project. The questions now are (1) what is the expected rate of inflation for the period 1974–79 and (2) given that the inflation has been identified as a terms-of-trade inflation, does it affect the net present value (NPV) of the project and, consequently, the accept/reject decision? As shown in chapter 3, the answer may be positive with regard to the two questions. If the project "buys" two inputs, and the expected inflation creates uncertainty with regard to the relative prices of the inputs, it may affect the technology chosen by the firm or, in other words, it may affect the choice between two mutually exclusive projects in favor of the one that allows for substitution of one input for the other. Thus, the choice between an investment in a fuel oil power plant, a coal power plant, or an interchangeable power plant (fuel oil or coal) is a function of the uncertainty with regard to the relative prices of oil and coal. An understanding of the inflationary process that begun in 1974 and its likely effects on the relative prices of oil and coal is necessary for a rational feasibility study. Even if information is hard to get, the questions have to be asked, and some answers should be provided. Assumption analysis or similar techniques can be employed, but ignoring the issue by assuming constant relative prices can lead to serious mistakes. (For an illustration of this case, see chapter 6.)

Another example involves the effect of an across-the-board inflation on the cost of funds. In order to highlight the issue, suppose that a certain corporation is considering financing a one-year investment. The required investment is one million U.S. dollars, and the project is being financed by a loan. The expected nominal rate of return on the project is 20 percent. The firm faces two options for financing the project. The first is a one-year loan with a nominally fixed rate of interest of 15 percent. The second option is a Consumer Price Index–linked loan with a rate of interest of 6 percent. The expected annual rate of inflation is 10 percent—a rate reflected in the expected nominal rate of return of the project. The decision concerning which way to finance the project depends on the type of the expected inflationary process. In a world of across-the-board inflation at a known rate, everybody will prefer the nominally fixed loan. This is so because the inflation-deflated rate of interest of the nominally fixed loan is 4.5 percent. The Consumer Price Index–linked loan carries an inflation-deflated rate of interest of 6 percent. In a world with an across-the-board inflation at an uncertain rate, the decision may reverse itself. The uncertain rate of inflation makes the inflation-deflated rate of interest of the nominally fixed loan a random variable. Corporate treasurers may prefer a certain rate of interest of 6 percent, inflation-deflated, to an uncertain rate of interest with an expected value of 4.5 percent. In addition to that, the distribution of returns from the project depends on the type of inflationary process. Different inflationary or disinflationary processes may yield different distributions of returns. These distributions in themselves have an effect on the cost of funds, the cost of capital, and the capital structure of the firm. This is so because as the distribution of the cash flows becomes more (or less) risky, the required expected rate of return on the firm's debt is increasing (or decreasing). The change in the financial risk of the firm affects the cost of funds from other sources and the capital structure. These issues are discussed in chapter 4 and applied in chapter 7.

An increase in the general riskiness in the economy may come from political uncertainty, from some structural instability in the prices of major commodities, or from both sources. Indeed, the distinction between general political economic factors and commodity-specific factors is not clear. At the very least, these two sources of risk are closely related. For example, one can argue that toward the end of the second term of the Reagan administration, the probability of a change in the underlying attitudes and preferences is possible. Those who believe in cycles can see a change that will cause a substantial increase in the rate of inflation in the United States. At the same time, OPEC may be successful in increasing the relative prices of oil once more. The outcome of the increased likelihood of such possibilities is to make the future more risky. An increase in the general riskiness may have several effects on financial decisions. Leverage may go down, and more flexible technologies may replace more dedicated technologies in capital-budgeting decisions. These and other changes in financial decisions will reflect the feelings of managers and shareholders alike that in a risky environment, one must be ready for any eventuality.

The focusing on financial decisions in an inflationary or disinflationary environment may look technical and narrow. This is not the case. Most, if not all, of the real changes in the economy are expressed in a combination of changes in price level and relative prices. This is true in a closed economy, but it is even more pronounced in a world of many currencies and a system of flexible exchange rates. Financial decisions are discussed, reported, and carried out in monetary terms. The abilities to identify the possible changes in the price levels and the associated changes in the relative price, and to adopt the financial decisions to these changes are real contributions to successful financial management. The following chapters are aimed at these goals.

2
Inflation, Changes in Relative Prices, and Financial Decisions: Some Evidence

I n chapter 1, we argued that the inflationary and disinflationary processes may have substantial effects on financial decisions involving capital budgeting, cost of funds, costing of products, and capital structure. The arguments depend to a great extent on the association between the inflationary processes and changes in relative prices. This line of argument will be developed further in the next three chapters, where the topics of capital budgeting, cost of funds, and costing will be discussed one by one.

However, before we embark on this task, we have to show that the association between inflation and the changes in relative prices is such that ignoring it does make a difference in terms of financial decisions. Another way to state this proposition is that the deviation in the changes of the prices of some inputs and outputs differs sufficiently from the changes in the general price index (the rate of inflation). If this were not the case, then our argument may be technically valid, but it will not have any practical value.

Two factors make the inflationary/disinflationary process relevant in terms of financial decisions. The first is the association between the rate of inflation and the changes in relative prices. The second is the uncertainty concerning the expected rate of inflation which is implicit in the nominal interest rate. These two factors are evident in the data presented in this chapter.

We will focus our analysis on the years 1972–86—a rather tumultuous period which began with the switch from the pegged exchange rate system to a flexible exchange rate system with intervention. This was followed by what is known as the "energy crisis" (a radical increase in the relative price of oil). The political and economic uncertainty was reflected by ever changing inflation rates, interest rates, and exchange rates.

The Uncertainty Factor

The behavior of the rate of inflation in the United States during this period is presented in table 2–1. The rates are quarterly rates of change of the Con-

Table 2–1
Consumer Price Index Quarterly Rates of Change, 1972–86

Quarter	CPI	Quarter	CPI
1	0.88	31	2.92
2	0.80	32	3.20
3	0.78	33	3.58
4	0.85	34	3.62
5	1.02	35	3.20
6	1.38	36	3.12
7	1.72	37	2.80
8	2.10	38	2.45
9	2.48	39	2.72
10	2.65	40	2.40
11	2.88	41	1.90
12	3.02	42	1.70
13	2.75	43	1.45
14	2.42	44	1.12
15	2.18	45	0.90
16	1.82	46	0.82
17	1.60	47	0.65
18	1.50	48	0.82
19	1.38	49	1.12
20	1.25	50	1.08
21	1.48	51	1.05
22	1.70	52	1.02
23	1.65	53	0.90
24	1.68	54	0.92
25	1.65	55	0.85
26	1.75	56	0.88
27	2.00	57	0.78
28	2.22	58	0.40
29	2.45		
30	2.68		

sumer Price Indeces (CPI). In table 2–2, we present the statistical nature of the time series of the rates of inflation.

Examining the data in the two tables, two characteristics emerge. The volatility of the rates of inflation was quite substantial, and the volatility is positively related to the mean value of the rate of inflation. This last trait is evident from the analysis of the subperiods presented in table 2–2.

We do not have a direct way to observe the real rate of interest or the expected rate of inflation. To derive one, we have to make some assumptions with regard to the other. Let us assume that the expected real rate of interest was constant at a level of 1 percent per quarter. Based on this assumption, the expected quarterly rate of inflation for the period 1972–86 is computed. This time series is presented in table 2–3.

Table 2–2
Mean, Standard Error, and Quartiles of Quarterly Rates of Inflation, 1972–86

Quarters	Mean	Standard Error	First Quartile	Third Quartile
1–58	1.778	0.852	1.000	2.455
1–7	1.061	0.358	0.800	1.375
8–14	2.614	0.310	2.425	2.875
15–28	1.704	0.281	1.494	1.869
29–41	2.850	0.494	2.450	3.200
42–58	0.969	0.293	0.825	1.100

Note: The first and third quartiles describe the range of the distribution.

Table 2–3
Quarterly and Annual Computed Expected Rates of Inflation by Quarter, 1972–86

Quarter	Rate	Annual Rate	Quarter	Rate	Annual Rate
1	0.3175	1.27	31	1.9150	7.66
2	0.2850	1.14	32	2.6750	10.70
3	0.3750	1.50	33	3.2775	13.11
4	0.4850	1.94	34	1.7875	7.15
5	0.8425	3.37	35	2.0200	8.08
6	1.1175	4.47	36	3.2750	13.10
7	1.7475	6.99	37	3.2025	12.81
8	1.5325	6.13	38	3.3975	13.59
9	1.2575	5.03	39	3.5950	14.38
10	1.8600	7.44	40	2.5850	10.34
11	2.2825	9.13	41	2.8850	11.54
12	1.6125	6.45	42	2.7675	11.07
13	0.8850	3.54	43	2.1475	8.59
14	0.6150	2.46	44	1.3650	5.46
15	0.7850	3.14	45	1.3200	5.28
16	0.7000	2.80	46	1.3325	5.33
17	0.3850	1.54	47	1.5100	6.04
18	0.4650	1.86	48	1.4500	5.80
19	0.4200	1.68	49	1.5450	6.18
20	0.3125	1.25	50	1.8400	7.36
21	0.2775	1.11	51	1.9550	7.82
22	0.3900	1.56	52	1.5075	6.03
23	0.5525	2.21	53	1.2575	5.03
24	0.7775	3.11	54	1.0650	4.26
25	0.8200	3.28	55	1.0350	4.14
26	0.9600	3.84	56	1.0375	4.15
27	1.1775	4.71	57	1.2275	4.91
28	1.7700	7.08	58	0.7775	3.11
29	1.7175	6.87			
30	1.6550	6.62			

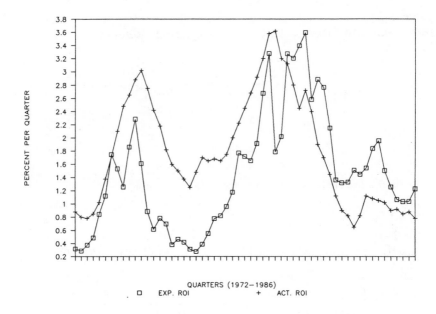

Figure 2–1. Expected and Realized Quarterly Rates of Inflation, 1972–1986

Figure 2–1 depicts the relationship between the expected quarterly rate of inflation and the realized, actual rate for the period under consideration. The calculation presented in figure 2–1 should not be taken literally. It is very sensitive to the assumption with regard to the real rate. The purpose here is to demonstrate the possible magnitude of the realized uncertainty or the deviation of the actual rate of inflation from the expected rate. This difference between the implicit expected rate of inflation and the actual, realized rate is a crucial variable in the determination of the required rate of interest on the corporate debt; therefore, it is an important component in the determination of the cost of capital. This issue is discussed in chapter 4.

Another facet of the same phenomenon is that the realized, inflation-deflated real rate of interest is highly volatile. This rate is calculated by dividing one plus the nominal rate of interest by one plus the actual rate of inflation for the same period. The time series for the quarterly realized real rate of interest for the period 1972–86 is presented in figure 2–2, and is statistically described in table 2–4. Tables 2–5 and 2–6 concern the mean, standard error, and quartiles of the realized rate of interest during these years. The data presented in tables 2–2 through 2–4 and in figures 2–1 and 2–2 show a substantial amount of uncertainty with regard to the rate of inflation in the period under consideration.

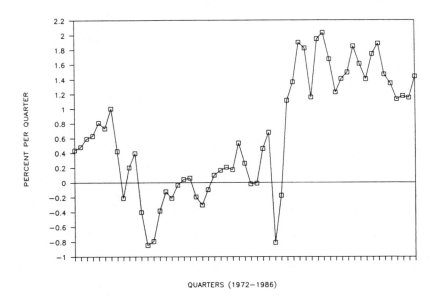

QUARTERS (1972–1986)

Figure 2–2. The Realized Inflation-Deflated Quarterly Rate of Interest, 1972–86

Table 2–4
The Realized Real Rate of Interest by Quarter, 1972–86

	Rate				Rate	
Quarter	Quarterly	Annualized		Quarter	Quarterly	Annualized
1	0.439	1.755		16	−0.123	−0.491
2	0.481	1.925		17	−0.212	−0.846
3	0.595	2.382		18	−0.034	−0.138
4	0.630	2.519		19	0.044	0.178
5	0.809	3.237		20	0.062	0.247
6	0.732	2.930		21	−0.195	−0.778
7	1.005	4.021		22	−0.305	−1.219
8	0.424	1.694		23	−0.096	−0.384
9	−0.212	−0.849		24	0.101	0.403
10	0.205	0.818		25	0.167	0.669
11	0.396	1.584		26	0.206	0.826
12	−0.400	−1.600		27	0.174	0.696
13	−0.842	−3.367		28	0.533	2.132
14	−0.791	−3.163		29	0.261	1.044
15	−0.382	−1.527		30	−0.019	−0.078

Table 2–4 (Continued)

Quarter	Rate Quarterly	Rate Annualized	Quarter	Rate Quarterly	Rate Annualized
31	−0.010	−0.039	46	1.495	5.981
32	0.460	1.841	47	1.848	7.392
33	0.678	2.713	48	1.612	6.447
34	−0.808	−3.233	49	1.404	5.617
35	−0.174	−0.698	50	1.746	6.985
36	1.115	4.461	51	1.885	7.541
37	1.364	5.457	52	1.467	5.870
38	1.901	7.604	53	1.345	5.382
39	1.820	7.281	54	1.130	4.518
40	1.157	4.629	55	1.175	4.700
41	1.948	7.792	56	1.152	4.610
42	2.033	8.132	57	1.441	5.765
43	1.673	6.693			
44	1.226	4.905			
45	1.407	5.629			

Table 2–5
Mean, Standard Error, and Quartiles of the Realized Rate of Interest by Quarter, 1972–86

Quarter	Mean	Standard Error	First Quartile	Third Quartile
1–57	0.652	0.798	−0.015	1.384
1–7	0.670	0.197	0.481	0.809
8–14	−0.174	0.533	−0.791	0.396
15–28	−0.004	0.240	−0.199	0.169
29–41	0.746	0.883	−0.014	1.592
42–57	1.502	0.276	1.256	1.728

Note: The first and third quartiles describe the range of the distribution.

Table 2–6
Mean, Standard Error, and Quartiles of the Realized Rate of Interest, Annualized by Quarter, 1972–86

Quarter	Mean	Standard Error	First Quartile	Third Quartile
1–57	2.608	3.192	−0.060	5.536
1–7	2.681	0.786	1.924	3.236
8–14	−0.700	2.130	−3.160	1.580
15–28	−0.017	0.959	−0.797	0.675
29–41	2.980	3.530	−0.060	6.370
42–57	6.010	1.100	5.020	6.910

Note: The first and third quartiles describe the range of the distribution.

Inflation and Changes in Relative Prices

Much of the development presented in chapter 3's analysis of capital budgeting rests on the assumption that the inflationary/disinflationary process is associated with changes in relative prices. In particular, we focus on cases where the rate of inflation as measured by the change in the CPI differs from the rate of change in the prices of specific inputs and outputs.

To illustrate this phenomenon, data on the quarterly rates of change in the prices of seven major inputs/outputs in the U.S. market are presented and analyzed. These are: hourly manufacturing wages, food grains, food consumed at home, housing, lumber and wood products, refined oil products, and new cars. The quarterly rates of change in the prices of the seven inputs and outputs are presented in table 2–7.

The relationships between the quarterly rates of change in the CPI and each one of the seven major inputs and outputs for the period 1972–86 are depicted in figures 2–3 through 2–9. These relationships are statistically summarized in table 2–8.

The data in table 2–8 show that the specific input or output inflations differ quite substantially from the general rate of inflation over the period 1972–86. In the case of the industries used as inputs to many other industries (food grains, lumber, and food products), the correlations with the CPI were zero and negative, respectively. These relationships suggest possible changes in the terms of trade between outputs and inputs which may be associated with the inflationary/disinflationary process. For example, in the case of food grains, the correlation between the quarterly changes in its price and that of the food industry is about .3, whereas the correlation between the quarterly changes in the prices of lumber and housing is about − .23.

Table 2–7
Quarterly Rates of Price Changes, Selected Items, 1972–86

Quarter	Manufac-turing Wages	Grains	Food	Housing	Oil	Cars	Lumber
1	1.351	0.000	0.490	0.860	4.347	−0.358	3.369
2	1.259	24.698	1.463	0.852	0.000	−1.527	2.982
3	1.755	36.715	0.961	0.845	0.000	0.912	0.875
4	0.934	−11.307	6.746	0.914	8.333	0.180	15.620
5	1.638	15.936	3.940	1.132	11.538	0.180	5.715
6	1.892	81.443	6.080	2.016	0.000	−1.711	−0.655
7	1.719	7.954	2.764	2.928	8.706	2.658	2.309
8	1.825	4.561	4.986	3.058	27.993	0.714	2.794
9	3.253	−25.167	0.250	2.967	16.790	3.191	0.470
10	2.636	9.865	2.867	3.820	4.721	1.718	−6.139

Table 2–7 (Continued)

Quarter	Manufac- turing Wages	Grains	Food	Housing	Oil	Cars	Lumber
11	2.568	7.346	4.060	3.227	−6.332	5.489	−8.314
12	2.443	−18.821	−1.048	2.313	3.353	1.921	2.539
13	1.967	−17.330	2.942	1.711	8.215	−0.235	6.721
14	2.046	31.161	1.772	1.502	13.007	−0.393	−0.607
15	1.776	−15.982	2.303	1.953	−1.797	5.928	1.778
16	1.858	2.570	−3.075	1.335	−3.442	0.373	10.486
17	1.492	−3.759	1.869	1.146	3.294	0.000	−1.235
18	2.450	−15.104	0.278	1.699	6.946	−0.223	6.456
19	1.541	−15.030	−0.332	1.169	−1.062	4.619	3.432
20	1.727	1.805	3.728	2.147	1.403	0.356	4.090
21	2.161	−13.120	3.057	1.886	5.415	0.567	−0.131
22	2.115	7.346	0.156	1.957	0.270	−0.423	10.362
23	1.874	17.870	0.675	−0.155	−1.463	6.661	−1.267
24	2.179	5.806	4.543	2.234	−1.485	0.398	6.821
25	1.753	2.743	5.629	2.694	3.412	1.588	4.620
26	1.956	−0.296	0.093	2.722	5.372	0.000	1.544
27	2.421	3.273	1.774	1.927	2.949	4.104	2.050
28	2.007	−0.864	5.507	2.884	6.084	1.814	4.123
29	2.273	22.965	1.870	3.630	16.472	2.212	−0.232
30	2.052	4.964	0.213	4.035	20.841	−0.120	3.302
31	2.262	−2.252	1.704	3.836	11.537	3.371	−6.328
32	2.498	−0.691	2.052	4.474	11.045	1.921	1.654
33	3.237	−0.696	1.806	4.793	5.011	2.000	−5.120
34	2.439	7.009	4.395	0.374	3.970	1.792	4.288
35	2.191	8.733	1.931	3.436	4.432	1.541	2.604
36	2.292	−2.409	1.780	2.058	14.611	−0.867	−1.670
37	2.241	−9.670	0.037	3.397	0.351	5.084	1.256
38	2.263	−2.505	1.674	3.935	−2.552	−0.468	−3.019
39	1.452	1.401	−0.549	0.493	−1.556	2.979	−1.279
40	2.044	−3.456	1.987	0.491	−5.564	−1.319	−0.035
41	1.703	−7.398	1.984	3.521	−6.182	1.903	1.296
42	1.444	−1.546	−0.707	0.692	8.254	−0.201	−2.076
43	0.712	4.188	−0.997	−1.063	−5.120	1.213	0.918
44	0.835	3.517	1.475	0.727	−10.860	0.549	7.072
45	0.446	−3.640	0.390	1.412	4.873	0.198	2.943
46	0.317	4.534	−0.176	1.021	1.447	0.545	−2.795
47	0.885	−4.096	0.176	0.306	−5.602	2.121	0.882
48	0.940	0.251	3.568	−1.802	−3.340	0.096	2.623
49	0.683	−1.754	−0.580	4.572	2.529	0.241	−3.061
50	0.678	−0.510	0.686	1.546	−5.612	0.240	−1.204
51	1.225	−1.282	−0.068	−0.058	0.159	1.825	−0.131
52	1.211	0.000	1.773	1.025	−6.932	0.990	0.033
53	0.717	−8.051	−0.804	1.653	14.661	0.280	3.299
54	0.297	−2.542	−0.135	0.970	−4.125	−0.093	−4.024
55	1.125	7.246	1.251	0.565	1.830	2.284	−0.798
56	0.468	0.540	0.634	0.337	−37.323	0.410	1.039
57	0.408	−25.806	0.132	1.176	10.250	1.770	1.726

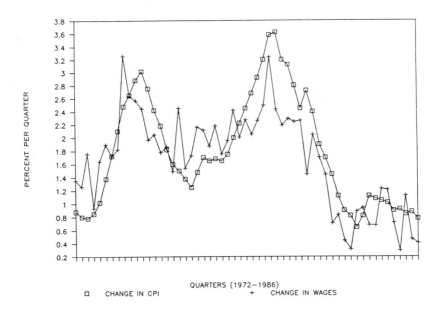

Figure 2–3. Relationship between Quarterly Rates of Change in the CPI and Hourly Manufacturing Wages, 1972–86

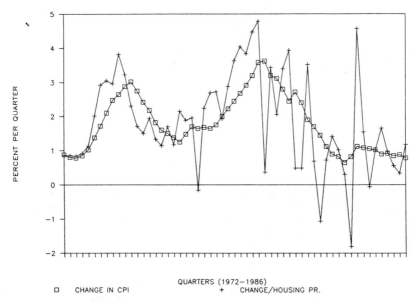

Figure 2–4. Relationship between Quarterly Rates of Change in the CPI and Housing Prices, 1972–86

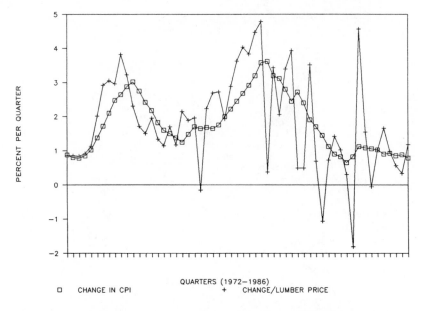

Figure 2–5. Relationship between Quarterly Rates of Change in the CPI and Lumber and Wood Products Prices, 1972–86

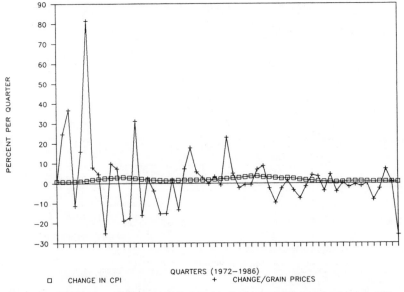

Figure 2–6. Relationship between Quarterly Rates of Change in the CPI and Grain Prices, 1972–86

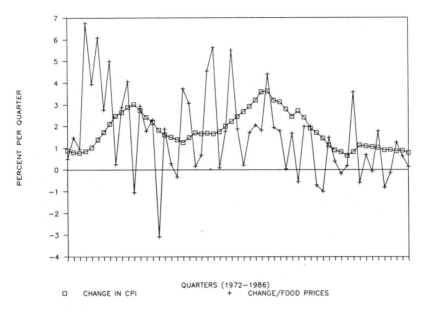

Figure 2–7. Relationship between Quarterly Rates of Change in the CPI and Food Prices, 1972–86

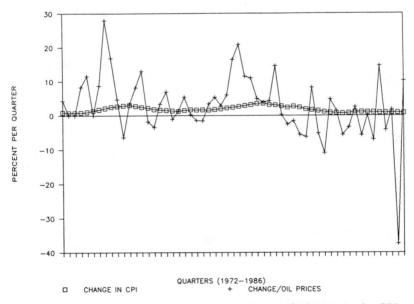

Figure 2–8. Relationship between Quarterly Rates of Change in the CPI and Refined Oil Products Prices, 1972–86

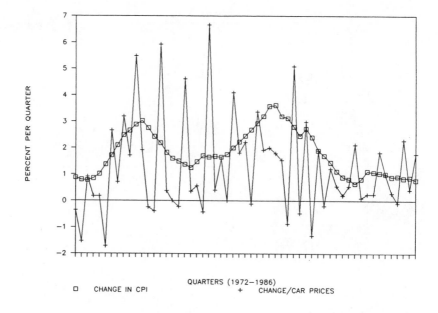

Figure 2–9. Relationship between Quarterly Rates of Change in the CPI and New Car Prices, 1972–86

Table 2–8
A Statistical Summary of the Relationship between CPI and Selected Inputs and Outputs, 1972–86

Item	Mean	Standard Error	First Quartile	Third Quartile
Manufacturing wages	1.684	0.719	1.168	2.217
Grains	1.950	15.990	−3.700	6.410
Food	1.614	2.006	0.144	2.816
Housing	1.848	1.418	0.856	2.948
Oil	2.880	9.270	−1.680	8.240
Cars	1.246	1.829	0.000	1.961
Lumber	1.473	4.174	−1.002	3.336

Correlation of CPI and hourly manufacturing wages	0.792
CPI and grain prices	−0.080
CPI and food prices	0.126
CPI and housing prices	0.567
CPI and oil prices	0.315
CPI and car prices	0.285
CPI and lumber prices	−0.232

Another source of changes in relative prices associated with the inflationary/disinflationary process is shifts in exchange rates. The 1972–86 period was characterized by very volatile changes in the exchange rates. Some of these changes were accounted for by the changes in the relative inflation rates in the countries involved. But, the lion's share of the volatility cannot be explained in this way.

Table 2–9 presents data on the quarterly rates of change in the major three currencies aginst the U.S. dollar. The changes are then decomposed into the anticipated change and the unanticipated change. The anticipated change is computed on the basis of the actual quarterly relative inflation—the ratio between one plus the rate of inflation in the foreign country divided by one plus the rate of inflation in the United States. This is an approximation only as the expected rate of inflation is not observable. (This calculation yields results similar to the one based on interest rates differentials.) The unanticipated changes in the exchange rates are reported in table 2–9. As we will see later, the unanticipated changes in the exchange rates may have an effect on financial decisions, in particular on some classes of capital budgeting decisions.

Table 2–9
Quarterly Unanticipated Changes in the Exchange Rates against the U.S. Dollar, 1972–86
(unanticipated changes are computed based on PPP)

Quarter	Yen	Pound	Deutsche Mark
1	3.49	2.39	3.16
2	1.03	− 6.54	0.38
3	0.00	− 0.94	− 1.44
4	− 0.30	− 2.98	0.00
5	11.86	5.50	12.83
6	1.77	4.23	17.03
7	− 27.45	− 6.54	0.21
8	− 30.60	− 3.74	− 10.47
9	1.45	3.06	7.14
10	− 3.19	− 37.37	− 0.82
11	− 4.65	− 4.66	− 4.00
12	− 0.54	63.38	9.46
13	3.23	2.89	3.26
14	− 1.72	− 9.17	− 0.66
15	− 2.11	− 6.85	− 10.35
16	− 0.98	− 0.52	0.39
17	2.04	− 6.12	3.85
18	0.60	− 7.57	− 1.90
19	3.80	− 4.65	5.39
20	− 1.91	1.93	3.96

Table 2–9 (Continued)
(unanticipated changes are computed based on PPP)

Quarter	Yen	Pound	Deutsche Mark
21	5.67	0.77	−1.69
22	3.67	0.03	2.16
23	1.83	2.09	2.13
24	10.63	10.63	8.93
25	8.21	−3.52	5.11
26	7.72	−0.60	−3.28
27	7.17	5.68	6.94
28	−3.66	3.97	6.93
29	−6.73	1.06	−3.86
30	−3.34	5.84	2.28
31	−3.02	0.09	5.91
32	−5.18	1.60	1.29
33	−5.19	−3.97	−13.28
34	13.71	10.29	12.06
35	5.15	1.25	−2.29
36	4.03	−0.40	−8.67
37	−5.04	−5.74	−5.71
38	−6.81	−14.82	−12.91
39	−2.49	−4.14	3.37
40	6.96	5.62	4.26
41	−11.91	−7.67	−7.23
42	−3.61	−2.88	−2.18
43	−4.57	−2.14	−2.46
44	17.14	−4.10	6.29
45	−3.81	−7.70	−1.78
46	0.00	2.13	−5.33
47	2.09	−2.91	−2.61
48	0.30	−3.55	−3.98
49	3.71	0.26	5.56
50	−5.66	−6.42	−7.54
51	−3.32	−8.53	−7.73
52	−2.20	−7.14	−4.45
53	0.90	7.62	2.65
54	0.79	6.80	2.08
55	14.53	6.85	13.08
56	7.17	3.39	9.61
57	13.33	0.76	4.57
58	9.65	5.27	7.03

3

The Effects of Inflation on the Value of Investment Projects: The Capital-Budgeting Decision

The capital-budgeting decision is one of the major activities of the financial manager. Interpreting the capital budgeting to include all capital outlays by the firm, it represents the demand for capital by the corporate sector. Although many books discuss issues and techniques of capital budgeting, the effects of inflation/disinflation are either ignored or treated as a marginal problem. This chapter shows inflation/disinflation to have a substantial effect on the value of investment projects. This result, consistent with the modern research on the macroeconomic nature of the inflationary/disinflationary process, is then translated into the actual mechanics of capital budgeting.

The Capital-Budgeting Decision

The capital-budgeting decision is viewed here within the context of the production decision by the firm. Suppose that a firm is considering the investment of a given amount in order to produce certain goods or services. We assume that the firm has decided on the technology—that is, how labor, L, and purchased materials, M, are going to be employed together with the prescribed capital investment in order to produce a stream of goods or services over the horizon of the investment project. In other words, the investment project under consideration can be described by using a production function in which the capital employed is given.

Formally, the investment project can be described as follows:

$$Q_t = KC_t^\alpha \cdot L_t^\beta \cdot M_t^\gamma \qquad t = 1, 2, \ldots n \qquad (3.1)$$

where: Q_t = the periodic stream of goods or services generated by the project under consideration

C_t^α = the contribution of the given stock of capital (in capital budgeting terms, the investment) to the production process

L_t = the number of units of labor employed at period t

M_t = the number of units of purchased materials employed at period t

We assume, following normal assumptions, that β and γ are positive. Also, KC_t is a constant once the investment decision has been made and I_o (present value of the capital investment) has been committed.

Given this presentation, it is easy to translate the normal cash flows (CF) used in the traditional capital-budgeting literature into terms of the production function.

This is done by the following definitions:

$$\text{Cash flows}_t = \text{Revenues}_t - \text{Cost}_t$$

$$\text{Revenues}_t = Q_t P_{Q_t}$$

$$\text{Cost}_t = L_t P_{L_t} + M_t P_{M_t} \tag{3.2}$$

where: P_{Q_t} = unit price of output (Q) at time t,

P_{L_t} = unit price of labor (L) at time t, and

P_{M_t} = unit price of purchased materials (M) at time t.

As we pointed out, the return for the capital is the residual revenue after all other costs have been paid. The return for the capital is usually presented as the net present value (NPV) of the project, where:

$$NPV = \sum_{t=1}^{n} [CF_t/(1+r)^t] - I_o \tag{3.3}$$

where r = appropriate discount rate.

The net present value of a single project j at period $t = 0$, with a horizon of n periods can be expressed as:

$$NPV_j = \left(Q_{1,j}P_{Q_1} - L_{1,j}P_{L_{1,j}} - M_{1,j}P_{M_{1,j}}\right)\frac{1}{(1+r)}$$

$$+ \left(Q_{2,j}P_{Q_{2,j}} - L_{2,j}P_{L_{2,j}} - M_{2,j}P_{M2,j}\right)\frac{1}{(1+r)^2} + \ldots$$

$$+ \left(Q_{n,j}P_{Q_{n,j}} - L_{n,j}P_{L_{n,j}} - M_{n,j}P_{M_{n,j}}\right)\frac{1}{(1+r)^n} - I_{oj}$$

$$= \sum_{t=1}^{n} \frac{1}{(1+r)^t}\left(Q_{tj}P_{Q_{tj}} - L_{tj}P_{L_{tj}} - M_{tj}P_{M_{tj}}\right) - I_{oj} \tag{3.4}$$

Given the nature of production function 3.1, the optimal combination of labor and purchased materials at any given period t is:

$$\frac{\gamma}{\beta} \cdot \frac{L_t}{M_t} = \frac{P_{M_t}}{P_{L_t}} \tag{3.5}$$

This combination of inputs will maximize profits and, thus, will yield the maximum cash flow for that period (given P_{Q_t}, the output price). Note that the planned quantity Q_t is assumed to be constant.

From equation 3.5, we can define M_t as:

$$M_{t_j} = L_{t_j} \frac{P_{Lt_j}}{P_{Mt_j}} \cdot \frac{\gamma}{\beta} \tag{3.6}$$

Substituting M_{t_j} into equation 3.4, we get the following NPV expression:

$$NPV_j = \sum_{t=1}^{n} \frac{1}{(1 + r)^t} \left(Q_{t_j} P_{Qt_j} - L_{t_j} P_{Lt_j} - L_{t_j} \frac{P_{Lt_j}}{P_{Mt_j}} \cdot \frac{\gamma}{\beta} \cdot P_{Mt_j} \right) - I_{o_j}$$

$$= \sum_{t=1}^{n} \frac{1}{(1 + r)^t} \left[Q_{t_j} P_{Qt_j} - L_{t_j} P_{Lt_j} \left(1 - \frac{\gamma}{\beta} \right) \right] - I_{o_j} \tag{3.7}$$

Equation 3.7 highlights the connection between the net present value of a given project, the relative prices of the inputs (P_L and P_M), and the output (P_Q). This connection is not immediately seen as $P_{M_{t_j}}$ is cancelled out in equation 3.7. However, the amount of L employed at time t is a function of its relative price in terms of materials. This relationship is expressed in equation 3.6. Different inflation/disinflation scenarios will have different effects on the net present value of a given project through the impact on the relative prices.

To see this point, let us define the cash flows at period t as

$$CF_t = (KC_t^{\alpha} \cdot L_t^{\beta} \cdot M_t^{\gamma}) P_{Q_t} - L_t P_{L_t} - M_t P_{M_t} \tag{3.8}$$

By assumption, $KC_t^{\alpha} = K'$. Substituting P_{M_t} we obtain:

$$CF_t = K' \cdot L_t^{\beta} \left(L_t \frac{P_{L_t}}{P_{M_t}} \cdot \frac{\gamma}{\beta} \right)^{\gamma} \cdot P_{Q_t} - L_t P_t - \left(L_t \frac{P_{L_t}}{P_{M_t}} \cdot \frac{\gamma}{\beta} P_{M_t} \right)$$

$$= K' P_{Q_t} L_t^{\beta + \gamma} \cdot \left(\frac{P_{L_t}}{P_{M_t}} \right)^{\gamma} \left(\frac{\gamma}{\beta} \right)^{\gamma} - L_t P_t \left(1 + \frac{\gamma}{\beta} \right)$$

$$NPV_j = \sum_{t=1}^{n} \frac{1}{(1 + r)^t} (CF_t)$$

Let us consider two main scenarios. The first one is of an across-the-board inflation. The second is an inflation with a change in the terms of trade.

The Case of Across-the-Board Price Change
(Textbook Inflation)

In this case, it is assumed that both upward and downward price changes are affecting the prices of all goods, services, and factors of production equally. The general price change is expressed as:

$$P_{it} = P_{io}(1 + \dot{P}_{i\tau}); \qquad i = 1, 2, \ldots n$$

where $\dot{P}_{i\tau}$ is the change in the pricing of item i over the period from 0 to t.

Specifically, in our model it is assumed that:

$$P_{Lt} = P_{Lo}(1 + \dot{P}_{L\tau})$$

$$P_{Mt} = P_{Mo}(1 + \dot{P}_{M\tau})$$

$$P_{Qt} = P_{Qo}(1 + \dot{P}_{Q\tau})$$

where $\dot{P}_{\tau}$ is the periodic change in the general price level (typically measured by the CPI). We assume that $\dot{P}_{\tau} = \dot{P}_{L\tau} = \dot{P}_{M\tau} = \dot{P}_{Q\tau}$. M_t is redefined now as:

$$M_t = L_t \frac{P_{Lo}(1 + \dot{P}_{\tau})}{P_{Mo}(1 + \dot{P}_{\tau})} \cdot \frac{\gamma}{\beta}$$

$$= L_t \frac{P_{Lo}}{P_{Mo}} \cdot \frac{\gamma}{\beta}$$

It follows that the NPV of project j is defined as:

$$NPV_j = \sum_{t=1}^{n} \frac{1}{(1 + r_o)^t (1 + \dot{P}_{\tau})} \left[Q_{tj} P_{Qoj}(1 + \dot{P}_{\tau}) \right.$$

$$\left. - L_{tj}\left(P_{Loj}\left(1 + \dot{P}_{\tau}\right)\left(1 - \frac{\gamma}{\beta}\right)\right) \right] - I_{oj}$$

$1,500

where

$$\dot{P}_{\tau} = \prod_{t=1}^{\tau}(1 + \dot{P}_t) - 1 \qquad (3.9)$$

and r_o is the zero-expected-inflation required return (the real return).

$$NPV_j = \sum_{t=1}^{n} \frac{1}{(1 + r_o)^t} \left[Q_{t_j} P_{Qo_j} - L_{t_j} P_{Lo_j} \left(1 - \frac{\gamma}{\beta} \right) \right] - I_{o_j}$$

Due to the fact that all prices have risen or fallen at exactly the same rate, the change of price is cancelled throughout. In other words, the case of an across-the-board inflation is similar to the case of constant prices. The latter is known in the literature of the financial management as the case of capital budgeting under constant prices.

The irrelevance of the across-the-board inflation to the capital-budgeting decision does not depend on a known rate of inflation. The result derived in equation 3.9 will be true even if the level of inflation or disinflation is unknown. The necessary and sufficient condition for this result to obtain is that the change in the price will be exactly the same across all goods, services, and factors of production, and equal to the change implied by the nominal interest rate.

In this case, there is no money illusion. People are able to make a distinction between monetary and real changes. In terms of monetary economics, one could say that in such a case, money is neutral. Cases such as this may happen in practice where the reference currency for the decision market is different than the currency in which the inflation is measured, and the exchange rates between the two currencies are free to move.

The corporate sector in Israel during 1983–84 provides an example of such a process. The inflation of the Israeli currency (the shekel) was very high and uncertain. However, most if not all firms moved to the U.S. dollar as their reference currency and, thus, avoided to a great extent some of the consequences of the high and volatile rate of inflation.

The Case of a Price Change that Causes a Change in the Relative Prices (a Change in the Terms of Trade)

Except in textbooks, inflation/disinflation has an effect on relative prices. In this case the "constant prices" technique does not hold. For purposes of capital budgeting, inflation cannot be treated simply by using the device of constant prices. Moreover, we have to specify the types of changes in the relative prices of outputs and inputs, as different types of changes in relative prices will have different effects on the capital-budgeting process.

We examine two general cases. The first is where the prices of the inputs change relative to the prices of the outputs. The second is where the relative prices of the inputs change as well. As we have shown earlier, different processes of inflation are associated with different paths of changes in relative prices.

Changes in the Relative Prices of Outputs and Inputs

Consider the following capital-budgeting decision. An investment is in a production facility where all the inputs, labor, and material are purchased in the domestic market (let us say the United States), and all the outputs are sold in a foreign market (let us say Germany). Assume further that the two markets are segmented. The prices of the inputs will vary with the price changes in the United States, and the prices of the outputs will vary with the price changes in Germany. Assume that for all periods:

$$1 + \dot{P}_{t,\text{US}} \neq 1 + \dot{P}_{t,\text{G}}$$

where $\dot{P}_{t,\text{US}}$ and $\dot{P}_{t,\text{G}}$ are the changes in the price levels over the period ending at t in the United States and Germany, respectively.

Redefining the NPV to account for the changes in the prices of the output and the inputs, we obtain:

$$NPV = \sum_{t=1}^{n} \frac{1}{(1 + r_o')^t (1 + \dot{P}_{\tau,\text{US}})} \left[Q_{oj} P_{Q_{oj}} \left(1 + \dot{P}_{\tau,\text{US}} \right) \right.$$

$$\left. - L_{tj} P_{L_{oj}} \left(1 + \dot{P}_{\tau,\text{G}} \right) \left(1 - \frac{\gamma}{\beta} \right) \right] - I_{oj} \qquad (3.10)$$

All prices and cash flows are measured in terms of U.S. dollars. r_o' is a risk-adjusted discount rate, where $r_o' > r_o$. The risk emanates from the uncertainty about the relative change of $\dot{P}_{\text{US}}$ and $\dot{P}_{\text{G}}$, not by the uncertain changes in the price level! This risk is expressed by a greater volatility of the cash flows. When volatile cash flows are discounted, r_o, the riskless discount rate, is replaced by a risk-adjusted and higher discount rate.

The relationship between uncertain price changes and the demand for, and supply of, capital for investment has been the subject of a number of studies. Dietrich and Heckerman (1980) have argued that due to the concavity of the process that generates the price changes (they have assumed Ito processes), the demand for capital may go up as price uncertainty increases because, according to their argument, higher volatility is associated with higher expected values. Indeed, given risk aversion, one would expect to find in equilibrium that the net present value of available projects discounted at a riskless rate will increase as perceived price volatility increases. Choosing the Ito process gives this empirical observation a mathematical interpretation in addition to the behavioral explanation.

If, however, we adopt either a strict economic interpretation of the decision making of the firm or an organizational approach, the demand for capital will decrease where relative price volatility increases. In the strict economic interpretation, the managers act as representatives of the shareholders, the owners. It follows that the managers will act as if they are risk-averse and will, therefore, discount the expected cash flows at a risk-adjusted discount rate r' which is higher than r_0. If, on the other hand, we adopt a more organizational approach, such as the agency theory, the same result will follow since, under the assumptions of the agency theory, the managers act to maximize their personal utility as if they are risk-averse. Therefore, a higher risk-adjusted discount rate will be imposed at the firm's level as a part of the capital-budgeting process, where relative prices become volatile and uncertain.

In a world of instantaneous adjustment and perfect capital markets, the rates of inflation in the two countries, expressed in terms of U.S. dollars, will be the same, and we will revert to the case of across-the-board inflation and constant prices. This, however, is not the general case. At the very least, there is a rather lengthy process of adjustment. Even if, at the end, prices follow the law of one price, the dynamics of the process are crucial for the capital-budgeting process. If projects and firms have finite horizons, in the presence of bankruptcy costs, the timing and pattern of the adjustment is very important. In other words (although in the long term and on the average, prices may move together), in a project with a finite horizon, the owners may not be around when the compensation arrives.

To illustrate, consider the following case. A U.S. brewery is selling beer in Germany. The inputs for the production, labor, and materials are purchased in the U.S. domestic market in U.S. dollars. The beer is sold in Germany for Deutsche marks. The proceeds from the sales are then converted into U.S. dollars and are transferred to the brewery.

Following an increase in the demand for American beer in Germany, the brewery is considering an investment in a new production facility dedicated to export to Germany.

At today's prices, the cost of the inputs per one unit of production is $1, and the output price in Germany for the same unit, net of transportation and related costs, is 3.125 Deutsche marks (DM). The current exchange rate is 2.5 DM for $1. The production line under consideration will function for five years. At the end of this period, it will have no value.

The five-year interest rate in the United States is 10 percent per annum (p.a.). The planned output of the proposed project is 100 million units per year. Production is evenly distributed over time. The required investment for the new facility is $90,000,000. The basic data is summarized in table 3–1.

Let us examine four different scenarios:

Scenario I: Constant Prices in the Two Countries. This is the base case used as a benchmark for the other scenarios. There are no price changes either in

Table 3–1
Brewery Case Basic Data

Item	Notation	Data
Required investment	I_o	$90,000,000
Cost of inputs per unit of output	$LP_L + MP_M$	$1
Unit price of output	P_Q	3.125 DM
Quantity produced (annual)	Q	100,000,000 units
Decision horizon	t	Five years
Five-year interest rate	r	10 percent
Exchange rate		2.5 DM/$

the United States or in Germany. Given the data, the net present value of the project is expressed as:

$$NPV_1 = \sum_{t=1}^{5} [(\$1.25 - \$1.00)100,000,000]/(1.1)^t - \$90,000,000$$

$$NPV_1 = \$4,770,000$$

If conditions were as assumed in scenario 1, the decision would be to accept the project as $NPV_1 > 0$.

Scenario II: Purchasing Power Parity World. Assume now that both $\dot{P}_{US,t}$ and $\dot{P}_{G,t}$ are positive and are the same for each country for $t = 1, \ldots 5$. However, $\dot{P}_{US,t} > \dot{P}_{G,t}$. Assume also that the exchange rate adjusts instantaneously such that the changes in the German prices times the changes in the exchange rate equal the change in the U.S. inflation. In this case, the purchasing price parity (PPP) or the law of one price (LOOP) hold. Given these assumptions, we can compute the NPV of the project (NPV_2).

Let $\dot{P}_{US,t} = 5$ percent p.a. and $\dot{P}_{G,t} = 2$ percent p.a. The change in the exchange rate that maintains LOOP or PPP is:

$$\Delta S_{t,t+1}^{\$/DM} = \frac{1 + \dot{P}_{US,t+1}}{1 + \dot{P}_{G,t+1}} - 1$$

All payments and receipts are made at the end of the period. Given PPP, the exchange rates at the end of each year of the five- year horizon of the project will be:

Year	$/DM Exchange Rate
Current	.400000
19X1	.411765
19X2	.423876
19X3	.436343
19X4	.449176
19X5	.462386

The five-year interest rate in the United States will change relative to the base case (scenario I) to reflect the expected inflation. The new rate r_n will be:

$$r_n = (1 + .10)(1.05) - 1 = .155 \, (\text{or } 15.5\%)$$

All other U.S. prices will rise by $1 + \dot{P}_{US}$ every year. The NPV of the project is:

$$
\begin{aligned}
NPV_2 = \Big\{ & \big[(3.125 \times 1.02 \times .411765) - (1 \times 1.05)\big] \frac{1}{1.155} \\
& + \big[(3.125 \times 1.02^2 \times .423876) - (1 \times 1.05^2)\big] \frac{1}{(1.155)^2} \\
& + \big[(3.125 \times 1.02^3 \times .436343) - (1 \times 1.05^3)\big] \frac{1}{(1.155)^3} \\
& + \big[(3.125 \times 1.02^4 \times .449176) - (1 \times 1.05^4)\big] \frac{1}{1.155^4} \\
& + \big[(3.125 \times 1.02^5 \times .462387) - (1 \times 1.05^5)\big] \frac{1}{1.155^5} \Big\}
\end{aligned}
$$

$$\times \, 100,000,000 - 90,000,000 = \$4,770,000$$

In a perfect market, where PPP holds all the time and where adjustments are costless, the value of the project is not affected by either U.S. or German inflation rates since PPP means that, in U.S. dollar terms, all prices in the United States or Germany are moving at the same rate of change.

Thus, the PPP case is similar to the aforementioned across-the-board inflation case. In both cases, the capital-budgeting decision is not affected at all by inflation/disinflation. In this case, the investment decision is invariable with regard to two different rates of inflation in the two countries.

Scenario III: Lagged Adjustment in the Exchange Rate. Although the PPP is a fair representation of the long-term tendency in the market, it does not hold instantaneously. Assume now that exchange rates do adjust with a one-year lag. The calculated exchange rates will be now:

Year	$/DM Exchange Rate
Current	.400000
19X1	.400000
19X2	.411765
19X3	.423876
19X4	.436343
19X5	.449170

The net present value of the project will now be:

$$NPV_3 = \left\{ [(3.125 \times 1.02 \times .40) - (1 \times 1.05)] \frac{1}{1.155} \right.$$

$$+ [(3.125 \times 1.02^2 \times .411765) - (1 \times 1.05^2)] \frac{1}{1.155^2}$$

$$+ [(3.125 \times 1.02^3 \times .423876) - (1 \times 1.05^3)] \frac{1}{1.155^3}$$

$$+ [(3.125 \times 1.02^4 \times .436343) - (1 \times 1.05^4)] \frac{1}{1.155^4}$$

$$\left. + [(3.125 \times 1.02^5 \times .449170) - (1 \times 1.05^5)] \frac{1}{1.155^5} \right\}$$

$$\times 100,000,000 - 90,000,000 = -\$8,768,534$$

As the calculated NPV, given the specific adjustment process assumed here, is negative, the project is rejected. Note that the discounted difference due to a one-year lag in the exchange rate is very substantial, $4,770,000 − (−$8,768,534) = $13,538,534.

Scenario IV: Overall, Uneven Adjustment in the Exchange Rate. Keeping all the data identical to that of the second scenario, we assume that the exchange rate does adjust according to PPP over the five-year period, but not every year. In other words, sometimes the exchange rate overshoots and sometimes it undershoots.

This situation can be summarized by the following two conditions:

$$\Delta S_{t,t+5}^{\$/DM} = \frac{1 + \dot{P}_{t,t+5}^{US}}{1 + \dot{P}_{t,t+5}^{G}} - 1$$

$$\text{and } \Delta S_{t,t+1} \neq \frac{1 + \dot{P}_{t,t+1}^{US}}{1 + \dot{P}_{t,t+1}^{G}} - 1; \quad t = 1, 2, \ldots 5$$

One possible assumed behavior of the exchange rate over the five-year horizon of the project is:

Year	$/DM Exchange Rate
Current	.400000
19X1	.405000
19X2	.430000
19X3	.432000
19X4	.455000
19X5	.462387

Fitting the new pattern of the exchange rate to the NPV model, we obtain:

$$NPV_4 = \left\{ \left[(3.125 \times 1.02 \times .4050) - (1 \times 1.05) \right] \frac{1}{1.155} \right.$$

$$+ \left[(3.15 \times 1.02^2 \times .4300) - (1 \times 1.105^2) \right] \frac{1}{1.155^2}$$

$$+ \left[(3.125 \times 1.02^3 \times .4320) - (1 \times 1.05^3) \right] \frac{1}{1.155^3}$$

$$+ \left[(3.125 \times 1.02^4 \times .4550) - (1 \times 1.105^4) \right] \frac{1}{1.155^4}$$

$$+ \left[(3.125 \times 1.02^5 \times .462387) - (1 \times 1.05^5) \right] \frac{1}{1.155^5} \right\}$$

$$\times 100,000,000 - 90,000,000 = \$4,596,800$$

Obviously, the NPV in this type of scenario is very sensitive to the precise pattern of the overshooting and the undershooting of the exchange rates. In particular, the timing is essential. Even if the decision maker knows that over the life of the project, PPP holds *on the average*, the timing is critical for the capital-budgeting decision.

For example, suppose that it is assumed that now we are in a "below-average" dollar-value period relative to European currencies and the yen. It is also assumed that there exists a high probability of a reversal such that the PPP will hold, on average, over the next five years. This information should be included explicitly in the capital-budgeting process as it affects the results.

In all the calculations we have presented, the riskless nominal rate of discount was employed. This is a correct procedure in scenarios I and II, where there is no risk. However, once the cash flows become volatile, as they do in the last two scenarios, a risk-adjusted, higher discount rate should be used. In this regard, NPV_3 and NPV_4 are too high.

The four scenarios are summarized in table 3–2. The data presented in table 3–2 show clearly that the net present value is affected by the nature of the assumed inflation in the output and input markets. In our specific example, the relative inflation is affecting the cash flows and, thus, the NPV through the changes in the exchange rates.

Obviously, there exist other scenarios where the NPV of the project is higher than the base case, NPV_1. For example, the exchange rates may be "overvalued" (that is, different than the PPP rate in a way beneficial to the project) for the whole of the five-year period. We choose, however, to focus on the downside risk rather than on the potential for profit.

In the case of the brewery, we have assumed that the prices of all the inputs are moving together. This is an unrealistic assumption. Also, it does not allow for compensating changes in the quantities of inputs employed as a response to changes in relative prices.

In the next section, we will relax the aforementioned limiting assumption and will move into a situation where the relative prices of the inputs may change with a shift in the rate of inflation/disinflation.

Table 3–2
A Comparison of the Four Scenarios Using Different Assumptions with Regard to Inflation

Scenario	Main Assumption	NPV ($)[1]
I	Constant prices	4,770,000
II	Instantaneous PPP	4,770,000
III	Lagged PPP (one period)	– 8,768,534
IV	Long-term average[2]	4,596,800

[1]Discounted at a nominal riskless rate.

[2]Short-term compensating movements. The results will differ if all the compensation will come in the last year.

Changes in the Relative Prices of Inputs,
Outputs and the Discount Rate

Following the discussion in chapter 2, assume a process of inflation/disinflation that has a varying effect on the prices of various goods, services, and factors of production. This situation can be expressed as:

$$\dot{P}_t \neq \dot{P}_{Q_t} \neq \dot{P}_{L_t} \neq \dot{P}_{M_t}$$

where $\dot{P}_t$ is the periodic change in the general price index. Assume further that all the relevant investment projects can be divided into two groups. The first group consists of those projects where it is relatively easy to substitute one input for another. The second group consists of those projects where such substitutability is limited by technological or cost reasons. To see how the inflation affects the net present value of a given project under those assumptions, let us consider the following case.

An apparel manufacturer is examining a proposed new production facility to produce shirts. The proposed project calls for a capital investment of $1,170,000. The life of the project is five years. At the end of the period, the equipment has no value. Output is produced by combining labor and materials. Formally, the production function can be written as:

$$Q = KC^{\alpha}L^{\beta}M^{\gamma}$$

where C, L, and M, are capital, labor, and materials, respectively. As before, we assume that Q, the planned production (let us say quantity of shirts) is given, and C, the capital outlay, is given. (The assumption of fixed capital is appropriate because this is the whole idea of the capital-budgeting decision. That is, does it make sense to carry out the proposed project?)

From the planned investment, and based on current prices, we derive the following information:

$$C = \$1,170,000$$
$$Q = 300,000 \text{ units}$$
$$P_Q = \$5/\text{unit}$$
$$L = 100,000 \text{ hours}$$
$$P_L = \$4.50/\text{hour}$$
$$M = 500,000 \text{ yards}$$
$$P_M = \$1.35/\text{yard}$$
$$P_L/P_M = 3.335; \quad \alpha = 1; \quad \beta = 0.2 \quad \gamma = 0.3, \quad K = 0.0005$$
$$i = 5 \text{ percent per annum (the riskless rate)}$$

Let us now examine a number of possible scenarios.

Scenario I: Constant Prices. As before, this is the base case. All the other scenarios are computed relative to this initial case.

$$NPV = \sum_{t=1}^{N} [Q_t P_{Q_t} - L_t P_{L_t} - M_t P_{M_t}] \frac{1}{(1 + r)^t} - I_o$$

Inserting the data, we obtain

$$NPV_I = \sum_{t=1}^{5} [(300{,}000 \times 5) - (100{,}000 \times 4.50) - (500{,}000 \times 1.35)]$$

$$\frac{1}{(1.05)^t} - 1{,}170{,}000$$

$$= \$1{,}623{,}554 - \$1{,}170{,}000 = \$453{,}554.$$

Scenario II: An Increase in the Input Prices Relative to the Output Prices (Income Effect Only). This case is similar in character to the case of the lagged exchange rates shown before. The change can be regarded as a shift in the terms of trade between inputs and outputs, without technological compensation. In other words, the way in which a given production is carried out, the combination of inputs will not change.

Suppose that the general price change is $\dot{P}_t = 5$ percent for every t, $t = 1, 2, \ldots 5$. It follows that the nominal riskless discount rate will be $r_{n_t} = (1 + r)(1 + \dot{P})^t$.

The changes in the prices of the output and the inputs are:

$$\dot{P}_Q = 5 \text{ percent p.a.}$$

$$\dot{P} = \dot{P}_L = \dot{P}_M = 7 \text{ percent p.a. where } \dot{P}' \text{ is the annual change in the price of the inputs.}$$

It follows that the net present value of the project is:

$$NPV_{II} = \sum_{t=1}^{5} [Q_o P_{Q_o}(1 + \dot{P}_Q)^t - (L_t P_{L_t} + M_t P_{M_t})(1 + \dot{P})^t] \frac{1}{(1 + i)^t} - I_o$$

$$= \sum_{t=1}^{5} 300{,}000\{5(1.05)^t - [(1/3)(4.50) + (5/3)(1.35)](1.07)^t\}$$

$$\frac{1}{(1.1025)^t} - 1{,}170{,}000 = 177{,}300$$

The decrease in the net present value in scenario 2, compared to scenario 1, is comparable to what is known in microeconomics as "income effect." The inputs have become more expensive relative to the output. This situation is defined as a worsening in terms of trade. The firm is seen here as a vehicle to trade a combination of inputs for a combination of outputs (in the case just described, a single output). It is useful to think of what happens to this trade between inputs and outputs as relative prices change and then to see how this information will affect current investment decisions.

Scenario III: A Change in the Relative Prices of the Inputs (Income and Substitution Effects). Assume now that the inflationary/disinflationary process affects the prices of different inputs in a different way. Specifically, let us assume that P_Q is increasing at a constant rate of 5 percent p.a.; P_M is also increasing at a constant rate of 5 percent p.a.; and P_L is increasing at an annual rate of 10 percent.

Given technology of combining labor and materials as given by the production function in equation 3.1, one response to a change in the relative price of labor in terms of material would be to change the proportions of the two inputs in producing the prescribed output. (It should be noted that we have assumed that the annual quantity of shirts to be produced is given and constant.) The substitution of labor for materials is carried out by moving to buy partially finished products. We regard these as purchased materials and express the quantity by the equivalent quantity (in terms of expenditure) of yards of materials. Thus, it would appear that the apparel manufacturer is substituting units of labor by units (yards) of materials.

In table 3–3, we present the unit prices of both labor and material, the relative price (P_L/P_M), and the resulting quantities to be employed in each one of the next five years. The quantities were derived from the production function and are based on the assumed patterns of the prices.

Given the information in table 3–3, we can procede now to calculate the net present value of the proposed investment project.

Table 3–3
Prices, Relative Prices, and Employed Quantities—The Apparel Case

Year	P_L ($)	P_M ($)	P_L/P_M	L (units)	M (units)
19X1	4.50	1.35	3.33	100,000	500,000
19X2	4.95	1.42	3.49	97,480	509,723
19X3	5.44	1.49	3.65	94,750	518,851
19X4	6.00	1.56	3.85	91,861	529,944
19X5	6.60	1.64	4.02	89,413	539,788

$$NPV_{III} = \left\{[5 - (.33 \times 4.50) + (1.66 \times 1.35)]\frac{1}{1.05}\right.$$

$$+ [5.25 - (.325 \times 4.95) + (1.699 \times 1.42)]\frac{1}{1.125}$$

$$+ [5.51 - (.316 \times 5.44) + (1.730 \times 1.49)]\frac{1}{1.158}$$

$$+ [5.79 - (.306 \times 6.00) + (1.766 \times 1.56)]\frac{1}{1.215}$$

$$\left.+ [6.08 - (.298 \times 6.60) + (1.799 \times 1.64)]\frac{1}{1.276}\right\}$$

$$\times\ 300,000\ -\ 1,170,000\ =\ 407,232$$

Both the terms of trade between the prices of the output and the inputs, and the relative prices of the inputs change. As a result, we have a reduction in the net present value, due to the worsening terms of trade (a negative income effect) and a correction by substituting materials for labor as the latter becomes more expensive. (This is a positive substitution effect, being positive as it increases the NPV relative to the former case.)

The sum total is still a lower NPV than in the base case, but it is higher than it would be if we could not optimize the production process as the relative prices of the inputs do change. As in the brewery case, we choose to focus on worsening terms of trade. If the terms of trade improve, inputs will become cheaper relative to output, and we will get the opposite results. The NPV will increase as the terms of trade improve.

In general, the case of a change in the relative prices can be described by taking the following partial derivative:

$$\frac{\partial NPV}{\partial(PL/PM)}$$

$$\frac{\partial CF}{\partial(P_L/P_M{}^*)} = \gamma K' P_Q L^{\beta+\gamma} P_M^{-\gamma} P_L^{\gamma-1}\left(\frac{\gamma}{\beta}\right)^\gamma - L\left(1 + \frac{\gamma}{\beta}\right)$$

$$= \frac{\gamma}{P_L}K' P_Q L^{\beta+\gamma}\left(\frac{P_L}{P_M}\right)^\gamma\left(\frac{\gamma}{\beta}\right)^\gamma - L\left(1 + \frac{\gamma}{\beta}\right)$$

$$= \frac{\gamma}{P_L}QP_Q - L\left(1 + \frac{\gamma}{\beta}\right)$$

$$\text{as } NPV = \sum_{t=1}^{n} CF_t/(1 + r)^t. \tag{3.11}$$

It follows that:

$$\frac{\partial NPV}{\partial (P_L/P_M{}^*)} = \sum_{t=1}^{n} \left[\frac{\gamma Q_t P Q_t}{PL_t} - L_t\left(1 + \frac{g}{\beta}\right) \right] \frac{1}{(1 + r)^t} - I_o$$

$P_M{}^*$ assumed to be constant, so all the *changes* in the relative prices are related to changes in P_L.

As P_L will go up, the expression $\partial Q_t P_{Q_t}/P_{L_t}$ will go down. This is similar to the income effect, and in the case of an increase in the relative cost of labor, the value of the project will go down. L, the number of hours or other units of labor, will also go down whereas P_L will go up. The expression $L_t(1 + \gamma/\beta)$ will go down. This is the corrective effect of the adjustment in the quantities of inputs to be employed as the relative prices change. In our terms, this is similar to a substitution effect.

In this analysis, we have assumed a constant discount rate. As was shown earlier, the discount rate will go up with an increase in the perceived volatility of the cash flows, and it will reduce the value of the project accordingly.

The net present value is calculated by discounting the cash flows by the appropriate discount rate. In this chapter the focus was on the way by which the cash flows are affected by the various types of the inflationary processes. In the next chapter we move to discuss the issue of what is the appropriate discount rate.

4

The Real Rate of Interest and the Cost of Funds

Inflation and the Real Rate of Interest

In the capital-budgeting model we have presented, the discount rate has been stated as a "basis" rate, r, plus an adjustment to the future changes in the relevant prices. Thus, in the case of across-the-board inflation, the discount rate for the first period was:

$$(1 + r)(1 + \dot{p}).$$

This presentation is similar to the well-known Fisher's statement where the observed interest rate (the nominal rate, i) has been decomposed into two parts: the real interest rate (r) and the price changes component ($\dot{p}$). Thus, the classic presentation is:

$$(1 + i) = (1 + r)(1 + \dot{p}) \tag{4.1}$$

where i is the observed nominal rate of interest, r is the real interest rate, and $\dot{p}$ is the change in the relevant price index over the period under consideration. r, the real rate, can be thought of as a general commodity rate of interest, and $\dot{p}$ is measured over a general price index. The real rate of interest is equal to:

$$r = [(1 + i)/(1 + \dot{p})] - 1 \tag{4.2}$$

This presentation is fraught with problems. First, at the time the interest rate is determined, $\dot{p}$ (the change in the price index) is not known. Assuming that $\dot{p}$ is a random variable and replacing $\dot{p}$ by $E(\dot{p})$, the expected value of the distribution of possible changes in the price index, does not solve the problem. This is so because the actual change in the price index (the rate of inflation, $\dot{p}$) will be different from the expected inflation over the relevant period. As a result of this difference, the actual inflation-deflated rate of interest will not be the same as the ex ante real rate of interest. This relationship is summarized in equation 4.3.

$$r = \frac{(1 + i)}{1 + E(\dot{p})} - 1 \neq \frac{(1 + i)}{(1 + \dot{p})} - 1 = r_a \qquad (4.3)$$

where r is the expected real rate and r_a is the actual inflation-deflated interest rate.

The distribution of the deviations $d = (r - r_a)$ has an effect on the risk associated with the cost of funds. Moreover, both logical analysis and a casual empiricism seem to suggest that the shape and the parameters of the distribution of the difference d are dependent on the direction and the volatility of the rate of inflation.

To illustrate, let us examine the one-year implied rate of inflation from the one-year interest rate. In doing this, we are following Fisher's equation. The implicit rate is then compared to the actual rate of inflation measured by the actual changes in the CPI over the twelve-month period for which the interest rate is applicable. Given these measures, the actual inflation-deflated rate of interest is computed.

Data for the period 1976–81 are presented in table 4–1. The twelve-month interest rate is defined as the market yield for that period at the Treasury bonds market. This rate is denoted i. The inflation rate $\dot{p}$ is defined as the change in the CPI over the same period for which the yield is applicable. r_a, the actual inflation-deflated cost of funds, is calculated as:

$$r_a = [(1 + i)/(1 + \dot{p})] - 1, \qquad (4.4)$$

i, $\dot{p}$, and r_a for the period 1976–85 are presented in table 4.1.

Table 4–1
Interest Rate, Actual Inflation, and the Inflation-Adjusted Cost of Funds, 1976–85
(annual percentages)

	Interest Rate, i	Inflation Rate, $\dot{p}$	Inflation-Adjusted Cost of Funds, r_a
1976	5.88	6.5	(0.58)
1977	6.09	8.9	(2.58)
1978	8.34	12.2	(3.44)
1979	10.67	12.6	(1.71)
1980	12.05	10.2	1.68
1981	14.78	5.1	9.21
1982	12.27	2.9	9.11
1983	9.57	4.2	5.15
1984	10.89	3.7	6.93
1985	9.86	1.6	8.13

Source: *Federal Reserve Bulletin.*

As is shown in figure 4–1 the rate of inflation changes over time, the inflation-adjusted cost of funds does not adjust immediately. In a period of unexpected rise in the rate of inflation, the inflation-adjusted cost of funds is low, sometimes negative. Where unexpected decline in the rate of inflation does occur, what we have defined as a process of unexpected disinflation— the inflation-deflated cost of funds—becomes very high.

The data presented in table 4–1 are consistent with a world of imperfect information. If one specifies a model of imperfect information, the data can be tested. One such model is the "delayed-information model" developed and tested by Choate and Archer (1975). According to this model, the participants in the capital market are using the following predictor for $\dot{p}$, the actual rate of inflation in the next period:

$$E(\dot{p})_t = \sum_{j=0}^{\infty} (1 - \Psi)^j \Psi (\dot{p}_{t-j-1} + \Delta \dot{p}_{t-j-1}) \tag{4.5}$$

$$j = t - 1, t - 2, t - 3, \ldots, t - \infty$$

where: $\Delta \dot{P}$ = an accelerating price term

Ψ = a constant rate of information dissemination, $0 < \Psi < 1$

$\dot{p}$ = the periodic rate of inflation

If the rate of inflation has been rising for a number of periods, let us say from 1976 to 1979, and then starts to decline, there will be a prediction error. This is so because, according to the view expressed in this model, the past record has an important role in predicting the future rate of inflation. Such a prediction error will result in "overshooting" or "undershooting" the real rate of interest, as is demonstrated by the data in table 4–1.

A volatile rate of inflation or disinflation is associated with an increase in the volatility of the inflation-adjusted cost of funds. Put in other words, a volatile rate of inflation tends to increase the expected cost of funds to the firm. To see how this result is obtained, let us examine the different sources of funds and ascertain how the costs of these sources of funds change with shifts in the rate of inflation. We will follow both logic and tradition. We will begin with debt instruments and move to equity next. Having done so, we will proceed next to derive appropriate funding policy for firms in different regimes of inflation or disinflation.

The Cost of Debt Instruments

Traditionally, sources of funds are classified as debt instruments and equity vehicles of various types. In a perfect market with certainty, there is no differ-

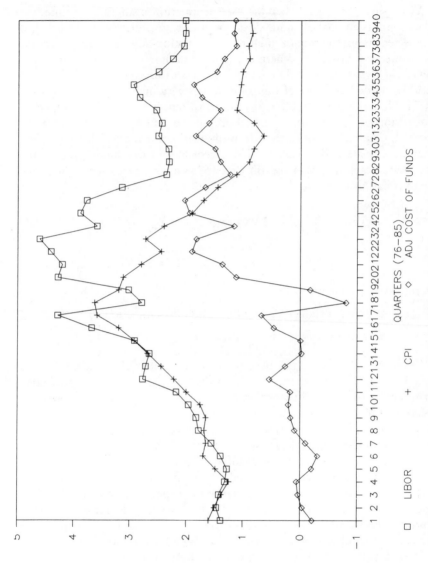

Figure 4–1. The Inflation Rate and the Inflation-Adjusted Cost of Funds, 1976–85

ence in the costs of funds for debt and equity. (Indeed, there is no distinction between the two categories.) Once uncertainty is acknowledged, the difference between the claims of debtholders and those of the shareholders is according to their seniority. As the firm generates cash flows, they are distributed to different claimants. Debtholders have priority over the shareholders. Their claims have to be settled before the shareholders can claim their part. However, the settling of any claim depends on the availability of cash flows to meet these claims.

To illustrate this point, let us assume that the free cash flows of a given firm are normally distributed where:

$$CF_t \sim N[E(CF), \sigma(CF)]$$

The distribution is assumed to be stationary. That is, the distribution of the free cash flows does not change from one year to the next. Cash flows (CF) are the cash flows available to meet financial obligations, usually defined as the EBIT (earnings before interest and taxes). Such a case is described in figure 4–2. Given this distribution, we define a default risk measure as the probability of not having sufficient cash flows to meet the financial obligations to the debtholders. If D is the amount of outstanding debt in dollars, and r_d is the interest rate charged by the debtholders (in nominal terms), then $d_t = D_{r_{d_t}}$ is the periodic interest payment. The probability of default is:

$$P_d\{CF < d\}$$

This probability is expressed by the shaded area under the curve. Note that this is an extremely simple model. It does not allow for partial payments or

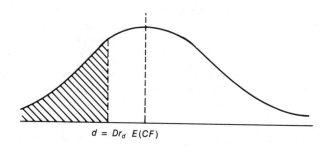

$$d = Dr_d \quad E(CF)$$

Figure 4–2. The Distribution of Cash Flows

for a source of payments outside the contemporaneous cash flows generated by the firm. However, the main conclusion of this model is not affected by its simplicity. The main conclusion is that, given the assumptions on the generating process of the cash flows, there is always some risk of default. This is so because in the normal distribution case:

$$P_d\{CF < d\} > 0$$

The probability of not having sufficient funds is always positive.

If r_f is a really default-free rate of interest, then it follows that the rate charged by lenders should be at least:

$$r_d = r_f/(1 - P\{CF < d\})$$

As $[1 - P\{CF < d\}] < 0$, $r_d > r_f$. r_d is an expected, or required rate; it may or may not be realized.

This is true even if the lender is risk-neutral, as with large financial institutions with large and diversified portfolios. The difference between r_d and r_f will be larger if the lenders are risk-averse.

Until now, we have assumed implicitly that there is no inflation and that nominal and real values are the same. This is clearly not the case in today's world. Once inflation (or disinflation) is introduced, the default risk becomes more pronounced and more important.

As was shown earlier, the effect of a given process of inflation on financial decisions depends on the nature of the inflationary process. As before, we will begin with across-the-board inflation.

The Case of Across-the-Board Inflation

Across-the-board inflation affects all prices equally. As we have seen earlier, across-the-board inflation has a scale effect in nominal terms, and it does not change the relative prices of either the outputs or the inputs. In terms of the distribution of cash flows, it will amount to a multiplication of the distribution (or the probability density function) by a scalar. In a world of a known rate of inflation for a given period, the periodic, nominally fixed interest rate will reflect the known rate of inflation for that period. If the firm maintains a constant level of debt in real terms (adjusted to the known rate of inflation), the interest payment in real terms will remain constant. Under these assumptions, the default risk will remain the same. The cost of debt in real terms will remain the same, and so will the cost of capital. Nominal changes will occur and everything will change in unison at the same rate, the rate of inflation.

If the rate of inflation is uncertain and the periodic interest rate is nominally fixed, there will be changes. Both lenders and borrowers have to agree on a nominally fixed rate which implicitly includes a prediction with regard to the periodic rate of inflation. As we have seen from the data presented in table 4–1, they may vary quite substantially. The distribution of the periodic cash flows is not changing in real terms (due to the assumption of across-the-board inflation), but the interest payment, in real terms, may change. Assuming a symmetric distribution of errors with regard to the rate of inflation in the next period (an equally likely chance of overshooting or undershooting), the measure of the default risk will go up. As $P\{CF < d\}$ will go up, r_d will go up as well. As was shown earlier, this will increase the cost of capital for the project.

The prediction error and the cost of an error will go down as the period for which the interest rate is nominally fixed becomes shorter. Consequently, we have observed a tendency in the financial markets to replace long-term nominally fixed interest rates with a string of short-term contracts, where the periodic rate of interest is adjustable.

Empirically, it has been shown that the variability of the rate of inflation is positively related to the level of inflation. As the prediction error of the next-period rate of inflation will increase with the period-to-period variability of the rate of inflation, so will the probability of default. This is similar to a contraction of the debt capacity. A contraction of the debt capacity will affect the optimal debt/equity ratio for any given firm. Given the fact that the cost of equity is greater than the cost of debt, the result will be an increase in the cost of capital.

One common way to reduce this type of financial risk is by varying the nominal rate of interest in such a way that the real, inflation-adjusted rate will remain constant. (In the case of across-the-board inflation, the real rate of interest and the inflation-adjusted interest rate are the same.) The best way to do that is to link the nominal rate of interest to the periodic changes in the general price level, the CPI. Some countries that have experienced a very high and volatile rate of inflation have developed a fairly universal linkage system. Such systems include linkage of savings deposits, loan contracts, bonds, and wages. Brazil and Israel are two cases in point. It has been argued that universal linkage tends to reduce the will to fight inflation at the political level. However, in the case of an across-the-board inflation with universal linkage, there are no real changes and, consequently, no need to fight inflation.

Linkage to CPI is rather rare and somewhat cumbersome as the changes in the CPI are computed and published at most on a monthly basis. A much more popular way to reduce the risk associated with an uncertain rate of inflation is linking the rate of interest to a short-term market rate of interest. The London interbank borrowing rate (LIBOR) is a common benchmark. Usually, the length of one period, the period between adjustments, is six months.

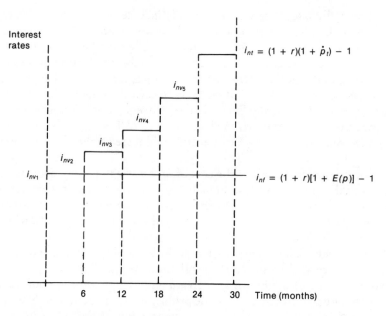

Figure 4–3. A Comparison between the Medium-Term Nominally Fixed Rate and Variable Rates of Interest

The linkage is based on the observation that every six months, the rate of interest for the next six months reflects the expectations of the market with regard to the rate of inflation for that period. Given a delayed information model such as the one presented earlier, the market will adjust the prediction in a stepwise fashion. This process will reduce the exposure to the risk resulting from the deviations between the actual and the expected (or implicit) rate of inflation. This process is described in figure 4–3.

If the expected rate of inflation at time 0 for the next thirty months is $E(\dot{p})$, and the real rate of interest is r, then the nominally fixed rate for the whole period, i_{nf}, is equal to the product of one plus the real rate times one plus the expected rate of inflation, minus unity. This nominally fixed rate is depicted by the straight line $(1 + r)[1 + E(\dot{p})] - 1$. If the actual rate of inflation $\dot{p}_t$ is monotonously increasing over the thirty-month period relative to the expected rate of inflation at the beginning of the period, then i_{nt} is the nominal rate which keeps r, the real rate, constant for all t. Obviously, as $\dot{p}_t$ is monotonously increasing, so should i_{nt}. Such an arrangement is not practical.

What is practical and is commonly done is to link the interest rate for the length of the contract to some market-determined rate of interest. Suppose that this rate is adjusted to the actual rate of inflation every six months. The

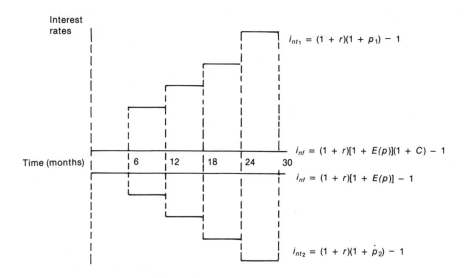

Figure 4–4. Nominal Rates of Interest in an Uncertain Inflation

resulting rate, i_{nv} (the nominal variable rate) is depicted in figure 4–2 by the step function below the rate i_{nt}.

In the case of a nominally fixed rate, the deviations between the contract rate and the nominal rate, which would keep the real rate constant, are represented by the area between the straight line, i_{nf}, and the upward-sloping line, i_{nt}. If only nominally fixed long rates are available and there is an unexpected increase in the rate of inflation, the lenders will suffer a substantial loss. If a variable rate such as i_{nv} is used, the deviation and the loss will be reduced to the shaded area between the step function, i_{nv}, and the upward-sloping line, i_{nt}.

If the actual inflation is decreasing relative to the expected inflation, we will get a mirror image of the situation presented in figure 4–2. The contract nominally fixed rate will yield an inflation-deflated rate higher than the ex ante real rate of interest.

As both lenders and borrowers expect deviations from the expected rate of inflation, the nominally fixed rate may include a risk premium. This case is presented in figure 4–4. To see how the risk premium is generated, consider the following illustration.

Example: Suppose that at time 0 a certain corporation has to borrow some money for a period of thirty months. The corporation can borrow at either a nominally fixed rate or a variable rate of interest linked to the six-month LIBOR. Let us assume that it is equally likely that the actual rate of inflation, $\dot{p}_t$, will decrease or increase, relative to the expected rate of inflation for the thirty-month period at the beginning of the period. (For simplicity, we assume that the actual inflation rate will be either increasing or decreasing monotonously for the whole period.)

In a world of risk neutrality, the market rate for nominally fixed, thirty-month contracts will be i_{nf}. However, in a more realistic world where risk aversion is a better descriptor of the behavior of both lenders and borrowers, the nominally fixed rate will contain a risk premium. Thus,

$$i_{nf}^* = (1 + r)[1 + E(\dot{p})](1 + C) - 1$$

where C is the risk premium, $C > 0$. It should be noted that by fixing the nominal rate, i_{nf}^*, for the maturity of the contract, the actual inflation-deflated rate is variable, and it will be determined by the differences between the expected rate of inflation and the actual rate of inflation in any given period.

The Case of Terms-of-Trade Inflation/Disinflation

Although it is not realistic, the case of an across-the-board inflation is very instructive. It points out what are the factors within the inflationary (or disinflationary) process that contribute to the risk and, therefore, to an increase in the cost of funds. However, most inflationary processes are of the terms-of-trade type. Such inflationary processes do change the relative prices of inputs and outputs.

In chapter 3, it was shown that, given an inflationary process associated with a contemporaneous change in the relative prices, three changes will occur in the cash flows generated by the firm. First, the volatility of the cash flows will increase. Second, there will be an income effect; if the relative prices move against the firm, the value of the firm will go down. If the relative prices will move "for the firm" (a positive change in the terms of trade), the value of the firm will go up. If it is equally likely that the change will go either for or against the firm, and given a general risk aversion, the value of the firm will go down, compared to a no-inflation situation. Third, if the changes in the relative prices affect the prices of various inputs differently, the income effect will be mitigated by a substitution effect. The technological ability to substitute one input for another determines the extent of the correction via substitution.

To see how this result is obtained in terms of the current analysis of the cost of funds, let us go back to the earlier example. Again, assume that the cash flows are normally distributed with the parameters $E(CF)$ and $\sigma(CF)$ as the expected value and the dispersion measure. The distribution is assumed to be stationary over time. $P\{CF < d\}$ is the default risk measure, and $d = Dr_d$ is the expected interest payment to be paid at t.

The possible changes in the relative prices introduce another dimension of uncertainty; in general, they increase the volatility of the cash flows. In the simplest case, this will produce "fatter tails" for the distribution. In other words, $E(CF)$ will remain the same, but the dispersion measure will go up from $\sigma(CF)$ to $\sigma_1(CF)$. This will result in a higher probability of default $P_1\{CF < d\}$ and, therefore, in a higher required interest rate on the debt. Thus:

$$r_{d_1} > r_d; \quad \text{this is so because}$$

$$P_1\{CF < d\} > P\{CF < d\}$$

where $P\{CF < d\}$ is the probability for default in an across-the-board inflation.

An Illustration of Uncertainty's Impact

To illustrate the effect of the uncertainty of the real cash flow (inflation-deflated cash flow) on the cost of funds, let us consider the following numerical example. Note that the uncertainty can be associated either with an across-the-board or a terms-of-trade inflation.

Let us define the inflation-deflated rate of interest for any given firm as:

$$r_j = \frac{1 + r_d}{1 + \dot{p}_j} - 1$$

where $\dot{p}_j$ is the changes in the prices of inputs and outputs of firm j. Under the terms-of-trade–type of inflation, $\dot{p}_{jt} \neq \dot{p}_t$, where $\dot{p}_t$ is the change in the CPI during t. r_j is then the firm-specific real rate of interest.

$\dot{p}_{jt}$ is a random variable (although we will see later that in some cases, we do know something about the distribution of $\dot{p}_{jt}$). Therefore, r_{jt} is a random variable. r_{jt} can be viewed as the real cost of debt, adjusted to the changes in the cash flows as a result of the changes in the relative prices. To see how this is derived, let us go back to the definition of the default risk. The interest payments are determined by the product of the outstanding debt, D, and the required nominal interest rate by the debtholders, r_d. The inflation-deflated (ex post real) rate of interest for the market as a whole is:

$$r_{a_t} = \frac{1 + r_{dt}}{1 + \dot{p}_t} - 1; \qquad \dot{p}_{t_{|}} = \text{CPI}$$

For the firm, the equivalent rate is $r_{jt} = 1 + r_{dt}/1 + p_{jt} - 1$. As $\dot{p}_j \neq \dot{p}_t$ so $r_{jt} \neq r_{a_t}$. The difference between these two rates depends on $\dot{p}_t/\dot{p}_j$. The more variable this ratio is, the more risky is the firm relative to the market. It should be emphasized that we are concerned here with financial risk as it is expressed in the probability of default. Also, as we pointed out earlier, it is assumed that this type of risk does matter.

To illustrate this point, let us examine the following example. Assume a firm with an expected value of annual cash flows of $1,000,000 and a standard deviation of the cash flows of $300,000. It follows that there is a probability of .95 that the annual cash flows will be equal to or greater than $496,200. Let us assume that the management of this firm has decided that they are willing to pay out this amount as the firm's debt service. Assume further that the riskless real interest rate, r_f, is 6 percent p.a. From our earlier discussion, it follows that the required rate of interest by debtholders will be:

$$r_d = r_f/(1 - p\{CF < d\})$$
$$.0632 = .06/(1 - .05)$$

Given the allocated amount for debt service of $496,200 and $r_d = .0632$, the firm can support an outstanding debt of $7,851,265. Now, assume that the interest rate is adjusted annually to reflect the expected rate of inflation for the next year. Assume further that lenders and borrowers are risk-neutral. If the expected rate of inflation for the next year is 5 percent, then the required rate of interest by the debtholders will be:

$$r_{dt} = \frac{1 + r_{d_{t-1}}}{(1 + \dot{p}_{t-1})}[1 + E(\dot{p})t] - 1$$

or in our case where the base year has zero inflation:

$$.1164 = (1.0632)(1.05) - 1$$

If at the same time the relevant prices for the firm go up by only 2 percent, the firm-specific actual rate of interest (nominal rate deflated by the firm-specific inflation) will be

$$r_j = (1 + r_{dt})/(1 + P_{jt}) - 1$$

or, given our example:

$$.0945 = (1.1164)/(1.02) - 1$$

whereas the market rate including default risk is .0632. Given the firm's specific r_{jt}, it also implies that the debt capacity of the firm, with the same default risk, has declined from \$7,851,256 to \$5,250,794. The difference in the debt capacity (holding the level of default risk constant) of \$2,600,462 reflects the increase in the risk due to the differences between $\dot{P}_t$ (the changes in the general price index) and $\dot{p}_{jt}$ (the changes in the firm's specific price index). Using the data in this example, but replacing the given probability of default

$$P\{CF < d\} = .05$$

by the implicit probability of default for the distribution of the firm's cash flows next period under relative price changes, we obtain

$$1 + r_j = [1 + r_f/(1 - P\{CF^* < d^*\})]/(1 + \dot{p}_{jt})$$

$P\{CF^* < d^*\}$ is the probability of default, or the financial risk measure in inflation-deflated terms, adjusted to the changes in the firm's specific price index, $\dot{p}_{jt}$.

In the case of our example, we get:

$$1.0945 = [1.06/(1 - p\{CF^* < d^*\})]/(1.02)$$

and $P\{CF^* < d^*\} = .053$.

In the case of a terms-of-trade inflation, the fatter tails of the distribution of the cash flows will increase the risk for any given level of debt. Hence, the cost of borrowed funds will increase as well.

Hedging

In the case of the across-the-board inflation, general and partial linkage systems were used as a way to reduce this type of financial risk. It has been shown that linkage of the interest rate to the CPI does eliminate this risk altogether, where linkage to a market-determined interest rate, such as LIBOR, does reduce the risk. In the case of a terms-of-trade–type inflation (or disinflation), this mechanism does not provide any relief. The deviations of the firm's specific price changes from their expected value will not, in general, be perfectly correlated with the period-to-period actual changes in the general price level. In some specific cases, the changes in the firm's specific price indices may be independent of, or even negatively correlated with, the changes in the general price level. Only a linkage with either the firm's specific price index (prices of inputs and outputs) or with a measure that is perfectly correlated with the possible changes in the firm's specific price index will provide a full hedge.

Firms' specific linkages or industry-specific linkages do exist. Such specific debt instruments may be linked to the price of a given input or an output.

Table 4–2
The Effect of Inflation on the Cost of Debt

| | | Type of Inflation | | | |
| | | Across-the-Board | | Terms-of-Trade | |
Contract Rate	*No Inflation*	*Known Rate of Inflation*	*Uncertain Rate of Inflation*	*With Substitution Among Inputs*	*Without Substitution Among Inputs*
Nominally fixed	r^*_{d0}	r^*_{d0}	r^*_{d2}	r^*_{d5}	r^*_{d8}
Variable, linked to the market rate	r^*_{d0}	r^*_{d0}	r^*_{d1}	r^*_{d4}	r^*_{d7}
Variable, linked to the general price index	r^*_{d0}	r^*_{d0}	r^*_{d0}	r^*_{d3}	r^*_{d6}
Variable, linked to the firm's specific price index	r^*_{d0}	r^*_{d0}	r^*_{d0}	r^*_{d0}	r^*_{d0}

Note: r^*_{d0} is the base rate in real terms. All the other rates are also presented in real terms, relative to r^*_{d0}. The rates are ranked by the subscripts; that is to say, $r^*_{d_{i+1}} > r^*_{d_i}$.

For example, some petroleum-related debt instruments were developed in the past decade, as well as other commodity-related debt instruments. These instruments provide the market with a way to diversify from one monetary rate of interest to commodities rates of interest. In a later chapter, we will see how the availability of such instruments and the ability of the corporate sector to design such debt instruments affect the financial policy of the firm.

The effects of different regimes of inflation and different contractual arrangements with regard to the interest rate on the cost of debt to the firm are summarized in table 4–2.

On the horizontal axis, we present five scenarios: no inflation, across-the-board inflation, across-the-board inflation with uncertain rate of inflation, terms-of-trade inflation with substitution among the inputs, and terms-of-trade inflation without substitution among the inputs. On the vertical axis, four contractual arrangements with regard to the interest rate are presented. These are: nominally fixed rate for the maturity of the loan, variable rate linked to a market rate of interest (LIBOR), variable rate linked to the general price index, and variable rate linked to a firm's specific price index.

The Cost of Equity

The issue of the relationship between the level and the changes of shares' prices, and the rate of inflation/disinflation has been the subject of many studies. Traditional wisdom has indicated that equity should be immune to inflation. When this expected relationship did not hold and share prices declined in real terms as the rate of inflation rose, many researchers tried to supply us with answers. These answers can be classified into three groups. The grouping is done by what the different researchers see as the main reason for the unexpected negative relationship between the changes in share prices and the rates of inflation.

The first group is concerned with taxes; the second group considers mainly the changes in the level of risk in the economy, and the third group of studies is concerned with myopic behavior by the market. Feldstein (1980) is an example of the first type of study. Pindyck (1984) is an example of the second group, and Modigliani and Cohn (1979) is an example of the third group.

As our earlier analysis indicated, we are focusing on an increase in the level of risk as the main explanatory variable. Moreover, we will focus in this section on the cost of equity to the firm. Obviously, this issue is closely related to the behavior of the price of shares of the firm under consideration. But the terminology, the purpose, and the point of view are different.

Given the perfect market equilibrium model known as the capital assets pricing model (CAPM), the expected return on the equity of a given firm j can be expressed as:

$$E(R_j) = r_f + [E(R_m) - r_f]\beta_{e,j} \tag{4.6}$$

where $E(R_j)$ is the expected return on the equity of firm j; r_f is the riskless rate of interest; and $E(R_m)$ is the expected return on the market portfolio. (The market portfolio is comprised of all the securities weighted by their market value. It serves as an anchor and a benchmark to measure the relative expected return of any given security.) $\beta_{e,j}$ is a measure of the systematic (nondiversifiable) risk of the equity of firm j.

The risk of the equity of firm j is composed of the basic business risk. This risk is a function of the volatility of the cash flows (relative to the volatility of the market) and the financial risk. This latter risk is directly related to the probability of default. As we have seen, the larger the debt/equity ratio, the higher the r_d (the required rate of interest of the debtholder). In the traditional analysis of the CAPM, it is assumed that the firm can issue default–risk-free debt and does so. That is the reason that in equation 4.6, r_f is used rather than r_d. Given this assumption, β_D (the measure of the systematic financial risk) is zero by definition. The systematic risk of the equity is then equal to:

$$\beta_{e,j} = \beta_{a,j} / \left(1 - \frac{D}{D + E}\right) \tag{4.7}$$

where $\beta_{a,j}$ is the measure of the systematic risk of the firm as a whole (assets' risk), D is the outstanding debt, and E is the outstanding equity, all at market values. It follows that the value of the firm is identically equal to:

$$V \equiv D + E.$$

In the more general case or risky debt, a case discussed previously and summarized in table 4–2, $\beta_D > 0$. In this case, equation 4.7 is replaced by:

$$\beta_{ej} = \beta_{aj} + \frac{D}{E}(\beta_{aj} - \beta_{dj}) \qquad (4.8)$$

β_{aj} depends on the correlation of the changes in the cash flows generated by the firm, with the changes in the market portfolio. β_{dj} (the risk measure for the debt) depends on the probability of default—which, in turn, depends on the debt/equity ratio—and the distribution of the cash flows generated by the firm. β_{aj} is a measure of the business risk of firm j. β_{dj} is a measure of the financial risk of firm j. β_{ej}, the risk of the equity, is determined by these two factors.

Inflation (or disinflation) will affect the cost of equity only if it affects its risk, β_{ej}. This will happen if the inflationary (or disinflationary) process will affect either the general riskiness of the firm (expressed by the systematic risk) or the financial risk, expressed by the volatility of the cash flows, or both. In the following, we will examine the effects of an across-the-board inflation and a terms-of-trade inflation.

The Case of an Across-the-Board Inflation

We will begin by assessing the effect of an across-the-board inflation on the systematic risk to the cash flows generated by the firm as a whole. Then, we will add the debt in order to compute the cost of the equity.

Assume that the economy is comprised of two firms only. These two firms trade with each other, so that the output of one firm serves as partial input to the other. In the initial stage, the trade between the two firms was determined by their respective demand for and supply of the inputs and the outputs, respectively. If, in the second period, the prices of both input and output change at the same rate, and there is no change in the physical streams between the two firms, the only change will be a nominal change. If prices are deflated by the rate of inflation (which in this case is equal to the changes in the prices of each and every input and output), nothing will change relative to the first period.

The cost of debt increases when the financial risk increases. As we have shown, the cost of debt increases in the case of across-the-board inflation, except in the special case where the interest rate is linked to the general price index. This causes the cost of equity to rise, too. It should be noted, however, in the case of across-the-board inflation, that the increase in the cost of the equity is due to an increase in the financial risk and not to an increase in the volatility of the cash flow per se. The source of the risk is that one particular item of the cost of doing business—the interest cost—is not perfectly correlated with the rate of inflation or disinflation. The only way to immunize the shareholders against this increase in the financial risk generated by inflation is to issue debt where the interest rate is linked to the general price level.

The Case of a Terms-of-Trade Inflation

As was pointed out in earlier chapters, inflation does affect relative prices. In some cases, it affects certain sectors of the economy in a predictable way. It follows that a terms-of-trade inflation or disinflation may affect the riskiness of a given firm in one or two ways. First, a terms-of-trade inflation increases the volatility of the cash flows of all the firms. If we adopt the traditional focusing on a single project as it is presented in chapter 3, this increase in the volatility means an increase in the business risk or the assets' risk (designated earlier as β_{aj}). This is similar to endorsing the view that total risk matters. Given managerial considerations, this may be an appropriate approach, at least for corporate finance. One can also maintain that as the inflation risk affects all firms (or at least most of them) and the policy of issuing debt with a nominally fixed interest rate is quite common, this risk cannot be diversified away. Another way to look at the same phenomenon is to regard the inflation risk as a political risk component introduced by the government. In this case, again one can regard this risk as a systematic risk.

In addition to that, the risk of certain industries (or firms) can go up if their cash flows are negatively affected by a specific process of a terms-of-trade inflation. Obviously, there may be other cases where the cash flows of other industries (or firms) may be affected positively by the inflation or disinflation.

To illustrate, consider the following two cases. The first case concerns a firm that buys the inputs in a market free of regulations and sells its output in a regulated market. The second case is the opposite of the first, a firm that buys one major input in a regulated market and sells its output in a free market. Now suppose that the government has initiated an inflationary process as a way to raise more income. Yet, for various political reasons, the government is trying to fight inflation. (The apparent inconsistency is not atypical of government policy.) The way to fight inflation is to keep prices constant in regulated markets. In a more practical way, the government can at least delay price adjustments in regulated markets through hearings and other attributes of the regulatory process. These delaying tactics are expected by the market as a part of the war against inflation. This knowledge will affect the value of the two firms in our example in two opposite directions, conditional on an expected inflation. The value of the first firm will go down and the value of the second firm will go up. In the terms used earlier, the first firm will experience a negative change in terms of trade, and the second firm will experience a positive change in terms of trade.

To the extent that an inflationary or a disinflationary process increases the general level of risk in the economy, the risk associated with firms of this type, conditional on the inflation, is higher. In this regard, the risk measure of these firms is higher than the risk measure of other firms, as their risk becomes higher when the general level of risk increases. (This is similar to the case of β_a greater than one in the framework of the capital assets pricing model.) In this case, the cost of capital will go up as all the components, assets, debt, and equity go up with inflation.

The effects of inflation (or disinflation) on the cost of equity are summarized in tables 4–3 and 4–4. For the purpose of the presentation in table 4–4, we assume a constant debt/equity ratio. As we will see later, this is not the general case. Also, the costs of equity are strictly comparable only within a given type of inflation and not across types of inflation.

In many cases, the inflation will have an effect on the cost of capital through the substitution of equity for debt. Assume that a given firm operates at an optimal capital structure which reflects tax and other considerations. Given inflationary or disinflationary expectations, the cost of debt may change relative to the cost of equity. Such a change in the relative cost will usually bring about an adjustment in the cost of capital.

In general, the cost of funds for any given firm is a function of the type of the inflation/disinflation and the nature of the financial instruments that the firm sells (and buys). The general characteristic of most inflationary and disinflationary processes is that they reflect an increase in the risk and, as such, they will drive up the costs of funds. Utilizing specific financial instruments by the firm may reduce the risk to the firm via a transfer of the risk to those better equipped to carry it.

Table 4–3
The Effect of Inflation/Disinflation on the Cost of Equity—No-Debt Situation

| | Type of Inflation | | | |
| | Across-the-Board | | Terms-of-Trade | |
No Inflation	Known Rate of Inflation	Uncertain Rate of Inflation	With Substitution among Inputs	Without Substitution among Inputs
K_0	K_0	$K_{0,1}$	$K_{0,2}$	$K_{0,3}$

Notes: K = the cost of equity.

$K_{0,3} \geq K_{0,2} \geq K_{0,1} \geq K_0$.

Table 4–4
The Effect of Inflation/Disinflation on the Cost of Equity—Firms with Debt

	Type of Inflation				
		Across-the-Board		Terms-of-Trade	
Type of Debt	*No Inflation*	*Known Rate of Inflation*	*Uncertain Rate of Inflation*	*With Substitution Among Inputs*	*Without Substitution Among Inputs*
Nominally fixed	$K_{e,0}$	$K_{e,0}$	$K_{e,2}$	$K_{e,6}$	$K_{e,10}$
Variable, linked to the market rate	$K_{e,0}$	$K_{e,0}$	$K_{e,1}$	$K_{e,5}$	$K_{e,9}$
Variable, linked to the general price index	$K_{e,0}$	$K_{e,0}$	$K_{e,0}$	$K_{e,4}$	$K_{e,8}$
Variable, linked to the firm's specific price index	$K_{e,0}$	$K_{e,0}$	$K_{e,0}$	$K_{e,3}$	$K_{e,7}$

Note: K = the cost of equity.

5
Costing

The costing process is aimed at the determination of the costs of the various components comprising any product, service, or other economic activity. Costing is a planning activity. It is an important part of the financial function in a corporation. Costing differs from cost accounting as the latter involves allocating actual costs among activities at the end of the reporting period, while the former involves calculating what the cost of a given product should be. In competitive markets, and if the costing includes returns to management and to equity, the costing process yields the price of the product.

In a world where firms have to inform the market about the prices of their products and services, costing is an essential activity. The array of such cases spans a whole range. Formal bids (where the bid price is a legal obligation) are one extreme where the price and, therefore, the costing process are strictly binding. Price lists and other non–legally binding messages are the other extreme. But even in this case, there are negative consequences for frequent changes in the announced prices. In all of these cases, the firm stands to gain from an appropriate process of costing.

The process of costing includes the following stages:

1. A quantitative determination of the inputs. This is usually done in terms of units of inputs per one unit of output.
2. Relating the appropriate prices to the inputs.
3. Adding the indirect production costs.
4. Adding selling and marketing costs per unit of output.
5. Adding the cost of financing per unit of output.

In this chapter, we will examine the process of costing given the different types of inflationary/disinflationary processes discussed earlier. However, as a base case and a source for comparison, we begin by a presentation of the costing process in a world of constant prices. We will follow the five stages just presented.

Costing in a World of Constant Prices

Quantitative Determination of the Inputs. In a world of constant prices, the input mix reflects the technology chosen by the firm. Given a technology, the first step is "physical budgeting" where the necessary quantities of inputs per one unit of output are determined. Once this is done, the same physical budget will apply as long as the selected technology remains the same.

Prices of Inputs. In general, the appropriate prices for the inputs are those that are contemporaneous with the purchasing time of the inputs. This date may vary with regard to the costing date. Obviously, this will not make a difference in a world of constant prices.

In the case of a continuous production process, average prices may be used to smooth over temporary changes. This is done to allow stable output prices where the prices of the inputs may vary.

Allocation of Indirect Production Costs. This activity will follow the two-stage process just described. First is a physical budgeting of units of inputs and, then, multiplication by the appropriate prices.

Selling and Marketing Costs. In general, the same process of physical budgeting is followed by choosing the appropriate prices is relevant here as well. However, it is a common procedure to fix the selling and marketing expenditure as a percentage of the direct costs or the selling price. This is an appropriate procedure as long as the selling and marketing costs are assumed to be linearly related to the sales.

Cost of Financing. The cost of financing depends on the amount of capital used for this purpose and on the costs of funds. The amount of capital needed is usually defined as the working capital needed for net production. In general it consists of (1) inventory financing and (2) credit financing (customers' credit-supplier's credit).

Inventory Financing. A typical production cycle is supported by three types of inventories:

1. Raw materials
2. Products in process
3. Finished goods

The level of each type of inventory is determined in such a way as to minimize the carrying costs of the inventory. The costs of the inventory are comprised of the holding costs and the shortage costs. For example, the well-

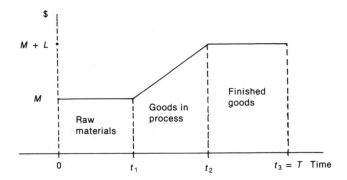

Figure 5–1. Inventories as a Function of the Production Cycle (per unit of output)

known economic order quantity (EOQ) is a nonlinear function of the demand for a given time interval, the carrying costs, and the ordering (transactions) costs. The EOQ is:

$$EOQ = \sqrt{\frac{2DC_o}{C_s}}$$

where D = demand per period

C_o = the ordering cost

C_s = the carrying costs (financial charge) per period

In the following period analysis, the cost of the inventory is divided into three parts: the financial charge, the cost of the tied-up capital, and all the rest. The nonfinancial elements of the costs will be added to the basic cost. The total cost is used as a basis for the calculation of cost of financing.

Figure 5–1 illustrates the production cycle. The cycle is based on material flows rather than on cash flow. As materials arrive at the production site, they are entered into the inventory regardless of the payments' arrangements.

M is the purchasing price of the materials needed for the production of one unit of output, including all transaction costs (such as ordering and shipping).

L is the cost of the labor per unit of output. Labor costs include direct and indirect labor, including management.

t_1 is the average holding period for raw materials.

t_2 is the average holding period for raw materials and goods in process. ($t_2 - t_1$ is the average duration for goods in process.)

$t_3 = T$ is the average holding period of all three types of the inventory for one unit of output. ($t_3 - t_2$ is the average holding period for finished goods.) T is also the average time for one production cycle.

The production cycle presented in figure 5–1 implies that the firm will have to finance the materials for the entire period T as well as the labor (broadly defined) for the period $(t_2 - t_1)/2 + (t_3 - t_2)$. Assuming that all inputs are financed (explicitly by some kind of debt or implicitly by retained earnings), the total cost of financing is:

$$C_1 = M \times \frac{r \times T}{365} + L \frac{r\left[\frac{(t_2 - t_1)}{2} + (t_3 - t_2)\right]}{365}$$

where r is the relevant cost of funds. C_1 is computed on a simple interest basis. If the nominal interest rate is high (say, 20 percent p.a. or higher), it is necessary to compute the financing cost using compounding.[1] In the computation of C_1, the holding periods are measured in days.

To illustrate, consider the following.

Example: ABC produces one unit of output by using materials and labor. For the production of one unit of output the firm needs:

M (materials)	3 units at $1 per unit
L (labor)	2 units at $5 per unit

The optimal level of inventories is a 90-days supply of raw materials, 30 days of products in process, and a 60-days supply of finished goods. The nominal interest rate of the firm, the relevant cost of funds, is 7 percent p.a. There is no inflation, current or expected.

The cost of inventory financing per unit of output is:

$$C_1 = 1 \times 3 \left(\frac{.07 \times 90}{365}\right) + 2 \times 5 \left[\frac{.07\left(\frac{30}{2} + 60\right)}{365}\right]$$

$C_1 = \$.1956$ per unit of output.

Credit Financing. The term *credit* is used here to denote the creation of a financial commitment by or to the firm to bridge the time difference between the purchase (sale) of an input (an output) and the payment (or receipt) of cash to the ultimate seller (buyer).

If payment for inputs is required t_n days after the purchase of the inputs, and the collection of cash for sold output occurs t_s days after the sale, the total cost of credit financing (computed by simple interest) is:

$$C_2 = (M + L)(1 + \alpha)\frac{r \times t_s}{365} - (M + L)\frac{r \times t_n}{365}$$

where α is the profit margin. The credit terms for all inputs are assumed to be equal to t_n, and for all outputs to t_s.

We assume an identical cost of funds for the purpose of both inventory financing and credit financing. This separation is not necessary given the assumption of constant prices (no inflation). We will see later that when inflation/disinflation is introduced, the separation is necessary.

Costing in a World of Across-the-Board Inflation

The outcome of the costing process is affected by what is assumed with regard to future changes in the price level as well as changes in relative prices. The latter may or may not be associated with the former. In this section, we trace the effects on an across-the-board inflation/disinflation on the prices of the inputs and the costs of financing. The results will determine the costs of the output and, given competitive markets, the prices as well.

Input Prices

Input prices can be adjusted backward or forward, given the price for a given input at some point of time and the rate of change in the price level. If we know the price at some point of time in the past, the price is brought forward by multiplying the base price by one plus the appropriate price change. If, on the other hand, we have information on the nominal price in some future time, the price is brought back using the expected rate of inflation. (If the rate of inflation is known, the expected rate of inflation and the actual rate of inflation are the same.)

Thus, P_o, the current price for a given output, will be equal to $P_o = P_{-t}(1 + \dot{P}_{-t_1 0})$ where P_{-t} is the known price in some past period and $\dot{P}_{-t_1 0}$ is the actual change in the price level from time $-t$ to the current time. If we have information on future nominal prices, then $P_o = P_t[1 + E(\dot{P}_{o_1 t})]^{-1}$

where P_t is the quoted price at some future date t, and $E(\dot{P}_{o_1 t})$ is the expected rate of price changes between the current time and t.

To illustrate, suppose that on January 1, 1987, the firm is reviewing its price list. The price list is based on the cost of production plus a given return for the equity capital computed on a per unit of output basis.

The firm collects information on inputs' prices. For input A, it has the per unit price as of January 1, 1986. At this time, the cost was $3 per pound. For input B, it has a binding offer from its supplier for June 30, 1987, also $3 per pound.

The actual rate of inflation in 1986 was 3.5 percent; the expected rate of inflation for 1987 is 5 percent, evenly distributed over the year. The prices of inputs A and B for January 1, 1987 will be:

$$P_A = \$3(1 + .035) = \$3.1050 \text{ per pound}$$

and

$$P_B = \$3(1 + .05)^{-\frac{1}{2}} = \$2.9277 \text{ per pound}$$

Cost of Financing

The nominal rate of interest is comprised of two parts. The first part is a compensation for postponed consumption. The second part is a purchasing power maintenance. The first part is usually called the "real rate of interest." The second part is often calculated as the expected rate of inflation.

The expression for the nominal interest rate is:

$$i = \{(1 + r)[1 + E(\dot{P})]\} - 1$$

where r is the real rate of interest, and $E(\dot{P})$ is the expected rate of inflation, expressed for the same holding period. To illustrate, suppose that the policy of the credit department of our firm is to charge an 8 percent real rate of interest per year. The expected rate of inflation, agreed by all, is 4 percent. Given this, the annual rate of interest charged by the credit department will be:

$$i = [(1 + .08)(1 + .04) - 1] \times 100 = 12.32 \text{ percent per annum}$$

Practically, the real rate cannot be observed on an ex ante basis, and the same applies to the expected rate of inflation. The only observable variable is the nominal rate of interest. We do have estimates for both the unobserved variables and, once one of them is estimated, the other variable is given. Another possibility is to compute the ex post realized real rate. In this case, the term *real* relates to the fact that this is an inflation-deflated rate of interest. This rate is given by the following equation:

$$\tilde{r} = \frac{(1 + i)}{(1 + \tilde{\dot{P}})} - 1$$

where $\tilde{\dot{P}}$ is the actual rate of inflation. $\tilde{\dot{P}}$ is a random variable. The difference between the expected rate of inflation, $E(\dot{P})$, and the actual rate creates a substantial degree of volatility in the realized rate of interest.

To illustrate, suppose that the firm considers a supplier's loan for one year at a nominally fixed rate of interest of 11 percent. The expected rate of inflation is 5 percent; however, let us assume that the actual rate can be lower, at 3 percent, or higher, at 7 percent per annum. The realized, ex post, real rate of interest is presented in table 5–1.

The realized rate is equal to

$$\tilde{r} = \frac{1 + i}{1 + \dot{P}} - 1.$$

The difference in realized cost of funds is not negligible even with low possible rates of inflation. In a period of high and volatile rates of inflation, the volatility in the actual costs of funds is more substantial.[2]

Inventory Financing. It has been shown that the cost of financing the inventory in an environment of constant price is equal to:

$$C_1 = M\frac{r \times T}{365} + L\frac{r\left[\dfrac{t_2 - t_1}{2} + (t_3 - t_2)\right]}{365}$$

where $T = $ the length of the production cycle (in days). The only variable that will change with the introduction of an across-the-board inflation is the cost of funds—the interest rate r.

M (the all-inclusive materials cost) and L (the all-inclusive labor cost) are measured in terms of some base period, $t = 0$. In an across-the-board inflation, the prices of all inputs and outputs change in an identical fashion, which is equal to the change in the general price index, $\dot{P}$. Hence, if a unit of inputs costs P_o at time o, it will cost $P_t = P_o(1 + \dot{P}_{ot})$ at time t. This new cost is

Table 5–1
The Realized Real Rate of Interest at Three Predicted Inflation Rates
(percentage p.a.)

	$\dot{P}$		
i	*3 Percent*	*5 Percent*	*7 Percent*
11 Percent	6.80	4.76	2.80

reflected in the price of the output which, in competition, reflects the cost of the inputs at the time of sale.

Thus, both materials and labor provide a certain hedge against inflation if the output prices are instantaneously linked to the rate of inflation. It follows that the financing charge for the carrying of the inventory should reflect the real component in the interest rate formula, not the inflation-adjustment part. This is so because the linkage of the prices of the output takes care of the inflation. Using the nominal rate of interest, which includes a compensation for the expected inflation, is like charging twice; it will increase the calculated costs. In a competitive market, it will lead to over-pricing and a possible loss of market share.

To illustrate, suppose that the firm maintains a pricing policy where the price of the output is twice the direct cost. The price list is adjusted once a month to reflect the changes in the price levels, measured by monthly changes in CPI. The nominal cost of funds available to the firm is 12 percent, while the expected rate of inflation for the coming year is 4 percent. The materials and labor costs per unit of output on January 1, 1987 are $3 and $10, respectively. The production cycle is six months, and during this period, an inventory of materials is maintained for six months. Labor inventory is held for 2½ months.

The total cost per unit of output at the base period is:

$$\bar{C}_o = M_o + L_o + M_o\frac{r \times 6}{12} + L_o\frac{r \times 2.5}{12}$$

Using at first the nominal cost of funds $r = 12$ percent, we obtain:

$$\bar{C}_o = \$3 + \$10 + \$.18 + \$.25 = \$13.43 \text{ per unit.}$$

Given the pricing policy, the price will be $2\bar{C}_o = 2(\$13.43) = \$26.86$. On December 1, 1987, the price list will be adjusted to account for the 4 percent increase in the price level. The adjusted price on that day will be:

$$\$26.86 \times 1.04 = \$27.93$$

This apparently straightforward adjustment contains "double counting," and, therefore, results in a higher than necessary adjustment. To see this, consider the cost composition (also adjusted for inflation). The cost per unit is composed of:

$$\text{Materials:} \quad M = \$3 \times 1.04 = \$3.12$$

$$\text{Labor:} \quad L = \$10 \times 1.04 = \$10.40$$

The total cost per unit is $13.52. Given the assumed relationship between cost and price, $P_t = 2\bar{C}_t$, the price per unit should be

$$\$13.52 \times 2 = \$27.04$$

The difference between the former and the latter price calculation is $27.93 − $27.04 = $.89. This amount is a contribution to cover the cost of financing for the inventory. However, we have shown earlier that this cost is only $.43 per unit of production. The difference of $.46 is due to a double counting. The double counting arises from counting the inflation once directly, through the change in the price level, and then again through the nominal interest rate.

Credit Financing. In most business activities, the cash cycle differs from the production cycle. For a given firm, the difference between the flow of materials and other inputs, on one hand, and the cash payments, on the other, is the credit given to the firm. The difference between the flow of products and services and the cash receipts of the firm is a function of the credit terms granted by the firm. The net cost of financing the credit is

$$Cr = (M + L)(1 + \alpha)\frac{r \times t_4}{365} - (M + L)\frac{r \times t_5}{365}$$

where t_5 is the duration (in days) of suppliers' credit. (We assume for simplicity that the suppliers' credit duration is the same for all outputs.) t_4 is the duration (in days) of customers' credit (again, assumed to be the same for all customers). α is the profit margin based on a full costing of M and L, and r is the appropriate interest rate. The question is what interest rate should be used here, the nominal or the real rate of interest? The answer is clearly the nominal rate. The reason is rooted at the nature of the credit transactions. Credit is a pure monetary transaction. A stated nominal amount of money is being "pushed forward" in time. Both the suppliers and the firm that sells the products can borrow against the future payments due to them. In this case, they will pay the nominal interest rate. It follows then that the nominal interest rate is the opportunity cost that should be applied to the financing cost of the credit. This rate, the nominal market rate of interest, contains the market's expectation of the rate of inflation for the credit periods both for suppliers and customers. In the expression for the cost of financing the credit, these periods are t_3 and t_4, respectively.

The cost of financing the credit just presented is a linear approximation of the true value. This linear approximation is a good representation of the true value if one wishes to discuss this cost element in general. For actual calculation, particularly in a period of high nominal rates of interest, it might be better to calculate the true value. This value is the difference between the actual cash price for both the inputs (labor and materials) and the output (the products) combined and for that loan which the payments (and receipts) at the actual dates of payments will support. The true value is calculated as:

$$C_r^1 \left[(M + L)(1 + \alpha) - \frac{(M + L)(1 + \alpha)}{(1 + r)t_4/365} \right]$$

$$- \left[(M + L) - \frac{(M + L)}{(1 + r)^{t5/365}} \right]$$

To illustrate, consider the following.

Example: A firm uses 3 units of materials at a cost of $1 per unit, and 2 units of labor at $5 per unit to produce one unit of output which is sold at twice the direct cost ($\alpha = 1$). The firm receives 30 days credit from the suppliers of both materials and labor, and it is granting 60 days of credit to its customers. The market nominal rate of interest is 11 percent. The true cost of financing the credit is:

$$C_r^1 = \left[(3 \times 1 + (2 \times 5)(1 + 1) + \frac{(3 \times 1) + (2 \times 5)(1 + 1)}{(1 + 0.11)60/365} \right]$$

$$- \left[(3 \times 1) + (2 \times 5) - \frac{(3 \times 1) + (2 \times 5)}{(1 + 0.11)^{30/365}} \right]$$

$$= \$.44 - \$.011$$

$$= \$.33 \text{ cost of financing credit per unit of output}$$

The Effect of Foreign Currency Transactions

Many firms in the world of today purchase inputs and/or sell outputs in the markets of the world. The volume of international trade as a proportion of world GNP is growing. Even large countries such as the United States find themselves more involved in international trade. In international trade, more than one currency is used. In practice, there are a number of what are called internationally traded currencies. Although the U.S. dollar is still the major currency in the world, many firms transact in other currencies such as the Japanese yen, the German mark, or the English pound—the other major currencies in the world trade.

Since the establishment of the flexible exchange rate in the period 1969–72, the world has witnessed substantial volatility in the exchange rates of the major currencies.[3] The shifts in the exchange rates can be decomposed into two parts: the anticipated and the unanticipated changes. The anticipated changes are calculated on the basis of what is known as the Purchasing Power Parity. The unanticipated changes are the observed changes minus the calculated PPP-based changes. According to the PPP, there is no change in real exchange rate (the actual exchange of goods and services), and the shifts in the exchange rates reflect only the relative rate of inflation in the two countries in question. In other words, PPP is consistent with the case of across-the-board inflation, as there is no change in relative prices.

In a PPP world, the shift in the exchange rates is given by:

$$\left(1 + \dot{S}_{t, \overline{\$}}^{\;*}\right) = \frac{1 + \dot{P}_t^*}{1 + \dot{P}_t^{\$}}$$

where $\dot{S}_{t, \overline{\$}}^{\;*}$ is the change in the exchange rate between the yen and the dollar (yens to dollars) from $(t - 1)$ to t, and $\dot{P}_t^*$ and $\dot{P}_t^{\$}$ are the respective rates of inflation in Japan and in the United States in the same period.

In a PPP world, there is no need for an adjustment in the costing beyond those suggested earlier in the case of an across-the-board inflation. Although the PPP may be a good description for the behavior of exchange rates on the average, and in the long term (five-to-ten–year horizon), it is not a good description of exchange-rate behavior for a costing decision. However, any deviation from the PPP is equivalent to either a real devaluation or a real appreciation of one currency in terms of another. To illustrate, consider the following two examples:

Example 1. The dollar was depreciated against the yen by 35 percent in one year. During the same period, the rate of inflation in the United States was 3 percent. In Japan, it was −1 percent. The real shift in the exchange rate (real devaluation) is computed as:

$$\dot{S}_{\underset{*}{\$}}^{r} = \frac{1 + S^{\$/*}}{(1 + \dot{P}^{\$})}(1 + \dot{P}^*)$$

In the case just specified, the real change is:

$$\dot{S}_{\underset{*}{\$}}^{r} = \frac{1 + .35}{1 + .03}(1 - .01) - 1$$

$$= .29$$

or a real depreciation of 29 percent. (An equivalent way is to calculate the real appreciation of the yen.)

Example 2: The Israeli shekel (Is) was devalued against the dollar at a rate of 10 percent per annum. The respective rates of inflation in Israel and the U.S. dollar over that year have been:

$$\dot{S}^r_{\frac{Is}{s}} = \frac{(1 + .1)}{(1 + .36)}(1 + .03) - 1 = -.167$$

As the expression is in terms of Israeli shekels per dollar, it means a real appreciation of 16.7 percent over that period.

Costing in a World of Relative Price Changes

As we have shown earlier in chapters 1 and 2, inflation and disinflation are usually associated with changes in relative prices. The idea of across-the-board inflation is a useful analytic device to explain when and in what way inflation matters for financial decisions, but it is always necessary to consider the case of changes in relative prices.

The published periodic rate of inflation is the average rate of price changes for various commodities, products, and services. As we demonstrated in chapter 2, the actual rates of price changes vary across industries. In some cases, they are not even positively correlated. It follows that for most commodities, goods, and services, the changes in the rate of inflation/disinflation are associated with relative price changes. This relative price change is defined as:

$$(1 + \dot{P}^r_i) = \frac{1 + \dot{P}^n_i}{1 + \dot{P}} \quad \text{all for the same period } t - 1 \text{ to } t.$$

$\dot{P}^r_i$ is the real change in the price or the change in the relative price for good i. $\dot{P}^n_i$ is the nominal price change for that specific good (or industry) i. P is the change in the general price level. To illustrate this point, consider the following examples.

Example 1: The price of an average house sold in the United States in 1986 increased by 11.8 percent relative to 1985. At the same time, the CPI rose by 3 percent. It follows that the real (relative) price of an average house rose by:

$$\dot{P}^r_{house} = \frac{1 + .118}{1 + .03} - 1 = .085$$

an increase of 8.5 percent.

Example 2. The general index in Israel rose during 1985 by 167 percent. In the same period, wages rose by 135 percent. The real (relative) change in the cost of labor in Israel during 1985 was:

$$\dot{P}^r_{labor} = \frac{1 + 1.35}{1 + 1.67} - 1 = -.12$$

a decrease of 12 percent.

The data presented in chapter 2 show that the correlation between the changes in the CPI and changes in the price indices of various industries is not always high and positive. In some cases, the correlation may be close to zero or even negative. This does not provide us with a way to predict relative price changes, but it does cast a big shadow on the practice of making financial decisions assuming our across-the-board inflation.

Prices of Inputs

In the case of continuous production, inputs are purchased in fixed intervals such that the overall inventory cost will be minimized. Unlike the case of across-the-board inflation, the relative prices of the inputs may change within the planning period. The planning period is defined as that period in which the only adjustments in the prices are due to changes in the general price level.

Barring frequent real price adjustments as impractical, a possible way to handle this case is to use the inputs' expected real price at the midpoint of the planning horizon as the inputs' reference price for costing purposes. This procedure will yield a too-high price in the first half of the planning period, to be compensated by a too-low price in the second half of the period.

Given this approach, input prices are calculated as follows:

$$M^1_o = M_o(1 + \dot{P}^r_m)^{1/2}$$

where M^1_o is the material cost to enter the calculation of the total cost for costing purposes. M_o is the observed cost of materials at the beginning of the period, the time of the actual costing. $\dot{P}^r_m$ is the real rate of change in the cost of materials; it is expected to prevail during the period for which the price of the product will remain unchanged.

To see how such a rule may work, consider the following. A unit of input was selling for $4 on January 1, 1987. The firm is preparing a list price to be in effect during calendar 1987. The price will be adjusted monthly by the change in the CPI. The firm expects the real (relative) price of the input to decrease by 3 percent during the year in a uniformly distributed rate over the period. The input price to enter the base price is:

$$M_o^1 = 4(1 - .03)^{1/2} = \$3.94 \text{ per unit of input.}$$

Labor cost can be treated in the same way. It should be noted that here we do not have to predict the changes in the general price index (CPI). It is sufficient to predict how the prices of a given input will behave relative to the CPI. This assessment can be assigned to specialists in the various fields (labor, certain commodities, or specific goods). Past history can be used to assess this relationship. A sample of such relationships is presented in chapter 2.

A more vigorous and precise procedure of accounting for future changes of real prices can be derived on the basis of the present-value concept. Specifically, assuming a uniform rate of using the input over time, the nominal constant price will be set in such a way as to make the present value of the expenditure equal to the present value of the expenditure given the true value of the actual and changing prices over time. Thus:

$$M \sum_{t=1}^{n} \frac{(1 + \dot{P})^{t/n}}{(1 + i)^{t/n}} = M_o \sum_{t=1}^{n} \frac{(1 + \dot{P}_m)^{t/m}}{(1 + i)^{t/m}}$$

where n is the number of purchases (spaced equally) in the planning period t, and t is equal to the period covered by the nominal interest rate i.

$$(1 + i) = (1 + r)(1 + \dot{P})$$

$$(1 + \dot{P}_m) = (1 + \dot{P})(1 + \dot{P}_m^r)$$

Substituting this into the preceding equation yields:

$$M = M_o \sum_{t=1}^{n} \left(\frac{1 + \dot{P}_m^r}{1 + r} \right)^{t/n} \bigg/ \sum_{t=1}^{n} (1 + r)^{-t/n}$$

The two expressions for the pricing of the input M yield similar results. Only when the deviations between $\dot{P}$ and $\dot{P}_m^r$ are very large will the adjustment by the two formulas differ substantially.

Inventory Financing

Earlier, we showed that the real rate of interest is the appropriate rate for the costing of the carrying cost of the inventory. This argument was based on the assumptions that the inventory maintains its real value and that the price of all goods, services, and factors of production are changing at the same rate. The more realistic case of terms-of-trade inflation requires some adjustments in the calculation of the financing charge of the inventory during the production cycle.

To make these adjustments, we first define the specific real rate of interest as that part of the nominal rate of interest that is not taken care of by the change in the price of the output. This rate, r_c is defined as:

$$(1 + r_c) = \frac{(1 + i)}{(1 + \dot{P}_c)}$$

where i is the nominal rate of interest over the production cycle, and $\dot{P}_c$ is the specific changes in the prices of the output. Using the relationships derived earlier from Fisher's equation, we get:

$$(1 + i) = (1 + r)(1 + \dot{P}) \text{ and}$$

$$(1 + \dot{P}_c) = (1 + \dot{P})(1 + \dot{P}_c^r)$$

We substitute real and relative measures for the nominal and the general price changes measures, and we obtain:

$$(1 + r_c) = \frac{(1 + r)}{(1 + \dot{P}_c^r)}$$

so that r_c, which is the appropriate rate of interest for the calculation of the cost of inventory financing, can be obtained from real or from nominal data. To illustrate this case, consider the following.

Example: The price of output x is expected to rise at a real (relative) rate of 2 percent per annum. Assuming a real rate of interest of 4 percent, the appropriate rate for inventory financing is:

$$r_x = \frac{1 + .04}{1 + .02} - 1 = .0196$$

$$r_x = 1.96\%.$$

Costing in a Multicurrency World

As it has been argued before, where there is no real devaluation or appreciation in the exchange rates, the purchasing powers of the different currencies do not change. In such a world, the relative prices would not change where nominal exchange rates changed. This, however, is not the case. Exchange rate changes do not usually follow the PPP pattern. Deviations from the PPP are persistent and do not average out over cycles of production of the type just described. The changes in the exchange rates minus the PPP-suggested changes are called the unanticipated changes. In table 2–9, we provided data on the quarterly unanticipated changes in the exchange rates of the Japanese yen, the British pound, and the German mark against the U.S. dollar for 1972–86. The data was presented on a quarterly basis and then summed up on a six-month basis to coincide with the production cycle. They were also summed up on an annual basis to coincide with the financial reporting cycle. As we can see, the unanticipated changes on the quarterly bases were significantly different than zero. Even if we calculate semiannual and annual changes they are significantly different than zero.

In other words, the changes in the exchange rates are a major force for changes in relative prices of inputs and outputs. (As before, all prices are measured in U.S. dollars). It follows that expectations with regard to the unanticipated (real) changes in the exchange rates should be part of the costing process.

A distinction should be made between the prediction of the nominal changes in the exchange rates and the prediction of changes in the exchange rates. The former involves a prediction of the rate of inflation in the two countries, whereas the latter involves changes in the real rate, which often are a subject of an explicit government policy.

Many small countries regard their exchange rates as policy variables. If the country is small enough and its currency has no external demand, such an approach is feasible. Countries such as South Korea, Brazil, and Israel are a few cases where the exchange rates are used as policy tools to encourage exports to control inflation and for other goals of economic policy. Even in the Japanese case, the government is trying to use the value of the yen vis-à-vis the U.S. dollar as a policy variable.

Whether the real changes in the exchange rates are caused by governments' policy decisions, or whether they are partially affected by the decisions of various actors in the marketplace, there is no question that real changes in the exchange rates are a constant feature of the world's markets. As such, they should be incorporated into the costing process. This is done in the following section.

Imported Input Prices

Assume that input x is an imported good. Assume further that the importing country has balance of payments and trade balance problems, and that the stated government policy is to discourage imports. A popular means for this end is to devalue and hope for a real devaluation. We expect the government to devalue at an annual rate of $\dot{S}^r_{1/2}$. The price M_x to enter the base cost figure should be the average M_x for the planning horizon. That average can be approximated by the price of x, in real term midpoint through the planning period. If we assume that the planning horizon is one year, the base price will be:

$$M_x = M_{x,o}(1 + \dot{S}^r_{1/2})^{1/2}$$

where M_x is the base price for the imported input. $M_{x,o}$ is the price of the imported input at the beginning of the period, which is the current foreign exchange price times the spot exchange rate. $\dot{S}^r_{1/2}$ is the expected real rate of change in the exchange rate. If the nominal price of x in the foreign currency is also subject to change, M_x becomes:

$$M_x = M_{x,o}[(1 + \dot{P}^r_x)(1 + \dot{S}^r_{1/2})]^{1/2}$$

where $\dot{p}^r_x$ is the expected rate of change of input x in real terms.

To illustrate, suppose that input x is a unit of photomask manufactured in South Korea. Assume that the current price is 16,000 Korean wons per unit. The won/dollar rate of exchange is 800 won/dollar. The Korean government is expected to devalue the won against the U.S. dollar at an annual (real) rate of 10 percent. Given constant won prices for the photomask unit, M_x will be:

$$M_x = \$20(1.10)^{1/2}$$
$$= \$20(1.0488) = \$20.976$$

If we assume a real rate of change in the won price of the photomask at an annual rate of 7 percent, we obtain:

$$M_x = \$20[(1.07)(1.10)]^{1/2}$$
$$= \$20(1.0849) = \$21.70$$

In the last three chapters we have discussed the three major components of corporate financial decisions—capital budgeting, cost of capital, and costing. In the next three chapters the main results of the analysis done earlier are applied to real cases.

Notes

1. The simple interest calculation neglects the compounding effect. In other words, we are using a linear approximation of the effective interest rate. If the interest rate is high enough, the difference between the approximation and the precise calculation is substantial.

2. For evidence with regard to the relationship between the mean value of the inflation and its volatility see chapter 2.

3. For a brief discussion, see chapter 2. The relevant data are presented in table 2–9.

6
Capital Budgeting in an Inflationary and Multiple-Currency Environment: An Application

I n chapter 3, the capital-budgeting decision was analyzed. We started the presentation with the production function and traced the changes in the net present value of a given investment project under different scenarios of inflation and disinflation. It has been shown that the value of an investment project is generally affected by the nature of the inflationary process. Where the cash flows of the project under consideration are generated by more than one currency, the value of the project depends also on the relative inflation and on the way in which exchange rates respond to changes in the relative inflation. In other cases, inflation may affect the product and/or the input mix of a certain investment project.

Chapter 3 presented the conditions under which the financial executive should be concerned about inflation in making investment decisions. Such decisions, however, require two additional pieces of information. The first is how much a project is affected by inflation or disinflation and, in particular, whether there are plausible cases where a proper accounting for inflation will reverse an investment decision. The second is the availability of the required information for decision making given expected inflation or disinflation.

These two questions are addressed in this chapter through a detailed case study and a section on data availability. The case study is based on an actual feasibility study. The situation described is common enough to allow us to generalize from this specific case.

The case deals with a production-facility investment aimed at import substitution. The focus of the analysis is on the integration of the various factors discussed in chapter 3 into one consistent managerial effort.

Import Substitution—The Chemical Factory

Integrated Materials is a medium-sized corporation which manufactures various chemicals for industrial and household use. One of the inputs used in many of its final products is a component known as X14. Currently,

Table 6–1
Annual Imports of X14, 1981–85

	Quantity (tons)	Price (DM/ton)
1981	1,400	3,400
1982	1,500	3,500
1983	1,100	3,300
1984	1,800	3,600
1985	1,600	3,500

Integrated Materials imports X14 from Germany. In the past ten years, the imports ranged between 1,100 and 1,800 tons per year. Over this period, the price of X14 varied between 3,000 and 3,900 DM per ton. Data on the imported quantities and prices for 1981–85 are presented in table 6–1.

The Product Development Group of Integrated Materials proposed to replace the import of X14 by in-house production of X14 in one of the firm's production facilities in Long Beach, California. The Product Development Group believed that such an activity would be profitable. The Product Development Group submitted a preliminary proposal to the investment committee of Intergrated Materials. The investment committee thought that the proposal was sound enough to warrant serious consideration. Therefore, the Product Development Group was asked to submit a full-scale feasibility study to the investment committee.

The Product Development Group appointed an internal task force to attend to the matter. The task force came back with the following preliminary report.

The Base Case—Certainty and Constant Prices

The task force decided to construct a base case first. The base case assumed certainty and constant prices. This case was considered the most favorable. If the project could not pass this test, there would be no need to proceed any further.

The following is the data for the base case:

1. Production capacity: 2,000 tons/year
2. Planned production: 1,480 tons/year
3. External price (in Germany): 3,460 DM/ton
4. Exchange rate: $.40 per DM

5. Production costs (dollars per ton):
   Materials: $500
   Labor: $360
   Energy: $360
6. Economic life of the project: ten years

Planned production and the import prices were calculated as a simple average of the data for the period 1981–85. The exchange rate reflects the task force forecast for the economic life of the project. Production costs were supplied by the Product Development Group. The cost of setting up the production line and the necessary investment in production equipment were estimated to be zero.

The feasibility study was based on a comparison between the costs of supplying X14 externally, of importing the material from Germany, and of internal production in Long Beach. As all the output of the proposed project was intended as input for Integrated Materials, the project was considered to be a low-risk investment and a 12 percent pretax nominal cost of capital was employed by the task force.

Given this information, and assuming no inflation and constant prices, the task force prepared a base-line calculation of the NPV of the project. The first run of the base-line case is presented in table 6–2.

Reviewing the results (a negative NPV of $132,650), the head of the task force realized that by using the nominal cost of capital and assuming constant prices, the nominal rate became a real rate. A 12 percent real discount factor was deemed to be too high. Assuming a 5 percent annual rate of inflation over the life of the project, the cost of capital was adjusted downward to 7 percent and the NPV was recalculated using the same cash flows as in table 6–2. The recalculation yielded a positive net present value:

$$NPV_2 = \$1,699,700 - \$1,500,000 = \$199,700$$

Given the base-line assumptions, the project was acceptable.

The results were reported to the investment committee. The members of the committee then asked the task force to prepare another report addressing the issues of inflation and shifts in the exchange rates. They asked that the task force specifically refer to the following scenarios:

1. Across-the-board inflation with uncertain rate of inflation
2. Terms-of-trade inflation—a 3 percent increase in input prices
3. PPP changes in the exchange rates
4. A 3 percent real devaluation
5. A relative price change with and without substitution

Table 6–2
Project X14 Cash Flows—Base-Line Case
(thousands of $, constant prices)

Item						Year					
	0	1	2	3	4	5	6	7	8	9	10
Investment	(1,500)	—									—
Sales[a]	—	2,048	—	—	—	—	—	—	—	—	2,048
Materials[b]	—	(740)									(740)
Labor[b]	—	(533)									(533)
Energy[b]	—	(533)									(533)
Cash flow	(1,500)	242									242

[a]Based on 1,480 tons per year at 3,460 DM/ton and $.40 per one German mark.
[b]Based on 1,480 tons/year and data from table 6–1.

Across-the-Board Inflation

Inflation and disinflation are an integral part of the economic environment. Usually, however, the rate of inflation is uncertain. As the data presented in chapter 2 illustrated, the rate of actual price changes varied greatly over the period 1972–86. It is likely that the rate of inflation will continue to vary in the future as well.

To examine the sensitivity of the proposed project, the task force selected two cases. In the first case, the rate of inflation was assumed to be higher than the expected rate of inflation. In the second case, the rate of inflation was supposed to be below the expected rate. For simplicity, it has been assumed that whatever the rate of inflation was, it would be the same over the life of the project.

For the first case, let us assume an annual rate of inflation of 6 percent. This rate is translated to an ex post real rate of interest of

$$r = \frac{1 + .12}{1 + .06} - 1 = .0566$$

That is, given a 12 percent nominal pretax cost of capital, the real discount rate is going to be 5.66 percent per annum. If we maintain the real-constant-prices assumption, the real cash flows will not change. The assumed actual rate of inflation affects the discount rate only. The real cash flows will be:

	Year 0	Year 1–10
Cash flows	$1,500	$242,000

Discounting these cash flows at a lower rate than before will yield higher NPV. Thus, given an actual rate of inflation of 6 percent and maintaining the nominal discount rate of 12 percent, higher inflation will yield an NPV of:

$$NPV_{3,r} = \$1,810,000 - \$1,500,000 = \$310,000$$

The higher NPV arises from the fact that all prices have adjusted themselves to inflation, but the real discount rate has declined.

A similar conclusion can be arrived at if we calculate the NPV on nominal terms. All prices will be inflated by 6 percent per annum (across-the-board inflation), and the nominal discount rate will remain at 12 percent. The nominal cash flows are presented in table 6–3.

Although both the cash flows and the discount rate differ from the previous example, the result is the same.

$$NPV_{3,n} = \$1,810,000 - \$1,500,000 = \$310,000$$

Table 6–3
Project X14 Cash Flows—Across-the-Board Inflation at a Known Rate
(*thousands of $*)

Item	0	1	2	3	4	5	6	7	8	9	10
						Year					
Investment	(1,500)	—	—	—	—	—	—	—	—	—	—
Sales		2,171	2,301	2,439	2,586	2,740	2,904	3,080	3,264	3,460	3,648
Materials		(784)	(831)	(881)	(935)	(990)	(1,049)	(1,112)	(1,179)	(1,250)	(1,325)
Labor		(565)	(599)	(635)	(673)	(713)	(756)	(802)	(850)	(901)	(955)
Energy		(565)	(599)	(635)	(673)	(713)	(756)	(802)	(850)	(901)	(955)
Cash flow	(1,500)	257	272	288	305	324	343	364	385	408	433

A less-than-expected rate of inflation will decrease the NPV of the project. This is so because the actual real discount factor will go up. To illustrate, assume that the actual rate of disinflation is 2 percent per annum (that is, a −2 percent rate of inflation). A 12 percent nominal discount rate (again, with all the analysis done on a pretax basis) is translated into:

$$r = \frac{1 + .12}{1 - .02} - 1 = .1429$$

The real cash flows will remain the same, but the NPV will decline.

$$NPV_{4,r} = \$1,248,000 - \$1,500,000 = -\$252,000$$

As demonstrated, the uncertainty about the rate of the inflation introduces uncertainty. Following our earlier assumption that project risk does matter, and assuming risk-averse behavior for managers and shareholders, one would expect a discount rate higher than 12 percent. The actual risk premium is hard to figure out. A better technique, adopted by the task force in this case, is to figure out the risk premium that will make the NPV equal zero. Management (in this case, the investment committee) is then presented with this information.

A risk premium of 3 percent (that is, a real discount factor of 10 percent) yields an NPV of zero. A risk premium of 4 percent (a real discount factor of 11 percent), yields an NPV of − $75,000.

If the investment committee regards the risk premium associated with the uncertain rate of inflation as less than 3 percent, the project is acceptable. If the appropriate risk premium is deemed to be around 4 percent or more, the project is unacceptable.

It should be emphasized that the only risk considered here is the risk associated with an uncertain rate of inflation. However, the sensitivity of the stock market to changes in the perceived future rate of inflation tells us that the market takes this risk seriously.

Changes in the Terms of Trade

In chapters 2 and 3, we argued that the inflation and disinflation are usually associated with changes in the relative prices. We have described this phenomenon as a terms-of-trade inflation. The task force decided to deal with this set of issues in a very specific way by examining a number of specific scenarios pertaining to the major components of the inputs and outputs of the proposed project.

A 3 Percent Deterioration in the Terms of Trade

Given the expected rate of inflation, the output prices are assumed to decrease by 3 percent relative to the rate of inflation. Formally we set:

$$P_t, \text{output} = P_0(1 + \dot{P})^t(1 - .03)$$

$$P_t, \text{inputs} = P_0(1 + \dot{P})^t$$

$\dot{P}$ (the rate of inflation) is known, or some agreed upon expected rate of inflation is used together with an appropriate rate of discount. (See the preceding section "Across-the-Board Inflation.")

Again, the NPV can be calculated either on a real basis or on a nominal basis. In both cases, the cash flows will go down. As we have shown earlier, the two methods yield the same results by definition. In table 6–4, the real cash flows are presented for the case just described. The NPV is negative at:

$$NPV_{5,r} = \$1,271,000 - \$1,500,000 = -\$229,000$$

If we add the effect of uncertain inflation, the NPV will be even lower as we will discount the cash flows at a higher rate than before.

The terms of trade may change in many different ways. One useful approach is to conduct a series of expert interviews to collect information on the likely changes in the relative prices of the inputs and the output. This is done next.

Specific Price Changes

The task force assembled information on the likely relative changes in the major inputs. Some of the prices were estimated on the basis of past data, and some were generated by experts. The data is presented in table 6–5.

$\dot{P}$ is estimated at 4.67 percent per annum, such that the real discount rate implied in a 12 percent nominal discount factor is 7 percent.

The cash flows, in real terms, are presented in table 6–6. The resulting NPV at 7 percent real discount rate is:

$$NPV_{6,r} = \$1,503,000 - \$1,500,000 = \$3,000$$

Clearly, an inflation rate below 4.67 percent will decrease the NPV, and an inflation rate above 4.67 percent will increase the value, as long as the 12 percent nominal pretax discount factor is constant.

Table 6–4
Project X14 Cash Flows—Terms-of-Trade Inflation with a 3 Percent Increase in Input Prices
(thousands of $, real numbers)

Item	Year										
	0	1	2	3	4	5	6	7	8	9	10
Investment	(1,500)	—	—	—	—	—	—	—	—	—	—
Sales	—	1,987									1,987
Materials	—	(740)									(740)
Labor	—	(533)									(533)
Energy	—	(533)									(533)
Cash flow	(1,500)	181									181

Table 6–5
Price Changes for Specific Inputs Relative to the Inflation Rate

Item	
X14	– 3%
Labor	+ 2%
Materials	– 4%
Energy	– 5%

Changes in the Exchange Rates

The proposed project was initiated as an import-substitution activity. As such, it depends crucially on the exchange rate. One way to look at the project is as a way to "buy" foreign exchange—in this case, German marks. Indeed, in many developing countries, the government views import substitution projects as a way to obtain foreign exchange, and it sets a "shadow price" of foreign exchange as a "hurdle rate" or the minimum required rate for such projects.

Looking at the base-line project, the task force figured out the shadow price of the exchange rate as follows: The cost of materials, energy, and labor needed to produce 1,480 tons of X14 is $1,805,600. The capital charge on an investment of $1,500,000 at a 7 percent real rate of return is $105,000. So, an expenditure of $1,805,000 + $105,000 = $1,910,000 buys DM 5,120,800. That implies an "internal" exchange rate of $.373 per one German mark or 2.681 DM per one U.S. dollar.

As the exchange rate assumed at the base-line case is $.40 per one DM, it is cheaper to "produce" one DM at the production facility (at $.373 per DM) than to buy it at the market for 40 cents. However, the base-line case assumes a constant exchange rate throughout the life of the project. If the past is a guide for the future, no one should expect the exchange rate to be constant. In the period 1972–86, the dollar/German mark exchange rate varied a great deal. The unanticipated changes in the exchange rate moved from – 15 percent per quarter to 17 percent per quarter. Therefore, the task force decided to subject the project to some sensitivity tests of changes in the exchange rates.

The Purchasing Power Parity—A Zero Real Change

The proposed investment can be looked upon as a way to substitute the need to purchase German marks in the world exchange market by domestic production in the United States. One possible criterion for such investment projects is to compare the implicit price of one German mark in production to the exchange rate at the market.

Given the base-line case just presented, we can derive the implicit exchange rate in production as follows: The variable cost of production per

Table 6–6
Project X14 Cash Flows—Specific Price Changes
(thousands of $, real numbers)

Item	0	1	2	3	4	5	6	7	8	9	10
						Year					
Investment	(1,500)										
Sales	—	1,987	—	—	—	—	—	—	—	—	1,987
Materials	—	(755)									(755)
Labor	—	(512)									(512)
Energy	—	(506)									(506)
Cash flow	(1,500)	214									214

one ton of X14 is $500 + $360 + $360 = $1,220. The necessary investment is $1,500,000 amortized over ten years at 7 percent real cost of capital. Using a "rental rate" for the capital, the annual charge for the capital is $180,000 for the total production or $121.60 per ton. The total cost per ton is $1,220 + $121.60 = 1,341.60.

The cost per ton of X14 in Germany is DM 3,460. It follows that Integrated Materials can save DM 3,460 by spending $1,341.60. The implicit exchange rate in production is $.388. The exchange rate in the market was assumed to be $.40. Therefore, the proposed project has a positive net present value, and it should be accepted.

This analysis highlights the crucial role of changes in the exchange rate in the determination of acceptability of the project. If exchange rates are fixed, the base-line calculation is sufficient. In the current system of managed flexible exchange rates, it is necessary to include in the analysis some process by which exchange rates are changing.

In a perfect market such a process of change is given by Purchasing Power Parity. The PPP results is no change in relative prices due to changes in the exchange rates. It is a similar process to the across-the-board inflation discussed already.

Assume that the rates of inflation in the United States and Germany are 4.67 percent and 2.00 percent per annum, respectively. That is:

$$E(\dot{P})_{US} = 4.67 \text{ percent}$$

$$E(\dot{P})_{G} = 2.00 \text{ percent}$$

Given PPP, it follows that the annual change in the exchange rate, dollars per marks, is given by

$$\Delta S \, \$/DM = \frac{1 + .0467}{1 + .020} - 1 = .0262$$

The relative inflation implies a continuous process of nominal depreciation of the dollar against the mark. The changes in the domestic prices of X14 both in the United States and in Germany are presented in table 6–7. The exchange rate (implied by PPP) and the dollar price of imported X14 are presented as well.

The PPP changes in the exchange rates do not affect the cash flows or, therefore, the NPV of the base-line case. As was pointed out before, this case is similar to an across-the-board inflation at a known rate. This is so because the changes of the exchange rates, given PPP, reflect the relative inflation in the two countries.

A Positive Real Devaluation

The decline in the value of the dollar over the past three years is viewed by many as a way to effect a real devaluation. The task force assumes that a real

Table 6–7
Changes in Domestic Prices of X14 in the United States and Germany, with the Dollar/Mark Exchange Rate

Item	Year									
	1	*2*	*3*	*4*	*5*	*6*	*7*	*8*	*9*	*10*
German prices (DM)	3,529	3,600	3,672	3,745	3,820	3,896	3,974	4,054	4,135	4,218
U.S. prices ($)	1,448	1,516	1,586	1,661	1,738	1,820	1,905	1,994	2,087	2,185
Exchange rate $/DM	.4104	.4212	.4322	.4435	.4551	.4671	.4793	.4919	.5048	.5180

devaluation of 3 percent per annum will hold for the ten-year period under consideration.

The process of annual change of the exchange rate, in this case, is given by:

$$\Delta S \, \$/DM = \frac{1 + .0467}{1 + .0200}(1 + .03) - 1 = .057$$

Given a real devaluation of 3 percent per annum, the dollar price of the imported X14 will rise by that amount. The resulting cash flows are presented in table 6–8. Here, $NPV_{7\%} = \$4,000,000 - \$1,500,000 = \$2,500,000$. A real devaluation makes the import substitution investment project more desirable. Obviously, a real appreciation of the dollar vis-à-vis the German mark will reduce the value of the project. The task force felt that given past experience, a real devaluation or appreciation of the U.S. dollar against the mark may affect relative prices as well, and that this case should also be considered.

Changes in Relative Prices and Real Devaluation or Appreciation

To examine the effects of possible changes in relative prices as a result of real changes in the exchange rates, the task force assumed a standard production function of the form:

$$Q = KC^{\alpha}EL^{\beta}M^{\gamma}$$

C, L, and M denote capital, labor, and materials, respectively. E is energy and K is a proportionality factor. Both K and E are assumed to be constant. The capital investment was taken as given ($\alpha = 1$), while a certain amount of substitution was allowed between labor and materials. (β and γ are less than one.) The data for the production function was given by the Product Development Group.

The task force was interested in answering the following question: Given a possible adverse change in relative prices, is there enough potential flexibility in the project to avert such a change? Put in terms of standard economic analysis, this question deals with the income effect and the substitution effect of a given change in relative prices.

The task force has assumed a deterioration in the terms of trade by an increase of the materials prices by 3 percent at period $t = 1$. For the rest of the time, the prices will remain at the same level as at $t = 1$.

The built-in flexibility of the project was estimated by calculating the NPV first without substitution and then with substitution. The cash flows for the case without substitution are presented in table 6–9.

Given substitution, the NPV has increased by $21,000. This is a result of using fewer materials and more labor. The cash flows of the project, given substitution, are presented in table 6–10.

Table 6–8
Project X14 Cash Flows at a 3 Percent Real Devaluation
(thousands of $, real numbers)

Item	0	1	2	3	4	5	6	7	8	9	10
						Year					
Investment	(1,500)	—	—	—	—	—	—	—	—	—	—
Sales		2,109	2,172	2,237	2,305	2,374	2,445	2,518	2,594	2,672	2,752
Materials		(740)									(740)
Labor		(533)									(533)
Energy		(533)									(533)
Cash flow	(1,500)	303	366	431	499	568	639	712	788	866	946

Table 6–9
Project X14 Cash Flows with an Increase in the Price of Materials and No Substitution
(thousands of $)

Item	0	1	2	3	4	5	6	7	8	9	10
						Year					
Investment	(1,500)	—									—
Sales	—	2,048									2,048
Materials	—	(762)									(762)
Labor	—	(533)									(533)
Energy	—	(533)									(533)
Cash flow	(1,500)	220									220

Note: $NPV_{7,r} = \$1,545,000 - \$1,500,000 = \$45,000$

Table 6–10
Project X14 Cash Flows with an Increase in the Price of Materials and with Substitution
(thousands of $)

Item	0	1	2	3	4	5	6	7	8	9	10
						Year					
Investment	(1,500)	—	—	—	—	—	—	—	—	—	—
Sales		2,048									2,048
Materials	—	(752)									(752)
Labor	—	(540)									(540)
Energy	—	(533)									(533)
Cash flow	(1,500)	223									223

Note: $NPV_{8,r} = \$1,566,000 - \$1,500,000 = \$21,000$

The Task Force's Conclusion

The task force presented its finding to the investment committee in a table form reproduced in table 6–11. It is clear from the report submitted by the task force that the project is sensitive to inflation-rate uncertainty. The project allows for a risk premium of about 3 percent. It is up to the investment committee to decide whether this premium is a sufficient compensation for the risk.

Table 6–11
Proposed Production of X14: Comparison of Scenarios with a Nominal Discount Rate of 12 Percent

Scenario	NPV($)
Base-line case (no inflation)	199,700
Across-the-board inflation of 6 percent	310,000
Across-the-board inflation of 2 percent	− 252,000[a]
Across-the-board inflation of an uncertain rate	0
Terms-of-trade inflation, 3 percent increase in the real prices of inputs	− 229,000
Specific multiple changes in relative prices	3,000
PPP changes in the exchange rates	199,700
3 percent real devaluation	$2,500,000
One-time change in relative price	$45,000
One-time change in relative price with substitution	$66,000

[a] A 3 percent risk premium.

7
Inflation and the Cost of Funds: Good Food Inc.

I n chapter 4, we showed that the cost of funds for a given project or a single-activity firm is affected by inflation/disinflation or, in a multiple-currency situation, by the relative inflation among the various countries. The only exception for this is the case in which the inflation rate is identical all over the economy and the rate of inflation is known with certainty. Such a case exists only in textbooks. The data presented in chapter 2 support the proposition that the inflationary/disinflationary process changes relative prices, and the rate of inflation/disinflation is not known with certainty for any length of time. The actual, ex post rate of inflation usually differs substantially from the expected rate of inflation for the same period.

We turn now to the question of what is the order of magnitude of the effect of inflation/disinflation on the cost of funds and the cost of capital. To put it differently, does inflation make a difference in financing decisions? Should management spend time and resources on understanding and estimating the inflationary process while making financing decisions? These questions are answered through a case study based on real data and actual company history. We feel that it is common enough to allow some level of generalization.

Good Food Inc.—A Description of the Case

Good Food Inc. is a medium-size producer of a corn-based cereal. Although the company produces a complete line of products, they differ only by their packaging. For the purpose of the financial analysis, we treat all of them as one product—corn-based cereals. The company confines its marketing and distribution to one region of the United States. For planning purposes, Good Food Inc. follows a scenario-generating approach. According to this approach, the planners produce three scenarios for each variable: reasonable, good, and poor. Thus, the planners produce three scenarios for the size of the relevant market for the products of Good Food Inc., three scenarios for the market share of the company, three for cost of production, and so on. Given the scenarios, the planners then use a computer program to generate a probability distribution of the cash flows for a given period. The variables for the scenario analysis were chosen based on their importance in the revenue-generating process and the availability of data for the three scenarios.

The planners decide to base their analysis on the following seven variables:

1. Market size
2. Market share of Good Food Inc.
3. Selling price per unit of product
4. Required number of units of labor for one unit of product
5. Price per unit of labor
6. Required number of units of materials for one unit of product
7. Price per unit of material

These seven variables create the contribution, which is an approximation to the cash flows:

$$C_t = (\text{market size} \times \text{market share})_t \times (\text{price per unit})_t$$

$$- (\text{market size} \times \text{market share})$$

$$\times [(\text{number of units per one unit of product})$$

$$\times (\text{price per unit of labor})$$

$$+ (\text{number of units of material per one unit of product})$$

$$\times (\text{price per unit of material})]$$

In generating the scenarios, each is assigned a subjective probability (.25 for the poor scenario, .60 for the reasonable scenario, and .15 for the good scenario). It is assumed that all the variables are statistically independent of each other. The data for the three scenarios are presented in table 7–1.

Given the basic structure, the contribution function, and a set of data, the distribution probability of the cash flows is derived by a Monte Carlo simulation. By running five hundred simulations, a bell-shaped distribution is produced.

Assuming that the periodic distribution of the cash flow is a good representation of a typical year, the data is used to derive the risk scenario, the market size from the good scenario, the price per unit of production from the good scenario, and so on. Six percent is the adjusted expected rate of return

Table 7–1
Data for the Scenarios Analysis

	Scenario		
Variable	Poor	Reasonable	Good
Market size	$7,000,000	$10,000,000	$15,000,000
Market share	.04	.07	.12
Selling price per unit of product	$140/unit	$200/unit	$300/unit
Quantity of labor per unit	14 hours	12 hours	10 hours
Price per unit of labor	$6/hour	$5/hour	$4/hour
Quantity of material per unit	50 units	40 units	35 units
Price per unit of material	$1.2/unit	$1/unit	$.8/unit

on the straight debt of Good Food Inc. The term *risk-adjusted* is used here with regard to default risk. Given the probabilistic nature of the periodic cash flow, the probability of default is always positive. The question is how significant is the default risk to the required rate of return on debt. In chapter 4, we showed that the required rate of return on straight debt is:

$$r_d = r_f / (1 - P\{CF < d\})$$
$$d = Dr_t$$

where r_f is a default-risk-free rate, $P\{CF < d\}$ is the probability of default, and D is outstanding debt.

r_d depends on the proportion of debt in the capital. In the following, we estimate r_d for Good Food Inc. based on the data presented in table 7–1 and two levels of outstanding debt—$100,000,000 and $50,000,000. The results are presented in table 7–2.

The rate r_d is computed based on the assumption that the cash flows are normally distributed. Given the central limit theorem and the nature of the Monte Carlo simulation, this is a reasonable assumption.

To illustrate the process by which r_d (the default-risk-adjusted rate of interest) is derived, let us examine the first case. The debt service, given an outstanding debt of $100,000,000 and a 6 percent risk-free rate, is $6,000,000 a year. We define a variable, Z, where

$$Z = \frac{M - Dr_f}{S}$$

where M = mean value of the cash flow distribution

Dr_f = debt service, evaluated at the risk-free rate of interest

S = standard error of the cash flow distribution

Table 7-2
Estimates of the Required Cost of Debt with No Inflation

Parameters			Variables		Results	
Risk-free Rate r_f	Debt D		Mean CF M	Standard Error S	Nominal r_d	Real r_d
6 percent	$100,000,000		$64,647,792	$49,483,000	6.8%	6.8%
6 percent	50,000,000		64,647,792	49,483,000	6.71	6.71

Table 7-3
Estimates of the Required Cost of Debt with Across-the-Board Inflation

Parameters			Variables		Results	
Risk-free Rate r_f	Debt D		Mean CF M	Standard Error S	Nominal r_d	Real r_d
16.6 percent	$50,000,000		$71,211,088	$54,718,792	18.97%	8.15%
16.6 percent	$100,000,000		71,211,088	54,718,792	19.08	8.91

aIn nominal terms.

As Dr_f, the debt service (evaluated at r_f) is given, Z will vary with the ratio of M/S. Given Z, we use the normal distribution tables to derive the value of

$$P(Dr_f \leq CF)$$

and, given that, we can compute the default-risk-adjusted rate of interest r_d. Any changes in the environment that affect M/S will affect r_d.

Table 7–2 illustrates two characteristics of the cost of funds. The first is that moderate deviations from the reasonable scenario, such as those presented in table 7–1, are sufficient to create a significant default-risk premium (an increase of 13.3 percent in the cost of debt). The second is that the premium depends on the outstanding debt level relative to the cash flow.

Across-the-Board Inflation and the Cost of Debt

As we have seen earlier, a case of an across-the-board inflation with a known rate of inflation is similar to the case of no inflation. However, if we introduce the more realistic assumption of an uncertain rate of inflation, r_d (the required rate of return on the debt obligations of Good Food Inc.) is affected. The possibility of having the actual rate of inflation substantially different than the expected rate of inflation makes the probability of default much higher. For example, given a $50,000,000 outstanding debt, the probability of the debt service being greater than the cash flow in the no-inflation case is about .10; it goes up to .125 when the rate of inflation can vary between 8 percent and 12 percent per year, with an expected value of 10 percent.

The additional extent of the default risk is translated into a higher required rate of interest on the debt. The estimates for the risk-adjusted interest rate are presented in table 7–3.

The data presented in table 7–3 can be interpreted to show that the general uncertainty in the rate of inflation affects the mean and the standard error of the distribution of the cash flow. However, whereas the mean value goes up by 10.15 percent, the standard error has increased by 10.6 percent. Assuming general risk aversion, it is not surprising that the default-risk premium rose from about ¾ of a percent to about 2.5 percent.

Terms-of-Trade Inflation and the Cost of Debt

Earlier, it was argued that most inflationary and disinflationary processes are associated with changes in the relative prices or changes in the terms of trade. In terms of the data presented in table 7–1, it means that the prices of the output (corn-based cereal) as well as the prices of the two inputs (labor and materials) will change at rates different than the rate of inflation. In general, we can denote such a case as:

$$\dot{P}_j, \text{output} \neq \dot{P}_i, \text{inputs} \neq \dot{P}$$

where $\dot{P}$ denotes the rate of change in the general price index. Such changes will produce a flatter distribution of cash flow where the mean value increases by 7.96 percent and the standard error increases by 9.26 percent (all relative to the no-inflation case).

If Good Food Inc. has an outstanding debt of $100,000,000, the probability of having insufficient funds will go up to .1620 and the resulting required rate of interest on the straight debt will go up to 19.81 percent in nominal terms and 8.91 percent in real terms. This is a default-risk premium of almost 50 percent relative to the base rate of 6 percent.

When inflation is associated with changes in the relative prices, the effects of the increased risk just described can be mitigated by a possible substitution effect. If the technology allows for a substitution between labor and materials, as the relative prices change with inflation, the resulting probability distribution of the cash flow will be less risky. In the case of Good Food Inc., this is unlikely as the production technology does not yield itself to such a substitution.

The changes in the environment, from no inflation to across-the-board inflation to terms-of-trade inflation, affect the probability distribution of the cash flow through changes in the prices of the inputs and the outputs. As was pointed out earlier, the important variable in the derivation of the default-risk adjusted in the ratio of the mean value to the standard error of the probability distribution of the cash flows. To illustrate this effect, we present in table 7–4 data on the nature of the inflationary process, the resulting changes in the distribution of the cash flow (the M/S ratio), and the nominal and real inflation-deflated rates of interest of the straight debt obligations of Good Food Inc.

Table 7–4
Changes in the Distribution of the Cash Flow and the Rates of Interest by Type of Inflation for $100,000,000 Debt

Type of Inflation	M/S	Nominal Rate	Real Rate
None	1.306	6.8%	6.8%
Across-the-board	1.301	19.08	8.91
Terms-of-trade	1.291	19.81	8.92

The Effect of the Cost of Debt
on the Cost of Capital

The reported changes in the cost of debt for Good Food Inc. reflect an increase in the risk to the company due to the nature of the inflationary process. It is, to a great extent, company-specific. The specificity comes from the relations between the output and the inputs, and it is expressed by the production function. (See, for example, the case of Integrated Materials in chapter 6.)

In chapter 4, the relationship between the required rate of return on the equity and the riskiness of the debt was postulated as:

$$\beta_{ej} = \beta_{aj} + \frac{D}{E}(\beta_{aj} - \beta_{dj})$$

where β_{ej}, β_{aj}, and β_{dj} are the risk measures of the equity, the assets, and the debt of corporation j, respectively. The partial effect of an increase in β_{dj} is to decrease the risk measure of the equity, all other things being equal.

This seemingly paradoxical result is the outcome of the willingness of the creditors to assume risk—risk for which they are compensated. In terms of our analysis, most inflationary processes will increase the total risk of the company in question, but only part of this risk is passed on to the shareholders.

To see how this result is obtained, let us examine the case of Good Food Inc. once more. A look at table 7–4 reveals that inflation makes the probability distribution of the cash flow more risky. (We ignore here portfolio risk mitigation.) This is expressed by the decline in the M/S ratio. However, the current financial structure in most developed capital markets does not provide a way to issue risk-free debt in a time of inflation. The lack of inflation-linked debt requires the suppliers of debt capital to take the inflation-related risk on themselves. Obviously, they require higher expected return for that risk. In the case of Good Food Inc., this premium ranges between 2 and 3 percent, depending on the debt/equity ratio (D/E). This premium is not passed through to the shareholders.

Inflationary and disinflationary processes eliminate the risk-free debt, unless a perfect hedge is possible. The cost of capital is going up, but the cost of equity will remain the same as before or, in some extreme cases, it may go down.

8
Costing in Two Currencies in an Inflationary Economy: An Application

In the idyllic world of the perfect market, where there are no transaction costs, where information is free and available to all, where all firms are price takers, and where the price reflects a constant equilibrium, there is no need for costing. But, real markets behave in a different way. In most industries, prices are set prior to the actual transaction, although a price list does not constitute a semicontractual obligation.

As was discussed in chapter 5, costing is affected by the existence and the nature of the inflationary/disinflationary process. Costing is more complex and more important where more than one currency is involved, and the foreign rate of inflation is entering the process of costing via shifts in the exchange rate.

To illustrate the various aspects of the costing process, consider the following example. A U.S. firm is manufacturing a product for the industrial market. The product is marketed both in the United States and Germany. The U.S. manufacturer buys inputs both in Germany (materials) and in the United States (labor and materials). The source of the inputs is given as well as their proportion in the production process. Due to the nature of the product, prices are published once a year. It is customary to adhere to the price list for that period.

The first stage in the costing process is to organize the necessary data. The data is classified into five categories. The categories are:

1. Selling price per unit in the two markets
2. Cost of various inputs
3. Credit terms
4. External financial data
5. Policy expectations

The classification of the data pertains both to the source of the information and to the level of uncertainty with regard to the information. The first three items are internal to the firm, although they are affected by industry and general market factors. Yet, it is likely that the firm has good information about the cost of various inputs. In the case of the prices of the outputs and the credit terms, the firm has some discretion. The extent of the discretion is decreasing as we move from a monopolist situation to perfect competition.

External financial data is marketwide information on such issues as changes in interest rates, inflation, and exchange rates. It is unlikely that a single firm will have a capability to generate such data internally, but there are a number of firms and organizations that specialize in the collection and communication of that kind of information. The fifth category (policy expectation) is a mixture of information, once again best provided by professionals, augmented by the views of the decision makers within the firm.

For the purpose of the illustration, we will provide all the data on the basis of certain quantities or expected value. (The issue of uncertainty and how to treat it was discussed in chapter 7.)

Data

1. **Selling prices (per unit)**
   Price in the U.S. market: $100 FOB factory.
   Price in Germany: DM 300 FOB factory.

2. **Cost of inputs per unit (for the date of the calculation)**
   Imported goods from Germany. Price given for the whole year: DM 60.
   Domestic materials, priced at market per date of purchase. Current price: $20.
   Fully loaded labor cost, which may change per market conditions. Current price: $30.

3. **Credit terms**
   Suppliers' credit.
   Imported goods from Germany, net 30 days.
   Domestic materials, U.S. market, net 60 days labor.
   Labor and indirect cost, cash.
   Customer credit.
   German customers, paying in DM, net 60 days.
   American customers, paying in U.S. dollars, net 30 days.

4. **Financial data**

Exchange rate: DM 3/$1.

Expected rate of inflation (for next year) in the United States: 3 percent.

Expected rate of inflation (for next year) in Germany: 0 percent.

Real rate of interest in both Germany and the United States: 7 percent p.a.

5. **Policy expectations**

A zero real devaluation throughout the year.

Labor and indirect costs will decrease over the relevant period (one year) by 10 percent in real terms.

In addition to the price information, we need to determine the levels of inventory in the various stages of the production. These are decision variables for the firms, and they are easily determined. The relevant data is reported under "*Production.*"

6. **Production**

Inventory of materials: 6 months.

Inventory of goods in process: 1 month.

Inventory of finished goods: 2 months.

To perform the costing, we need to calculate the cost of the different components. Following the general presentation in chapter 5, we proceed on the basis of the data provided under categories 1 through 6. We begin with the calculation of the cost of various inputs.

Cost of Inputs

Cost of Imported Goods.

$$DM\, 60/\{3[1/(1\, +\, .05)^{1/2}]\}\, =\, \$.19.52\, \text{per unit}$$

The middle-of-the-year price is assumed to be the average price. Given the assumption of a fixed DM price contract, fixed exchange rate, and a relative dollar inflation of 5 percent, the standard price is lower than the current price which is DM $60/3 = \$20$.

Cost of Domestic Goods.
Here, the current price of $20 per unit is a good

standard given the assumption of continuous adjustment to the changes in the price level:

$$P_t = P_0(1 + \dot{P}_t) \text{ for all } t.$$

Labor and Indirect Cost

$$30/(1 + .10)^{\frac{1}{2}} = \$19.52 \text{ per unit}$$

Given the rate of decrease in real wages assumed in the preceding data section, we use a linear approximation and choose the midyear point as the standard price for the year as a whole.

The total cost of the inputs is:

Cost of imported goods + cost of domestic goods + labor
$28.60   + $20.00   + $19.52 = $68.12

In order to arrive at a complete costing, we have to add two more cost elements. These are the cost of the net credit and the cost of financing the inventory.

Cost of Credit

We assume no quantitative restrictions or credit rationing. Therefore, all credit components can be expressed in monetary terms as the cost of financing the credit. This approach assumes that the firm buys and sells packages that include interest charges. An alternative view is to buy inputs and to sell output only on a cash basis, to provide credit for customers, and to arrange for credit for the purchases of inputs as a separate activity. Although this approach is more consistent with the theory of finance than the "packages" approach just described, the latter is much more common in practice, and, therefore, we follow it.

Suppliers' Credit

Imported Goods

$$\$19.52\left[1 - \frac{1}{(1 + .07)^{\frac{1}{12}}}\right] = \$.38$$

The credit component is calculated at the real rate, 7 percent, as the rate of inflation in Germany is zero.

Domestic Goods

$$\$20.00\left[1 - \frac{1}{(1 + .07)(1.05)^{2/12}}\right] = \$.11$$

The two-month credit is calculated at the U.S. nominal rate of interest. We assume that the Fisher equation holds. It follows that the annual nominal rate of interest is:

$$[(1 + .07)(1 + .05) - 1] \times 100 = 12.35 \text{ percent}$$

When the firm buys domestic and imported goods, it pays an annual interest charge of $.11 + $.38 = $.49 per unit. It follows that the cash price of these inputs should be:

$$\$19.52 - \$.11 = \$19.41$$
$$\$20.00 - \$.38 = \underline{\$19.62}$$
$$\$39.03$$

Customers' Credit

German Customers

$$\frac{300}{3} \times \frac{1}{(1 + .05)^{1/2}}\left[1 - \frac{1}{(1 + .07)^{2/12}}\right] = \$1.09$$

The first component in the equation is the dollar equivalent of the DM price. As we have assumed zero real devaluation and 5 percent inflation in the United States, the midyear price (used here as the representative price) is

$$\frac{300}{3} \times \frac{1}{(1.05)^{1/2}} = \$97.59$$

This price is what the firm is financing for two months at the real rate of interest.

Domestic Customers

$$100\left[1 - \frac{1}{(1.07)(1.05)^{1/12}}\right] = \$1.01$$

Due to the assumed adjustment of the price in real, inflation-deflated dollars is always $100. The relevant rate of interest for the calculation is the nominal rate of interest in the United States, and the nominal price will reflect the nominal interest rate.

Cost of Financing the Inventory

Materials

$$\$39.03\left[(1 + .07)^{6/12} - 1\right] = \$1.34$$

Materials are carried through all the phases of the inventory (raw materials, work in process, and finished goods). The appropriate rate of interest here is the real rate, as it is assumed that the materials maintain their real value.

Labor and Indirect Cost

$$\$28.60\left[(1 + .07)^{\frac{2.5}{12}} - 1\right] = \$.41$$

Labor is carried in the inventory for half the time of the work in process (½ month) and for all the time of the finished goods (2 months). It follows that the total cost of financing the inventory is:

$$\$1.34 + \$.41 = \$1.75 \text{ per unit}$$

The results are summarized in table 8–1, where the financing costs are divided into two parts. The financing cost of the credit, both supplier and

Table 8–1
Summary of Costing in the United States and Germany

		German Market		U.S. Market
Selling price		97.59		100.00
Customer credit		(1.09)		(1.01)
Cash-basis selling price		96.50		98.99
Production cost				
Materials (cash basis)	(39.03)		(39.03)	
Labor and indirect				
costs	(28.60)		(28.60)	
Operating cost		(67.63)		(67.63)
Operating profit		28.87		31.36
Financing cost (inventory)		(1.75)		(1.75)
Profit after financing cost		27.12		29.61

Note: The difference in the profit stems from the adjustment of the price in the U.S. market. This adjustment (or the lack of it in the German market) reduces the cash-basis selling price in Germany by 2.5 percent relative to the price in the United States.

customer, is deducted from the calculation. Assuming that all financing is done at market rates, as we have done previously, means that the cost of the credit covers the cost of providing the credit, and there are no losses or gains involved in this operation.

The financing costs of inventory are a part of the financing cost of the firm. In this, they are similar to the cost of debt which finances a part of the assets of the firm.

Inflation and disinflation are part and parcel of the world in which we live. Even at a time of a low rate of inflation, people are concerned about the recurrence of inflation. In this book we have demonstrated that the major corporate financial decisions are affected by both the inflationary and the disinflationary processes. We have proceeded to show how corporate financial decisions are affected and what can and should be done about it.

Bibliography

Agmon, T. *Political Economy and Risk in World Financial Markets.* Lexington, Mass.: Lexington Books, 1985.

Agmon, T., and M.C. Findlay, "Domestic Political Risk and Stock Valuation," *Financial Analysts' Journal,* November/December 1982, 74–77.

Bodie, Z. "Common Stocks as a Hedge against Inflation," *Journal of Finance,* May 1976, 459–70.

Brealey, R., and S.C. Myers. *Principles of Corporate Finance,* 2nd ed. New York: McGraw-Hill, 1984.

Choate, G. Marc, and Stephen H. Archer. "Irving Fisher, Inflation, and the Nominal Rate of Interest," *Journal of Financial and Quantitative Analysis,* November 1975, 675–85.

Dietrich, J.K, and D.G. Heckerman. "Uncertain Inflation and the Demand for Capital," *Economic Inquiry,* July 1980, 461–71.

Feldstein, M. "Inflation and the Stock Market," *American Economic Review,* December 1980, 839–47.

Modigliani, F., and R.A. Cohn. "Inflation, Rational Valuation, and the Market," *Financial Analysts' Journal,* 1979, 3–23.

Myers, S.C. "The Capital Structure Puzzle," *Journal of Finance,* July 1984.

Parks, R.W. "Inflation and Relative Price Variability," *Journal of Political Economy,* February 1978, 79–97.

Pindyck, R.S. "Risk, Inflation, and the Stock Market," *American Economic Review,* June 1984, 335–51.

Sargent, T. *Inflation and Rational Expectations.* New York: Harper & Row, 1986.

Index

About the Authors

Tamir Agmon is a professor of finance and business economics in the graduate school of business administration at the University of Southern California, where he serves as IBEAR Research Professor. He is also an associate professor of international finance in the faculty of management at Tel Aviv University. Professor Agmon has written many articles in scholarly journals, has edited two books, *Multinational Corporations from Small Countries* (MIT Press, 1977) and *The Future of the International Monetary System* (Lexington Books, 1984), and is the author of *Political Economy and Risk in World Financial Markets* (Lexington Books, 1985).

Professor Agmon has extensive experience in consulting in corporate finance, international finance, and international banking. He has worked as a consultant in Israel, the United States, and the Pacific Basin countries. His work in Israel has made him an expert on the effects of inflation and disinflation on corporate finance.

Reuven Horesh is the dean of the Management College in Tel Aviv, as well as the academic director of Koor Industries school of management. Dr. Horesh has an extensive experience in the field of executive development. His research focuses on the economics of research and development and on corporate finance.

Dr. Horesh has consulted with business firms in Israel, Mexico, and with the World Bank, where his expertise in financial management under inflation was put to use. He is a member of the board of two Israeli firms and is involved in a number of business ventures.

STRATEGIC
MANAGEMENT of
TECHNOLOGICAL
LEARNING

Learning to Learn and Learning to
Learn-How-to-Learn as Drivers of
Strategic Choice and Firm Performance
in Global, Technology-Driven Markets

By
Elias G. Carayannis, PhD, MBA, BScEE
Associate Professor of Management Science
and
Director of Research on Science, Technology,
Innovation, and Entrepreneurship
European Union Center
School of Business and Public Management
George Washington University

CRC Press
Boca Raton   London   New York   Washington, D.C.

Library of Congress Cataloging-in-Publication Data

Carayannis, Elias G.
    Strategic management of technological learning / by Elias G. Carayannis
        p. cm. — (Technology management series)
    Includes bibliographical references (p.) and index.
    ISBN 0-8493-3741-0 (alk. paper)
    1. Organization learning. 2. Technological innovations--Study and
teaching—Management. 3. Employees—Training of—Management.. I. Title.
II. Series. III. Technology management series (CRC Press)
    HD58.82 .C37 2000
    658.3′124—dc21
                                                   00-057165
                                                         CIP

This book contains information obtained from authentic and highly regarded sources. Reprinted material is quoted with permission, and sources are indicated. A wide variety of references are listed. Reasonable efforts have been made to publish reliable data and information, but the author and the publisher cannot assume responsibility for the validity of all materials or for the consequences of their use.

ΕΝ ΟΙΔΑ, ΟΤΙ ΟΥΔΕΝ ΟΙΔΑ

ΣΩΚΡΑΤΗΣ ΣΩΦΡΟΝΙΣΚΟΥ

I know one thing, that

I know nothing

Socrates

Zum sehen geboren;

zum schauen bestellt

Born to see;

meant to Look

Goethe Faust

Preface

The purpose of this work is to isolate and better understand strategic decision-making frameworks as they are used in practice; and the role that feedback and learning processes play in reaching a decision within an entrepreneurial or strategic investment decision context and in technologically intensive, dynamic, and uncertain environments. It starts from a continuing schism between two diverging perspectives or schools of decision making. According to Schoen (1983, p. 237), the first is the view that "the manager is a technician;" the second is that "the manager is a craftsman." By following the Hegelian approach of thesis, antithesis, synthesis (Dewey, 1917, p. 71), we attempt to outline a third alternative to the two prevalent and conflicting schools of decision making, namely, the analytic or synoptic vs. the experiential or incremental school. This third alternative consists of the *metacognitive Paradigm* and the *strategic* or *active incrementalism framework of decision making* (Carayannis, 1992a, 1993, 1994a, 1994b, 1994c).

We formulate our third proposed alternative following a hybrid of the hypothetico-deductive and the inductive approaches to developing new insights and knowledge in the area of strategic decision making. We rely on both a review of the current divergent theories of decision making as they apply to an entrepreneurial/strategic investment decision context and the findings from our field research with several technologically driven enterprises. Thus, we attempt to identify empirically the presence of strategic incrementalism within the context of the strategic management of technology, through in-depth–interview-driven, ethnographic case studies of 13 companies from four industries (process, automotive manufacturing, aerospace, and power generation) headquartered in the United States, Canada, Germany, and France. The firms studied operate in business environments of high risk and/or uncertainty, very dynamic conditions (due to intensity of competition and/or technological complexity), and technological intensity (where technology has strategic import, and in many cases one has to "bet the company" when deciding for or against a certain project or technology).

The study was designed to cover at least three companies from each of three major sectors of industrial activity (transport manufacturing, process, and power generation sectors). Included are at least two business cycles, with products of short-, medium-, and long-term development and life cycles; and with domestic and international operations. Moreover, the firms studied are from four very competitive markets (industrial materials, health care products, automotive manufacturing, and aerospace), and one regulated market (nuclear power generation) used as the control group.

Specifically, the firms studied are as follows:

Industries and Corporations of Research Focus

Industry	Country	Corporation
Process industries	United States	Bristol-Myers Squibb Inc.
	Germany	Bayer AG
	France	Compagnie De Saint Gobain SA
Automotive manufacturing	Germany	BMW AG
	Germany	Daimler-Benz AG
	France	Matra Automobile SA
Aerospace	France	Airbus Industrie SA
Power generation	United States	Consolidated Edison Inc.
	United States	Rochester Gas & Electric Inc.
	United States	Tennessee Valley Authority
	United States	Duke Power Inc.
	Canada	Ontario Hydro Ltd.
	France	Electricité de France

The literature review and the empirical findings are synthesized to develop an organizational architecture of multiple-level technological learning (strategic or learning to learn how to learn from experience, tactical or learning how to learn from experience, and operational or learning from experience), that is the *strategic management of technological learning* (SMOTL). SMOTL is analyzed and discussed as the engine for building firm core competencies and sustainable competitive advantage, and an empirically validated philosophy and practice of strategic technology management.

The SMOTL framework for studying and interpreting firm behavior may lead to a new and emerging theory of the firm, one built around the strategic management of organizational knowledge and technological learning (Carayannis, 1992a, 1993, 1994, 1994a, 1994b, 1994c, 1996, 1996a, 1997, 1998, 1998a, 1998b, 1998c, 1998d, 1998e, 1998f, 1998g, 1998h, 1999, 1999a, 1999b, 1999c, 1999d, 1999e).

Acknowledgment/Dedication

Στην Μήτέρα μου
(To My Mother)

and to the following people who really made this work possible:

Mr. Jeffrey Alexander, Vice President and Director of Research, Washington CORE; Mr. Marc Aubert, Manager Associate President/VIP Programme, Airbus Industrie SA; Mr. Jean-Louis Caussin, Technical Director, Matra Automobile SA; Dr. Richard Elander, Senior Vice President, Research and Development, Bristol-Myers Squibb Inc.; Mr. Friedrich Hujer, Board of Management Member, Bayer/AGFA-Gevaert AG; Mr. Eberhard von Kuenheim, Chairman (Retired), BMW AG; Dr. George Laidlaw, Operations Manager, BASF Corp.; Mr. Edzard Reuter, Chairman (Retired), Daimler-Chrysler AG; Mr. Siegfried Schlesinger, BASF Corp.; Dr. Manfred Schneider, Chairman Bayer AG; Dr. Dieter Stein, President, BASF Corp.; Mr. Eggert Voscherau, Vice President BASF Corp.; Mr. Wolfgang Wehmann, Engineering and Services Manager, BASF Corp.; Mr. Mark Yogman, Head of Strategic Planning, Bayer Corp.

Elias G. Carayannis
George Washington University

About the Author

Dr. Elias G. Carayannis (e-mail: caraye@gwu.edu) is on the faculty of the School of Business and Public Management (SBPM), George Washington University (GWU), Washington, D.C. He is also Director of Research on Science, Technology, Innovation, and Entrepreneurship, European Union Center, SBPM, GWU, and faculty member of the GWU SBPM Environmental Studies Center and the GWU SBPM Center for Organizational Learning Studies.

Dr. Carayannis received his Ph.D. in technology management from the Rensselaer Polytechnic Institute in Troy, New York, in 1994; his M.B.A. in Finance from Rensselaer in 1990; and his B.S. in electrical engineering from the National Technical University of Athens, Greece, in 1985.

His teaching and research activities focus on the areas of strategic government–university–industry technology partnerships, business/war gaming and technology roadmapping, technology transfer and commercialization, international science and technology policy, technological entrepreneurship, and regional economic development.

Dr. Carayannis has several publications in both academic and practitioner U.S. and European journals such as *Research Journal*, the *Journal of Engineering and Technology Management, International Journal of Technology Management, Technovation, Journal of Technology Transfer, R&D Management, Growth and Change, The Review of Regional Studies, International Journal of Global Energy Issues, International Journal of Environment and Pollution, Le Progres Technique*, and *Focus on Change Management*.

He has consulted for several technology-driven governments, universities, and industries — foreign and domestic, large as well as small organizations — such as the NSF SBIR, the NIST ATP, Sandia National Laboratories' New Technological Ventures Initiative, the USC IMSC, the General Electric Corporate Training and Development Center, Cowen & Co., First Albany International, Entreprises Importfab, Bekaert NV, and others.

Carayannis, a citizen of the United States and the European Union, is fluent in English, French, German, Greek, as well as having a working knowledge of Spanish.

Table of Contents

Chapter 9

Chapter 10

1 Introduction

Existing concepts in the theory of the firm, especially those focused on strategic issues, tend to be constrained along two dimensions. First, past theory development has been static, analyzing the nature of a firm and its competitive position at a given point in time. Second, past analyses have emphasized homogeneity, so that firms are perceived to function in the same way, with variations in performance attributed to subtle differences in conceptual constructs not readily apparent (such as organizational culture, managerial talent, core competencies and knowledge, as well as technological learning processes).

Further extensions to the theory of the firm need to challenge the static, homogeneous approach, and move toward the creation of a theory of the firm that accommodates their dynamic and heterogeneous nature. Some recent works have a greater focus on dynamism and differences in firms as key determinants of competitive advantage (Porter, 1991). Examples include the development of the dynamic capabilities theory (Teece et al., 1992 and 1997), which attempts to identify the differences among firms with greatest strategic significance (Nelson, 1991). Other examples could be the way that the particular nature and environment of firms, especially in high-technology fields, leads to a new basis of competition and competitive advantage in those firms (Granstand, 1998). Competitive advantage in these industries is not based simply on the construction of barriers to the entry or establishment of market dominance, because the hypercompetitive environment of high-technology industry renders such advantages only temporary (D'Aveni, 1994). Instead, competitive advantage is derived from the ability to develop and commercialize new technologies more rapidly than other firms, by promoting and facilitating the creation and dissemination of technological and organizational innovations. In this environment, strategy becomes "a series of quests for the next technological winner" (Arthur, 1996).

A promising path toward the evolution of this new theory of the firm is to focus on the role of organizational learning in competitive advantage (Edmondson and Moingeon, 1996). This choice of research focus is supported by the examination of the nature of knowledge, and how the acquisition and integration of knowledge leads to the development of new competencies through organizational transformation (Morone, 1989; Nonaka and Takeuchi, 1995; Spender, 1996; Rosenbloom, 1996; Christensen, 1999). These processes of knowledge-based transformation are organizational learning activities. The result of improved organizational learning is enhanced strategic flexibility (Sanchez, 1993), meaning that the firm faces a greater range of potential options for action that then can be leveraged to achieve a better fit to its competitive environment. Such a view of organizational learning is analogous to the general concept of learning advanced by Huber (1991, p. 89): "An entity learns if, through its processing of information, the range of its potential behaviors is increased." Thus, a learning-based theory of the firm would advance our understanding of the dynamic construction of competitive advantage by (Carayannis, 1994b):

> ... focusing on the ways that organizations and the people therein generate, process, and alter their explicit knowledge and tacit skills, as well as the paths of change that such styles of organizational cognition can follow ... and [thereby] create questions and motives for further research on the dynamics of the creation and evolution of firm core competencies.

We address a specific area of organizational learning, which we term *technological learning*. Technological learning (TL) is defined as the process by which a technology-driven firm creates, renews, and upgrades its latent and enacted capabilities based on its stock of explicit and tacit resources (Aaker, 1989; Amit and Shoemaker, 1993; Bahrami and Evans, 1989; Barney, 1991; Carayannis, 1992a, 1993, 1994a, 1994b, 1996a, 1999, 1999a, 1999b).

The management of technological capabilities produces increasing economic returns as they focus more narrowly on knowledge assets and processes that are nonsubstitutable, imperfectly imitable, rare, and valuable (Carayannis, 1994b). To probe the relationship between technological learning, strategic management, and firm performance, we identify and study specific dimensions of technological learning at various levels of competitive significance as shown in Figure 1.1 and explained through this work. In this book we look at three main levels (operational, tactical, and strategic), four aspects (content, context, process, and impact), and two dimensions (qualitative and quantitative), that form part of the organizational knowledge generation, diffusion, and management architecture.

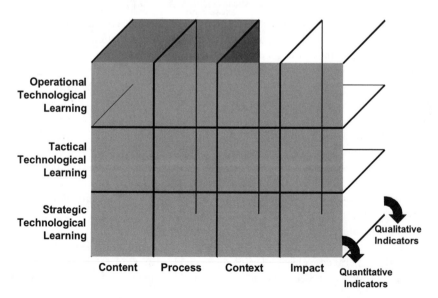

FIGURE 1.1   An architecture of concepts in technological learning.

1.1 CONCEPT OF DECISION MAKING UNDER UNCERTAINTY: INTERDISCIPLINARY OVERVIEW OF DECISION MAKING THEORIES

The problem of decision making under uncertainty is pervasive to modern life. It arises in virtually all domains of public policy, from social and urban policy, to foreign and national security policy, to science and technology policy; it arises in crisis decision making as well as in more routine conditions, and in judicial and regulatory bodies as well as in the legislative and executive branches. Decision making under uncertainty is also common to the private sector, in issues ranging from new business development to technology management to virtually all aspects of strategic management; moreover, "much recent literature has emphasized the importance of addressing decisions about business strategy, technology, and organizational structure as part of a coherent whole, rather than in isolation" (Adler, 1992, p. 269).

As pervasive as decision making under uncertainty is to human behavior, contemporary scholarship on the subject reflects a deeply rooted and long-standing schism between two schools of thought. On the one side stands the *analytic school* (Steinbruner, 1974), which suggests that in one form or another decisions should be made on the basis of expected value calculations. The decision maker should array his/her options, calculate the consequences of each of these options, evaluate those consequences, and finally select an option that satisfies an appropriate decision rule (e.g., maximize expected value, minimize expected loss, or maximize the minimum benefit). The second school of thought, the *experience-based school*, suggests that decision makers rely less on analysis to see their way through uncertain problems than on what is variously referred to as *learning from experience, selective trial and error*, and *learning by doing*.

We explore the empirical validity of these two models. Are both employed in practice, and specifically in the area of the strategic management of technology? Is one (or specific variations of one of the two schools) more commonly used than the other? If both are found in practice, which one, and in particular, which specific variation of the school in question, is more commonly associated with success than the other? We present an interdisciplinary literature review of decision-making paradigms from such fields as adaptive and self-organizing control theory, information theory, artificial intelligence, induction theory, cybernetics, management science, thermodynamics, cognitive science, military science, political science, game theory, utility theory, risk management, nonparametric statistics, catastrophe theory, and chaos theory.

1.2 STRATEGIC DECISION MAKING: ESSENCE OF STRATEGIC MANAGEMENT OF TECHNOLOGY

By relying on the one hand on the fundamental commonalities detected through our interdisciplinary investigation of published academic knowledge in the area of decision making (the "should" or normative dimension), and on the other hand by deriving corroborating conclusions from our empirical research on how decision making is actually being conducted in the real world (the "is" or descriptive dimension), we propose to formulate and qualitatively test comprehensive hypotheses as answers to the questions outlined in Section 1.1.

The motivation of such an effort is to bring conceptual clarity, and thus simplicity, to the prevailing divergent views of strategic decision making as it is being practiced in the real world. In our effort we were inspired by Forrester's comment on precision and accuracy: "…accuracy must be achieved before precision is useful. The ability to precisely state a hypothesis and to examine its consequences can be tremendously revealing even though the accuracy of the statement is low" (Forrester, 1960). That statement on the revealing power of a precisely stated hypothesis, regardless of its degree of accuracy, has partly motivated our hybrid research approach and our proposal of the strategic incrementalism framework of decision making.

The following quote from Nelson and Winter (1982) also constitutes a major reason for motivating our proposed framework of decision and focuses on the tacit dimension of learning and knowledge (Nelson and Winter, 1982, p. 82):

> Efforts to articulate complete knowledge of something by exhaustive attention to details and thorough discussion … of preconditions succeed only in producing an incoherent message…. In short, *much operational knowledge remains tacit* because it cannot be articulated fast enough, because it is impossible to articulate all that is necessary to a successful performance, and because language cannot simultaneously serve to describe relationships and characterize the things related. The knowledge contained in the how-to-do-it book and its various supplements and analogues tends to be more adequate when the pace of the required performance is slow and pace variations are tolerable, where a standardized, controlled context for the performance is somehow assured, and where the performance as a whole is truly reducible to a set of simple parts that relate to one another only in very simple ways. *To the extent that these conditions do not hold, the role of tacit knowledge may be expected to be large* [emphasis added].

Technology is a word with Greek roots that in free translation means *the logic or method of an art*, implying that it is what allows one to engage in a certain activity, initially considered as part of the state of the art, with *consistent quality of results*. This term currently has a multitude of definitions, but we prefer the one by Rogers: "A technology is a design for instrumental action that reduces the uncertainty in the cause–effect relationships involved in achieving a desired outcome" (Rogers, 1983, p. 12). His definition allows us to perceive the strategic management of technology as an "information-seeking and information-processing activity" (Rogers, 1983, p. 13) that tries to build advantage on the basis of technology (Morone, Summer 1989, p. 94) or "bring the potential opportunities that technology creates to bear on the formulation of corporate strategy" (Morone, Summer 1989, p. 96).

This emphasis on the informational theoretical dimension of technology and thus the importance of information in the technology-driven strategic decision-making process — allows us to look at decision making from several interdisciplinary perspectives. This refers to both our survey of theories of decision making and our clusters of case studies of successful companies, in particular, their top decision makers or problem solvers (Marone, Summer 1989, p. 98) who exhibit similar information acquisition and processing patterns. This emphasis also allows us to establish the link between learning and decision-making processes, particularly between the strategic management of technology and the management of technological learning, which refers to a company's ability to "rapidly acquire and diffuse technological knowledge, both theoretical and practical" (Dodgson, 1991).

Sahal (1982) distinguishes between "technological learning" and "manufacturing (or operational) learning," and defines technological learning as "a metalevel process in relation to manufacturing learning" (Dodgson, 1991; (Sahal, 1982).

Simon in his seminal 1969 Karl Taylor Kompton lecture at MIT, defined the meaning of *artificiality, complexity,* and *design* as well as the boundaries of the *sciences of the artificial,* at a very fundamental and pervasive (hence universally useful in the form of conceptual guides) level (Simon, 1969).

Seen from this perspective, the goal of this book is to answer some fundamental questions about the nature, the content, and the process of formulating and implementing the frameworks for making choices, which are after all the essence of strategy (Porter, 1990). Put in Simon's terms, to outline the design and the boundaries for a framework of decision making constitutes the driving force behind the revolutionary science of the artificial (Simon, 1969), which is the strategic management of technology. In Schoen's terms, decision making deals with the "predicament of the professions" and the "rigor or relevance dilemma" as they apply to strategic management (Schoen, 1983). Thus, strategic decision making can be seen as a science of the artificial (Simon, 1969), with the added dimension of an *actively dynamically adaptive and self-organizing nature*, in short, a decision-making framework that approximates dynamically and on a contingency basis, the right mix of both analysis and synthesis.

Using Kuhn's terminology, it is more a revolutionary than a normal science (Kuhn, 1970) within the context of the strategic management of technology, because by the definition of that context, it tries to usher in new technological paradigms on a continual basis, thus maintaining the comparative technological advantage, the intangible asset, and the core competencies base of technical enterprise.

The underlying common thread between the scientists and the top managers is that they both have to solve highly ambiguous and complex problems with limited resources. Thus, both groups are in essence problem solvers who are trying to effectively deal with the uncertainty and complexity inherent in their operating universes, in that sense they have to rely heavily on a set of assumptions and/or technologies as "means of uncertainty reduction" (Kuhn, 1970). In the same way that much of the scientist's success depends on *tacit knowledge* (i.e., *knowledge that has been acquired through practice and that cannot be articulated explicitly*) (Polanyi, 1958), much of the success of a top manager depends on knowledge and experience acquired through practice, learning from experience (Morone, Summer 1989, p. 105), or learning by trying. These forms of learning are members of a family of learning processes, which implies that learning can be viewed as a multidimensional phenomenon whose main dimensions or family members are (1) learning by doing (LBD), (2) researching and developing (or learning by studying and developing, R&D), and (3) imitating others (diffusion between firms, or learning by imitating).

The top managers are therefore perceived as *problem solvers* confronted with three levels of technology-driven complexity, change, and uncertainty:

1. *Changing problems* (operational loop)
2. *Changing ways of applying rules and assumptions* or starting points (tactical loop)
3. *Changing the rules and the assumptions themselves* (strategic loop) when trying to solve a problem

As outlined by Simon (1969, p. 5–6), the boundaries:

(1) Artificial things are synthesized (though not always or usually with full forethought) by man; (2) artificial things may imitate appearances in natural things while lacking, in one or many respects, the reality of the latter; (3) artificial things can be characterized in terms of functions, goals, adaptation; (4) artificial things are often discussed, particularly when they are being designed, in terms of imperatives as well as descriptives.

As paraphrased from Mintzberg (1989, p. 254), this enriched version of the science of the artificial means the right combination of "lumpers" that categorize; they are the synthesizers and "splitters" that provide nuance; they are the analyzers because "No organization can afford the luxury of being purely analytic or purely intuitive" (Mintzberg, 1989, p. 69). Contrary to Simon's view that intuition is inextricably intertwined with analysis, so that the "two processes are essentially complementary components of effective decision-making systems" (Simon, 1987, p. 60), Mintzberg believes that creative insight cannot be explained by seeing intuition and good judgment as "simply analyses frozen into habit" (Simon, 1987, p. 61).

We agree with Mintzberg that the concept of near decomposability (Simon, 1969) is not tantamount to recombination, in other words that "synthesis includes analysis" (Mintzberg, 1989, p. 69), but instead that synthesis "is rooted in the mysteries of intuition." If we see strategic management as the management of meaning: "The meaning is essentially wordless. Yes. Words are always qualifications and limitations" (Campbell, 1988, p. 231); or as Drucker (1989) says, "management by results," then the strategic management of technology is the conceptual management of "a process, or a set of processes, which, through an explicit or implicit phase of research and development (the application of scientific knowledge), allow for commercial production of goods and services" (Dussauge, 1988, p. 19); this is exactly one of the most comprehensive definitions of technology, suggested by Dussauge.

Burgelman and Rosenbloom's (1989, p. 2) definition of technology is focused more on the content than on the process of technology: "... the ensemble of theoretical and practical knowledge, know-how, skills, and artifacts that are used by the firm to develop, produce, and deliver its products and services."

Itami and Roehl (1987, p. 88) view technology with a nontrivial payoff value as "a ring of logic" where "each bit of knowledge must be in place to create the ring and render the technology functional."

Also from Dussauge (1988, p. 10) we learn that "a 'strategic' approach to technology ... requires that technology be viewed not only as an external factor whose evolution a firm can at best anticipate, but also *a factor which can be utilized to create competitive advantage*" [emphasis added]. Hence, concerning the dual (proactive and reactive) identity of the strategic management of technology (Dussauge, 1988, p. 35):

> Managing technology strategically implies going beyond the anticipation of technological change and combining the external and reactive approach of forecasting and scenario methods with the internal and proactive perspective of management of innovation techniques. The strategic management of technology is not so much the anticipation of technological change as it is the *determination of how technology can be used to create competitive advantage* [emphasis added].

The strategic decision maker has to contend with three kinds of uncertainty when managing a particular technology: "discovery does not always result from technology development efforts; markets do not always accept products from new technology; and newly developed technology can become obsolete" (Itami and Roehl, 1987, p. 89). These uncertainties, especially the third one, bring out the importance of learning and of continuous improvement in strategic decision making.

Itami and Roehl (1987, p. 132) connect the concept of dynamic imbalance with strategic decision making and dynamic resource fit through an overextension strategy, as they describe Casio's calculated risk taking with its jumping into integrated circuit design:

> Casio began with less than adequate resource backing, less than fully balanced resources. This short-term imbalance led to the creation of a solid base for future strategy that enabled Casio to beat back the competition in this market. This I call dynamic imbalance.

2 Overview of Decision- and Strategy-Making Schools

As pervasive as decision making under uncertainty is to human behavior, contemporary scholarship on the subject reflects a deeply rooted and long standing schism between two schools of thought on decision-making styles, whose presence was acknowledged as early as 1938 by Barnard when he wrote about the divergence between what he called *logical* and *nonlogical processes* that underlie decision making (Barnard, 1938, p. 36):

> By *logical processes* I mean conscious thinking which could be expressed in words or other symbols, that is, reasoning. By *nonlogical* processes I mean those not capable of being expressed in words or as reasoning, which are only made known by a judgment, decision, or action [emphasis added].

Barnard's statement on nonlogical processes can be considered the preamble to Polanyi's (1966) concept of tacit knowledge, knowledge that cannot be expressed (nonarticulable and perhaps even nonteachable knowledge).* In terms of strategy and structure formation, that translates to what Mintzberg calls "two feet walking: strategy always precedes structure and always follows it too" (Mintzberg, 1991b, p. 465), and this view is reinforced by Varela et al., "Experience and scientific understanding are like two legs without which we cannot walk" (Varela et al., 1991, p. 14). Itami and Roehl refer to the same phenomenon as the "logic of dynamic imbalance": "The logic of dynamic imbalance is not limited to the successful applications cited here from business. It is universal." (Itami and Roehl, 1987, p. 164).

If one reflects on the actual process of walking, one would realize that it consists indeed of a continuum of dynamic imbalances: one starts falling as one starts walking from rest, and then has to put one foot forward to arrest his/her fall, and so on and so forth. Alternatively, the *strategy–structure* duality can be perceived as the two extreme points between which a pendulum swings and can from time to time even shift across pivot points — when strategy shifts occur (see analysis on metastrategies in Chapter 9).

Mintzberg (1991b) uses the phraseology first coined by Drucker: "do the right thing" vs. "doing things right," to distinguish between the two diametrically opposed views of strategy making, the "Porterian" or *normative view* espoused by the *design*

---

* See also David Teece's Taxonomic Dimensions of Knowledge Assets: (Teece, 1987: 170).

school of strategy vs. the "Peterian" or *descriptive view* espoused by the *planning school* of strategy.

Along these lines we propose a synthesis of the two sides, a prescriptive view that synthesizes elements from both the design and the planning school. This view conceives of strategy formation as a process that is par excellence a learning one. It sees the formulation and the implementation of strategy, or thought and action, as closely intertwined in most cases and especially "during or immediately after a major or unexpected shift in the environment" (Mintzberg, 1990, p. 187), when one faces conditions that are uncertain, complex, unique, and may cause serious conflict of values. Under such conditions "thought must be so bound up with action in an interactive and continuous process that learning becomes a better label" (Mintzberg, 1990, p. 187).

What we see as the most intriguing pattern emerging from Mintzberg's (1990) critique of the design school, Ansoff's (1991) reply and counter-critique of Mintzberg's views on emergent strategy formation, and Mintzberg's (1991b) counter-counter-critique, is that *both sides agree on at least one point: the pervasive role that learning plays in the formation of strategy and that its essence is making decisions.*

Although each uses different terminology and places emphasis on different points, this common underlying strand of their diverging views on strategy making is what confirms and corroborates our emphasis on learning and our focus on highlighting its anatomy as it pertains to the strategy formation process. We believe that the most important element of learning, within a strategic decision-making context, is that of *tacit knowledge formation.* We also believe that kind of tacit knowledge, skills, and technological competencies, which is very difficult to analyze and comprehend explicitly, is where competitive advantages emanate from that are sustainable and reinforcible over time. Thus, to the extent to which one could understand the dynamics of the process of tacit knowledge formation or at least discern some ways that enhance and accelerate such a process, both, on an individual and an organizational level, as well as the anatomy of the related learning process, one could enjoy a substantial and lasting advantage over competitors who view strategy formation through a more static and rational prism resulting in *strategic myopia.*

In this chapter, we review briefly the two main schools of decision making — the *analytic school* and the *experiential school* — and the three major schools of strategy making — the *design school* (Andrews, Arrow, and Porter), the *planning school* (Ansoff), and the *Austrian (or experiential) school* (Mintzberg, Quinn, and Jacobson) — because they form the philosophical context that undergirds the conceptual foundations for our typology of schools of strategic decision making and strategy making, respectively (Figure 2.1).

2.1 ANALYTIC OR SYNOPTIC SCHOOL OF DECISION MAKING

On the one side stands the analytic school of strategic decision making (under which we classify the analytic paradigm [Steinbruner, 1974]), which suggests that in one form or another, decisions should be made on the basis of expected value calculations.

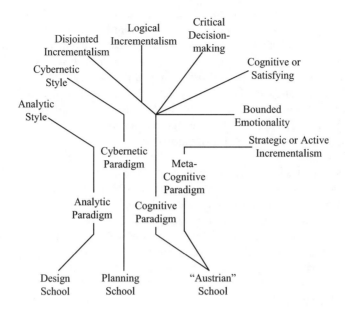

FIGURE 2.1 The tree of schools of strategic thought.

The decision maker should array his/her options, calculate the consequences of each of these options, evaluate those consequences, and finally select an option that satisfies an appropriate decision rule (e.g., maximize expected value, minimize expected loss, or maximize minimum benefit).

Analysis-based decision-making models come in many forms. Common examples in the public policy arena are cost-benefit analysis, risk benefit analysis, and probabilistic risk assessment. In the private sector, net present value analysis and some forms of market analysis are the primary examples. Whatever its particular form, analytic decision making rests on several core assumptions: first, that the most important features of the decision problem can be reliably represented in a model; second, that uncertainties associated with the problem (as represented in the model) can be treated probabilistically; and third, that the decision maker's values can be ordered in some sort of consistent fashion.

From these assumptions follow the general characteristics of analytic decision making, which for our purposes in this text, we have divided into three general stages — problem definition; identification, evaluation, and selection of alternative courses of action; and implementation.

2.2 EXPERIENTIAL OR INCREMENTAL SCHOOL OF DECISION MAKING

The second school of thought, the experience-based school of strategic decision making, under which we classify the *cybernetic* and the *cognitive paradigms* (Steinbruner, 1974; Allison, 1971; de Mey, 1982), as well as the metacognitive paradigm we propose, suggests that decision makers rely less on analysis to see their way through uncertain problems than on what is variously referred to as learning from experience, selective trial and error, learning by doing, and even learning by failing; and finds expression in a family of dynamically incremental decision-making styles with varying emphasis on *multiple-loop feedback* and *strategic learning* (Machlup, 1946, pp. 524–525): Businessmen do not always "calculate" before they make decisions, and they do not always "decide" before they act. For they think that they know their business well enough without having to make repeated calculations; ... The feeling that calculations are not always necessary is usually based upon an ability to size up a situation without reducing its dimensions to definite numerical value.

This second school thus covers the realm of *nonrational* (intuitive and judgmental decision making) and *irrational* (Simon, 1987) decision making (emotional decision making) in addition to the rational one.

These areas of managerial decision making have been investigated by Simon: "We will be concerned, then, with the nonrational and irrational components of managerial decision making and behavior. Our task, you might say, is to discover the reason that underlies unreason." (Simon, 1987, p. 24).

2.2.1 PROBLEM DEFINITION

Experience-based decision making begins the analytic approach. Lindblom's decision makers focus only on those aspects of the problem that directly concern their political interests; Simon's decision makers break the problem down into "nearly decomposable parts" and then deal with each part in relative independence; and Quinn's decision makers tend to limit attention to a domain shaped by a broadly defined strategic focus.

2.2.2 IDENTIFICATION, EVALUATION, AND SELECTION OF ALTERNATIVES

Identification of alternatives is explicitly constrained in this second school. Indeed, the notion of "search" for alternatives is emphasized by Simon to demonstrate that the process of identifying alternatives is itself a resource-consuming, ambiguous activity. Simon's decision maker considers alternatives sequentially; Lindblom's limits attention to alternatives marginally or incrementally different from existing policies; and the cybernetic decision making falls back on a limited and previously learned repertory of possible courses of action.

Analysis and evaluation of the consequences of each alternative are also simplified. Lindblom's decision makers limit consideration to those consequences that directly affect their political interests, and tend to restrict considerations of value to trade-offs at the margin among a restricted set of values (again, those of direct political concern to the decision maker). For Simon's decision maker, the task of evaluation and selection is simplified in a number of ways: alternatives are considered one at a time, and less analysis is required; the consequences of each alternative are limited to those that affect the part of the "nearly decomposed" problem to which the decision maker is attending; and, of course, evaluation proceeds by "satisficing" — instead of seeking the optimal solution, the decision maker is content to seek the first acceptable one. For the cybernetic decision maker, the need for analysis and evaluation is even more simplified, and approximates a learned stimulus–response pattern.

2.2.3 IMPLEMENTATION

For all the differences between the two schools in the problem definition and identification, evaluation and selection stages of decision making, the most striking and important difference comes in this third stage of the decision-making process. Whereas analytic decision making ends with selection, it is only just beginning for experience-based decision making. Implementation becomes a central part of the decision-making process. The decision maker implements the selected alternative, monitors feedback from the results of that implementation, adjusts his/her policy or choice on the basis of that feedback, monitors the results again, adjusts again, and so on. As Mintzberg describes, the key to successful strategic decision making is not "foresight, but a capacity and willingness to learn" from experience; whereas the analyt school leads decision makers to "retreat to their offices and mire them-selves in detached analysis," and experience-based decision makers emphasize "getting out in the field and learning."

Like the analytic school, experience-based models of decision making take a variety of forms. Among the leading examples are Lindblom's *disjointed incrementalism* (1980) and Quinn's *logical incrementalism* (1980), and what Steinbruner (1974) describes as the *cybernetic model*. Mintzberg (1978), Etzioni (1986), and Fredrickson (1990) also have made important contributions.

Each of the leading experience-based models were developed independently with largely different contexts in mind. Simon's model grew out of his attempts to explain general human problem solving; Lindblom's focuses on political environments; Quinn's, on strategic decision making in firms; and Steinbruner's, on bureaucratic decision making. Although they grow out of different intellectual traditions, and apply to different institutional settings, the experience-based models of decision making all begin with the premise that in practice, the conditions needed to pursue the analytic approach are rarely, if ever, achieved in real decision-making contexts. What is far more common in both private and public sector decision making, is that the alternatives facing decision makers are at best "dimly perceived" (Nelson and Winter, 1982, p. 171). Knowledge about the consequences of those alternatives is *incomplete*, sometimes grossly so; the time and resources required to generate the information needed for proper analysis of decision alternatives are *rarely available*; and decision-making objectives and values are themselves *ambiguous* and *often in conflict*.

What separates the variants into the two schools is the *relative emphasis* they place on the different stages of decision making, especially on feedback and strategic learning. Variants of the analytic school place a premium on the first two stages (problem definition; and identification, evaluation, and selection of alternatives), whereas variants of the experience-based school place a premium on the third stage (implementation that through feedback reception and strategic learning, particularly in the case of strategic incrementalism, drives the entire decision-making process). This is not to say that analytic decision makers eschew feedback, or that experience-based decision makers eschew analysis. On the contrary, the former continually upgrade their models as information becomes available, and the latter engage in extensive analysis. The difference lies in the center of gravity of the two approaches. In the end, the analytic approach assumes that the solution to a decision problem can be uncovered primarily through the application of model-based, analytic tools, whereas the experience-based approach assumes that the solution can be uncovered primarily through learning by doing and that "we shall go nowhere without emergent learning alongside deliberate planning" (Mintzberg, 1991b, p. 465).

2.3   DESIGN SCHOOL OF STRATEGY MAKING

Over the last three decades there has been a lot of theoretical and empirical research in the realm of strategy. However, due to the interdisciplinary and very dynamic nature of the subject, consensus has been consistently eluding the major intellectual powers in the academic arena of strategy making and the field of strategic management. The Schumpeterian processes of "creative destruction" and "organized abandonment" are all too evident if one were to try to devise a metatheory about the formation of theories of strategy making and by extension of strategic decision making.

The purpose of such an intellectual exercise would be to better understand the premises on which any such edifice is built and thus through a critical review of the diverging schools of strategy making manage to synthesize their underlying common threads to a potentially overarching paradigm of strategic decision making.

The main proponents of the *design school* are Selznick (1957), Chandler (1962), Ansoff (1965), and Porter (1980, 1985, 1990). The model proposed by the design school "places primary emphasis on the appraisals of the external and internal situations, the former uncovering threats and opportunities in the environment, the latter revealing strengths and weaknesses in the organization" (Mintzberg, 1990, p. 173) (Figure 2.2).

According to Mintzberg (1990, pp. 175–179), the premises underlying the design school are

1. Strategy formation should be a controlled, conscious process of thought.
2. Responsibility for that control and consciousness must rest with the chief executive officer: that person is *the* strategist.
3. The model of strategy formation must be kept simple and informal.
4. Strategies should be unique: the best ones result from a process of creative design.
5. Strategies emerge from the design process fully formulated.
6. These strategies should be explicit and, if possible, articulated, which also favors their being kept simple.
7. Finally, only after these unique, full blown, explicit, and simple strategies are fully formulated can they be implemented.

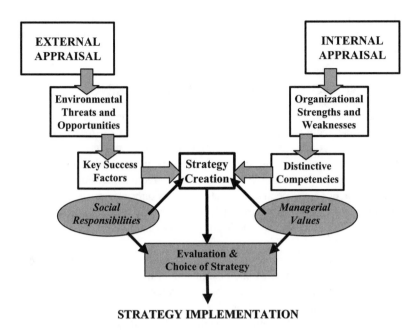

FIGURE 2.2   Strategy formulation and implementation in the design school.

The main weakness of the school as Mintzberg notes is that it has designed into its conceptual framework a rigidity that means that *"the school has denied itself the chance to adapt"* [emphasis added] (Mintzberg, 1990, p. 181). Mintzberg considers making strategies explicit as a kind of straightjacket or blinder that enforces a what we call *impaired strategic focus:* "Explicit strategies, as implied in the reasons for wanting them, are blinders designed to focus direction and so to *block our peripheral vision* [emphasis added]" (Mintzberg, 1990, p. 184). This impairment of strategic focus calls for its redefinition that we attempt to accomplish via our proposed decision-making framework of strategic incrementalism.

The design school's main shortcoming is, in our opinion, the fact that it *de-emphasized learning* by considering it a form of opportunism and by that token decoupled the formulation of strategy from its implementation and suppressed its dynamically evolving nature. In reality, formulation is intertwined with implementation in a close and dynamically evolving relationship centered around *strategic learning*: "Both situations — 'formulators' implementing and 'implementers' formulating — amount to the same thing in one important respect: the organizations are *learning,*" and "… especially during or immediately after a major unexpected shift in the environment [*what we refer to as paradigm shift — added*], thought must be so bound up with action in an *interactive and continuous* {emphasis added} process that learning becomes a better label and concept, for what happens then is *formulation–implementation* [emphasis added]" (Mintzberg, 1990, p. 187).

The main contribution of the Design School is that it provided the conceptual context, or appropriate basic vocabulary, that allowed effective higher order thinking and expression concerning strategy making and the notion that "strategy represents a fundamental congruence between external opportunity and internal capability" (Mintzberg, 1990, p. 193).

2.4 PLANNING SCHOOL OF STRATEGY MAKING

Ansoff refers to the *planning school of strategy making* as the school of holistic strategic management (Ansoff, 1991, p. 452) and presents 12 theses as the premises that help profile its identity and differentiate it from the other schools.

Concerning learning, this school recognizes it explicitly, unlike the design school, although in our opinion it suggests a less effective and representative of what is actually practiced perspective of strategic decision making.

Ansoff (1991, p. 457–458), refers to three models of learning, tracing the evolution of learning models from medieval to modern times:

1. The *existential learning* model he considers to be the oldest and the one implicitly referred to by the design school of strategy. This is the model of learning practiced by the master builders in the Middle Ages who created the architectural miracles that are the European cathedrals.
2. The *rational learning* model was the outcome of the age of enlightenment and emphasized the role of cognition. Here, decision making is the first stage, and the second is implementation of the decision. That was the driving force behind the early version of strategic planning.
3. The *strategic learning* model is the outcome of adding strategic control capability to the rational learning model. This model is effectively a "chain of cognition-trial-cognition-trial, etc." (Ansoff, 1991, p. 458).

The premises underlying the Planning School are (Ansoff, 1991: 449–461):

1. Revised concept of strengths and weaknesses
2. Structured method for analytic strategy formulation
3. Concept of organizational capability
4. Concept of strategic bicentralization
5. Concept of strategic myopia and resistance to strategic change
6. Diagnostic procedure for sequencing strategy/structure development
7. Concept of strategic management
8. Concept of real-time response that includes three procedures (1) strong signal issue management, (2) weak signal issue management, and (3) surprise management
9. Applied theory of strategic behavior
10. Strategic success hypothesis
11. Practical strategic diagnosis procedure
12. Interactive computer software for strategy formulation

2.5 EMERGENT LEARNING AND DELIBERATE PLANNING OR "AUSTRIAN" SCHOOL OF STRATEGY MAKING

The *Austrian* or *experiential school,* with proponents such as Mintzberg (1989, 1990, 1991a, 1991b), Quinn (1992), and Jacobson (1992), is the one to which our meta-cognitive paradigm of strategic decision making is the most akin, because it provides the conceptual foundations for integrating multiple-loop learning, metalearning, and metacognition in the domain of strategy making. The major premise of that school is the emphasis on dealing with change, uncertainty, and disequilibrium. It is called the Austrian school of strategy by Jacobson (Jacobson, 1992), because like the Austrian school of economic thought (von Mises, von Hayek, Schumpeter, Kirzner, et al), it focuses on "strategic issues relating to: (1) continuous innovation, (2) flexibility, (3) intertemporal heterogeneity, and (4) unobservable influences of business performance" (Jacobson, 1992, p. 784).

Like the Austrian economists, this school views "markets as processes of discovery that mobilize dispersed information" (Jacobson, 1992, p. 785). Moreover, it places explicit emphasis on the "role of *knowledge and learning* [emphasis added] in dynamic competitive markets" (Jacobson, 1992, p. 789) and treats competition as "a process rather than as a static notion [emphasis added]" (ibid: 789). The notion of static equilibrium is prevalent in the models of the design school (Porter's models) (Figure 2.3).

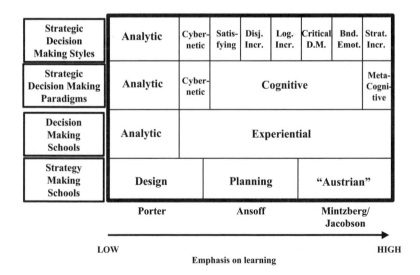

FIGURE 2.3 Typology of strategic decision making: schools, paradigms, and styles.

3 Concept of Paradigms in Decision Making

Paradigms are conceptual entities that share two main characteristics: they are "sufficiently unprecedented" and "sufficiently open-ended" (Kuhn, 1970, p. 10). A fuller definition of a paradigm is as follows: "a paradigm is an accepted model, or pattern, ... like an accepted judicial decision in the common law, it is an object for further articulation and specification under new or more stringent conditions" (Kuhn, 1970, p. 23); or "universally recognized scientific achievements that for a time provide model problems and solutions to a community of practitioners" (Kuhn, 1970, p. viii) (in our case the practitioners are the strategic decision makers). Allison quotes Merton to give a sociological definition of a paradigm: "According to Merton, a paradigm is a systematic statement of the basic assumptions, concepts, and propositions, employed by a school of analysis" (Allison, 1971, p. 32).

A *technological paradigm* is a sufficiently unprecedented and open-ended, widely accepted model or pattern as it relates to the fundamental views that guide the strategic management of the technology in question. Thus, the strategic relevance of the concept of a technological paradigm, as well as of the process through which a shift in the dominant paradigm takes place, is multiple:

1. It lies in the fact that managements with different established paradigms have different perspectives of the world and hence can consistently differ in their respective patterns of strategic decisions: "when paradigms change, the world itself changes with them ... paradigm changes do cause scientists [read managers] to see the world of their research-engagement [read area of strategic management] differently" (Kuhn, 1970, p. 111).

2. It provides for those who accept the same paradigm with its possible nuances a common language or cognitive protocol, that in itself is a very powerful source of sustainable competitive advantage vis-a-vis those with nonuniform paradigms: "... once the reception of a common paradigm has freed the scientific [read strategic management of technology] community from the need constantly to reexamine its first principles, the members of that community can concentrate exclusively on the subtlest and most esoteric of the phenomena that concern it. Inevitably, that does increase both the effectiveness and the efficiency with which the group as a whole solves new problems" (Kuhn, 1970, p. 163–164). That is primarily due to the higher rates of learning, in our case technological, made possible through the facilitation of an intellectual free trade: "The real subjects of the new intellectual free trade among the many cultures

are our own thought processes, *our processes of judging, deciding, choosing, and creating."* [emphasis added] (Simon, 1969, p. 83).

3. It creates new strategic opportunities and threats when there is a paradigm shift through what Kuhn calls a "scientific revolution," that is, "noncumulative developmental episodes in which an older paradigm is replaced in whole or in part by an incompatible new one" or "the extraordinary episodes in which that shift of professional commitments occurs ... the tradition shattering complements to the tradition bound activity of normal science." (Kuhn, 1970, p. 6).

In our case this would take place against the dominant, established paradigm(s) of strategic decision making and technological worldview(s). The opportunities and threats are created because identification of an emerging new paradigm is very difficult, not just because looking for the guiding elements in scientific activity or strategic decision making is not like looking for a wholesome, unitary entity that either is there or is not. To understand this difficulty in identifying a new paradigm a quote from James (1950) might be useful: "Man is born with a tendency to do more things than he has ready-made arrangements for in his nerve centers." The reception of a new paradigm often necessitates a redefinition of the corresponding science or norms and standard practices in the strategic management of technology. In other words, it entails dealing with what Veblen (1924) called "trained incapacity."

Rogers (1983, p. 85) refers to that concept with regard to innovation diffusion:

... by being taught to "see" innovativeness, opinion leadership, and other aspects of the classical model of diffusion, we failed to see much else. *Acceptance of an intellectual paradigm by scholars in a research field enables them to cope with uncertainty and information overload, through the simplification of reality that the paradigm represents.* [emphasis added].

It is also important to remember that the new normal scientific tradition or strategic management practice that emerges from a scientific revolution not only is incompatible but also is often incommensurable with what has gone before. In our terms, old practices such as the concept of strategic business units and formal, comprehensive strategic planning through detailed business plans may be not only useless but also actually harmful to the new realities and challenges confronting the modern practitioners of the strategic management of technology.

The evolution of paradigms should therefore be considered as a continuum of discontinuities because the transition between competing paradigms cannot be made a step at a time, forced by logic and neutral experience. Like the Gestalt switch: *"it must occur all at once (though not necessarily in an instant) or not at all"* [emphasis added] (Kuhn, 1970, p. 150). According to Itami and Roehl (1987, p. 133), it also must occur through a process of dynamic imbalances, which in the strategic management context work as "an impetus to achieve dynamic resource fit" and through an overextension strategy that is "crucial to accumulating sufficient resources to become competitive." These resources or assets can be both visible (economic) and invisible (consumer trust, brand image, control of distribution, corporate culture, and management skill [Itami and Roehl, 1987, p .12]) to which we add the ability to learn and adapt at an increasing rate and find maximum leverage points for change implementation. See also Stata's comments about comparatively higher rates of organizational learning as the only sustainable competitive advantage in Kochan & Useem (Kochan and Useem (1992, p. 377–380) and Senge's (1990, p. 128) system dynamics approach to leverage points, accumulated through processes of *single* and *double loop learning* and *deuterolearning* (Bateson, 1972; Argyris and Schoen, 1978). These invisible assets are "the real source of competitive power and the key factor in corporate adaptability for three reasons: they are hard to accumulate, they are capable of simultaneous multiple uses, and they are both inputs and outputs of business activities" (Itami, 1987, p. 12–13). To that we would add the fact that invisible assets, due to their predominantly tacit nature, are very difficult if not impossible to imitate and/or transplant and can be only truly acquired through internal development. This trait corroborates their strategic importance for the tech-nological enterprise.

The three major paradigms of strategic decision making that constitute our frame of reference were adapted to the realm of strategic management from similarly named paradigms that were initially developed for a wide range of disciplines and are complemented by the metacognitive paradigm we developed:

1. *Analytic* (Steinbruner, 1974)
2. *Cybernetic* (Steinbruner, 1974)
3. *Cognitive* ((Steinbruner, 1974; Allison, 1971)

To those paradigms we add the one we propose, the metacognitive paradigm (see Figures 2.2 and 2.3).

3.1   ANALYTIC PARADIGM

The analytic paradigm falls under the analytic school; and the cybernetic, cognitive, and metacognitive paradigms fall under the experiential or experience-based school of strategic decision making. The analytic paradigm contains the analytic, synoptic, or comprehensive style.

3.2   CYBERNETIC PARADIGM

The cybernetic paradigm contains the cybernetic or hierarchical stimulus-driven style.

3.3   COGNITIVE PARADIGM

The cognitive paradigm can be further expanded into five frameworks or styles of strategic decision making:

1. Cognitive style, also akin to the "satisficing" or "bounded rationality" style (Simon, 1987)
2. Disjointed incrementalism or "muddling through" style (Braybrook and Lindblom, 1963), also akin to the *bureaucratic* or *governmental politics paradigm* proposed by Allison
3. Logical or "evolutionary" incrementalism style (Quinn, 1980), also akin to the *organizational perspective* proposed by Andersen and the *organizational process paradigm* proposed by Allison
4. Critical decision-making or Neo-Popperian style (Collingridge, 1982), also akin to the *devil's advocate* and *dialectic inquiry* styles
5. Bounded emotionality style, that focuses on four premises (Mumby and Putnam, 1992, p. 478):
   a. Centrality of the cognitive metaphor
   b. Emphasis on a mind–body dualism
   c. Devaluing of physical labor
   d. Treatment of emotion as form of labor

4 Concepts of Culture, Feedback, and Learning in Decision Making and Strategy Crafting

4.1 CULTURE AS A MEDIUM FOR LEARNING

Culture is the invisible force behind the tangibles and observables in any organization, a social energy that moves people to act. Culture is to the organization what personality is to the individual — a hidden, yet unifying theme that provides meaning, direction, and mobilization.

Killman, R., Gaining Control of the Corporate Culture, 1985

One way of looking at culture is as a "phenomenon that surrounds us at all times, being constantly enacted and created by our interactions with others" (Schein, 1992, p. 1). In other words, it is a living, evolving protocol of action and interaction among members of a group or an organization. This modus operandi consists of both tangible, explicit and intangible, implicit dimensions. Schein (1992, p. 5) believes that the major driving force behind shaping and legitimating cultures are the leaders of a group of people: "leaders create and change cultures, while managers and administrators live within them."

A formal definition of culture is as follows: Culture is a "pattern of shared basic assumptions that the group learned as it solved its problems of external adaptation and internal integration, that has worked well enough to be considered valid, and therefore, to be taught to new members as the correct way to perceive, think, and feel in relation to those problems" (Schein, 1992, p. 12). The emphasis on dealing with problems of adaptation and integration is akin to the manager as a problem solver that learns continuously and whose survival and success hinge exactly on this ability to learn and more importantly to disseminate within the organization the capacity to *learn how to learn* and to *learn to learn-how to learn* (Carayannis, 1992a, 1993, 1994a, 1994b, 1994c).

Culture is perceived as a system with three interacting layers of increasing visibility and decreasing decipherability (Figure 4.1) (Frost, 1991, p. 21–23):

1. Basic assumptions that reflect the relationship of the members of the organization to the environment and the nature of humans and the contingencies surrounding them, and are invisible or taken for granted

2. Values that reflect the prevailing organizational culture and are driven by the underlying basic assumptions, and are more visible than the Basic Assumptions themselves

3. Artifacts and creations that reflect technological and artistic organizational endowments as well as visible and audible behavior patterns, and are visible but often hard to decipher.

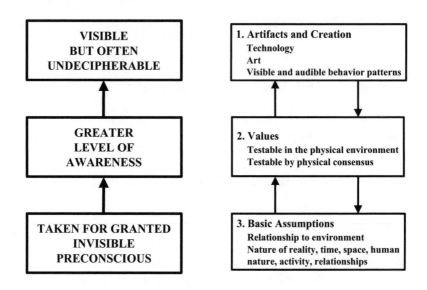

FIGURE 4.1   The tree of schools of strategic thought.

4.1.1   CONCEPT OF ORGANIZATIONAL CULTURE FROM THREE PERSPECTIVES: INTEGRATION, DIFFERENTIATION, AND FRAGMENTATION

Martin developed a critical analysis of three perspectives on organizational culture, those of integration, differentiation, and fragmentation, that she feels are simultaneously present and valid in most organizations with one temporarily prevailing from time to time.

The integration perspective is defined by "organization-wide consensus, consistency, and clarity" (Martin, 1992, p. 45) and views culture as "the pattern of shared beliefs and values that give the members of an institution meaning, and provide them with the rules for behavior in their organization" (Davis, 1984, p. 1).

The differentiation perspective is defined by "inconsistency, subcultural consensus, and the relegation of ambiguity to the periphery of subcultures" (Martin, 1992, p. 83) and views culture as "a set of understandings or meanings shared by a group of people. The meanings are largely tacit among members, are clearly relevant to a particular group, and are *distinctive* to the group" (Louis, 1985, p. 74).

The fragmentation perspective is defined by "focus on ambiguity, complexity of relationships among manifestations, and a multiplicity of interpretations that do not coalesce into a stable consensus" (Martin, 1992, p. 130); and views culture as "a web of individuals, sporadically and loosely connected by their changing positions on a variety of issues. Their involvement, their subcultural identities, and their individual self-definitions *fluctuate*, depending on which issues are activated at a given moment" (Martin, 1992, p. 153).

4.1.2   ORGANIZATIONAL CULTURE AS A FACILITATOR/INHIBITOR OF TECHNOLOGICAL LEARNING: A METACULTURE PERSPECTIVE

From Martin's definitions we can elicit a common underlying pattern, that of culture being a "conduit" or guide to continuous change and adaptation of members of a group or organization in a concerted manner, and in response to evolving internal or external contingencies, such as technological innovation or technology transfer. The validity and effectiveness of culture as such a guide hinges mainly on the degree to which the culture in question is focused on and facilitates learning, and in particular *technological learning* among the organizations in our study: "Knowledge does not grow in a linear way, through the accumulation of facts and the application of the hypothetico-deductive method, but rather resembles an *upward spiral*, so that each time we reevaluate a position or place we've been before, we do so from a new perspective" (Jaggar, 1983, p. 368).

Martin's exposé of the continuum of the three perspectives on culture where each perspective dynamically exchanges the predominant position with a repressed one, with the other two perspectives brings forward the dynamics of the learning process itself: "When one perspective seems to be the 'best' way to regard a context, the other two, forbidden perspectives may be particularly useful sources of insight" (Martin, 1992, p. 177). The pathological, persistent predominance of one cultural perspective or worldview to the detriment of the others leads to *organizational learning disabilities*. Then the prevailing culture becomes a barrier to learning or an organizational learning inhibitor, a "cultural blinder," because: "Culture is the invisible force behind the tangibles and observables in any organization, a social energy that moves the membership into action. Culture is to the organization what personality is to the individual — a hidden yet unifying theme that provides meaning, direction, and mobilization" (Killman, 1985). In that sense, culture can act as a blinder or "mental restraint" affecting adversely the present and future organizational welfare with the *organizational and technological momentum* of the past.

Hughes (1983, p. 140) outlined the concept of technological momentum using the case of the polyphase universal electric supply system:

> During the 1890's the polyphase system gathered momentum. Because it encompassed the old contenders in "the battle of the systems" (direct current versus single-phase alternating current), the new system gained widespread support from men and institutions in the rapidly growing field of electrical engineering, science, and industry. A supportive context, or culture, formed rapidly. Men and institutions developed characteristics that suited them to the characteristics of the technology. And the systematic interaction of men, ideas, and institutions, both technical and nontechnical, led to the development of *a supersystem — a sociotechnical one —* with mass movement, and direction. *An apt metaphor for this movement is "momentum"* [emphasis added].

4.2 FEEDBACK AS A TOOL FOR LEARNING

4.2.1 INTERDISCIPLINARY OVERVIEW

Truth emerges more readily from error than from confusion.

Sir Francis Bacon

The history of feedback can be traced to the golden age of ancient Greece. Mayr (1970) credits Ktesibios (250 B.C.) with designing the first known feedback device: a float valve that served as a moderator of the water flow into a cylindrical vessel, thus making possible the construction of an accurate water clock. In western Europe, the *thermostatic device* invented by Cornelius Drebbel (1572–1633) was the first known feedback mechanism of western European origin (Mayr, 1970).

The Epimenides "liar's paradox" (all Cretans are liars) introduced the concept of the "vicious circle" or self-referential loop very much in use and abuse nowadays and in all walks of life (Epimenides was Cretan and hence a liar himself). This same concept was used by Bertrand Russell to question the very foundations of mathematical thought. Russell defined the set R of all sets that are not members of themselves and then asked whether R is a member of itself. The answer is paradoxically enough, that it is if and only if it is not and vice versa.

In the social sciences, Verhulst (1838) developed the logistic population differential equation to predict population growth trends, Lotka (1925) and Volterra (1931) developed the differential equations to model the evolution of a closed-loop ecosytem, and Richardson (1991) developed a linear arms race model.

Hegel's (1948) *thesis–antithesis–synthesis* driven dialectic pivots implicitly around the idea of a negative feedback loop. Maxwell in his 1868 paper, "On Governors," showed that it was possible to represent the dynamic characteristics of a feedback system with a set of differential equations. He thus started the process for shifting the design of feedback mechanisms from the purely experimental to one that relies on differential calculus.

Bateson's (1972) *schismogenesis*, the creation of divisions, or *progressive differentiation* between cultural groups, represents a family of positive feedback loops in society. Following Maxwell, scientists and engineers, such as Routh (1877), Lyapunov (1892), Hurwitz (1895), up to Brown (1948) and Bode (1960), developed and applied the ideas of feedback loops and servomechanisms. Starting in the 1940s, Wiener, Lewin, Deutsh, Ashby, Tustin, Simon, and others spread the concept of feedback throughout the social sciences following two main threads, the servomechanism thread and the cybernetics thread, albeit in a nonuniform and incomplete manner (Figure 4.2).

Within the cybernetics thread, Rosenblueth and co-workers (1943), first outlined *the connection between human systems and feedback loops*, in "Behavior, Purpose, and Teleology." The authors' thesis was that any system, animate or inanimate, that is controlled by negative feedback, should be called purposeful. Similarly, Wiener (1948) aimed at identifying the conditions under which negative feedback in linear systems can lead to explosive oscillations, a precursor to nonlinear dynamics, such as chaos theory (Gleick, 1987).

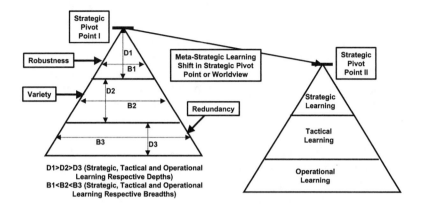

STRATEGIC PIVOT POINTS REPRESENT THE CURRENT
PREVALENT BUSINESS/TECHNOLOGICAL WORLDVIEW

ROBUSTNESS, VARIETY, AND REDUNDANCY ARE THE
FOCAL POINTS FOR THE RESPECTIVE LEARNING LEVEL

FIGURE 4.2

Within the servomechanism thread, economists started around 1950 to interpret economic fluctuations and business cycles by means of servomechanisms founded on the concept of feedback loops. Goodwin (1951) argued that feedback systems are useful to understand business cycles because of their potential to overshoot and oscillate. Goodwin was followed by Tustin (1953), the famous Phillips curve, Simon (1952), and Forrester (1960).

4.2.2 MULTILAYERED FEEDBACK AND STRATEGIC DECISION MAKING

Demming was clearly speaking in a *feedback-driven* spirit when he added the strategic management perspective to Plato's philosophical and Freud's psychological/cognitive ones: "*A president should see his company as a system and the whole world as a system*" (Demming, PBS, The American Interests Interview, February 1992).

These worldviews form the core of the *invisible asset base* or *tacit knowledge reservoir* of the technological enterprise: "The learning-by-doing effect enables the firm to accumulate the necessary invisible assets to carry out future strategy in the course of its everyday operations" (Itami, 1987, p. 161). Follett's poetic thoughts on the value of experience and the challenging nature of the learning-from-experience *process*, are very insightful: "Experience may be hard, but we claim its gifts because they are real, even though our feet bleed on its stones" (Follett, 1924, p. 302).

This perspective of strategy making puts a lot of emphasis on learning, both individual and organizational, through multilevel feedback. We quote from James (1950, p. 92) to express this view from a psychological/cognitive point of view: "If practice did not make perfect, nor habit economize the expense of nervous and muscular energy, he [man] would be in a sorry plight." For a strategic management point of view Itami (1987, p. 14) says, "People are important assets of the firm, but they are important because much of the invisible assets of the firm are embodied in people; ... People are important resources, not just as participants in the labor force, but as accumulators and producers of invisible assets." Also according to Itami (1987, p. 161): "When a firm participates in a market in which there are strong competitive pressures, it gains a great deal of information as a result. The pressure-cooker atmosphere of such markets provides high-quality feedback. ... *The firm's invisible assets are no more or less than the accumulated efforts of everyone in the organization*" [emphasis added].

According to Varela et al. (1991, p. 9) it takes an "enactive" or strategic meta-cognitive approach to better understand the process and content of strategic thought and decision making and highlight its essentially dynamic and experiential nature: "We propose as a name the term enactive to emphasize the growing conviction that cognition is not the representation of a pregiven world by a pregiven mind but is rather the enactment of a world and a mind on the basis of a history of the variety of actions that a being in the world performs."

4.2.3   FEEDBACK AND SELF-ORGANIZATION IN THE STRATEGIC MANAGEMENT OF TECHNOLOGY

We especially focus on the tacit dimension of learning as what drives the dynamically adaptive, self-organizing component of the proposed decision-making framework, which through strategic insight leads to the perception of new, improved worldviews or the process that Polanyi (1966, p. 48) calls "ideogenesis:" "When originality breeds new values, it breeds them tacitly, by implication; we cannot choose explicitly a set of new values, but must submit to them by the very act of creating or adopting them" (Polanyi, 1966, p. xi) and also: "Knowing is an *indwelling* [emphasis added], that is, a utilization of a framework for unfolding our understanding in accordance with the indications and standards imposed by the framework" (Polanyi, 1969, p. 134). We are thus motivated by Polanyi's writings about tacit knowing that is produced by tacit learning or *learning without awareness* (Polanyi, 1969, p. 143) as well as *discovery without awareness* (Polanyi, 1969, p. 143). This leads to strategic insights or perceptions: "Perception has this inexhaustible profundity, because what we perceive is an aspect of reality, and aspects of reality are clues to boundless undisclosed, and perhaps yet unthinkable experiences" (Polanyi, 1966, p. 68).

Polanyi says that identifying a problem whose solution leads to a great discovery is equivalent to seeing something invisible to the rest of the people: "Such tacit knowledge can be discovered, without our being able to identify what it is that we have come to know" (Polanyi, 1969, p. 142). Motivated from Plato's *Meno* he considers this an oxymoron: "For either you know what you are looking for, and then there is no problem; or you do not know what you are looking for, and then you cannot expect to find anything" (Polanyi, 1966, p. 22). Polanyi believes that this oxymoron is solved by the admission that a substantial amount of important knowledge is tacit, that is, to know important things that we cannot tell or that "to know that a statement is true is to know more than we can tell" (Polanyi, 1966, p. 23): "For the Meno shows conclusively that if all knowledge is explicit, i.e., capable of being clearly stated, then we cannot know a problem or look for a solution" (Polanyi, 1966, p. 22). In addition, *"While tacit knowledge can be possessed by itself, explicit knowledge must rely on being tacitly understood and applied. Hence all knowledge is either tacit or rooted in tacit knowledge* [emphasis added]. A wholly explicit knowledge is unthinkable" (Polanyi, 1969, p. 144).

The preceding statements are crucial to better understanding the content and process of strategic decision making, exactly due to the premise that the essence of knowledge is tacit, and hence what guides our strategic choices is never explicit nor is it acquired in an explicit fashion, but instead without awareness. We agree with Polanyi (1966, p. 60) that "tacit thought is an indispensable element of all knowing" and "the ultimate mental power by which all explicit knowledge is endowed with meaning."

Polanyi (1966, p. 91) also recognizes the fundamental nature of learning: "It seems that even protozoa have the faculty of learning" and the importance of accepting the validity of tacit knowing for successful decision making or "how man can exercise responsible judgment when faced with a problem" (Polanyi, 1966, p. 87): "Since a problem can be known only tacitly, our knowledge of it can be recognized as valid only by accepting the validity of tacit knowing; and the same applies to truth in its bearing on reality." The focus is also on the strategic role of actively open-minded thinking and learning in the decision-making process, because "one of the main biases in hypothesis testing, the failure to consider alternative hypotheses (possibilities)" (Baron, 1988, p. 240), can be reduced or eliminated.

The importance of *learning by doing* (a term first coined by John Dewey circa early 1900s) and *trial and error* (a term first coined by Alexander Bain circa 1854), in short learning from experience, cannot be emphasized too much with regard to the formation and reformation of strategic thought and worldviews. The word *world-views*, derived from the German word *Weltanschauung*, was first coined by Freud (1973, p. 193):

> ... a Weltanschauung is an intellectual construction which solves all the problems of our existence uniformly on the basis of an overriding hypothesis, which accordingly, leaves no question unanswered and in which everything that interests us finds its fixed place.... Possession of a Weltanschauung of this kind is among the ideal wishes of human beings.

Although Freud's powers of conceptual insight are formidable, he may well have been preceded by Plato, who in our opinion referred to a worldview as a "comprehensive intuition" and furthermore assigned to it the highest position in his hierarchy of forms of thinking: "The lowest form of thinking is the base recognition of the object. The highest, the comprehensive intuition of the man who sees all things as part of a system."

4.3 LEARNING: AUTONOMY AND RESPONSIBILITY

4.3.1 INTERDISCIPLINARY OVERVIEW

Uncertainty, complexity, ambiguity, uniqueness, and *value conflict* are the five main factors that securely maintain decision making in the realm of art, all the human attempts to claim it for the realm of science notwithstanding. These five factors are prevalent in varying degrees, in virtually all areas of human endeavor, from politics to business to sports, science, research and development (R&D), corporate strategy, and — in particular — in the area of the strategic management of technology.

Hence, the decision-making styles that try to deal with those *five pathologies of decision making* are also of paramount importance in all the preceding areas. The experiential school of strategic decision making comprises the styles that attempt to deal par excellence with the five pathologies of decision making, and the higher the emphasis on strategic learning (Ansoff, 1984) the more explicit the focus on those pathologies is.

The following excerpts show:

1. Feedback and multiple-loop strategic learning underlie to varying degrees all the models within the experiential school of strategic decision making,
2. Results from empirical studies show that strategic decision making proves comparatively more successful the more feedback and learning driven it is.
3. There is strong evidence for the presence of a tacit component of strategic learning (Nonaka, 1988) that bears major influence on the creation and dynamic maintenance of comparative advantage, expressed by the creation and introduction of successful products or services that are the outcome of a process of nonobvious and often unexpected strategic choices.

Whereas all the authors quoted next propose different kinds of strategic decision making within different contexts (political, military, and business), there are few studies that contain empirical evidence and explicitly emphasize the feedback (learning) stage of the decision-making loop (Quinn, Hammermesh, Pascale, De Geus, and Morone). All the studies contend that the second family of decision-making styles have been shown to be superior in terms of the results achieved, especially those documented within a business context with studies done on corporate decision making by Quinn (1980, 1992), Pascale (1984), and Morone (1993).

Simon (1957, p. 104), states, "... human problem solving from the most blundering to the most insightful involves nothing more than varying mixtures of trial and error and selectivity... ." Concerning human problem solving processes, Simon (1957, p. 104) says, "The process usually involves a great deal of trial and error. ... At the same time the process is not completely random or blind, it is in fact rather highly selective.... Problem solving requires selective trial and error."

Simon (1957, p. 104) recognizes two different kinds of selectivity: "There are two basic kinds of selectivity. One we have already noted: various paths are tried out, the consequences of following them are noted, and this information is used to guide further search.... The second source of selectivity in problem solving is from previous experience." He also believes that: "One way to solve a complex problem is to reduce it to a problem previously solved."

Simon and March (1958, p. 137) compare and contrast between rationality of the classical "homo economicus" and the "administrative man:"

> How does the rationality of "administrative man" compare with that of classical "economic man" or with the rational man of modern statistical decision theory? The rational man of economics and statistical decision theory makes "optimal" choices in a highly specified and clearly defined environment....

Simon and March (1958, p. 137) also go on to classify the theories about the outcome of decisions in three groups:

> (a) Certainty: theories that assume the decision maker complete and accurate knowledge of the consequences that will follow on each alternative. (b) Risk: theories that assume accurate knowledge of a probability distribution of the consequences of each alternative. (c) Uncertainty: theories that assume that the consequences of each alternative belong to some subset of all possible consequences, but that the decision maker cannot assign definite probabilities to the occurrence of particular consequences.

Concerning the way the decision is made Simon and March (1957, p. 138) recognize: "In the case of uncertainty, the definition of rationality becomes problematic."

The authors emphasize their bias toward satisficing overoptimizing as a more realistic representation of decision-making criteria. They also give their version of mechanistic or cybernetic incrementalism, which they call "performance program or strategy" and which they view as: "A program may specify only general goals, and leave unspecified the exact activities to be used in reaching them" Simon and March (1958, p. 148) and: "... adaptation takes place through a recombination of lower level programs that are already in existence" (Simon and March, 1958, p. 150).

The core of March and Simon's (1958, p. 169) philosophy and the philosophy of the *bounded rationality school*, the precursor of the experiential school, lies in the following phrase: "Because of the limits of human intellective capacities in comparison with the complexities of the problems that individuals and organizations face, rational behavior calls for simplified models that capture the main features of the problem without capturing all its complexities."

We believe the following excerpt reflects the core difference between the "satisficing" or traditional and more static experiential school and the more dynamic or strategic version of *active incrementalism* we propose, and which we believe is widely prevalent (Simon and March, 1958, p. 169–170):

> Action is goal oriented and adaptive. But because of its approximating and fragmented character, only a few elements of the system are adaptive at any one time; the remainder are, at least in the short run, "givens".... This "one-thing-at-a-time" or *ceteris paribus* approach to adaptive behavior is fundamental to the very existence of what we call "organization structure." Organization structure consists simply of those aspects of the pattern of behavior in the organization that are relatively stable and that change only slowly. If behavior in organizations is "intendedly rational", we will expect aspects of

the behavior to be relatively stable that either (a) represent adaptations to relatively stable elements in the environment, or (b) are the learning programs that govern the process of adaptation.

The core difference lies in the static nature of adaptation that March and Simon see as the premise of organizational structure and hence the staggered nature of change occurring in organizations.

Steinbruner (1974, p. 78) states that

... The learning process which would characterize the cybernetically operating organization manifests itself in terms of changes in behavior rather than changes in outcome calculation.... Learning occurs in the sense that there is a systematic change in the pattern of activity in the organization... such learning is of the kind known as instrumental learning ....

Steinbruner (1974) further asserts that

... outcomes which emerge from a decision process operating according to the analytic paradigm may be incremental in character without any contradiction in logic or even natural expectation.... A decision process working in this fashion may still proceed by marginal adjustment, and indeed often does ... often proceed in practical application by a process of successive approximation in reiterated cycles of setting and adjusting constraints.... One set of experiments lend direct justification to the assumption that the analytic and cybernetic paradigms describe distinct, independently complete, and coherent decision processes which operate at least in some circumstances as substitutes for one another.... The major theme is the decision process which is organized around the problem of controlling inherent uncertainty by means of highly focused attention and highly programmed response.

Finally, *"The learning process is not causal but, rather, instrumental"* (Steinbruner, 1974, p. 81–86).

Lindblom (1959) distinguishes between what he calls the "root" (rational–comprehensive) and the "branch" (successive limited comparisons) approach in decision making:

Curiously, however, the literatures of decision making, policy formulation, planning, and public administration formalize the first approach rather than the second, leaving public administrators who handle complex decisions in the position of practising what few preach.... Accordingly, I propose in this paper to clarify and formalize the second method, much neglected in the literature. This might be described as the method of successive limited comparisons. I will contrast it with the first approach which might be called the rational–comprehensive method.... They could be characterized as the branch method and the root method, the former continually building out from the current situation, step-by-step and by small degrees; the latter starting from fundamentals anew each time, building on the past only as experience is embodied in a theory, and always prepared to start completely from the ground up.... Ideally, rational-comprehensive analysis leaves out nothing important. But it is impossible to take everything important into consideration unless "important" is so narrowly defined that analysis is in fact quite limited.... In the method of successive limited comparisons, simplification is systematically achieved in two principal ways. First, it is achieved through limitation of policy comparisons to those policies that differ in relatively small degree from policies presently in effect.... Policy is not made once and for all; it is made and re-made endlessly. Policymaking is a process of successive approximation to some desired objectives in which what is desired itself continues to change under reconsideration.

About the wise policymaker, Lindblom (1959, p. 44) believes that:

If he proceeds through a succession of incremental changes, he avoids serious lasting mistakes in several ways. In the first place past sequences of policy steps have given him knowledge about the probable consequences of further similar steps. Second, he need not attempt big jumps toward his goals that would require predictions beyond his or anyone else's knowledge, because he never expects his policy to be a final resolution of a problem. His decision is only one step, one that if successful, can quickly be followed by another. Third, he is in effect able to test his previous predictions as he moves on to each further step. Lastly, he often can remedy a past error fairly — more quickly than if policy proceeded through more distinct steps widely spaced in time. Comparative analysis, as in the branch method, is sometimes a systematic alternative to theory.

Etzioni (1986) proposes a third approach that he states "was developed in contrast to rationalist models of decision making and to incrementalism" and he calls "mixed scanning." Mixed scanning is a hierarchical mode of decision making that combines higher order, fundamental decision making with lower order, incremental decisions that work out and/or prepare for the higher order ones. Etzioni (1986) claims, "This approach is less demanding than the full search of all options that rationalism requires, and more 'strategic' and innovative than incrementalism" and "Mixed scanning... is akin to scanning by satellites with two lenses: wide and zoom... the wide lenses provide clues as to places to zoom in, looking for details."

As opposed to incrementalism, mixed scanning through the fundamental decisions (deciding where to zoom in), provides direction for the ensuing accumulation of incremental changes, whereas in incrementalism this is more of a random process. Etzioni (1986) quotes Bradley as stating: "Mixed scanning seeks to avoid the most serious problems of both the overly rationalistic model and the excessively pragmatic model;" and also Morrow (1981) as concluding, "Incrementalism leans toward consensus whereas rationalism tends toward optimization and hence to disregard of consensus. Mixed scanning is viewed as seeking to provide a 'compromise' of the two approaches." One of the main issues in Etzioni's article is the distinction between fundamental and incremental decisions. Etzioni suggests using relative size or a nesting relation to determine the kind of decision made.

Etzioni (1989) proposes and analyzes a model of decision making that he calls "humble decision making," which "understands that executives must often proceed with only partial information, which, moreover they have had no time to fully process or analyze." This model is a version of his mixed scanning model presented earlier:

"I call it humble decision making, but a more descriptive title might be adaptive decision making or mixed scanning" (Etzioni, 1989). Etzioni contrasts his decision-making model against both rationalism and incrementalism (muddling through), finding the first too optimistic and the second too conservative and self-defeating, whereas he qualifies mixed scanning as "an adaptive strategy that acknowledges our inability to know more than part of what we would need to make a genuinely rational decision" (Etzioni, 1973). Finally, Etzioni lists several adaptive techniques that highlight the "essential qualities of effective decision making... : flexibility, caution, and the capacity to proceed with partial knowledge" (Etzioni, 1973). These adaptive techniques are "Focused trial and error.... Tentativeness.... Procrastination (decision staggering, fractionalizing).... Hedging bets.... Maintaining strategic reserves.... Reversible decisions ... " (Etzioni, 1973).

These techniques coincide to a considerable extent with the qualities associated with Quinn's logical incrementalism and even more with the adaptive nature of strategic or active incrementalism we propose. The humble decision-making model comes very close to our model of strategic incrementalism; however, it does not outline as succinctly the structure of the feedback mechanisms that are at the heart of any adaptive decision-making model and it does not try to conceptually integrate the qualities of adaptive decision making in an explicit decision-making model.

Ansoff (1988) proposes an adaptive research method for strategic decision making. This method has the following salient characteristics:

1. Cascade procedure of successive narrowing and refining the decision rules
2. Feedback between stages in the cascade
3. Gap-reduction process within each stage
4. Adaptation of both objectives and starting point evaluation

This method has what Reitman (1976, p. 26) calls an "open constraint" property, in that "both the objectives and the evaluation of the present position are subject to revision as a result of insights obtained in the process of solution."

De Geus (1988) focuses on corporate or *institutional learning* and the role that strategic planning can play in the learning process. He summarizes conclusions from a study conducted by Royal Dutch Shell on 30 companies with life spans of at least 75 years, and hence proven successful corporate learners, to answer two questions: "How does a company learn and adapt?" and "What is planning's role in corporate learning?"

The conclusions drawn from this study we believe corroborate our conclusions and lead into the model of strategic incrementalism that we propose as a premise for corporate survival and success. Their study complements ours in the sense that they studied "older" companies. They found that the old but vigorous ones are those that (De Geus, 1988, p. 70):

"... depend on learning. Or, more precisely, on institutional learning, which is the process whereby management teams change their shared mental models of their company, their markets, and their competitors. For this reason we think of planning as learning and of corporate planning as institutional learning."

De Geus defines as "high-level, effective, and continuous" the process of learning and change that leads to corporate success. These are exactly some of the main features of strategic incrementalism with also added focus on the use of feedback as a strategic management tool.

Another important aspect of De Geus' (1988, p. 71) institutional learning is *speed*, which is also the reason why we call strategic incrementalism *active*, to give in other words emphasis on the importance of both the feedback loop and the speed by which it can advance the corporate learning process: "the ability to learn faster than your competitors may be the only sustainable competitive advantage."

There is another reason eloquently expressed a few hundred years ago by Machiavelli that complements the previous excerpt and that makes active incrementalism more valuable to management because of the effectiveness and speed it endows its decisions with: "In the beginning of the malady it is easy to cure but difficult to detect it and later it is easy to detect it but difficult to cure."

Ways to accelerate the learning process can be to *learn by playing* because "games could significantly accelerate institutional learning" (De Geus, 1988, p. 73), also "changing the rules, or suspending them, could be a spur to learning" (De Geus, 1988, p. 72) and "for the purpose of learning, it is not the reality that matters but the team's model of reality" (De Geus, 1988, p. 73).

The most important aspect of institutional learning according to De Geus (1988, p. 74) is the fact that *"the institutional learning process is a process of language development,"* because "When people play with models this way, they are actually creating a new language among themselves that expresses the knowledge they have acquired." De Geus further states the condition under which planning can be effective and constructive, which again points toward the three levels of strategic incrementalism, "So the real purpose of effective planning is not to make plans but to change the microcosm, the mental models that these decision makers carry in their heads."

Finally, De Geus (1988, p. 74) states the three reasons why people at Shell focused and tried to understand better the corporate learning process:

> First, ... most people can deal with only three or four variables at a time and do so through only one or two time iterations.... The second reason for putting mental models into computers is that in working with dynamic models, people discover that in complex systems (like markets or companies) cause and effect are separated in time and place.... Lastly, by using computer models we learn what constitutes relevant information. For only when we start playing with these microworlds do we find out what information we really need to know."

Quinn is a proponent of a version of incrementalism that he calls logical incrementalism. He elaborates on this version of incrementalism also using empirical evidence to support his claims, in his book (1980) and in his article (1982): "... a synthesis of various behavioral, power-dynamic, and formal analytical approaches more closely approximates the processes major organizations use in changing their strategies." Managers purposely blended these processes together to improve both the quality of the decisions and the effectiveness of their implementation. Although the processes they used at first appeared to be disjointed or "muddling," they actually embodied a strong internal logic that is consistent among companies and among action sequences within individual companies. Upon analysis, this logic appeared to many central elements of both the formal systems planning approach and the power-behavioral approach. But neither of these paradigms adequately characterized the way successful strategic processes operated. Instead, my studies showed:

1. Effective strategies tended to emerge from a series of strategic formulation subsystems. Each subsystem involved a somewhat different set of players.
2. The logic patterns underlying the formulation of effective strategies for each subsystem were so powerful that they could serve as normative approaches for creating these key components of strategy in large organizations.
3. Because each subsystem had its own cognitive limits and process limits, its strategies tended to be arrived at logically and incrementally. "The incremental manager is a shrewd, resourceful problem solver, wrestling bravely with a universe he is wise enough to know it is too big for him" (Lindblom, 1965). Time is one of the major process constraints as Mintzberg (1971) notes, "the top manager is a juggler who must constantly make small decisions whether or not he is ready for them." Consequently, the total enterprise's strategy that had to deal with the interactions of all the subsystem strategies was also arrived at by an approach most appropriately described as logical incrementalism.
4. In the hands of a skillful manager, such incrementalism was not muddling. It was a purposeful, effective, proactive management technique for improving and integrating both the analytic and the behavioral aspects of strategy formulation. This is not a reactive technique or "maintainer of equilibrium" as Ansoff (Summer 1972, p. 16–17) has suggested.

Quinn (1980, p. 24) believes:

Highly adaptive learning interactions with outside information sources and strong incentives to use the information obtained are among the primary reasons why high-morale, small companies can so often outdesign larger electronics companies.... Conscious incrementalism often helps in three important process dimensions: (1) coping with the varying lead times and sequencing arrangements demanded by interacting major decisions, (2) overcoming important political and informational barriers to needed changes, (3) creating the personal and organizational awareness, understanding, acceptance, and commitment needed to implement strategies effectively.

Quinn (1980) further believes that formal corporate planning does play a role in strategic management and specifically: "Examining and maintaining the potential meshing of the various subsystems with ongoing operating committees was one of the main functions of formal corporate planning. All companies in the study did have some form of formal planning procedure embedded in their management direction and control systems." These seemed to serve certain essential functions; in a decision-making sense they:

1. Formalized and calibrated strategic decisions already made
2. Provided a systematic means for evaluating and fine-tuning annual budgets
3. Formed a basis for protecting longer term investments and commitments that might otherwise have been driven out by budgetary pressures
4. Helped implement strategic changes once decided

All these were important functions; however, formal planning systems rarely formulated a corporation's central strategy. Perhaps the most important contributions of formal corporate planning systems were in the "process" realm:

1. They created a network of information that would not otherwise have been available.
2. They periodically forced operating managers to extend their time horizons and see their work in a larger framework.
3. They required rigorous communications about goals, strategic issues, and resource allocations.
4. They systematically taught managers about the future so they could better intuitively calibrate their short-term or interim decisions.
5. They often created an attitude about and comfort factor concerning the future, that is, managers felt less uncertain about the future and consequently were more willing to make commitments that extended beyond short-time horizons.
6. They often stimulated longer term "special studies" that could have high impact at key junctures for specific strategic decisions.

Quinn (1980) also believes formal planning practices that are usually perceived to lean toward the rational/comprehensive style of decision making are actually part of an incremental process. Quinn (1980, pp. 40–44) says:

> Formal planning practices themselves usually institutionalized a form of incrementalism. There were two reasons for this. First, in order to utilize specialized expertise and to obtain executive involvement and commitment, most planning occurred "from the bottom up".... Second, management purposely designed their plans to be "evergreen." They were intended only as frameworks to guide.... Formal planning to a large extent provided the interface between strategic and tactical decisions.... Most of the important strategies that were supported by formal plans were determined in processes separate from the formal planning cycle."

In all the companies that were part of his research sample, Quinn (1980, p. 43) found "a mixture of all three of Mintzberg's 'modes' of strategy formation — entrepreneurial, adaptive, and planning."

As for the timing of decision making Quinn (1980, p. 52) states, "Logic dictates that the prudent and rational executive make final commitments as late as possible consistent with the information available;" and (Quinn, 1980, p. 56) "Hence it is logical that one proceed flexibly and experimentally from broad concepts toward specific commitments, making the latter concrete as late as possible in order to benefit from the best available information. This is the process of logical incrementalism."

Quinn's (1980, p. 58) comments about the way the companies he examined formulate and implement their strategies are

> The most effective strategies of major entreprises tend to emerge step-by-step from an iterative process in which the organization probes the future, experiments, and learns from a series of partial (incremental) commitments rather than through global formulations of these strategies.... The process is both logical and incremental. *Such logical incrementalism is not "muddling,"* as most people understand that word. Properly managed, it is a conscious, purposeful, proactive, executive practice. Logical incrementalism honors and utilizes the global analyses inherent in formal strategy formulation models. It also embraces the tenets of the political and power-behavioral approaches to such decision making. But it does not become subservient to any one model.

Quinn (1980, p. 145) also cautions against another trap that purists tilting either toward rationality or *"muddling through"* might fall into:

> These executives and their companies have generally fallen into the classic trap of thinking of strategy formulation and implementation as separate sequential processes.... By the time strategy begins to crystallize in focus, pieces of it are already being implemented.... Significant strategic shifts in large entreprises take years, if not decades to accomplish.... What one sees in the short run as an important strategic shift very often turns out to be part of a much larger continuity ... this continuously evolving consensus-creating process."

The shortcomings of formal planning as it is usually practiced decoupled from any incremental flexibility include (Quinn, 1980, p. 154)

1. [Has] formless wordy statements ...
2. Deals inadequately with the multiple goals and psychological commitments ...
3. Uses formal analytical techniques ... which militate against generating the coordinated cross-divisional thrusts ...
4. Overemphasizes financial analysis ...
5. Converts planning departments into bureaucratized agencies ...

Quinn (1980, pp. 162–164) believes that an effective strategy has *three basic dimensions*:

> First, effective formal strategies contain three essential elements: (a) the most important goals to be achieved, (b) the most significant policies guiding or limiting action, (c) the major action sequences that are to accomplish the defined goals within the limits set.... Second, effective strategies develop around a few key concepts and thrusts.... Third, strategy deals not just with the unpredictable but also with the unknowable.... Consequently, the essence of strategy, ... is to build a posture that is so strong (and potentially flexible) in selective ways that the organization can achieve its goals despite the unforeseeable ways external forces may actually interact when the time comes.

Finally, Quinn (1980, p. 203) explicitly connects logical incrementalism with more formal (rational/comprehensive) management methodologies: "Knowledgeable top executives consciously design logical incrementalism into their decision processes. They also wisely use more formal management practices to ensure the continuity, balance, and cohesion of actions taken in this incremental mode."

Morone and Woodhouse (1986) lay out five strategies that they consider constitute the main elements of a catastrophe aversion system when managing high-risk technologies, such as nuclear power. These five strategies follow.

1. *Protect against the potential hazard through*:
   a. Prohibition of use of risky technology
   b. Limits on use of risky technology
   c. Prevention of errors from resulting in hazardous outcomes
   d. Containment of error repercussions
   e. Mitigation of error impact
2. *Proceed cautiously when using risky technology*
3. *Test the risks involved* (reducing uncertainties about the hazard's likelihood and magnitude)
4. *Learn from experience* (an alternative and complement to testing for the risks involved) and a trial-and-error policy that comprises five stages:
   a. Establish a policy
   b. Observe the effects of the policy
   c. Attempt to correct for any undesired effects
   d. Observe the new outcome
   e. Make corrections again
5. *Prioritize the risks in terms of urgency and seriousness*, a strategy that complements the previous two.

Strategic incrementalism builds on all the preceding strategies, but mostly on the last three (Morone and Woodhouse, 1986, pp. 124–135):

> These five strategies for coping with the potential for catastrophe jointly compose a complete, integrated system to:
>
> 1. Protect against the possible hazard; do so conservatively (strategies 1 and 2).
> 2. Reduce uncertainty; do so through prioritized testing and monitoring of experience (strategies 3, 4, and 5).
> 3. As uncertainty is reduced and more is learned about the nature of the risk, revise the original precautions: strengthen them if new risks are discovered or if the risks appear to be worse than initially feared; weaken them if the reverse proves true.

Morone and Woodhouse (1986, p. 138) refer to two main schools of decision making, the rational/analytic and the strategic school. They contend all the different approaches that belong to the strategic school of decision making have as common denominator the fact that "... decision makers respond ... by monitoring feedback from their choices and then adjusting those choices accordingly. All of those approaches are elaborate variations on a trial-and-error strategy." They also state that existing theories expounding on this trial-and-error approach do not focus as much on learning by doing as their study of managing risky technologies showed (Morone and Woodhouse, 1986, p. 138): "If there is a difference between our cases and the literature on strategic decision making, it is that in our cases there is more orientation to learning as an explicit and deliberate part of decision making than it is implied by existing theory."

Morone and Woodhouse classify decision problems in four categories:

1. Normal policy issues
2. Some social issues
3. Risky technology issues
4. Crisis decision making

Strategic incrementalism becomes more effective the more severe the consequences are and the less available the feedback is, because by its nature it compensates for such adversities. Therefore, as we move from normal policy issues to crisis decision making, it increasingly helps differentiate between more and less effective decision makers.

Weiss (1989) compiled the main criticisms against incrementalism in the following eight categories:

1. It exhibits randomness or a lack of goal orientation.
2. It is conservatism with respect to increment size.
3. It is not useful in crisis situations.
4. It is shortsighted.
5. It cannot deal with threshold and sleeper effects.
6. It favors organized elites.
7. It is reactive.

All these criticisms are successfully rebutted by Quinn (1980) in paragraphs quoted earlier, and by Quinn's (1982) paper, and they are more relevant to Lindblom's disjointed incrementalism model of decision making instead of the logical incrementalism or the strategic or active incrementalism decision-making models. In fact, active incrementalism expressly tries to deal with those pathologies or weaknesses detected in incrementalist strategies.

Morone (1989) distinguishes between a technology strategy and the strategic use of technology, the latter being possible through the recognition and exploitation of opportunities created by technology. That means that where the decision-making style is incremental and even more so, *actively incremental* as we call it here, corporate strategy can be built around opportunities created by technology (Morone, 1989, p. 96): "... But it is one thing to make technology decisions consistent with corporate strategy, and quite another to bring the potential opportunities that technology creates to bear on the formulation of corporate strategy. If the former is technology strategy, the latter is strategic use of technology."

From his research work and the evidence accruing from the work of other researchers, Morone (1989, pp. 104–106) formulates the following hypotheses that link an experiential learning or actively incremental decision-making style and a contingency-based concept of strategic fit with successful strategic use of technology:

> … Hypothesis 3: Firms that tend to make strategic use of technology place more weight than their counterparts on how well the option "fits" with their representation of the strategic issues before them, and less weight on more formal financial and market analyses.

> … Hypothesis 4: Firms that succeed in using technology for strategic advantage exhibit a high degree of learning from experience. Successful new products and processes emerge gradually, over the source of a sequence of earlier product and process introductions.

> … Hypothesis 4a: Firms that succeed in using technology for strategic advantage exhibit consistent and stable strategic management.

This last hypothesis supports the view that stable and consistent management is not necessarily driven by formal and comprehensively analytic planning, because in hypothesis 3 he links use of technology with more of a contingency based fit and less with formal planning. In other words, incrementalism and learning by doing instead of formal planning are linked with a successful, stable, and consistent strategic management of technology.

Burgelman and Rosenbloom (1989) present an evolutionary process perspective of technology strategy that "focuses on variation, selection, retention mechanisms for explaining dynamic behavior over time" and recognizes the importance of "history, irreversibilities, invariance, and inertia" and "the effects of individual and social learning." This perspective views "strategy making as a social learning process." Thus, incrementalism is considered to be pervasive in strategy making and, in particular, technology strategy crafting, which relates to highly uncertain and dynamic events and frequent major changes (Burgelman and Rosenbloom, 1989): "The essence of this perspective is that strategy is built on capabilities and tempered by experience.… Capabilities give strategy its force; strategy enacted creates experience that modifies capabilities."

The three central ideas of the work by Burgelman and Rosenbloom (1989) bring forth the importance of learning by doing in the strategic management of technology: "the reality of a strategy lies in its enactment, not in those pronouncements that appear to assert it;" and, in particular, of strategic incrementalism: "the on going interactions of capabilities–strategy–experience occur within a matrix of generative and integrative mechanisms that shape strategy" and "it is advantageous to attain a state where a strategy is both comprehensive and integrated." The last two quotes focus on the conceptualization of strategic incrementalism on three levels (strategic, tactical, and operational) and the feedback mechanisms that interconnect those levels in the formulation and implementation of strategy (the generative and integrative mechanisms and the comprehensive and integrated nature of an advantageous strategy).

Itami and Roehl (1987) focus on what they call "invisible assets" (knowledge, skills, and experience of committed people), "the vital contribution of accumulated experience and information to a corporation's strategic resources," and "overextension as an unbalanced growth strategy that stimulates resource accumulation and organizational vitality." Itami and Roehl (1987, p. 1) use many examples of Japanese companies to show that their success is a result of achieving "a dynamic strategic fit," the match over time between external and internal factors and the content of a corporation's strategy.

They see five kinds of strategic fit: customer fit, competitive fit, technological fit, resource fit, and organizational fit. In their technological fit elaboration, Itami and Roehl (1987, p. 87) bring forth evidence clearly showing that strategic or active incrementalism is the secret of success of Japanese companies when using technology as a competitive weapon: "... The paradox of technology is that it is both uncertain and logical, ... technology development is a mixture of chance and inevitability."

The strategies that Itami and Roehl (1987, p. 89) suggest as possible choices for dealing with the uncertainty inherent in dealing with technology are very similar to those proposed by Morone (1989):

> ... In dealing with the uncertain nature of technology, a firm can choose a passive response, perhaps undertaking a series of parallel projects in developing new technology to spread the risk. Or it can choose a strategy that actively tries to reduce uncertainty. Or it can seize the opportunity to identify the logic of technologies hidden in nature. Because technology is uncertain, the strategy may have to serve as a lever of certainty to guide people.

In the following excerpt we see clearly that Itami and Roehl (1987, p. 89) believe, although they do not use the words, that active incrementalism and learning by doing (as opposed to comprehensive, analytic planning) is the recipe for success in dealing with technological uncertainty:

> ... three types of uncertainty are important to the strategist: discovery does not always result from technology development efforts; markets do not always accept products from new technology; and newly developed technology can become obsolete.... The results can never be forecast; the process is inherently risky and requires continuous struggle. From the various possible sets of logic, a firm must choose the one that meets its technological development goals.... It is like sailing a ship into uncharted waters.... By the time the firm goes through the learning process and finds which elements are necessary to complete the ring of logic, it may be too late to make the resulting product a commercial success....

Also (Itami and Roehl, 1987, p. 90) state:

> Companies must learn to deal with these three types of uncertainty. The following strategies are useful: maintaining a deep pool of core technological assets, combining the different types of technology risk, conducting more and earlier experimentation in the field, and keeping up with technology trends.

Another view from Japan comes from Nonaka (1988, p. 59) who focuses on using organizational chaos for creating order and sustaining self-renewal in firms: "Chaos widens the spectrum of options and forces the organization to seek new points of view. For an organization to renew itself, it must keep itself in a nonequilibrium state at all times." In addition (Nonaka, 1988, p. 64) comments:

In order to create continuous fluctuations within an organization, the behavior and ideas of managers should not be fixed. When the managers' decision making is patterned in a certain style, the subordinate information processing will also be patterned because they will know how to respond to their bosses and they will not be willing to challenge existing information.

Nonaka (1988, p. 65) sees "the emphasis on action," avoiding assigning too much weight to analytic techniques, and the reliance on feedback from concrete actions as the recurring pattern among successful firms:

The common feature among the "excellent companies" was their emphasis on action. Emphasis on action means experimentation and the principle of trial and error. Taking action first while avoiding the attachment of too much importance to analytical techniques, which tend to be conservative by nature, is emphasized. Only after a concrete action has been taken will a concrete response come back.

Nonaka (1988, p. 67) considers self-organizing groups within an organization as the crucial unit of renewal and he describes their function as: "The group begins to experiment with a trial-and-error method for both thought and action. Action clarifies and generates meaning, thus execution is analysis and implementation is formulation."

Hence he considers trial and error (or learning by doing) the appropriate mode of operation for the cornerstone unit of an organization. Nonaka (1988, p. 70) considers learning and feedback from actions taken to be important features of an organization for another reason as well:

A learning organization transforms the flow of information into a stock of knowledge, and at the same time, spreads it to other departments and stimulates the systematic self-organizing of information.... Success and failure should be analyzed logically. This can be accomplished with a retrospective point of view.... This kind of systematic evaluation of the so-called learning and unlearning is important strategically.

Hammermesh (1985) elaborates on tools that make corporate strategy effective and specifically on portfolio planning techniques. What is pertinent for our case is that he makes it clear that even the quintessential planning tool (portfolio analysis) can be successfully applied only with a strong dose of incrementalism, to the point that he actually quotes Quinn (1980):

In managing the development and implementation of the three levels of strategy, the CEO has to keep all three of the strategies consistent with the demands of the external environment and with each other. One view of how CEOs manage this process is the sequential one.... While this sequential view is quite rational and is consistent with common prescriptions of how to use portfolio planning, it is not an accurate description of the strategic process. In most companies, strategy is set and achieved as the result of a continuous process of adjustment between the formulation and implementation of each level of strategy.... Admittedly, this view is more complicated than the sequential one, but it does describe common strategic processes not accounted for in the sequential view. The first of these is the bottom-up strategy development.... The interactive view is also consistent with the notion that strategies emerge over time, rather than being conceived at one point in time by "one big brain" at the top of the organization.

This notion is similar to Quinn's conclusion after studying strategic change in nine companies (Hammermesh, 1985, pp. 47–49):

Dramatic new sets of strategic goals rarely emerge full blown from individual bottom-up proposals or from comprehensive strategic planning. Instead, a series of individual, logical, and perhaps somewhat disruptive decisions interact to create a new structure and cohesion for the company. Top managers create a new consensus through a continuous, evolving, incremental, and often highly political process that has no precise beginning or end.

Hammermesh (1985) includes three case studies about corporate success and failure involving Dexter Corp. (a failure), General Electric (a success), and Memorex (a failure). The evidence presented in those cases corroborates our empirical findings and specifically that the most successful approach is what we call an actively incremental approach (Hammermesh, 1985, p. 170): "Dexter had standard capital appropriation procedures that did not explicitly link capital investments to the strategy of the SBS.... All investments were evaluated on a discounted cash flow basis and were required to exceed the 15% hurdle rate. The hurdle rate was applied to all SBSs, regardless of their strategy, ..." Hammermesh (1985, p. 182) further states:

When I began my research at General Electric, I expected to find a very orthodox implementation of industry attractiveness, business position portfolio tools and a heavy reliance on PIMS (profit impact marketing strategy).... When the first manager that I interviewed told me that GE had not seriously used PIMS in several years, I knew that my initial hypothesis was going to be revised.

In addition, Hammermesh (1985, p. 192) says:

It is significant to note that this portfolio planning technique was developed as a way to address the administrative problem of how to compress information for a busy CEO, rather than as a rigorous technical tool of strategic analysis.... The nine block summary had tremendous appeal to us, not only because it compressed a lot of data, but also because it contained subjective evaluation to appeal to the thinking of GE management.

Welch is quoted (Hammermesh, 1985, p. 206) as being "... the ultimate believer in people first, strategies second. To me strategy starts with the person you hire."

Finally, Hammermesh (1985, p. 212) articulates an approach to corporate strategy similar to Active Incrementalism:

> In my view, General Electric's approach to strategic planning well deserves the publicity and recognition that it has received, not because the company has been the most vigorous and persistent in the implementation of portfolio planning techniques but because it has been able to revise and abandon some techniques and to create new ones to respond to the changing agendas and strategic management approach of its chief executives.

The Memorex corporation applied a very rigid form of portfolio planning, refusing to respond to any feedback information from the results of allocating its resources among its divisions. As a result the company ran into serious trouble.

The final comment by Hammermesh (1985, p. 229) about all three cases underlines again the advantages of the incremental or learning-by-doing approach even when applying analytic planning tools to strategy formulation and implementation: "And when considered together, the three cases point to the necessity of the CEO's modifying the portfolio approach not only to serve specific purposes but also to maintain consistency with the company's financial condition and administrative constraints."

In their article Bahrami and Evans (1989, p. 107) focus on the value of "a capacity for continuous learning" to make effective strategies. They determined that the successful high-technology companies they observed, go through a three-stage, strategy-making process, which they call the "empiricist process:" experimentation, escalation, and integration. Bahrami and Evans, (1989, p. 119) state:

> However, in the firms we observed, this was largely accomplished through action and experimentation, rather than detailed analysis of data and preparation of product/market plans. As indicated in previous studies, these early experiments may be set up in parallel in order to speed up the learning process. In retrospect, experimentation provides a basis for selecting viable pathways and recasting the forged vision.

Bahrami and Evans (1989, pp. 123–124) draw three conclusions about strategy making by medium-sized, high-technology firms:

> First, the process reflects ongoing recalibration efforts and continuous refinement of policy ends and strategy means.... Second, the processes of strategy formation and implementation are closely intertwined and fused together in an iterative process, especially during the early stage of experimentation.... Third, the process incorporates both deliberate and emergent components.

Thus, the main conclusion of Bahrami and Evans (1989, p. 125) is that the efficacy of strategy making "depends not on how well the original intentions can be realized in their exact form, but on their ability to adapt to unenvisioned developments." These conclusions in our view clearly support the case for incrementalism and specifically what we call active, self-organizing, or adaptive incrementalism.

Romanelli (1987, p. 161) reached conclusions through her research on new high-technology ventures that corroborate our case for active incrementalism: "… more successful or longer living firms engage in less change than firms which fail." This is apparently contradictory with our viewpoint and is actually very strong evidence pointing to the opposite direction, if examined more carefully. Firms that are operating in an actively incremental way are not constrained by long-term, inflexible plans, but have a flexible, responsive, gradually emergent strategy that is indeed a "living document." Hence, there is a continuous learning process and adaptation that renders bigger scale changes unnecessary. In the same vein, Romanelli (1987, pp. 170, 172) concludes that "fast-moverness not first-moverness, appears to be the common denominator" for the successful ventures and also that "firms which adopt a conservative generalist strategy, during any stage of industry development, fare much worse than firms adopting any other strategy." That contrasts with the strategy she calls "specialist:" "specialism seems to provide the greatest chance of survival." In other words, the rigid planning approach comes out clearly as a loser and the winner is again a fast-moving specialism that is a form of active incrementalism.

Pascale (1984, p. 51) outlines the philosophy behind the actions of Honda's management, after interviewing many senior Honda executives, stating that: "The story that unfolded … highlights miscalculation, serendipity, and *organizational learning* — counterpoints to the streamlined 'strategy' version."

Pascale calls the way Honda became a powerhouse, first in the motorcycle and then the automobile business, "the Honda effect," which at its core has the concept of active incrementalism. That becomes obvious in Pascale's (1984, pp. 57, 59) following statements: "How an organization deals with miscalculation, mistakes, and serendipitous events outside its field of vision is often crucial to success over time." In addition, "Military science is the kin of managerial science. The stable industrial world culminating in the sixties was accompanied by a body of managerial beliefs which in the hindsight of the eighties, endowed us with the tactics of Gallipoli in a theater more akin to Vietnam." By contrast Pascale (1984, p. 64) refers to the Japanese view of strategy as follows:

> The Japanese don't use the term "strategy" to describe a crisp business definition or competitive master plan. They think more in terms of "strategic accommodation," or "adaptive persistence," underscoring their *belief that corporate direction evolves from an incremental adjustment to unfolding events* [emphasis added]. Rarely, in their view, does one leader (or one strategic planning group) produce a bold strategy that guides a firm unerringly…. Strategy is defined as all the things necessary for the successful functioning of organization as an adaptive mechanism.

Eisenhardt (1990, p. 53) focuses on the importance of speed in decision making: "Previous scholarly research on decision making has ignored speed in favor of topics such as the breakdown of rationality and the difficulty of identifying goals" and she explains how managers can "make fast, yet high-quality, strategic decisions:"

1. Before decisions arise track real time information….
2. During the decision process, immediately begin to build multiple alternatives using your intuitive grasp of the business ….

3. Ask everyone for advice, but depend on two counselors....
4. When it is time to decide involve everyone....
5. Ensure that you have integrated your choice with other decisions and tactical moves....

This "algorithm" we believe is essentially extolling the virtues not of speed but of active incrementalism (flexible, responsive to real time information, and participative). One of the positive side effects of such an approach to management is certainly better quality and more expedient decisions. Hence speed is a symptom of following the right recipe. Eisenhardt (1990, p. 53) acknowledges that "knowing how to be fast is difficult" and we completely agree with her.

Bourgeois and Brodwin (1984, p. 177) state, "Research shows that managers do not analyze opportunities exhaustively before taking action; rather, they shape strategy through a continuing stream of individual decisions and actions."

Bourgeois and Brodwin (1984, p. 177) also ask a very pertinent question: "How can we reconcile the static academic dogma, 'First formulate strategy and then implement it,' with the dynamic reality of managerial work?" They in essence support as well our view that active incrementalism lies at the core of managerial action.

The authors classify any management style of formulating and implementing strategy in five categories:

1. *Commander approach*
2. *Organizational change approach*
3. *Collaborative approach*
4. *Cultural approach*
5. *Crescive approach*

The crescive approach is what Bourgeois and Brodwin (1984, p. 188) consider the most effective and they directly link it to logical incrementalism: "... This process has been described as 'logical incrementalism' because it can be a rational process that proceeds in small steps rather than by long leaps." Bourgeois and Brodwin (1984, p. 189) actually outline the four main elements that constitute the crescive approach to management:

1. Maintain the openness of the organization to new and discrepant information
2. Articulate a general strategy to guide the firm's growth
3. Manipulate systems and structures to encourage bottom-up strategy formulation
4. Use the "logical incrementalism" manner described by James Brian Quinn, to select from among the strategies that emerge

Two other empirical studies of corporate decision making by Fredrickson and Iaquinto (1989) and Eisenhardt (1989) in our opinion corroborate the case for experience-based decision making, although the authors of those studies claim the opposite. Specifically, Fredrickson and Iaquinto contend that continuity, tenure, and size lead to what they call "creeping rationality," whereas Eisenhardt interprets her findings from a high-speed decision-making environment as showing a trend toward more comprehensiveness under more stringent process (time) constraints. We believe that what is enhanced in both cases is the emphasis on strategic, incremental, information-rich, and responsive but not rational/comprehensive decision making. We believe they have added to the empirical evidence supporting the case for learning-by-doing decision-making style.

An illuminating example arises in a cluster of works by Fredrickson (1984), Fredrickson and Mitchell (1994), Fredrickson and Iaquinto (1989), and Eisenhardt and Bourgeois (1988), and Eisenhardt (1989). All the authors equate *comprehensive* decision making with what we refer to here as the analytic school and *"noncomprehensive"* decision making with the experience-based school. Whereas Fredrickson offers evidence that suggests noncomprehensive decision making tends to be associated with unstable decision environments, Eisenhardt offers evidence that suggests precisely the reverse. Fredrickson and Iaquinto (1989, p. 517) argue:

> Several contributors to the strategy formulation literature have suggested that synoptic (i.e., analytic) processes … are appropriate for firms in stable environments … they have also suggested that firms should use incremental (i.e., experience-based) processes when their environment is unstable. Since comprehensiveness is a major feature of synoptic models, this view implies that a comprehensive decision process will result in superior performance in a stable environment. In contrast, a noncomprehensive process, with its speed and flexibility, would be expected to have a similar effect in an unstable environment. Both assertions have received empirical support.

Eisenhardt (1989, p. 545) challenges these views:

> The evidence suggests that fast decision makers use more, not less information, than do slow decision makers…. The existing views rest on the assumption that fast decisions are achieved through a less thorough strategic decision-making process involving limited information, analysis, participation and conflict. However, as Bourgeois and Eisenhardt noted, there is pressure for both a rapid and high quality decision process, especially in high velocity environments. Is the snap decision process described by existing views realistic?

We believe these two positions are largely in agreement, and that the real problem here is less empirical than it is conceptual. Once the distinguishing characteristic between the two schools is seen as the degree of reliance on experience instead of degree of comprehensiveness of analysis, the arguments of Fredrickson and Eisenhardt take on a very different cast. The evidence of noncomprehensiveness in unstable environments provided by Fredrickson does not necessarily imply use of experience-based decision making. It may very well imply a deterioration of the quality of decision making.

Low comprehensiveness, without a corresponding reliance on learning from experience, simply represents poor decision making. The only way to determine if the phenomenon uncovered by Fredrickson does represent a shift to a more experience-based approach would be to provide evidence of some form of learning by doing.

Conversely, the evidence of comprehensiveness in high-velocity environments provided by Eisenhardt does not necessarily imply use of analytic decision making. The real issue is, Is there a greater reliance in "high-velocity environments" on model-based analysis or on learning from experience? We interpret Eisenhardt's work to suggest exactly the latter. One of the most striking characteristics of "fast decision making" described by Eisenhardt (1989, pp. 569, 570) is an immersion of the decision maker in "real-time information on their environment and firm operations," whereas slower decision making is characterized as "analysis paralysis." However, attention to real-time information is nothing more or less than attention to experience. Eisenhardt's fast decision makers are continually monitoring results of past decisions and new developments in the environment, rapidly adjusting their policies according to those results and developments, monitoring the results of those adjustments, and then rapidly adjusting again. This sounds very much like a sophisticated and well-developed exercise of experience-based decision making and more specifically strategic incrementalism. In other words, Fredrickson and Eisenhardt seem to be arguing in favor of the same basic approach to decision making, but because they focus on comprehensiveness instead of on degree of reliance on experience, they find themselves in apparent opposition.

4.3.2 MULTIPLE-LEVEL LEARNING: INDIVIDUAL, GROUP, INTRAORGANIZATIONAL, INTERORGANIZATIONAL, AND SUPRAORGANIZATIONAL

The self-organizing learning takes place on four levels: individual, intraorganizational (functional/business strategy at the firm level), interorganizational (corporate/institutional strategy at the industry level), and supraorganizational (metastrategy or strategy-about-strategies level) (Tables 4.1, 4.2A to 4.2C) for the four-dimensional process and three-level content of technological learning).

TABLE 4.1
Process Typology of Technological Learning Dimensions and Respective Levels of the Strategic Management of Technology

Level 1	Individual learning	Functional/business strategy
Level 2	Intraorganizational learning	Business/corporate strategy
Level 3	Interorganizational learning	Corporate/institutional strategy
Level 4	Supraorganizational learning	Institutional strategy/metastrategy

Adapted from Hedberg, B., Handbook of Organizational Design, Oxford University Press, New York, 1981.

4.3.3 MULTIPLE-LOOP LEARNING: OPERATIONAL, TACTICAL, STRATEGIC, AND METASTRATEGIC

The strategic or active incrementalism style of decision making studied throughout this book has a multiple-loop learning architecture. That is, it consists of a triple

TABLE 4.2A
Level One Learning

| | Content Typology of Operational Technological Learning | |
	Individual	Group
Tacit	Know-how, expertise	Group texture, work practice
Explicit	Rules of thumb, procedures	Drills, stories

TABLE 4.2B
Level Two Learning

| | Content Typology of Tactical Technological Learning | |
	Individual	Group
Tacit	Common sense, good judgment	Work practice, core competencies
Explicit	Design rules, procedures	Best practices, work processes

TABLE 4.2C
Level Three Learning

| | Content Typology of Strategic Technological Learning | |
	Individual	Group
Tacit	Wisdom, intuition	Organizational intelligence
Explicit	Design metarules	Business reengineering

feedback loop to facilitate *strategic*, *tactical*, and *operational* self-organizing learning, which all feed into the level of *metastrategic* learning, where the decision maker learns about strategy making per se. This learning is conceived as a dynamically evolving synthesis of causal learning (underlying the analytic paradigm), instrumental learning (underlying the cybernetic paradigm), and constrained learning (underlying the cognitive paradigm) (Figure 4.3). The concept of self-organizing learning was explored in a limited fashion in the form of strategic learning by Ansoff (1984), who prescribes it as the appropriate mode of strategic management behavior under conditions of high complexity, low predictability, and high novelty, which form a subset of the five pathologies of strategic decision making (uncertainty, complexity, ambiguity, uniqueness, and value conflict). We singled it out as defining the operating realm of the strategic management of technological learning (Ansoff, 1984, p. 93):

> Complex and discontinuous reality and speed of change make it necessary to anticipate and to plan as far as possible, but the unpredictability also makes it necessary to make up for the shortcomings of planning by continually testing and learning from reality.

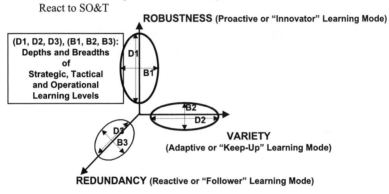

TECHNOLOGICAL LEARNING PROCESSES:
Scanning, Diagnosis, Response

TECHNOLOGICAL LEARNING MODES:
ROBUSTNESS (Strategic Learning Level)
React to, foresee, and create strategic opportunities & threats (SO&T)
VARIETY (Tactical Learning Level)
React to and foresee SO&T
REDUNDANCY (Operational Learning Level)
React to SO&T

FIGURE 4.3   Technological learning dimensions.

Thus a synthesis of the opportunistic and planned approaches is necessary. This synthesis must combine the advantages of rational analysis with a sensitivity and responsiveness to the unpredictable environment.

4.3.4   METAPROCESSES OF LEARNING, AUTOPOIESIS, AND TECHNOLOGICAL PARADIGM SHIFTS

Out of the link between the strategic management of technology and the management of technological learning emanates the concept of the strategic management of technological learning (SMTL), which highlights the unfair competitive advantage that accrues for a firm with an operating bias for a layered, dynamically adaptive archetype for its learning and decision-making processes.

Such an archetype is partly motivated from Simon's (1967) *hierarchical approach to complexity,* Prigogine and Nicolic's (1989) *chaotic and symbolic dynamics approach to complexity and change,* as well as Saridis's (1987) *Principle of Increasing Precision with Decreasing Intelligence.* Its roots, however, lie in Clausius's *second law of thermodynamics* and Heisenberg's *uncertainty principle.* The link with these fundamental concepts of modern physics and the strategic management of technological learning is brought forth by Prigogine and Nicolic (1989, p. 32):

... physico-chemical systems giving rise to transition phenomena, long-range order, and symmetry breaking far from equilibrium can *serve as an archetype for understanding other types of systems that show complex behavior* — systems for which the evolution laws of the variables involved are not known to any comparable degree of detail.

Moreover, a given paradigm can be perceived in different ways by scientists or top managers: the scientists "… can, that is, agree in their identification of a paradigm without agreeing on, or even attempting to produce, a full interpretation or rationalization of it" (Kuhn, 1970, p. 44) or equivalently for the top managers: "… it was the companies with the inferior technological capabilities that succeeded in using technology for strategic advantage…. … suggest that part of the reason stems from a fundamental divergence in how the different companies viewed their businesses (i.e., defined the problem) (Figure 4.4).

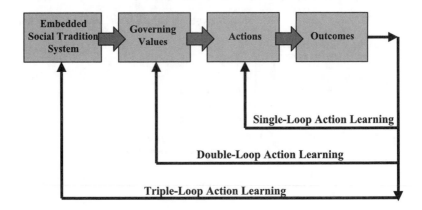

FIGURE 4.4

Krogh and Vicari (1993) focus on the dual nature of the human brain (rational/analytic and emotional/synthetic) to conceptualize organizations as cognitive learning systems. We espouse their integrative view of organizations as cognitive systems and not just as a collection of individual cognitive units (Gioia and Sims, 1986). Moreover, their emphasis on *autopoiesis* (a Greek word meaning *self-creation* or *self-organization*) when viewing strategic learning, corroborates and complements the organizational learning architecture of strategic incrementalism (Krogh and Vicari, 1993, p. 395): "The theory of autopoiesis provides a new understanding of strategic learning … the firm may be understood as an autopoietic system … firms may learn by creating errors."

In essence, Krogh and Vicari (1993, p. 401) show the need for and the potential of strategic learning (experimental learning by erring) over the limited capacity of adaptive-rational learning. This line of arguing lays the foundation for strategic incrementalism, which postulates that the truly, long-term successful organization must be endowed with a capacity for multiple-loop, multiple-level learning (Carayannis, 1992a, 1993, 1994a, 1994b, 1994c), thus transforming the debate from an "either-or" to an integrative, comprehensive mode.

Simply put, strategic incrementalism recognizes the value of experimental or strategic learning as the tool for creating new worldviews and escaping the "mental grooves" of traditional organizational routines, while stressing at the same time, the need for a capacity to engage in *operational* or *routine* as well as *tactical* or *adaptive-rational* learning. Without those lower forms of learning, strategic learning can only have a limited effect on organizational effectiveness and thus is not a solid basis for long-term competitive advantage. Moreover, all three types of learning can provide an insurmountable barrier to entry and an inimitable core competence, when integrated in the form of metastrategic learning (see Figures 4.2 and 4.3), which is the capacity to learn how to invent new strategies based on the triple-level acquired experience (operational, tactical, and strategic). Metastrategic learning is a path to influencing positively one's creative powers; and while it may have very tangible lasting results, it is intangible in its form and very difficult to articulate and codify. It can only be internalized by people with the appropriate intellectual, cultural, and linguistic patrimony, through a lengthy process of *iterative learning by example* and *by analogy*. This integrative, multiple-loop, multiple-level learning architecture facilitates and accelerates the continual transition from outdated to emerging technological paradigms, thus enabling strategic incrementalists to outmaneuver and outperform their competition by being at the right technological juncture at the right moment of technological evolution seen as a process of ongoing *Gestalt Wechsel und Gestalt Schaffung* (see the following section with company case studies as empirical evidence) (Kuhn, 1970, pp. 85, 112):

> The transition from a paradigm in crisis to a new one from which a new tradition of normal science can emerge is far from a cumulative process, one achieved by an articulation or extension of the old paradigm. Rather it is a reconstruction of the field from new fundamentals, a reconstruction that changes some of the field's most elementary theoretical generalizations as well as many of its paradigm methods and applications.

and "... at times of revolution, when the normal-scientific tradition changes, the scientist's perception of his environment must be re-educated — in some familiar situations he must learn to see a new gestalt."

4.3.5 STRATEGIC MANAGEMENT OF TECHNOLOGICAL LEARNING, ORGANIZATIONAL RENT, AND SUSTAINABLE COMPETITIVE ADVANTAGE

This research integrates three streams of literature relating to organizational learning, strategic management, and technology management, to create an empirical model for detecting and measuring organizational learning activities and connecting them to changes in firm performance. This model should suggest how learning can lead to new insight about a theory of the technology-based firm (Granstand, 1998).

Early research on organizational learning in the context of organization theory focused most substantially on attempting to describe learning processes in organizational settings, without necessarily assigning a normative value to learning (cf. March and Simon, 1958; Cyert and March, 1963; Nelson and Winter, 1982; Levitt and March, 1988). Learning as an organizational activity is perceived as an integration of individual efforts and group interactions. Thus, organizational learning becomes a process embedded in relationships among individuals; some authors argue that organizational culture is the outcome of shared learning experiences.

The field of organizational development popularized the concept of organizational learning in the business community, linking the development of the "learning organization" to the efficiency and effectiveness of a company (Senge, 1990). More recent research has generated descriptive analyses of organizational learning to identify paths to the improvement of organizational learning (Senge, 1990; Ciborra and Schneider, 1992), under the presumption that firms that are better at organizational learning perform better than others in the market. Preliminary efforts have been made to delimit and explore the intersection of the microeconomic understanding of the organizational dynamics of learning contributed by the organizational development perspective and the macroeconomic analysis by strategy researchers on how learning enables firms to develop the basic elements of competitive advantage (Edmondson and Moingeon, 1996).

Learning on its own may not qualify as a source of competitive advantage, because there are varying degrees to which learning contributes to firm performance. As noted by Huber (1991), "Entities can incorrectly learn, and they can correctly learn that which is incorrect." Ineffective or inappropriate learning processes can erode firm competitive advantage if they reinforce incorrect linkages between managerial activities and firm performance (Levitt and March, 1988). Even effective learning processes can be undermined by changes in market and environmental conditions that render them irrelevant, or worse, damaging to firm performance. Thus, learning activities can change from core competencies to core rigidities (Leonard-Barton, 1992). It is also possible that competence-destroying technological learning can limit firm performance in the short run, but lead to superior performance in the long term when market conditions adapt to new technologies (Christensen, 1999). Any attempt to link learning activities to firm performance must consider the alignment of internal learning activities and attitudes to the firm's external environment.

The field of strategic management is dedicated to the explanation of differences in firm performance, and further to the understanding of how to replicate conditions that lead to improvements in performance. As noted earlier, a significant subset of current work in this field is focused on developing a "dynamic theory of strategy" (Porter, 1991). Teece et al. (1997) expand on the resource-based view of the firm, with its analysis of strategic resources, capabilities, and competencies to explore the possibility of a theory of "dynamic capabilities." Central to this analysis is the role of learning in building new competencies (Nanda, 1996). Teece et al. (1992) link learning explicitly to improved firm performance by defining learning as "a process by which repetition and experimentation enable tasks to be performed better and quicker and new production opportunities to be identified." Learning is conceived as an *individual and organizational process*, so that improvements in organizational processes lead to the creation of new strategic capabilities (Teece et al., 1992):

> Learning processes are intrinsically social and collective phenomena. Learning occurs not only through the imitation and emulation of individuals, as with teacher–student, or master–apprentice, but also *because of joint contributions to the understanding of*

complex problems. Learning requires *common codes of communication* and coordinated search procedures.

Adopting a learning-based view of competitive advantage changes the basis for understanding what aspects of firms are linked to improved performance. Under the older conceptions of strategy as the domain of top management, performance improvement was attributed to the assumed "superior knowledge" of executives compared with employees, and the ability of those executives to create rules and structures for executing plans based on that knowledge. While top management still has an important role in learning-based strategic management, the top-down approach to strategy is no longer valid (Spender, 1996, p.95):

> ... top management would do better to provide a context in which employees at every level become independent agents, take responsibility, experiment and make mistakes and learn as they strive for continuous improvement in every aspect of the firm's total transformation process.

For learning processes to qualify as a source of competitive advantage, they must meet the tests developed under the resource-based theory of the firm. That is, the learning processes must possess the attributes of (see Barney 1986, 1991; Grant, 1991; Peteraf, 1993):

- Heterogeneity — processes are not identical across all firms.
- Durability — learning processes must endure over time.
- Causal ambiguity — basis and development of learning processes are not immediately apparent.
- Imperfect mobility — learning processes are difficult to transfer across organizational boundaries.
- Nonreplicability — learning processes cannot be easily imitated.
- Appropriability — firms are able to profit from learning.

It is clear that for the concept of organizational learning to be useful to strategic management, it must be unbundled to identify different dimensions of organizational learning, so that these can then be used to evaluate and even predict firm performance (DiBella et al., 1996; Carayannis and Kassicieh, 1996).

Adopting the tests applied to strategic resources from the resource-based view of the firm (Peteraf, 1993) to the findings of the organizational learning literature, a particular style of organizational learning can be considered a "strategic capability" if it satisfies the following criteria:

- Distinguishability — good learning can be seen as distinct from bad learning.
- Pervasiveness— learning style is present throughout the organization, thus representing organizational learning instead of individual or group learning.
- Communicability — new employees can learn the new style of learning through explicit teaching, tacit socialization, or other processes.

- Firm-specificity — style of learning is valuable only in the context of that firm, so that it loses its strategic value if replicated in another organization.
- Flexibility— learning style can be changed to meet new needs and new conditions.

The premise of our work that we attempt to illustrate conceptually and validate empirically is that long-term, sustainable competitive advantage and market performance derive from the strategic management of multiple, mutually complementing and reinforcing levels of technological learning.

In other words, we attempt to derive insights for the real and hard to appropriate (von Hippel, 1988; D'Aveni, 1994) explicit and tacit sources of sustainable competitive advantage from a marriage of three perspectives of technological learning (operational, tactical, and strategic) (Carayannis, 1992a, 1993, 1994a, 1994b, 1994c, 1997, 1998, 1999, in press) (see Figure 4.4) for a similar model in the Organization Design field, namely, *triple-loop action–learning* (Argyris, 1990):

1. *Operational learning level perspective:* The short- to medium-term perspective that focuses on managing core organizational capabilities (Prahalad and Hamel, 1990), resource allocation (Andrews, 1965), and competitive strategy (Porter, 1980, 1985, 1990, 1991)
2. *Tactical (learning to learn or metalearning) level perspective:* The medium- to long-term perspective that focuses on a strategy of reinventing and reengineering the corporation (Argyris, 1985; Argyris and Schoen, 1978; Bateson, 1972; Schoen, 1983, 1991; Mintzberg, 1979, 1985, 1990, 1991a, 1991b; Quinn, 1980, 1992; Senge, 1990)
3. Strategic (*learning to learn how to learn or meta-meta-learning) level perspective:** The very long-term perspective that focuses on reshaping our reinventing and reengineering organizational tools (methods and processes) (Bateson, 1972; Krogh and Vicari, 1993).

On the operational learning level, we have accumulated experience and learning by doing: *we learn new things* (Carayannis, 1994b). This is the short- to medium-term perspective on learning, focusing on new or improved capabilities built through the *content* learned by an organization. This learning contributes to the management of core organizational capabilities (Prahalad and Hamel, 1990), resource allocation (Andrews, 1965), and competitive strategy (Porter, 1991).

On the tactical learning level, we have learning of new tactics about applying the accumulating experience and the learning *process* (redefinition of the fundamental rules and contingencies of our short-term operating universe) (Carayannis, 1994b): *we build new contingency models of decision making by changing the rules for making decisions and/ or adding new ones.* This is the medium- to long-term

---

* At the level of strategic learning, the *speed of change is very low, the breadth and depth (or impact) of change, however, are substantial* and may indeed constitute a radical and permanent departure (or bifurcation) from the status quo once it takes hold: "Learning organizations evolve slowly and will keep on evolving slowly. *But the results are solid, tangible, and most importantly sustainable"* [emphasis added] (Day, M., October/November 1993).

perspective on learning, resulting in a process of reinventing and reengineering the *corporation* (Argyris and Schoen, 1978; Schoen, 1983, 1991; Mintzberg, 1979, 1985, 1990, 1991a, 1991b; Quinn, 1980, 1992; Senge, 1990). Tactical learning enables firms to approach new organizational opportunities in a more efficient and more effective manner, and to leverage or combine existing core capabilities in novel formations for greater competitive advantage.

On the strategic learning level, we have development *and* learning (*internalization and institutionalization*) of new views of our operating universe or *Weltanschauungen* (Hedberg, 1981),* hence we learn new strategies of learning (Cole, 1989). Thus, we redefine our fundamentals (our rules and contingencies) for our decision making, or we redefine the fundamentals of our operating universe. This is the very long-term perspective on learning, that focuses on reshaping our reinventing and reengineering organizational tools (methods and processes) (Bartunek, 1987; Bateson, 1972; Krogh and Vicari, 1993; Nielsen, 1993). The strategic learning level involves the expansion and reformulation of concepts about the limits and potential of the firm's strategic environment, where the older framework is seen as simply a "special case" within the new, more inclusive framework (akin to the relationship between normal and revolutionary science developed by Kuhn, 1970).

Strategic learning serves to "leapfrog" to a new competitive realm and "to increase the slope of the learning curve as well as the rate by which the slope per se increases by means of enhanced and innovative *organizational routines*" (Carayannis, 1994b, p. 582–583). The result is what other authors refer to as "changing the rules of the game" (Brandenburger and Nalebuff, 1996; D'Aveni, 1994) or creating new "ecologies of business" (Moore, 1996). The firm pioneers a new conceptualization of its business, its market, and/or its overall competitive environment, which gives it greater strategic flexibility not only in its own course of actions but also in influencing and leading the firms around it.

These three levels of learning activities are linked through a series of feedback and feed-forward loops as shown in Figure 4.3, so that cumulative learning at lower levels may lead to improved learning at higher levels, while learning at higher levels can reconfigure learning processes occurring at lower levels. The patterns of learning at each of the three levels present in a given firm at a specified point in time denote the particular "learning style" of that firm, with the implication that we can begin to differentiate the nature and effects of different learning styles (Edmondson and Moingeon, 1996).

Firms exhibiting tactical and/or strategic technological learning but not operational technological learning may be vulnerable in the short run, but have long-term advantage if they manage to survive. Conversely, those focused on lower order learning activities vs. lower order activities may excel in the short term but see their advantage erode over time. The various configurations of learning may be a factor in the formation of learning alliances (i.e., firms may form alliances if they have complementary strengths in different levels of technological learning).

---

* A Weltanschauung is a definition of the situation: it influences what problems are perceived, how these problems are interpreted, and what learning ultimately results (Hedberg, 1981).

The effect on firm performance of activities at each level of technological learning (operational, tactical, and strategic) initially appear difficult to discern, but are brought into sharp relief by considering the performance effects of the *absence* of each type of learning:

- Firms that are unable to learn (absence of operational learning) are quickly eliminated from competition, because they are unable to develop new capabilities to match changes in their environment and to maintain performance parity with other firms.
- Firms that are unable to learn how to learn (absence of tactical learning) are able to compete in the short term, but in the medium term are unable to adopt new learning strategies that could enable them to make discontinuous leaps in performance (analogous to changes in quanta). Thus, such firms are unable to maintain the same rate of performance improvement as firms that engage in tactical learning.
- Firms that are unable to learn to learn how to learn are able to compete in the medium term, but in the long term are eliminated because they cannot maintain a consistent rate of improvement in learning processes, and therefore cannot control the timing and scale of quantum leaps in performance. Such firms are outmaneuvered at the hyperlearning level by firms that have developed the organizational capacity to generate new strategic learning processes through self-regulating, emergent, and adaptive mechanisms.

Finally, the reflexive analysis of strategic technological learning styles enables a firm to identify and leverage instances of strategic pivot points (Carayannis, 1999, 1999a, 1999b), when a particular strategic approach to learning becomes inappropriate and must be changed. This metastrategic level of technological learning becomes embedded in the organizational culture as *organizational wisdom* — the implicit understanding of the context, dynamics, and implications of shifting strategic inflection points. In other words, metastrategic technological learning is seen in changes in the cognitive maps utilized by top management to analyze the competitive environment and to generate new strategies.

4.3.6 General Framework of Technological Learning

Differentiating among the learning styles of various firms requires further decomposition of technological learning within each of the three levels. In our model, we identify and study four general aspects of technological learning present at each level. Each of these aspects itself has several dimensions, enabling a greater degree of specification in describing the particular approach to technological learning adopted by a firm. The four aspects are

1. *Content — what* is being learned, whether it is a skill, a theory, or a new way of thinking

2. Process — the *conceptual level* of learning, whether it is simply learning new content, learning to learn, or learning to learn how to learn
3. Context — the *environmental conditions* of the learning activity under study
4. Impact — the *change resulting from learning* on the firm

Table 4.3 shows the range of dimensions found within each aspect.

The content of the learning describes the nature of the corporate capability that is improved or added through organizational learning. One breakdown of learning content distinguishes among learning facts, learning rules, and learning metarules (or know-what, know-how, and know-why). Facts are codified and tacit understandings are reached about the nature of the physical world and its contents. Rules are procedures, practices, and routines that dictate or guide the activities of members in an organization. Metarules are the culture, shared social experiences, and world-views that shape the organization's perception of reality and the resulting rules that it develops. Table 4.4 illustrates various forms of learning content at the individual and organizational level in an integrated fashion.

TABLE 4.3
Framework for the Assessment of Learning

Aspect	Description	Dimensions
Learning content	Nature of the capability added or improved through learning	Facts (operational) Rules, theories, models (tactical) Metarules (strategic)
Learning process	Nature and effectiveness of the mechanism of learning	Learning (learning new capabilities or improving existing capabilities) Learning to learn (learning how to improve firm performance through learning) Learning to learn how to learn (learning how to redesign organizational paradigms to generate improved learning)

Learning context	Environmental conditions affecting and affected by learning content and process	Focus (administrative vs. technical)
		Scope (individual, group, firm, industry)
		Nature, including
		    Timeframe (short, medium or long term)
		    Structure (formal to informal)
		    Tangibility (explicit to tacit)
		    Magnitude (radical to incremental)
		    Relation (competitive to cooperative)
		    Function (sociocultural change, socioeconomic change, etc.)

Learning impact	Nature and function of the change that results from learning in the technological operations and activities of the firm	Instrumental change (operational) Innovative change (tactical) Creative change (strategic)

The process of learning concerns whether the learning is limited to the improvement of existing capabilities or the creation of new capabilities (technological learning), or if learning encompasses new ways to learn (learning about learning) and the development of a new capacity to synthesize and manage learning capabilities (learning to learn how to learn) (Carayannis, 1994a, 1995, 1996). Note that these categories are not mutually exclusive or interdependent; that is, one can have higher order technological learning independent of simple technological learning, although in practice one would expect that the presence of higher order learning is correlated with the presence of simple technological learning. The implication is that any level of technological learning impacts firm competitive advantage, but is not always a necessary or sufficient factor in competitive advantage.

TABLE 4.4
Typologies of Technological Learning Content: Strategic, Tactical, and Operational

	Individual	Group
Typology of Operational Technological Learning		
Tacit	Know-how, expertise	Group texture, work practice
Explicit	Rules of thumb, procedures	Drills, stories
Typology of Tactical Technological Learning		
Tacit	Common sense, good judgment	Work practice, core competencies
Explicit	Design rules, procedures	Best practices, work processes
Typology of Strategic Technological Learning		
Tacit	Wisdom, intuition	Organizational intelligence
Explicit	Design metarules	Business process reengineering

From Carayannis, E., 1994b, 1995, 1996, and 1997.

The context of learning refers to the level and scope within which a learning activity is analyzed and measured. Context consists of many different variables, each measured along a continuum, which together is analogous to the "magnification" of the lens used to view learning. For example, learning can be analyzed at several different organizational levels (individual, team, plant, division, company-wide, or even industry-wide); across time periods of varying length (from immediate or static to very long term); or with various ranges of impact (isolated to systemic). Context also characterizes the nature of the knowledge gained through learning and its effects, including its structure (formal or informal), tangibility (explicit or tacit), magnitude (radical or incremental), and so on.

To these three dimensions we add a fourth aspect of learning, namely, impact (the nature of the resulting change due to learning). This impact operates on three levels as well:

- Instrumental impact, corresponding to operational learning, which produces incremental change in firm processes, outputs, operations, and performance
- Innovative impact, corresponding to tactical learning, which produces radical change in firm processes, outputs, operations, and performance
- Creative impact, corresponding to strategic learning, which produces architectural change in firm processes, outputs, operations, and performance.

Together, these four aspects of learning can be used to specify the essential features of a specific instance of learning, project the nature of its likely outcomes, and compare it with other observed instances of learning. While the categories used are not entirely mutually exclusive (a learning activity may have multiple values within the same element of the framework, for example, comprising both technical and administrative learning), the framework is useful in the development of a typology that can link specific types of learning to specific outcomes. Furthermore, the scale and scope of the outcomes depend on the extent to which each aspect is emphasized in the technological learning activities of the firm. Table 4.2 illustrates that reengineering that emphasizes process and content dimensions instead of context and impact empowers more the tactical level of technological learning. Emphasizing the context and impact dimensions enables more strategic technological learning.

5 Study of Methodology

5.1 EMPIRICAL EVIDENCE: STRATEGIC MANAGEMENT OF TECHNOLOGICAL LEARNING FROM FIVE ETHNOGRAPHIC PERSPECTIVES

Until philosophers are kings, or the kings and princes of this world have the spirit and power of philosophy, ... cities will never have rest from their evils — no, nor the human race as I believe... [emphasis added].

Plato, *The Republic*, Vol. 5, p. 492

In this chapter, we propose to empirically show the presence of the decision-making model of strategic incrementalism within the context of the *strategic management of technological learning* (SMOTL). We attempt to do so through in-depth–interview-driven, ethnographic case studies of companies that:

1. Operate with varying degrees of sucess in high risk and/or uncertainty
2. Are very dynamic (due to intensity of competition and/or technological complexity)
3. Are technologically intensive business environments (where technology has *strategic import*, and in many cases one has to "bet the company" when deciding for or against a certain project or technology)

In particular, the focus of the empirical component of the thesis has been on five technologically driven industries (Table 5.1) to derive the framework(s) of strategic decision making actually being practiced — a "theory-in-action" vs. "an espoused theory" of strategic decision making (Argyris, 1985, 1990). "As long as the building of frameworks is based on in-depth empirical research, it has the potential to not only inform practice but to push the development of more rigorous theory" (Porter, 1991, pp. 95–117).

In those industries there is pronounced competitive turbulence (Emery and Trist, 1965), or *hyperturbulence* (McCann and Selsky, 1984), hyper-competition (D'Aveni, 1994). Perhaps more appropriately, there is a continuous process of paradigm shifts (Kuhn, 1970), or a *continuum of dynamic imbalances*, with several technological paradigms, designs, and standards overlapping timewise and competing for predominance.

The study was designed to cover at least two companies in a similar technological and business environment from four major areas of industrial activity, for at least two business cycles; to encompass products of short, medium, and long-term development, as well as life cycles; and to include domestic and international operations.

TABLE 5.1
Industries and Corporations of Research Focus

Industry	Country	Corporation
Process industries	United States	Bristol-Myers Squibb Inc.
	Germany	Bayer AG
	France	Compagnie de Saint Gobain SA
Automotive manufacturing	Germany	BMW AG
	Germany	Daimler-Benz AG
	France	Matra Automobile SA
Aerospace	France	Airbus Industrie SA
Power generation	United States	Consolidated Edison Inc.
	United States	Rochester Gas & Electric Inc.
	United States	Tennessee Valley Authority
	United States	Duke Power Inc.
	Canada	Ontario Hydro Ltd.
	France	Electricité de France

We selected the firms from three very competitive markets (industrial chemicals, health care products, and transportation means), and one regulated (power generation) used as the control/contrast group (see Appendix for interview questionnaires used in this study). See Table 5.1 for the list of companies studied and their industries.

One of the areas of focus of the study is the power generation industry, in particular, nuclear power. This is because it is an especially challenged industry undergoing radical sociotechnical change, including deregulation and decentralization/decoupling of the generation, transfer, and distribution components of the business as well as convergence of the energy sector with other utility-based sectors (such as telephony or cable). Moreover, the extra interest in this industry is due to the *commonalities* (high levels of risk and technological intensity and complexity) as well as the *differences* (more regulated) compared with the other four industries.

By using the insights from both the interdisciplinary survey of theories of decision and the empirical data from the case studies, we validate the formulated decision-making model (of *strategic incrementalism*) for the strategic management of technology and technological learning. Moreover, we propose ways to optimize its implementation, that is maximize the minimization of uncertainty on all three levels or loops of technological learning, both individually and cumulatively. We thus attempt to validate the decision-making framework of Strategic Incrementalism and the organizational architecture of the strategic management of technological learning (SMOTL) (Carayannis, 1994a, 1994b, 1994c).*

---

* *Ethnography* is derived from the synthesis of the Greek words *ethnos*, which means nation and *graphia*, which means detailed and in-depth description. The term was originally used in anthropology, another Greek word meaning the study of humans, and has now been "transliterated" in management thought.

6 Transport Manufacturing Sector Case Studies (Automotive, Aerospace, and Defense)

6.1 INDUSTRY OVERVIEW

The global automotive and aerospace industries experienced a sweeping transformation during the 1990s driven by deregulation, technology, trade competition, and consolidation. We studied four enterprises operating in this sector: Bayerische Motoren Werke AG (BMW), DaimlerChrysler, Matra Automobile, and Airbus Industrie. The strategic environment facing these companies is radically different from the situation in the late 1980s.

In the automotive industry, the 1980s were a time of intensely national competition, with various "champions" from each country battling for market share in the industrialized economies. Japanese manufacturers had made major inroads into the U.S. and European markets, leading governments to impose import restrictions and other trade barriers. The U.S. industry, focused on the Big Three manufacturers (Ford, General Motors, and Chrysler), were still operating in a crisis mode stemming from their near-bankruptcy in the late 1970s and early 1980s. The European champions (e.g., Renault and Peugeot in France, BMW and Daimler-Benz in Germany, and Saab in Sweden) were also under intense competitive pressure, struggling to restructure for more efficiency while maximizing employment to maintain social stability.

The strategic challenges facing automotive companies today stem from three sources.

6.1.1 GLOBALIZATION

The integration of national markets into a global automotive market and industry accelerated during the 1990s. The major manufacturers now realize that scale is absolutely essential to developing the resources to sell across all markets and in all product segments. Also, the automotive supply chain is becoming global, as assemblers form partnerships with best-of-breed component manufacturers around the world. As a result, many of the marginal national manufacturers are being bought up by foreign competitors, as shown in the Table 6.1. One development is the increased ownership of Japanese car makers by foreign competitors, a situation enabled by the financial weakness of those firms in the late 1990s and the removal of political and economic barriers to foreign investment in Japan. Access to a global supply chain management is another reason why auto companies are eager to acquire the operations of their overseas competitors.

6.1.2 COMPETITION

The cross-entry of auto manufacturers into each other's market has put tremendous pressure on each company to improve efficiency and productivity. This is a primary factor driving the recent wave of mergers, which are intended to achieve greater economies of scale. The drive for efficiency is shown in other ways, including frequent corporate restructurings and layoffs, increased flexibility in work assignments and labor relations, investment in new production technologies, and outsourcing to suppliers. As a measure of increased efficiency, plant capacity utilization in U.S. auto factories increased from 84% in 1993 to 92% in 1998 (Ford averaged 100% capacity utilization in its 16 U.S. plants in 1998).

TABLE 6.1
Global Acquisitions of Auto Manufacturers

Auto Manufacturer	Foreign Acquisitions
General Motors Corp. (United States)	100% of Saab (Sweden)
	49% of Isuzu (Japan)
	10% of Suzuki (Japan)
	20% of Fiat (Italy)
	100% of Opel (Europe)
	21% of Subaru (Japan)[a]
Ford Motor Co. (United States)	100% of Jaguar (United Kingdom)
	100% of Aston Martin (United Kingdom)
	100% of Volvo (Sweden)
	100% of Rover (United Kingdom)[a]
	33% of Mazda (Japan)
	100% of Think electric cars (Sweden)
DaimlerChrysler AG (Germany–U.S.)	100% of Chrysler Corp. (United States)
	100% of Mercedes-Benz (Germany)
	34% of Mitsubishi (Japan)[a]
Renault SA	36.7% of Nissan (Japan)
Volkswagen AG	Automobili Lamborghini (Italy)

[a] Pending.

Source: Daimler to buy 34% stake in Mitsubishi, *Washington Post*, March, 28, 2000.

6.1.3 TECHNOLOGY

Underscoring the globalization and competitive intensity of the auto industry is the influence of technology. Much of the focus of technological change in the 1980s and early 1990s fell on production technology, especially the global adoption of the "Toyota" system of lean production. Several significant product innovations also emerged, mainly related to the increased computer control of car functions (e.g., the introduction of antilock braking systems). For the year 2000 and beyond, some significant product innovations are expected to be introduced in such areas as fuel systems (with the first commercial introduction of hybrid electric–gasoline cars) and telematics (smart cars with integrated global positioning systems and Internet connectivity). The Internet is also in the process of changing the entire way of doing business in the auto industry, affecting supplier relations, labor relations, marketing, sales, and distribution.

In aerospace and defense manufacturing, many of these same tendencies are emerging, although at a somewhat slower pace. The key development of recent years is the emergence of a duopoly in commercial jet aircraft manufacturing, as Boeing merged with McDonnell-Douglas and Airbus Industrie reached parity in market share with Boeing. Other aspects of the industry also saw consolidation, although without the transoceanic mergers and acquisitions found in the automotive industry. DaimlerChrysler Aerospace acquired CASA of Spain, and is now merging with Matra Aerospatiale of France to form the European Aeronautical, Defense and Space Co. In the United States, Boeing also acquired the space and defense unit for Rockwell International.

In this industry, technology is again the key resource for competitive advantage. With air travel volumes increasing (especially in Asia), airline operators need longer operating lifetimes, greater fuel efficiency, and increased capacity. Airbus captured the technological lead by being first to introduce the "fly-by-wire" technology in commercial aircraft, but Boeing has gained an advantage in production technology by introducing some aspects of lean manufacturing during the development of the 777 model aircraft.

In the face of this period of dramatic changes in business and technology, the strategic management of technological learning gives companies the flexibility and resilience to deal with their shifting environment while capturing new gains through innovation.

6.2   BAYERISCHE MOTOREN WERKE AG: FROM CRAFT EXCELLENCE TO LEAN LEARNING

It is our task to think the unthinkable.

> Eberhard von Kuenheim, 1970–1993 BMW AG Chairman, January 1992

We have visions, but we have always compared them carefully to reality. As long as we fulfill the demand for mobility in a modern, up-to-date manner, our strength and competence for the future will be further reinforced.

> Eberhard von Kuenheim, 1970–1993 BMW AG Chairman, May 1993

Womack et al. (1989) define *lean production* as a production system that combines teamwork, communication, efficient use of resources, elimination of waste, and continuous improvement. Moreover, they characterized the European automobile manufacturers as high-cost, low-quality, mass producers, frozen into patterns of inefficient manufacturing, partly because of protectionism against leaner Japanese companies. That was in 1989, when Womack et al. touted the model of the post-national corporation and Ford as the exemplar the Europeans should emulate. Today, the authors of this report would probably benefit if they looked again (*Wall Street Journal*, May 4, 1994):

> The conventional wisdom in the auto industry is that you need to go global to survive. Then there is *Renault SA*. The No. 2 French car maker, behind Peugeot SA, doesn't sell a single car in the world's hottest car market, the U.S. But after skidding to the brink of bankruptcy in the mid-1980's, *Renault has made money every year for each of the past seven*, a record unmatched by most of the big global producers [including two champions of leanness, *Ford* and Nissan].... They are kind of the miracle of Europe, says automotive analyst and managing director of Furzman-Selz, Maryann Keller.... Only Toyota and Honda have better profitability track records than Renault.... Indeed, together with Chrysler, Bayerische Motoren Werke AG, and Mitsubishi Motor, Renault offers what some say is *an alternative model for the car company of the future*. We used to think "the big will eat the small," says Robert Lutz, the president of Chrysler; *"Now it's the swift who eat the slow."*

Thus, we see that compared with the other 22 major car manufacturers world-wide, BMW is the only one that, according to this study, has followed a truly independent, alliance-free path over the years. That seems to have actually facilitated *a more focused process of technological learning* reflected in the excellence of BMW's product line and in the savvy of its marketing and pricing strategies.

6.2.1 OVERVIEW OF BAYERISCHE MOTOREN WERKE AG

Bayerische Motoren Werke AG (BMW) was a company founded in 1916 as a manufacturer of aircraft engines* to supply the German Empire, at war with the rest of the world at the time. The company started making motorcycles in 1923 and automobiles in 1929 and had modest automotive beginnings; however, by the 1930s, the company had become a pioneer of technological excellence in performance starting with the 1936 328 Roadster and carried through to today's models.

Today, the company is, as its ex-chairman articulated in his farewell address, *in the* "business of individual mobility" (*Roundel*, September 1993). BMW developed a tradition that can be found in modern models: "transferring lessons learned on the race track to production sedans, convertibles and coupes so that BMW drivers could enjoy performance and practicality at the same time" (*BMW Today*, 1993). This tradition has imbued the company's *product philosophy of commitment and consistency* to "the pleasure of driving, combined with practicality, the highest standards of quality, and active and passive safety features that improve driving confidence" (*BMW Today*, 1993).

BMW has five major divisions (BMW Automobile, Rover Automobile, financial services, engines, and BMW motorcycles), and generated $37.9 billion in sales in 1999. However, BMW has no intention of becoming one of the largest car

---

* That is the origin of the blue-and-white propeller that is the BMW distinctive emblem.

manufacturers: "BMW's size allows the efficiency and quality benefits of up-to-date automation in production, yet maintains its position as a premium, exclusive make." (ibid.). *In essence, the company's goal is to be both, a high caliber craft and lean car manufacturer.* There are three assembly factories in Germany, in Munich (the original one), in Dingolfing (the largest one), and in Regensburg (opened in 1986). To those BMW added the plant in Spartanburg, South Carolina, which initiated production in September 1994* and an assembly plant in Mexico (*Wall Street Journal*, June 13, 1994). In the German plants more than 1000 robots perform various production operations; however, as the following two quotations from the *Wall Street Journal* (June 13, 1994) state, "BMW applies handwork where it is crucial to quality" thus seeking to attain an optimal mix of craft and lean manufacturing profile:

> And though all of BMW's chemical baths, spraying booths, and drying and baking ovens are automated, *careful handwork again plays a role in the final finishing.* A team of checkers marks every spot on the body that shows the slightest roughness; at the next station, another team swarms over those spots, sanding them with extra care before the final coat of paint goes on.

BMW's commitment and consistency of product philosophy** focusing on pleasure of driving,*** practicality, highest quality, and active and passive safety (*Wall Street Journal*, June 13, 1994), reflects as well the continuity in top management from which the company has benefited. Eberhard von Kuenheim was BMW AG's chairman for 23 years**** before he retired in 1993 and was succeeded by Bernd Pischetsrieder. In his farewell speech, he outlined his views of BMW's past and his visions about BMW's future (*Roundel*, September 1993):

> During the last five years, BMW has invested $6.5 billion in the expansion and modernization of its plants, in preparing the production of new vehicles and major components, and in the enlargement of our sales organization. Averaging seven percent, our investment ratio is higher than the average in our industry as a whole.... Sales of the BMW Group increased in 1992 to $20 billion ... the year's net income amounted to $454 million...The year's net income of BMW AG amounts to $282 million...The success of your company is attributable first and foremost to the cars we build.... It has always been BMW's policy to concentrate on our core business, the automobile and the motorcycle ... for diversifications, we have always asked ourselves whether they help safeguard our main business and provide an efficient exchange of technology. And precisely this is the case in *aviation technology, financial services, and electronics* [the *BMW Rolls-Royce GmbH* founded in 1990 to manufacture civilian use aeroengines, the *Financial Services Division* that provides credit to BMW customers through leasing

---

* In June 1992, BMW announced plans to build a showcase 1.9 million sq ft manufacturing facility in Spartanburg, SC. The new facility represents an initial investment of $300 million and will employ roughly 2000 people by the year 2000. BMW plans to build a new model there for the United States and to export worldwide (*Wall Street Journal*, June 13, 1994).
** Seven years of painstaking engineering, testing, and development go into every new BMW model (*Wall Street Journal*, June 13, 1994).
*** BMW's traditional slogan is "*Freude am Fahren*" joy in driving.
**** The longest tenure of any chairman of any carmaker worldwide since World War II.

and loan contracts and had a volume of $7 billion in 1992, and the *SoftLab GmbH*, a wholly owned subsidiary since August 1992, that specializes in large EDP projects for both BMW and other customers: these three make up along with *BMW AG* the BMW Group].

BMW also has moved into new product classes that seem to contradict its image of high-performance automobiles. The company has considered production of a station wagon model, and even a minivan (the epitome of suburban family transportation). According to Robert Warner (member, BMW Strategic Planning Group, in an interview with the author):

> We see minivan type vehicles as a very lucrative emerging niche in the US as the baby-boomers and their families come of age, and we feel that a car can satisfy more utilitarian purposes while providing its driver all the enjoyment that the driving characteristics of a BMW provide. Thus we decided to start selling the Touring Sedan model last year, since we feel that our motto implies both performance quality and quality performance.

In what is perhaps a market even more difficult than the U.S. car market, the Japanese market, BMW has been enjoying the fruits of its philosophy of commitment and consistency enlightened by an overarching emphasis on technological learning. In May 1994, sales of BMWs jumped 52% from a year earlier (*Wall Street Journal*, June 7, 1994) and its stock price in the Frankfurt stock exchange* went from DM480.5 in April 1993 to DM834 in March 1994 (*Die Welt*, March 30, 1994). It is instructive to put this in context, especially with regard to the ongoing debate about import quotas of American products to the Japanese market (*Wall Street Journal*, March 30, 1992):

> The most pointed question on the auto issue ... is the complaint of the Europeans that it is unfair for Japanese to offer assistance to Americans who have shown little interest in this market, while Europeans have made huge investments to adapt their products and build profits.... Overall, 199,992 foreign cars were imported last year [1991], and of 107,228 units with engines of two-liter capacity or more, three German makers — BMW, Mercedes-Benz, and Volkswagen — accounted for more than 98,000 units.... Even though 1991 sales dropped 7.5%, BMW Japan had sales of close to $1 billion, including parts, service, used cars, and motorcycles.

---

* Although in a multiniche, multimodal expansion mode, BMW is not likely to place its stock on the New York Stock Exchange (NYSE) like Daimler-Benz did last year. BMW chairman, "Mr. Pichetsrieder said his company *still objects to the U.S. standard of reporting financial results on a quarterly basis*" (*Wall Street Journal*, June 13, 1994). BMW thus foregoes a "golden" opportunity to raise "cheap" capital while in a major expansion mode, thus stressing its commitment to long-term horizons and *avoiding short-term-oriented technological learning disabilities*.

6.2.2 MAJOR RESEARCH ACTIVITIES AND TECHNOLOGICAL POSITION

In 1990, the company opened its Research and Engineering Center in Munich that employs approximately 4500 people and engages in the research, design, development, and planning of future models, enhancing the capability of BMW to the world of tomorrow with advanced projects such as an advanced four-wheel steering system, electric- and hydrogen-powered cars, and a system that automatically monitors a car's tire pressure for the driver. Moreover, BMW is part of *Prometheus*, a joint research project conducted by European carmakers and more than 50 scientific institutes to create a safer, more efficient, and more environmentally friendly traffic system for the future (*Wall Street Journal*, June 30, 1992). These are instances of the BMW strategic commitment to long-term technological learning through interdisciplinary and cooperative research and development (R&D) projects.

6.2.2.1 BMW's Electric-Powered Vehicles

BMW Technik GmbH's latest creations are the E1 and E2 electric cars, the former destined for European and the latter for American roads. The E2 is geared to meet California's zero emission vehicle (ZEV) requirements (*Roundel*, November 1992). With a seating capacity of four people, projected range of 161 mi, top speed of 75 mi, and 15.6 s for 0 to 50 mi/h, the E2 is very good personal urban transportation (assuming its price is value driven). The E2 is the first design project to come from DesignWorks/USA, a California design studio 50% owned by BMW since 1991 (*Roundel*, November 1992).

6.2.2.2 BMW's Californian Car Design Subsidiary

DesignWorks is BMW's eyes and ears for emerging American trends; according to the BMW Design Director (*BMW Mag.*, January 1994), "DesignWorks helps BMW recognize American trends at an early stage. We think of DesignWorks as a part of BMW." Besides the E2, DesignWorks also designed the seats for the new 8 Series BMWs.

The design firm spends about a third of its time on detailed applications, a third into developing BMW models with designers from Munich, and the remaining time to develop concepts for the future. To facilitate the potential synergies and foster creativity, BMW allows DesignWorks people access to all its departments — ergonomics, aerodynamics, marketing, and BMW of North America (*BMW Mag.*, January 1994).

6.2.2.3 BMW's Motorsport or M Division

The BMW M GmbH is BMW's laboratory for the pursuit of technological excellence and is the embodiment of BMW holistic approach to car design and manufacturing that views the driver and the car as an open, feedback-driven system. According to Dr. Wolfgang Reitzle, member of the Board of Management, BMW, January 1994):

The BMW Research and Development Center (*Forschung und Innovation Zentrum*) is the spiritual stronghold of BMW technology. Engineers from all areas work together under a single roof to form a unified, highly motivated team. This arrangement combined with the most modern tools provides us with the necessary prerequisites to tackle the complex challenges of the future. The new BMW M GmbH complements this organisation with a very special team. With its unique technical competence, it enhances the BMW product range with extraordinary products. A technical outpost for special projects.

The M GmbH subsidiary of BMW produces 8500 cars annually (M3, M5, and 850 Cs models) (*BMW Mag.*, January 1994) and is built around five concepts (BMW Motorsport International, BMW Individual, BMW M Fahrzeuge, BMW Fahrer-Training, and BMW Systemtechnik) that revolve around the themes of excellence in technology, safety, and joy-in-driving (*Freude am Fahren*). As Paul Rosche, Technical Director BMW M GmbH (January 1994) states:

> What inspires me is the desire to reconcile mutually conflicting objectives: high [engine] output together with lower emissions and fuel consumption. With the high levels of technological development our firm has reached with *atmospheric engines,** we can do it. I am certain of it.

Additionally, Otto Pukl, BMW M GmbH Manager of Engine Development (January 1994) comments:

> The BMW M3 can certainly be regarded as the forerunner of a new automotive generation.** It has the power of a super sports car, offers the driving pleasure of an agile compact coupe, and features the economy of a standard mid-range car.

Finally, Josef Buecherl, Chief Instructor, BMW M GmbH Fahrer-Training (June 1993) says:

> We are investing a great deal of money in safety technology. From now on, all additional improvements in the system of human and machine will assign the driver a priority position. The Compact-Training, in which the driver is acquainted with the problems arising in daily traffic, should be mandatory.

6.2.2.4 BMW Recyclable Parts and Cars

Although currently 75% of a vehicle is recyclable, the other 25% still ends up in a landfill. To deal with this 25%, BMW has been conducting research for several years.

---

* A worldwide premiere in technological innovation can be found in the new BMW M3 engines: multi-variable camshaft control (VACC). This system ensures that the intake valves open at precisely the right instant for any given engine speed and load factor — with response times of just a few thousandths of a second. *The result is flatter torque curve, maximum output, smoother idle, enhanced fuel economy, and lower emissions* (BMW M GmbH document, 1993).

** The M3 has a 286 brake horsepower (bhp), six-cylinder engine that allows accelerations of 0 to 60 mi/h in less than 6 s, yet has an average highway fuel consumption of 26 mi/gal (*Automobile Mag.*, Fall 1993).

In 1988, the Z-1 sports car (available only in Europe) was introduced, one of the first *wholly recyclable* cars. In the United States, BMW has joined hands with the Automobile Dismantlers and Recyclers Association to designate three BMW-authorized dismantlers in California, Florida, and New York (*BMW Mag.*, January 1994). These dismantlers facilitate *two-way technological learning* in dismantling and recycling, by sharing experiences and ideas with the BMW pilot facility in Munich, Germany, that opened in 1990.

6.2.2.5 Research and Development in BMW's Strategic Technological Learning Posture

One clear measure of BMW's emphasis on strategic technical learning is its effort to balance emphasis on both product and process innovation. As Robert Warner (member, BMW Strategic Planning Group) in an interview with the author, points out here and the following quotation, this balance is prompted both by the changed nature of BMW's market environment and its intentional strategy of using a broad spectrum of innovations to stay ahead of competitors:

> Again ... we are *undergoing a transition in placing our emphasis not only on radical and product innovation but on process and incremental and generational innovation as well.* This more evenly distributed emphasis has become a strategic imperative in itself for us as we move to respond to competitive and market pressures that were simply not there in the past when we enjoyed oligopolistic (duopolistic) profit margins worldwide.... We religiously follow the path of continuous improvement which means that we constantly renew our stock of utilized technologies using predominantly strategic, engineering, and marketing feedback criteria. Until recently, financial imperatives had no say in our pursuit of automotive excellence. We are currently though trying to become more value-driven in response to a changing worldwide market and that implies that cost will now also play a role in managing our portfolio of technologies.

6.2.3 MAJOR CORPORATE DEVELOPMENTS AND STRATEGIC DECISION-MAKING FRAME

6.2.3.1 The Acquisition of Rover Cars

BMW, which was close to extinction in the 1960s and which ironically, Daimler-Benz considered buying at the time, has climbed to rank 28 among European industrial enterprises, and with the acquisition of 80% of Rover Cars for $1.2 billion in January of 1994, nearly doubled its sales:* "This is different from the normal takeover," a triumphant Chairman Bernd Pischetsrieder said during a London news conference. In this case, he said, "two plus two is five" (*Wall Street Journal*, February 1, 1994).

BMW and Rover Cars enjoy significant synergies because Rover is strong where BMW is weak and vice versa. Moreover, the new BMW-Rover concern can offer a full range of vehicles from the Rover Mini subcompact to BMW's large 7 Series,

---

* In 1993, Rover sold 442,000 vehicles worldwide and BMW, 534,000 (78,010 in the United States).

without incurring any additional R&D expenses; and this synergy can provide BMW with a huge time jump on Mercedes-Benz, which is trying to enter many of the same niches (*Wall Street Journal*, February 1, 1994).

The Rover Cars acquisition was put into strategic perspective by BMW's Chairman: "What we want to become is *the world's largest specialty-car manufacturer without becoming a mass manufacturer*" (*Wall Street Journal*, June 13, 1994) [emphasis added]. Emerging markets which were previously inaccessible to upscale BMW models are now fair game: Latin America, India, Indonesia, China, and the Philippines (*Wall Street Journal*, June 13, 1994), will become acquainted with BMW through the less costly Rover cars opening huge opportunities as their emerging middle classes start buying more expensive cars.

6.2.3.2 BMW's Spartanburg, South Carolina Plant

BMW's decision to build its new plant in Spartanburg, South Carolina, was the outcome of many converging reasons, both in Germany and in the United States: the wage and benefits levels of the German workforce have made it the most highly paid in the world, while the workforce of South Carolina combines skills and with an average cost of labor that meets worldwide standards. BMW looked at 250 sites worldwide and narrowed the list to ten before choosing Spartanburg. Many factors played a role for choosing Spartanburg, such as financing, tax incentives, infrastructure, labor–management relations, and unionization levels. However, the primary reason was South Carolina's intensive preemployment worker training program (*Wall Street Journal*, May 15, 1993):

> BMW found qualified workers and a flexible educational structure ready and waiting…. This ongoing, *high-quality training program* was modified and tailored especially for BMW…. The South Carolina education package included training in technical skills, leadership–team building, new management techniques and youth apprenticeship programs. They will be developed jointly by BMW and South Carolina.

The new BMW facility will be *a lean and flexible operation*, with many parts and services locally sourced, and it will inject $6 billion in the region over the next 10 years. Its engineers will work alongside production employees after undergoing team training in Germany and the United States, building *a culture that fosters organization-wide learning* from the bottom up (*Wall Street Journal*, May 15, 1993).

Other manufacturers in this same period were moving to relocate more manufacturing to domestic facilities or to lower cost locations. Volkswagen AG had to close down its plant in Pennsylvania and move to Mexico. Japanese transplant factories in the United States were facing quality control problems vis-a-vis their peers based in Japan; while Honda and Toyota have plants that produce cars in the United States, they chose to keep the production of the Acura and Lexus lines (BMW's direct competitors) based exclusively in Japan. In an author interview with Rober Warner (member, BMW Strategic Planning Group), he explains BMW's analysis:

Our decision was driven clearly by strategic imperatives. BMW chose to show its commitment to the U.S. market, the most important market for our company worldwide and at the same time enjoy economic advantages that will accrue from insulating the company from labor wages, currency exchange rates, and import tariffs risks by producing in the U.S.

As far as Lexus and Acura are concerned, they do not produce their cars here because they have no need to do so, in terms of their available manufacturing capacity, not because they were concerned with the quality standards that American produced Lexus and Acuras would have attained.

We are not concerned that transferring our manufacturing outside Germany will affect adversely the quality of our products because we strongly feel that their technological excellence is a derivative of BMW's commitments and imperatives and not due to BMW's location in Germany. In other words, we want to emphasize that our cars enjoy their good reputation because they are built by BMW and not because they are built in Germany.

The Spartanburg plant also is not an attempt by BMW to simply replicate its German operations on U.S. soil. As reported in the trade journal *Assembly*, "BMW's Spartanburg assembly plant emphasizes quality over quantity. There's not as much innovation at the plant as there is a synthesis of the best practices of U.S., Japanese and European carmakers" (*Assembly*, June 1998, p. 22). The company used the opportunity to learn from the experiences of Japanese auto firm transplant factories (*U.S. News & World Rep.*, July 30, 1997, p. 43):

… BMW didn't do everything the same way Japan's transplants did. Unlike Japanese car makers, which hired mostly 20-somethings when they started up, BMW has American workers whose average age is about 33; the German company also pays U.S. employees an average of about $20 an hour. The reason BMW didn't go for younger and therefore cheaper labor is that it needed a higher degree of handcrafting, which a more mature work force can better provide.

BMW is thus leveraging the human capital available in South Carolina to complement its German workforce (*U.S. News & World Rep.*, July 30, 1997, p. 43):

… Average labor costs at BMW Spartanburg are roughly on a par with those for German workers (taking into account their 36-hour workweeks and six weeks of summer vacation). The real difference is the flexibility of the work-force…. Attendance rates also are much higher in South Carolina. Other major savings come from lower taxes, cheaper utility costs, and easier distribution.

6.2.3.3　Introduction of the Z3 Roadster

The Spartanburg plant was opened as the main assembly plant for BMW's newest product, the Z3 Roadster. This new car was launched with a major marketing campaign, centered on the car's featured role in the 1995 James Bond movie *Goldeneye*. Demand for the new model spiked after the movie's release. The company immediately received 10,000 orders. By mid-1998, more than 32,000 had been sold in the United States, and the Z3 had captured 40% of the global market share for roadsters (*Assembly*, June 1998).

The Z3 also launched a new manufacturing approach by BMW as a global auto assembler. The car was designed in Munich, with engineering data transmitted to the South Carolina plant, six time zones away. "Being so far away from the design facility was an issue," reported Rick Graham, assembly coordinator. "We had to solve problems that the designers couldn't physically touch or see" (quoted in *Assembly*, June 1998, p. 43). The Z3 went from concept to full-scale production in 36 months, a record for a new BMW model.

While final assembly occurs in Spartanburg, the components are produced in locations ranging from Austria to Mexico to Australia. More than 65 North American companies supply components for the Z3 on a just-in-time basis. This tremendous outsourcing of production is also relatively new to BMW.

6.2.3.4 Human resources policy

In 1995, BMW introduced a new compensation plan for its 58,000 workers in Germany. As part of this system, employees were able to earn a personal supplement on a monthly basis, depending on their individual contribution to their group's results. A worker's contribution is assessed at one of four levels (*Eur. Ind. Relations Rev.*, August 1996):

1. The initial level, carrying no supplement, applies to an employee who meets the agreed quantities to the agreed quality standards.
2. The "target level," which carries the basic supplement of DM98, applies when the employee fulfills the expectations for cooperation, overall quality, flexibility, and initiative.
3. A stage one increment, worth DM196, applies when the employee has made a particular positive contribution.
4. A stage two increment — the highest level and worth DM294 per month — is attained when an employee has a significant influence upon the group result.

The employee and his/her supervisor determine the expected level of performance on an annual basis. At the end of the year, the employee's success in achieving that level is assessed and the supplement to be paid for the following year is determined.

A further component of the pay system is a one-time payment in the form of a bonus — payable to the individual or the group — which is awarded for a specific contribution to improved productivity as part of the process of continuous improvement. In 1995, BMW paid out around DM14 million in annual bonuses. The objective of these two new bonus opportunities is to encourage teamwork.

BMW also began to introduce more flexibility into the historically rigid job scheduling system by setting up working hour credit accounts for each worker. Under this plan, workers who work overtime can earn additional vacation instead of additional pay. This plan gives BMW the ability to adjust its workforce levels to fit unusual demand increases, or to reduce the number of workers during slow periods (*Eur. Ind. Relations Rev.*, August 1996):

> With high labour costs, averaging around 45 DM (approx. L19) per hour, overtime is too expensive and inflexible to respond to changes in demand. By introducing flexible working time arrangements throughout the company, the quota of overtime worked per worker has been reduced from 2.1% to 1.4% of normal hours between 1991 and 1995.

6.2.3.5 Analytic Posture for Strategic Decisions

BMW combines qualitative assessments of the environment and quantitative analysis to support decision making on strategic investments in businesses and technologies. In an author interview with Robert Warner (member, BMW Strategic Planning Group) he states:

> We rely more on our experience and the strategic imperatives that define our objectives than any quantitative approaches. Once we decide to embark on a certain technology, however, we use a *Strategic Discounting Factor* to find the optimal or most affordable way for proceeding with the development of the chosen technology. This approach is a hybrid between the two approaches you refer to (NPV and LBD), since it discounts expected future cash flows by a factor that is determined and continually updated via feedback from our engineering and marketing functions.

> The approach is at the same time structured and informal; what I mean by that is that, while we always try to maintain our strategic focus and thus filter out projects that do not exhibit a satisfactory fit with BMW's core business, we nonetheless evaluate, acquire, and utilize emergent technologies under the guidance not of net-present-value-dependent but of strategic imperatives: continued technical and qualitative excellence and unsurpassed innovativeness in a well defined segment of the worldwide automotive market. Within that context we pursue a portfolio of emergent technologies at any given time and we are constantly looking for new ones as well.

6.2.4 EVIDENCE OF STRATEGIC TECHNOLOGICAL LEARNING AT BAYERISCHE MOTOREN WERKE

According to Robert Warner, Senior Member of Strategic Planning at BMW, technology and strategy are inextricably interlinked at BMW; he further states in an interview with the author:

> BMW uses a combination of all modes of strategic planning: it reacts to major opportunities/threats (the recent decision to build a factory in South Carolina was made to insulate the company against future labor and currency exchange risks), *it takes proactive measures leveraging off its technological expertise to benefit from expected future market needs and regulations* (development and production of electric and hydrogen cars), and finally it is clearly *technology-driven* in constantly seeking to push the envelope of automotive technology with each generation of new cars.

> The *Learning by Doing* approach is clearly favored, or as we call it the *Engineering Benchmarking* approach: how viable a technology proves for a given testing stage determines the additional investment to develop it further. Of course, we always try to

get the best value out of our investment at any stage, once we have decided to commit our money, so at that point we use NPV type methods to select among alternate paths. Thus our investigation of new technologies proceeds incrementally and the Learning by Doing approach used for strategic decisions is complemented by Net Present Value type approaches for operational decisions.

In its quest to further enhance technological learning links throughout its operations, BMW commenced building a global network of videoconferencing systems at its offices and manufacturing plants worldwide (*Edge*, November 1, 1993):

> VTEL equipment was chosen after an extensive trial of available equipment and delivery of the initial systems commenced in August.... As a leading manufacturer of quality motor cars, BMW AG invests heavily in the training of its engineering, maintenance, and service staff. The primary requirement for the VTEL systems was for the *training department*, where huge gains in productivity and efficiency already have been achieved by conducting training courses from headquarters in Munich to subsidiary offices.

The emphasis on technological learning through customer, dealer,* and supplier feedback is also shown by the efforts BMW makes to solicit such feedback; in a March 10, 1994 interview with James McDowell, Vice President Marketing, BMW North America, he explains:

> BMW solicits feedback from its customers at four different points during their BMW car-ownership lifetime: at 90 days, one year, three years, and at five years since purchase. Moreover, we have set up a database to which BMW dealers are linked and it is getting continuously updated and enriched with customer complaints, suggestions, and ideas. Furthermore, I personally talk continually to customers through focus groups and then I follow-up with questionnaires trying to capture both the short- and long-term customer response to exposure to our products.

Learning from customer feedback is what made possible BMW's successful repositioning of itself and its product line away from the pejorative "yuppy toy" image that its cars acquired in the 1980s partly because of misdirected advertising. BMW now takes dramatic efforts to respond to customer concerns. Realizing that scheduled maintenance alone cost owners $1180 in the first 3 years of ownership, BMW decided to make all normal maintenance services free on all cars. Responding to customer concerns about safety, comfort, and price, BMW redesigned its 3 Series model in 1999 to include more interior room, side and passenger airbags, while increasing the list price by 1.8%. Also, the 1998 J. D. Powers survey rated the three BMW plants in Germany to be top in the world in manufacturing quality.

---

* BMW has made a lot of effort to improve customer service offered by its dealers, while there is still room for improvement: "We've made incredible strides with our dealers. They know they have to change and we're supporting them. We've reduced our field organization from seven to four regions; we've put more people on the field; and we've got new policies on parts and sales (Carl Flesher, Vice President Marketing BMW NA, *Roundel*, June 1992).

Learning from its errors, the company radically revamped the image it projects with its current advertising campaign. The image projected now differentiates BMWs from other high-performance, luxury cars by emphasizing the feedback that BMWs provide to their drivers, as cited by Carl Flesher, Vice President Marketing BMW NA (*Roundel*, June 1992):

> We had to look for a quality that would differentiate BMW from the competition. We decided that it was performance — performance in a very simple sense: acceleration, braking, cornering, evenness in handling.... In a BMW, the car's precision and accuracy will make you a better driver, a driver who is alert, secure, and in control — quite the opposite of all the cocoon-like "commodity" nature of competition.

BMW also has instituted higher quality in its manufacturing operations. The company has developed a new manufacturing vision using the acronym OPTIMUM, which emphasizes:

- Optimum quality as the decisive factor
- Productivity as a measure of efficiency
- Time to market and time to customer (agility = speed + flexibility)
- Innovation in processes, technologies, and organization
- Market orientation through individuality and flexibility
- Understanding of the natural and business environments
- Motivation of the workforce as a fundamental requirement

BMW is redesigned as a network, according to Ernst Bauman, Project Manager for Medium and Large Car Production: "The BMW production system is designed as a network, not as a number of isolated 'islands'. Each location or division forms a link in this network. However, each link is only viable as part of the overall network" (*Automot. En. Int.*, May 1, 1999). As an example, each of BMW's plants builds at least two models and there are examples of a single model being built at two plants. This makes it easier to switch production across plants as needed to adjust to differing demand across model lines. Thanks to these and similar initiatives, a BMW 325i model now retains over 69% of its value after its first 3 years, compared with 31% in 1991.

Still, BMW's learning orientation shows that there is room for improvement. Most difficult has been the management of Rover after its acquisition. Due to continuing financial losses in the Rover division, two key executives lost their positions in February 1999: chairman Bernd Pischetsrieder and production development chief Wolfgang Reitzle (also formerly chairman of Rover). In early 2000, BMW reached an agreement to sell Rover to Ford Motor Co. for slightly less than $3 billion (*Wall Street Journal*, March, 17 2000). BMW announced that it would also write off just over $3 billion in losses accrued during its ownership of Rover. Although the sale of Rover is in part an admission of defeat in its attempt to use Rover to revive BMW's overall brand portfolio, it also helped to improve the company's financial standing against a possible takeover or merger. Thus, shedding

Rover reinforces BMW's longer term strategy of remaining independent in an industry where mergers are increasingly commonplace.

Thus, the overall BMW strategy consists of restructuring (*Umstrukturierung-sprozess*) and reengineering its operations, at the operational, tactical, and strategic levels (Carayannis, 1992, 1993, 1994a, 1994b, 1994c). This is done by focusing on core competencies (*Kernkompetenzen*), on the customer (*Kundenorientierung*), and on lean production (*schlanke Produktion*) by following a market-adaptive pricing policy (*marktgerechten Preispolitik*), and by building a manufacturing facility at the heart of their second largest market, the United States (*Frankfurter Allgemeine Zeitung*, April 15, 1994).

Furthermore (*Wall Street Journal*, March 10, 1994):

> ... A survey of the winners and losers in the European auto wars shows that those companies that are aggressively following the U.S. model — cutting costs and trimming work forces — are the ones that are currently profitable: GM's European unit, BMW AG, and Renault SA.... The irony for European governments is that their efforts to protect jobs at their "national" companies have given the edge to foreign-owned companies and independent-minded manufacturers such as BMW.

6.3 DAIMLER-BENZ AG: MOVING FROM A CENTURY-OLD TRADITION OF TECHNOLOGICAL EXCELLENCE TO EXCELLENCE IN TECHNOLOGICAL LEARNING

> In addition, we have launched broad-based measures to make our organizational structures more flexible.... These policies are not empty phrases, but are quickly becoming the reality of our day-to-day operations. They are key components of a corporate culture characterized by creative unrest and intradivisional, intrahierarchical cooperation.
>
> Edzard Reuter, 1987– Daimler-Benz AG Chairman, January 1992

> Wir haben auf dem Weg zum integrierten Technologie-Konzern natuerlich teilweise auch Fehler gemacht. [We have naturally made mistakes as well, on the way to become an integrated technologies enterprise]
>
> Edzard Reuter, 1987– Daimler-Benz AG Chairman, November 1992

6.3.1 OVERVIEW OF DAIMLER-BENZ/DAIMLERCHRYSLER

Daimler, the largest German conglomerate and employer in Germany, in 1999 produced cars, light trucks, commercial vehicles, aircraft, and financial services. Also in 1999, the company had consolidated sales revenue of approximately $151 billion. Approximately 41% of sales are generated by the car division of the former Chrysler Corp., and 24% by Mercedes-Benz. The company maintains 180 manufacturing facilities, of which 50 are in Germany and 40 are in the United States.

In November 1998, DB merged with Chrysler Corp., forming a new entity called DaimlerChrysler. By the time of the merger, DB had shed many of its former businesses, including AEG. In 1999, DASA announced a merger with Matra Aerospatiale of France and CASA of Spain. Thus, the company was radically transformed between 1994 and 1999.

Daimler is a truly global and integrated technology group with business activities in over 170 countries, whose various business areas are interconnected by technologies and system structures focused, in particular, on the group's know-how in traffic management systems and transportation technologies. The *core businesses* of Daimler include vehicles for passenger and freight transportation, rail systems, aerospace, propulsion systems, defense systems, automation, power transmission and distribution, and information–technology services.

Parts of the company are more than a century old (Mercedes-Benz was founded in 1886), thus imbuing the group with a strong tradition of technical excellence shaping its corporate principles, and according to Edzard Reuter (November 1992):

> Our work at Daimler-Benz serves people and their environment. We aim to offer the world's most advanced products, systems, and services. This requires a continual commitment to technical, business, and social innovation as well as a corporate culture characterized not by complacency, but by *creative unrest....*

> Our customers are the focus of our efforts. We must strive not just to meet their expectations, but *to exceed them.* Cooperation and the open exchange of know-how throughout all areas of our companies are central to meeting this goal....

> We aim *to learn better and faster than our competitors.* To achieve this, we need not only flexible organizational structures but also employees who think entrepreneurially*....

> Our cooperation aims to: combine know-how and experience to create new dimensions — responsibly promoting progress for everyone.

We see from the company's corporate credo that top management assigns explicitly a lot of emphasis on learning as a competitive weapon and on building on explicit and tacit expertise to introduce new competitive worldviews. Moreover, the integrated systems approach to technological innovation as well as to global competition** permeates the company's modus operandi. This is the outcome of the current top management of Daimler and originated in 1989 (Mercedes, 1992/1993):

> It was 28 June, 1989. The stockholders' meeting of Daimler-Benz AG passed one of the most important resolutions in the company's more than 100-year-old history: *to change from a pure automobile manufacturer to an integrated technology group.* This

---

* A widely circulated anecdote is that when the engineers at Stuttgart wanted to make the point to top management for the need for a new generation of engines, they put a BMW engine in an E Series Mercedes and chained the hood shut. They then had top management drive the car on all kinds of roads and then revealed the engine that made them so excited. That really drove the point home and R&D for new engine development was swiftly commissioned (Internal Daimler-Benz document).

** Instead of following a "world car" or "world truck" strategy — like Ford's costly and not so successful Mondeo project that required $6 billion in R&D (*Wall Street Journal*, June 15, 1993) — DB follows a multidomestic strategy whose goal is "to safeguard world leadership by gearing production concepts to the relevant market requirements, the intensive use of the respective local resources, and the networking of industrial locations in different countries" (Mercedes, 1992/1993).

move thereby provided the organisational structure for the strategic goals of the Board of Management, namely, to combine classic fields of activity with new technology and to derive innovative ideas from that new technology.... The newly created corporate structure is geared towards the group's ambitious strategic aims: comprehensive know-how in all branches of vehicle technology on the road, on rails and in the air, with a high degree of competence in information technology and the ability to manage complex systems.

Thus, DB's century-long experience in high-quality automobiles was transformed into the modern version of multimodal and multifuel transportation of people and transfer of information: by land, by air, and by electronics (information technologies), as well as hydrogen-powered engine technology.

6.3.2 MAJOR RESEARCH AND DEVELOPMENT ACTIVITIES AND TECHNOLOGICAL POSITION

Specific instances of technological learning at Daimler can be found:

1. In the 1970s decision to develop *hydrogen-powered engines*, which is still being pursued through the development of hydrogen battery cells for automobiles (such as the Study A prototype scheduled for 1997 mass production) and hydrogen-powered airplanes (such as the Cryoplane, currently being jointly developed by DASA and Tupolev)
2. In the development and introduction in 1982 of the 190 Series *compact Mercedes Benz*
3. In the mid-1980s introduction by Mercedes-Benz of a series of *drivetrain and active safety innovations*, such as the automatic locking differential (*Automatisches Sperrdifferential* or ASD), the high-efficiency torque converters, the automatic slip control (*Antriebs Schlupfregelung* or ASR), and the *4MATIC* all-wheel drive*
4. In the 1989 decision to move from a purely automotive niche of excellence to the realm of *integrated transportation technologies*
5. In the introduction in 1993 of the *C Class* to succeed the 190 Series
6. In the 1993 decision to support the development of the *Swatch-mobile* with the creator of the watch that revived the Swiss watchmaking industry, Nicholas Hayek
7. In the *expansion and consolidation of Deutsche Aerospace* following the 1989 move into the transportation technologies arena, that made it the leading partner of the Airbus Industrie consortium and the major aerospace company in Europe
8. In the building of a plant to manufacture Mercedes-Benz cars *for the first time in the United States*, at Tuscaloosa, Alabama (may have been partly

---

* 4MATIC's control unit continuously monitors wheel slip, progressively engaging or disengaging the different modes as necessary from Mode 0 to Mode 3.

prompted by BMW's decision to build a plant in Spartanburg, South Carolina, and certainly by sky-high German wages and labor costs)

9. In setting up Mercedes-Benz Japan in 1986, *as the exclusive authorized importer of Mercedes-Benz cars in Japan*

By 1988, registrations had reached 31,511, almost one third of peak sales level in the United States. In 1991, the company had 228 dealers with 34 exclusive outlets and invested $180 million in two comprehensive, new vehicle preparation centers and aims at capturing 1% of the total market by 1996. As Rainer H. Jahn, president of Mercedes-Benz Japan put it: "Japan is a tough market. Japanese consumers are among the toughest in the world. They have a definition of service and quality you are not likely to find in a standard English or German dictionary" (*Fortune*, June 15, 1991).

6.3.2.1   Mercedes 190 Series: Resistance to Learning

The Mercedes-Benz 190, the entry-level car that broke with the firm's century-old tradition of building behemoths of technological excellence with little concern for affordability, was the outcome of careful market research and a painstaking process of strategic decision making by the board of management of DB.

The project was triggered by the *customer feedback* that Heinz C. Hoppe, the head of sales for DB of North America for the 1954 to 1970 period, received on the need to offer a smaller Mercedes (Mercedes, April 1993):

> Time and time again while I was in the USA I was confronted by the wives of Mercedes owners with the question why there was no small Mercedes, which could be driven by families as a second car, to take the children to school in for example.

A market research survey conducted by Ogilvy and Mather showed there was an urgent need for a compact Mercedes; and, moreover, small car manufacturers had started entering the luxury car class niche putting pressure on Mercedes dealers to incorporate their cars as entry-level luxury models. However, there was still no decision to build a compact Mercedes until the 1973 oil crisis and the introduction of the corporate average fuel economy (CAFE) standard by the U.S. government in 1975.

Even then, Mercedes at first introduced a higher proportion of lower consumption diesel models on the market, refusing to learn from its recent experiences: "the company still saw itself as a producer of big, expensive saloons — and did not want to become involved in the tough battle of selling medium-sized cars" (*Mercedes*, April 1993). Heinz C. Hoppe did an internal study that radically altered the world-view of the Board of Management in 1976 which then concluded that (*Mercedes*, April 1993):

> Taking into account a whole host of data concerning range structure, choice of engine, quality, design, and price, *Daimler-Benz can only continue its successful history in the car market if the range is extended at the lower end at the right time.*

The internal code name for the model was W 201. It took a little time from the first ideas until the people in Stuttgart finally made up their mind for a small Mercedes. However, once the decision was made, no effort and resources were spared to ensure that the small Mercedes would incorporate successfully the tradition of technical excellence and safety of its predecessors along with a host of new concepts.

For that purpose, 6 years of intensive research and development (1976–1982) led to such major industry innovations as the *rear multilink independent suspension,* for which eight basic principles of rear wheel suspension were investigated, 77 prototype versions were built to the smallest details, and 23 were actually manufactured and road tested.

Proof of the technical excellence designed and built into the W 201 is the longevity of its model life cycle: 11 years (1982 to 1993) and the 2 million units sold (Mercedes, April 1993).

6.3.2.2 Technological Learning

The C class with the C 220 and 280 models was the Mercedes reaction to criticism over its introducing the over-the-top S class in the midst of a world recession in 1991 with prices ranging from $50,000 to $120,000 dollars; to losing market share to competitors Lexus, Infiniti, BMW, and Acura; and to being pointed to as the model of old-world inefficiency in the new age of automotive lean production.* Instances of the Mercedes design and manufacturing philosophy that until very recently at least was geared almost exclusively toward technical excellence and safety, completely ignoring cost considerations and bordering on a sort of *technological hubris,* can be found in any document describing their product line, such as in the case of the Mercedes-Benz SL Roadster priced from $75,000 to $100,000 introduced in 1990 (Mercedes-Benz 1990 SL Roadster Coupe Manual):

> Initial design exploration for the new SL began in the early 1980s and was deliberately unrestrained in the interest of exploring every useful possibility — including radical styling designs.... The Mercedes-Benz SL has evolved through four body designs since it was launched as a passenger car in 1955. Each new SL pays respect to its predecessor, and leaps decisively forward.... For the SL, Mercedes-Benz virtually reinvented automobile manufacture. Its Bremen, West Germany, assembly plant *produces a handful each day — approximately ten per hour — under full production.* Each car is clamped to its own rigid multi-point platform...The new SL has 536 body panels, more than any previous Mercedes-Benz.... *Human inspectors use a full week to check a single body."*

The 1994 C class is a *critical link* in the Mercedes evolving strategy of repositioning itself to focus on cost as well as technological excellence and safety; and Dieter Zetsche, Daimler-Benz Board of Management member (*Investors' Business*

---

* In the 1989 MIT study on lean manufacturing techniques by Womack et al. (1989), DB was used, but not referred to by name, as the benchmark of craft-oriented, inefficient manufacturer. However, as we have seen with the trials and tribulations of the Japanese cars in the U.S. market, lean is a necessary but not sufficient quality for long-term market success. The Germans are learning, perhaps slowly but surely....

Daily, May 27, 1993) states: "This is the first car our company has produced at the same cost as the previous model [with substantial improvements made]. The vehicle has become more valuable but not more expensive."

In fact, the new C class motto is, *More car for your money*, which is indeed true, despite the fact that developing and tooling for the C class cost $1.7 billion. A Wertheim Schroeder car analyst called the introduction of the C class "a watershed event for Mercedes because it is the first time the company has not been able to get premium pricing but has had to focus on value" (*USA Today*, September 23, 1993). That is the outcome of the radical changes in the competitive environment of Mercedes-Benz according to Juergen Hubbert, DB Board of Management in charge of Car Division of Mercedes-Benz AG, *Automobile* (September 1993): "This company had very good engineering in the past, and they decided what to do. There was no competition, and they were very successful. Now, we have competition in all sectors. This is painful but healthy for us."

In the same vein, the prices for the other Mercedes-Benz models have actually been reduced (with the help of the mark–dollar exchange rate (*Wall Street Journal*, September 23, 1993): "Mercedes-Benz of North America Inc., trying to position itself as a 'value' player in a sluggish U.S. market for luxury cars, said it is cutting prices as much as 14.8% on some of its best-selling models for the 1994 model year."

Under the leadership of the new chairman of Mercedes-Benz, Helmut Werner, the company "... appears eager to shed its old and arrogant ways. Indeed, Mr. Werner notes that his parent company, Daimler-Benz AG, has adopted English as its official second language. It also has tried to cut costs.... Mercedes-Benz wants to prove it can play the price-to-value game as well as any other auto maker ..." (*Wall Street Journal*, October 10, 1993). This attempt is for good reason, because the company's share has been declining after the peak year of 1985–1986: "Since 1986, Mercedes-Benz's U.S. sales have declined steadily from a peak of nearly 100,000 cars to a low of about 59,000 in 1991.... Its share of the German market, its largest, has fallen from 11.6% in 1985 to 6.4% last year" (*Wall Street Journal*, October 10, 1993).

Moreover, DB has been listing its stock in the NYSE since 1993, deciding to adapt to U.S. accounting rules that require reporting of financial results on a quarterly basis — a much shorter term than the German standard.

Some subtle changes in the C class, such as the addition of cupholders and the discontinuation of a no longer needed oil–pressure gauge that nevertheless survived with previous models for over 20 years, present strong evidence that the company's attitude has changed from the past when it felt it "knew what was good for you, even if you did not." (*Automot. News*, September 27, 1993).

6.3.2.3 Fuel Cell Technology

On the expansion side, DB has been consistently and confidently making progress in two areas of personal transportation technologies slated for explosive growth both in the United States and abroad: *electric vehicles* and *small, low-cost but high-quality and safety cars*. In its approach the company is trying to leapfrog the competition by introducing novel, superior technologies (the development of hydrogen fuel cell technology) and taking an *iconoclastic approach* to small car design (teaming with the designer of Swatch watches for building the Swatch-mobile). Specifically, in April 1994, DB unveiled a no-battery electric vehicle as a viable alternative to the internal combustion engine. DB said that the vehicle "relies on fuel cells, a technology that allows gases such as hydrogen and oxygen to react, yielding energy that can be used as electrical power" (*Wall Street Journal*, April 14, 1994).

Also according to the *Wall Street Journal* (April 14, 1994): the company showcased a fuel cell powered Mercedes-Benz van claiming it had solved all the fundamental challenges associated with mass-producing such vehicles; fuel cells are emission-free, because their chief by-product is water, and equally important, they have energy-storage capabilities comparable to gasoline-powered cars: "... with a German company like Daimler pushing the technology so confidently, the question now remains whether Detroit and Washington must respond swiftly or risk forfeiting a potential technological edge to foreign competitors."

In September 1997, DB announced development of a fuel cell engine powered by liquid methanol, which does away with the need for bulky tanks. The methanol is converted into hydrogen, which is fed into fuel cells where it reacts with oxygen to produce electricity. The electricity powers an electric motor that gets nearly 23 mi/gal. The car could go into production in less than 10 years.

6.3.2.4 The Swatch-Mobile

Nicholas Hayek, the Swiss creator of the Swatch watch, the popular plastic watch that reinvigorated the Swiss watchmaking industry in the face of an apparently fatal Japanese onslaught, joined forces with DB to build the Swatch-mobile targeted at younger and more frugal buyers (*Wall Street Journal*, February 23, 1994). This was a radical move for a colossus like DB, perhaps a strong sign that following its competitive identity crisis, DB has learned new ways to learn from its experiences at both the tactical and the strategic levels, and thus to reformulate appropriately its worldviews: "For Mercedes, it was a daring — some analysts said dangerous — bid to broaden its presence in the mass market. The company already is planning to introduce a series of small 'A-class' luxury cars in 1997" (*Wall Street Journal*, February 23, 1994).

Hayek said that the project would aim to sell 100,000 cars by 1996 or 1997, compounding the fears of some analysts (*Wall Street Journal*, February 23, 1994): "It's already a massive gamble for someone like Mercedes to build the A-class. To build a small Swatch car in addition is completely illogical." Others, however, felt that the alliance was "smart strategic move that would enable Mercedes to make better use of its overcapacities in production and engineering. Moreover, by marketing the cars under the Swatch label, Mercedes would be able to enter the subcompact market without stretching the brand image of Mercedes too far downward" (*Wall Street Journal*, February 23, 1994). In essence, the company would thus find a productive outlet for its existing core competencies and would be able to maintain and grow them appropriately in a move with both defensive and offensive strategic import.

6.3.2.5 "Technology for Life" and Other Key Projects

The DB R&D department has embarked on several key projects over the last few years. The "Technology for Life" project is one example. This project's subtitle reads: "Technology for People, Networked Thinking and Acting, Materials Cycles" (Daimler-Benz [DB] High Tech Report, February 1994). The central theme of this project, whose lifecycle extends to the year 2000, is the networking of different scientific endeavors within the framework of an interdisciplinary mission. The motivation emanates from the rationale that technologically oriented innovation alone does not suffice to solve tomorrow's problems, necessitating a more holistic, interdisciplinary approach. This approach covers the spheres of work, leisure, and home, "whereby mobility, as a central element, also plays a central role" (DB High Tech Report, February 1994). The DB people involved in this project in essence try to predict future patterns of work and leisure as well as future aspects of information technology (including multimedia applications in transportation technologies), future traffic and infrastructure systems, and true environmental impact of product and production cycles. They use "scenario techniques" that enable them to learn from past and present experience to glimpse into the future.

The project itself allows DB not only to learn about the technological, social, and ecological future, but as importantly, to learn new ways to learn by redefining fundamental human-oriented, economic, and ecological concepts as well as technological problem definition and problem solving. As Walter Ziegler, coordinator of the Technology for Life project puts it (DB High Tech Report, February 1994, p. 15):

> The start of networked action must be based on the cooperation of the most varied disciplines within research. Expert know-how must be constructively superimposed. Just as important are the goals reached by consensus. These must provide the specialists with orientation as they continue to work in their individual fields."

Concerning the emphasis on the environmental dimension of these key projects, this reflects the technological learning processes through which Germany went during its *Wirtschaftswunder* period of explosive economic growth. Appropriately, the DB environmental maxim is, "In the future, the environment's resources should be used — they should *not* be used up!" DB High Tech Report, February 1994, 15).

Germany as a whole has become a pacesetter in environmentally-sensitive economic development throughout Europe: "In *a completely new type of learning process* we are beginning to fully comprehend the global nature of many environmental problems" (Werner Pollmann, DB Environmental Commissioner, DB High Tech Report, February 1994). Examples of this emerging mentality that aims at striking a balance among economy, ecology, and technology is the German–Russian, hydrogen-powered Cryoplane, with hydrogen tanks in the upper section of the fuselage and the pioneering of CFC-free vehicles with the S class Mercedes in 1991. The strategic context for these key projects is laid out by the DB Head of R&D, Hartmut Weule, who characterized them as integral to the company strategic planning activities since 1990, as the means for devising holistic solutions for critical present and future challenges and job-creating concepts at the company, the national, and the European Union levels (Werner Pollman, DB Environmental Commissioner, DB High Tech Report, February 1994).

In an interview with the author, Peter Merten, Comptroller, Daimler-Benz, states,

> Historically, Daimler-Benz has been a pioneer of both product and process innovations seeking to continuously push the envelope of feasible technologies and attain higher levels of excellence in its product lines, both the industrial- and the consumer-oriented ones. However, while that passion for excellence was and remains our prime directive, we are increasingly becoming aware of *the strategic importance of cost containment through continuous improvements and process innovations*. For example, we are currently developing radically new automobile engines and we have a joint venture with Boeing and some Japanese companies to develop a space shuttle for commercial use. Such a means of transportation would radically shorten trips around the world since it would be able to fly through both the atmosphere and the stratosphere.

6.3.3   MAJOR CORPORATE DEVELOPMENTS AND STRATEGIC DECISION-MAKING FRAME

In 1995, Edzard Reuter was replaced as chairman by Jurgen Schrempp. The new chairman immediately promised a radical change in Daimler's organization, strategy, and culture. As a start, he retained the investment bank Deutsche Morgan Grenfell to advise on a comprehensive corporate restructuring. Most of the engineering group AEG was slated for sale. In all, 12 of the 35 business units in existence at the start of Schrempp's tenure were eliminated through sale or consolidation. To stave off fears about the effect of the restructuring on employment, in 1995 Schrempp personally led negotiations with Daimler's unions to guarantee job security through the year 2000, in exchange for concessions that increased the flexibility of Daimler's human resources systems.

Schrempp also oversaw the transition of the company to a listing on the NYSE, which carried with it the move to U.S. accounting practices, thereby promoting transparency and emphasis on shareholder value. Schrempp himself adopted a "management by objectives" approach comparable to the legendary Jack Welch of General Electric. Under Schrempp, any business unit that did not meet a goal of 12% return on capital would be a candidate for divestiture.

The move to the NYSE made Daimler more "American" in culture as well as financial management. In the words of Schrempp (*Forbes*, September 8, 1997), "The company has become more open to the outside world, looking more carefully at what suppliers can offer, at what the customers want, at how the market is developing."

The company also pursues a product strategy contrary to most auto manufacturers, based on selling smaller volumes of niche models in each market segment and relying on the Mercedes brand to support premium pricing for those cars. Each new model uses a different vehicle platform, vs. other manufacturers who share platforms across models. Mercedes has even been very successful with its M-class sport utility vehicle (SUV), when many analysts believed that a SUV offering would "cheapen" the Mercedes brand.

In overall strategic planning, Daimler tends to look at which positions would give it favorable leverage instead of straight financial returns. The assumption is that profits follow when the strategy is sound, as shown in an interview with Peter Merten, Comptroller, Daimler-Benz, in which he states:

> High risk and uncertainty investments are assessed predominantly by using strategic (qualitative) criteria and secondarily financial (quantitative) ones. In other words, once we have found a project that we believe fits well within one of our core businesses, we then try to determine which is the most affordable way to embark on it.

> When major projects are being reviewed, we perform a deep analysis of cash flows, but we again use the information derived from such analysis in a supportive manner. It is clearly not the determinant factor in our strategic asset allocation process. What really drives this process, are strategic and technological imperatives.

By far the most significant strategic decision was to merge with the Chrysler Corp. in November 1998. This made DaimlerChrysler the largest automotive firm in the world. The major objective of the merger is not to completely combine operations, but to exploit specific synergies, including

1. Using common supply chains and pooling purchasing power for negotiations with suppliers (Chrysler having superior supplier relations, thanks to its successful SCORE program)
2. Sharing of key technologies, especially engine and transmission systems (an area where Daimler has historical strength)
3. Pooling resources to exploit international markets not accessible to the companies independently; current efforts focusing on Latin America (especially Brazil) and China (Daimler with a more extensive global distribution network, while Chrysler with widely recognized brands such as Jeep)

Analysts believe that with the acceleration of consolidation in the auto industry (such as the sale of Volvo's car division to Ford and the acquisition of Mazda by Renault), there will be only 20 auto manufacturers left in the world by the next decade. DaimlerChrysler is clearly moving into position as one of these surviving giants.

6.3.4   EVIDENCE OF STRATEGIC TECHNOLOGICAL LEARNING AT DAIMLERCHRYSLER

The chairman of DB in 1992 openly admitted that "we have committed errors" concerning the specifics but not the overall strategy of technological integration and consolidation around four business units since 1989 (*Der Spiegel*, April 6, 1992). This admission was corroborated when the results for the Daimler-Benz 1993 bottom line were out* (*Wall Street Journal*, April 13, 1994):

---

* These results are the latest in a series. DB reported that net income plunged 96% to DM20 million in the first quarter of 1993 from DM 480 million in the year-earlier quarter (*Wall Street Journal*, May 14, 1993).

Daimler-Benz AG crashed to a DM1.8 billion ($1.05 billion) net loss in 1993, its worst performance since World War II. But Chairman Edzard Reuter expressed confidence for a "clear reversal" of the losses this year as the company steers toward a "recovery with lasting effect."

It was also evident in the fact that for the first time arch rival BMW surpassed Mercedes-Benz in cars produced and sold in 1992.

However, it seems that Mercedes-Benz has been learning from its trials and tribulations. This technological learning has been having effects on organizational culture, engineering philosophy, manufacturing policy, outsourcing focus, internationalization of production and financing,* and pricing strategies adopted by this company (*Wall Street Journal*, January 28, 1993) : "Marking a fundamental change in direction, Mercedes-Benz AG embarked on a plan to embrace lean manufacturing, broaden its range of models, and make its cars more cost-competitive;" and the chairman of Mercedes-Benz, Helmut Werner, called this radical transformation "a 'strategic realignment' of its product policy."

This realignment includes the addition of a multipurpose vehicle, akin to a minivan, a small city car for tooling around town (perhaps the Swatch-mobile), and a four-wheel drive leisure car (to be manufactured in the Mercedes-Benz new plant in Tuscaloosa, Alabama) that would compete with Range Rover (now a BMW marque) (*Wall Street Journal*, January 28, 1993).

Werner acknowledged that in the past, "overengineering"** at Mercedes-Benz (with such examples as the S class introduced in 1991 with prices currently ranging from $52,000 to $139,000) would lead to "outpricing" and stated that his company's new strategy will focus on engineering "new products 'with clearly defined cost and sale price targets' [as opposed to the firm's traditional cost-plus pricing approach] and on adopting a 'Mercedes-specific lean logic' " (*Wall Street Journal*, January 28, 1993).

Moreover, the company reorganized its manufacturing around performance centers, that is, small groups of workers with broad responsibilities for production, parts logistics, maintenance, and quality control. In essence, Mercedes-Benz adopted a *concurrent engineering* and *lean manufacturing* approach abandoning the traditional craft approach.***

Werner also said that the company needed "rigorous pruning" of its administrative functions, and to that effect the management hierarchy levels were reduced from six to four (*Wall Street Journal*, January 28, 1993). Furthermore, Werner said that the new C class is being introduced at the same price as the preceding 190 Series

---

* DB started listing their stock on the NYSE in late 1993 and thus started reporting quarterly earnings, a break with the German accounting practices tradition, which is more long-term oriented and keeps companies immune to stock market pressures.

** Mr. Werner said that in the 1995–2000 period, R&D spending for new products will be cut by 11% over the preceding period to DM18.7 billion ($10.74 dollars) (*Wall Street Journal*, January 13, 1994).

*** "The *craft* producer uses highly skilled workers and simple but flexible tools to make exactly what the consumer asks for — one item at a time.... The *mass* producer uses narrowly skilled professionals to design products made by unskilled or semiskilled workers tending expensive, single-purpose machines.... The *lean* producer, by contrast, combines the advantages of craft and mass production, while avoiding the high cost of the former and the rigidity of the latter" (Womack et al., 1989, pp. 12–13).

reflecting "a significant reduction in internal costs* " and that parts outsourcing will be emphasized further to reduce the percentage of parts made in-house from 50% in 1993 to 40% by 2000 (*Ward's Automot. Int.*, July 1993). Part of this strategic realignment is the internationalization of MB's manufacturing base with the new plant in Tuscaloosa, Alabama and a spare parts plant that will be built in Mexico (*Ward's Automot. Int.*, July 1993).

These changes, in conjunction with the improvement of the European economies, seem to be taking effect because Mercedes-Benz sales in January 1994 jumped 54% over the same period in the previous year (*Wall Street Journal*, February 11, 1994). In an interview with the author, Peter Merten, Comptroller, DB, states:

> Feedback from our engineers and scientists drives the continual evaluation of technologies, both old and new, that Daimler-Benz relies upon. This is coupled with the impetus of our strategic imperatives and the Board of Management (*Vorstand*) assessment as to whether the emergent technologies exhibit a satisfactory fit with our core businesses.

> The primary focus has been predominantly on meeting and even exceeding the customer's needs with the quality of our products and their technological superiority. However, recently strategic considerations have been increasingly directing attention to the overall total costs of our production processes, and with that I mean both domestic conditions such as increasing pressures on labor costs, and external ones such as the worldwide slowdown of the automotive and aerospace markets.

> We emphasize all kinds of innovations depending on the phase the specific product lines and the company itself are going through. For instance, in 1985–1986, we went through a period of intense radical innovations in several of our product lines and in the strategic mix of our core businesses. Currently, we are going through a phase of emphasis on incremental innovation and careful reassessment of our strategic imperatives.

More recently, Daimler has become a major practitioner of "knowledge management" in its product development operations (*Prism*, 2Q98, p. 41):

> In early 1997, Daimler-Benz's management recognized that its new-car projects — and the new ways of doing things it developed concurrently with the new cars — held rich potentials for learning which the company did not want to lose. So the executives decided to have a team look into the transfer of learning from these projects. While the immediate objective of the project was to identify, codify, document, store, and transfer learning from the passenger-car division's three new-car projects into other new and existing ventures, its overriding objective was to establish a continuous learning process within the passenger-car division that would support the sharing of experience and knowledge among all parts of the division.

In the early phase of the project, the team identified nine key strategic learning fields involved in the auto industry: organization, cultural diversity, strategic planning/product development, marketing, production, logistics, supply chain

---

* DB cut its workforce by 18,000 in 1992 and plans another 15,000 cuts in 1993 to level off at about 360,000 workers (*Wall Street Journal*, May 27, 1993). For 1994, DB plans to cut another 51,000 from its four business units (*Wall Street Journal*, December 16, 1993).

management, customer management, and cross-functional areas. For each strategic learning field, they then defined knowledge objectives. After identifying key goals, they interviewed managers to derive common key learning processes. There were three criteria for selecting a process as key:

- Were the methods/practices different from what had been done before?
- Did the methods/practices influence the overall project result?
- Acid test: "You have 10 min to explain the most important issues from your field to a board member. Which ones do you choose?"

The team then created a master plan to promote learning with four components: content, culture, processes, and infrastructure. These components were used to construct a database of lessons from projects, not intended as a catalog of best practices but simply as a way to identify different approaches specific to each project. The project team decided not to dissolve after 6 months, as had been originally planned, but to manage several follow-on tasks. These included input into and follow-up of important management decisions, such as changing the incentive and reward system, and designing pilot learning and knowledge-exchange sessions at specific milestones in the car development process. As Kohler, the head of the effort, puts it, "The team has prepared the ground for a better knowledge exchange. Our long-term success will depend on how we build on this ground." To continue the promotion of knowledge identification and knowledge sharing, the project team decided to abandon its original plan to terminate its operations after 6 months, and is now an ongoing management system for corporate knowledge.

6.4   MATRA AUTOMOBILE SA: A FLAIR FOR LEARNING

Matra constitue le pôle "Haute Technologie" d'un groupe plus vaste, parfaitement contrôlé comprenant la communication multimedia avec Hachette et la finance avec la Banque Arjil. [Matra constitutes the *high technology pole* of a larger group, that is effectively controlled and also includes *multimedia communications* with Hachette and *finance* with the Arjil Bank.]

Jean-Luc Lagardère, Chairman, Matra-Hachette Groupe, February 1992

6.4.1   OVERVIEW OF MATRA AUTOMOBILE

Matra Automobile is a subsidiary and 99% owned by Matra SA, a company of the Matra-Hachette Groupe, a major European and international force in high-technology, publishing and multimedia, and banking services.

Matra SA is a world-class competitor in five high-technology areas important for helping people defend themselves, increase their productivity, improve their quality of life, and protect the environment (Matra SA, Annual Report, 1992):

1. *Defense systems* — integrated systems of observation and response, satellite image-processing systems, and ground-to-air intelligent combat systems that can react in real time to any kind of threat

2. *Space Systems*—Telecommunication and earth photography satellites, satellites for space exploration, manned space flights technology, and electronic brain of the European missile Ariane

3. *Telecommunications and flexible manufacturing systems (FMS)*— Telecommunication fixed and mobile to accelerate image-voice-written communication, FMS that allow manufacturing industries shorter response times to the needs of the market

4. *Automobile*—pioneer of the "monospace" van; Matra conceived, manufactured, and commercialized for Renault* the van Espace,** real "liberation tool" for the car driver

5. *Transportation systems*—Automatic systems for urban transportation, for instance, the VAL system installed in Taipei, Taiwan, and O'Hare airport in Chicago

6.4.2 MAJOR RESEARCH ACTIVITIES AND TECHNOLOGICAL POSITION

Matra's competitive advantage accrues from its technological competencies and expertise. For instance, the company in Espace created a vehicle more technically advanced than any competitor and was recognized by being awarded the "Volant d'Or 1991" in November 1992 in Germany. This is an award for technical automotive excellence and the competing vehicles over which the Espace prevailed were Toyota's Previa, Mitsubishi's Space Wagon, and Chrysler's Voyager. In an interview with the author, Jean-Louis Caussin, Technical Director, Matra Automobile, states:

> The R&D effort is tightly coupled with an approach to market research that again differs from the conventional approaches: it does not use the traditional marketing tools, neither does it follow the rationale of total market coverage but rather, it focuses on market niches. It also takes a more conceptual approach and instead of relying on, for example, focus groups, it takes a step back and looks at how the potential customers conduct their lives, their habits, and the way they spend their free time. Thus, MA while sensitive to the market's idiosyncrasies, it is much more technology than market driven. It asks the question: *"What do we want to give to the customer?"* rather than just *"What do we think that the customer wants?"*

> In that sense MA tries to keep redefining the market on a continuous basis and thus maintain its "unfair" competitive advantage. It complements these efforts with frequent solicitation by phone or mail of feedback from its clients to:

> 1. Gauge their satisfaction with the product (several times a year)
> 2. Assess their overall perception of the product's quality (once a year).

> *Customer feedback constitutes a major part of our organizational learning and adaptation process.*

---

* Renault is considered the most improved automaker in Europe (*Fortune*, May 15, 1994).
** Matra also created the concept-car Zoom for Renault, an electric vehicle ideal for cities, because its rear part folds into the body of the car to reduce its length to just 2.1 m (*Paris-Match*, May 1992).

Another very relevant fact is that MA subcontracts the manufacturing of the engine of the Espace to companies such as *Renault, Talbot, and Chrysler*. This mode of operation, *vertical de-integration and strategic focus through outsourcing (subcontracting)*, which is again a la mode, has been an SOP with MA for 20 years now. The choice not to manufacture but to subcontract the heavy engine components was thus a deliberate one that allows MA to perfect and continuously improve the quality and value of the overall product and fits strategically with the most defining imperative for MA, the *total quality management imperative*. This is the outcome of the synthesis of the *strategic imperative, the leadership in innovation imperative,* and the *champion culture imperative* that we will explain later.

We rely on specific technologies and *incremental* as well as *radical* innovations to improve both the overall value of our products and the customer benefit/cost ratio. Our innovations are also both, *product- and process-based*.

For example, we pioneered *the "hot dip" galvanization process* for the Espace's underbody, a process that is much more effective than what is used by the other manufacturers as anticorrosive methods. This approach also improves the rigidity and sound insulation qualities of the car and, moreover, it is much cheaper than the alternative approaches.

Another example has to do with panels assembly: here we pioneered the use of *SMC compounds*, a method solely used by Matra. By using such composites technology, which was partly *the outcome of synergistic learning and cross-fertilization between our aerospace and space research divisions with the automobile division*, we achieved substantial *economies of scale, scope, and time*: we saved 100 million francs and cut the development and manufacturing time from 18 to 12 months (a reduction of more than 30%).

A third example has to do with the structural assembly of parts: we pioneered *a "bonding" method* that again allows us to attain significant economies of scale and time.

All three examples point to the fact that the top management of MA perceives *the strategic management of technology as a coherent system* whose parts (such as concept R&D, design and manufacturing, organizational learning, and process and product innovation) must coexist in harmony and support each other with the overall goal of satisfying MA's three pronged *strategic imperative*.

6.4.3   MAJOR CORPORATE DEVELOPMENTS AND STRATEGIC DECISION-MAKING FRAME

The Espace has been a Europe-wide commercial success with 20% annual sales growth (interview with Jean-Louis Caussin, July 1993). The Espace's success is tangible evidence for the ability of Matra Automobile to bring about technological innovations very quickly and cost efficiently. This is the outcome of the strategic role the company assigns to R&D and to continuously improving its capacity for technological learning that builds creative know-how. With the U.S. withdrawal and the Maastricht agreement, the technological core competencies of companies such as Matra Automobile become crucial for the articulation and safeguarding of Europe's emerging identity and responsibilities as an economic and technological superpower (interview with Jean-Louis Caussin):

The three main components of MA's strategic imperative are:

1. *The originality of the product:* we believe that what many larger manufacturers do, which is to build good products but without originality, is a self-defeating and potentially very costly enterprise.
2. *A short response time to market changes:* for example, for more than 10 years now, the product development life cycle (from product conception to commercialization), has been less than 36 months compared to the average of 60 months for the other automobile manufacturers. The attainment of this objective is further aided by the emphasis we assign on organizational learning throughout MA and across management levels and functions.
3. *A small required project development investment* and thus lower manufacturer suggested retail price (MSRP) resulting from much lower feasibility study, development, and manufacturing costs compared to the other car manufacturers: it is about 1 billion francs ($200 million) compared to 5 or 6 billion francs in the case of other car producers.

In 1998, Matra Automobile gained a new corporate owner as Matra Haute Technologies was sold to Aerospatiale. While Matra Automobile is still owned by the Lagardere Group, the corporation works closely with Aerospatiale, which has more than 40% ownership by the French government. Matra Automobile is therefore a minor player compared with the other French automotive giants, Renault and Peugeot. It is also a small part of Lagardere, which is now principally concentrating on its publishing business, Matra-Hachette. This makes it very likely that Matra Automobile will be swept up in the rash of mergers in the global auto industry.

6.4.4 EVIDENCE OF STRATEGIC TECHNOLOGICAL LEARNING AT MATRA AUTOMOBILE

In an interview with the author, Jean-Louis Caussin, Technical Director, Matra Automobile, comments:

MA has long been the pioneer of many manufacturing concepts that eventually become very popular worldwide, such as *concurrent engineering*. Concurrent engineering has been the routine approach at MA, thanks to its *small size, for the last 20 years*.

Moreover, the concept of *organizational learning* which is presently becoming increasingly popular, is a concept we implemented in specific ways years ago: we kept our size and the number of our management levels small so that intra-organizational communications could remain effective and we have the smallest number of functions, with the highest degree of fit, however, of any other car manufacturer. We consciously and continuously safeguard the *flat nature* of our organization and give *wide span of control and responsibilities* to our managers; for example, the manager of the initial concepts study is in direct contact with the purchasing and manufacturing managers.

In this manner, we prevent the *erection of psychological barriers* (turf mentality and NIH syndromes) and we attain higher speed in our decision-making processes. As a result of this, MA has done 53 major project studies in the last 28 years, it has manufactured seven individual models, it has sold 8 of its studies to major car manufacturers, and it has also developed numerous models for futuristic car exhibitions.

6.5 AIRBUS INDUSTRIE: HIGH-TECH, TRANSNATIONAL, COOPERATIVE LEARNING

In dieser Branche ... du kannst nicht gewinnen, aber du kannst auch nicht aussteigen.
[In this industry, you cannot win, but you can also not give up.]

Jean Pierson, Airbus Industrie President, March 1993

The U.S. aerospace industry is one of our last remaining crown jewels.

Albert Gore, U.S. Vice President, 1993

Like basketball, airplane building is no longer strictly an American game.

Fortune Magazine, June 1, 1992

6.5.1 OVERVIEW OF AIRBUS INDUSTRIE

Airbus Industrie was created in 1970 as a two-nation, single-project undertaking, because Europe's major aircraft manufacturers realized that cooperation was the only alternative to the gradual decline of the European civil aerospace industries.

The first airplane made by Airbus Industrie entered service in May 1974; and since then, the company had produced 500 planes by June 1989 and 1000 planes by March 1993 to rank number two (in terms of market share)*, ** in the worldwide aerospace industry after Boeing Corp. (*Airbus Today*, 1993).

Airbus Industrie in its current form is a *Grouping of Mutual Economic Interest (Groupement d'Interet Economique [GIE])* headquartered in Toulouse, France. It is made up of four of Europe's major civil aviation manufacturers: Deutsche Aerospace Airbus (DASA), a unit of Daimler-Benz, Germany's largest corporation), and Aerospatiale of France, each participating with 37.9%, British Aerospace Airbus (BAA) with 20%, and CASA of Spain with 4.2% of ownership. Two other companies are also associated with the GEI, namely, Fokker and Belairbus (*Airbus Today*, 1993).

The GIE is a system introduced under French law in 1967 and has proved appropriate for cross-border corporate cooperation (akin to the German corporate governance model of *Interessengemeinschaft*). GIEs are required by law to have neither profits nor losses; thus, the operating results of Airbus Industrie are passed on to the partner companies in proportion to their shareholding. Airbus employs 1,600 people of 25 nationalities in its Toulouse headquarters, France; 200 people staff the Airbus subsidiaries in North America; 375 operate the Airbus spare parts center, Airspares, in Hamburg, Germany; and 382 operate the Airbus training

---

* The Airbus Industrie share in civil aviation units increased from 5 to 30% of the worldwide market, in less than 10 years (*Der Spiegel*, March 1993).

** The big break in the U.S. market came for Airbus in 1977, when AMR's chairman, Robert Crandall, looking for fuel-efficient planes with a lot of cargo space, bought 35 A300s (*Fortune*, June 1, 1992).

subsidiary Aeroformation at Toulouse, which has trained over 44,000 flight and fixed base operator (FBO) personnel since 1972 (*Airbus Today*, 1993).

The main policymaking instrument is the five-member Supervisory Board (*Aufsichtsrat* or *Committee de Surveillance*) whose decisions are implemented by the seven-member executive board (*Vorstand* or *Conseil Administratif*). These structures ensure *leanness* of operation and effective coordination among partners facilitating and enhancing inter- and intra-organizational technological learning in the areas of R&D, engineering, marketing, and customer service.

6.5.2 Major Research Activities and Technological Position

Since its inception and as a means to carve its own niche in an essentially duopolistic market dominated until the late 1980s by Boeing and McDonnell-Douglas, Airbus Industrie had to offer products and services superior in technological and economic value. In a mature industry that is intensively high tech and requires tremendous upfront R&D investments as the price of (potential) market share access, a company's capacity for and quality of technological learning, both across functions within the organization and through supplier and customer feedback, has always been the driving force and the prime determinant of success. This also has been very much the case with the current market leader Boeing Corp., which "bet the company" on the new Boeing 777 (or "Triple Seven" as it is called by Boeing employees). The Triple Seven is the first plane ever designed entirely by computer simulation,* bypassing costly prototypes, while Boeing "went to unprecedented lengths to involve airline customers in its design" (*Albany Times Union*, April 3, 1994) to capitalize on the benefits accruing from an accelerated R&D learning curve thanks to early customer and supplier feedback and to a concurrent engineering approach to product development (Boeing, Annual Report, 1992):

> In developing the 777, the company has worked more closely with its airline customers than ever before. Customers have been invited to play an integral part in the design process to ensure that every feature of the new aircraft will be configured to meet their needs. The 777 design-build teams include people from engineering design, manufacturing, finance, and support — as well as customers and suppliers. The teams evaluate a design from many perspectives before it is released to manufacturing. The various disciplines working together help ensure that the 777 will be produced in an efficient, cost-effective manner, and that the end product will have superior quality and reliability.

These best practices have certainly been benchmarked and applied throughout the industry and by Airbus Industrie par excellence (see Interview with AIP/VIP Program Director). The product line offered by Airbus Industrie today matches that of Boeing segment by segment;** and in some cases its products are of superior

---

* Thanks to the emerging *multimedia* and *virtual reality* technologies, simulation-based R&D is quickly becoming the standard in many high-tech industries with high R&D costs (in addition to aerospace) such as the biotechnology–pharmaceutical industry.

** Only Boeing's 747 Jumbo has no Airbus competitor, but for the future *Superjumbo* of the twenty-first century, Boeing and Airbus have joined forces to spread the huge R&D costs and risks (*Wall Street Journal*, March 4, 1994).

design and technology, for example, the A300 wing design and the A320 "fly-by-wire" electronic flight control technologies.

Airbus Industrie introduced as its first product, the first twin-engined, wide-bodied airliner worldwide, the A300,* that first flew in October 1972 and entered service in 1974 (*Airbus Today*, 1993):

> The economic superiority of the "twin-aisle twin" concept increasingly showed to advantage as fuel prices increased throughout the 1970s.... The A300's advanced wing took full advantage of Europe's unmatched length of experience in jetliner wing design. The twin-aisle fuselage cross-section was dimensional to create minimum drag while providing full wide-body comfort for passengers in all classes.... The A300 has been progressively developed as the market and technology have evolved. ... Improved systems management technology made it possible for a reduced crew to operate large aircraft safely: The A300 was the first two-person crew wide-body to be certified in 1982....

The second airliner introduced by Airbus Industrie, the A310, launched in July 1978, is still one of the world's most advanced commercial airliners both structurally and aerodynamically. Its design and flight technologies have been continually improved, driven by both direct R&D experience and customer and supplier feedback. For instance, its wing design was further enhanced by the addition of drag-reducing wing-tip fences on the A310-300, which entered service in December 1985. Moreover, the A310-300 was the first subsonic civil aircraft that employed automatic center-of-gravity control, which considerably improves fuel efficiency (*Airbus Today*, 1993).

The third Airbus product, the A320, was launched in March 1984 and entered service in 1988; and its electronic flight control system is recognized as the most advanced in operation or under development worldwide (*Airbus Today*, 1993):

> Electronic "fly-by-wire"** enables design engineers to dispense with highly cumbersome mechanical controls, and leads naturally to a complete reassessment of the relationship between the pilot and his aircraft. This was the subject of a lengthy research and development programme in which practising line pilots were actively involved.... Airbus products enable operators to realise the considerable economies of Cross-Crew Qualifications, thanks to their shared technologies, reducing the cost of training flight deck, cabin and grained crews, and increasing flight crew productivity.

In May 1996, Airbus Industrie established a team to begin development work on a "superjumbo" airliner called the A3XX project. The jet will seat 480 to 656 passengers, using a double-decked fuselage. It is also targeted to achieve a 15 to 20% operating cost advantage over the Boeing 747 series aircraft. The project is very controversial in several respects. First, Boeing has abandoned a similar project (after holding exploratory meetings on a collaboration in superjumbo design with

---

* The A300 is about 15% cheaper to operate than its direct competitor, the Boeing 727-200, thanks to advanced wing design and its efficient twin engines (*Fortune*, June 1, 1992).

** Airbus Industrie pilots use joy sticks and all their commands are transmitted by computers instead of manually. Boeing did not offer such "fly-by-wire" technology until 1995 in the new 777 (*Fortune*, June 1, 1992).

Airbus), claiming that there is not sufficient demand for this configuration of aircraft. Second, with an estimated development cost of $7 billion, the Airbus partners are planning to tap government funds using loans guaranteed or provided by their respective national governments. Third, the Airbus partners essentially need to convert from their current GIE corporate structure to a more traditional, public corporation structure (see later) to tap public capital markets for development funds. The problems in all three areas threaten the viability of the A3XX project.

The Airbus design and manufacturing philosophy is thus one of continuous improvement through consistent technological commonalities* across its product lines to provide customers with economies of scope and scale in their own technological learning processes, which cumulatively can make a big difference. The reason is that the main factor behind the high training and maintenance costs associated with the operation of a civil airliner is the technological complexity and risks inherent in modern commercial aviation. In the words of Marc Aubert, during 1993/1994 interviews with the author:

> In our business, we have so many highly complex and dynamic technologies whose evolutionary paths are intertwined and interdependent, that I would like to suggest to you that the concept of a technological paradigm or "established way of perceiving and utilizing technologies" simply does not apply. We remain always engaged in a mode of continuous improvement, innovation, and "scheduled obsolescence."

> This might perhaps serve as the closest to a technological paradigm that fashions our industry's modus operandi, with the note that the lifetime of a project for the development of a commercial airplane is roughly 20 years, and that change in aerospace technology is punctuated by evolutions occurring both during and especially at the end of such a project's lifetime.

> For the purpose of monitoring the performance and promise of emergent technologies, Airbus coordinates monthly meetings among design, manufacturing, and marketing representatives from the four partners. In those meetings *"modification proposals"* are reviewed and acted upon. Actually, we end up having too many of those proposals with all sides trying to make improvements constantly. In assessing the feasibility and usefulness of those proposals we follow first the *safety imperative* and subsequently considerations of cost of operation, passenger comfort, pilot workload reduction, ease of maintenance, resale value, etc.

Hence, the Airbus marketing strategy of differentiation against its competitors has as one of its main pivotal points the commonality of the technological and structural features among its various products (Marc Aubert interviews, 1993/1994):

> We are currently in the position of challenging the worldwide aerospace market leader (Boeing Inc. of Seattle, Washington), hence we are mostly proactive and technology driven as well. We are continuously trying to integrate over time all the competitive advantages accruing from the plethora of technologies involved in aerospace design

---

* Air Canada recently chose the A319 over Boeing and McDonnell-Douglas airliners, partly because of common features the A319s have with the A320s Air Canada already operates. Thus, Airbus won a $1 billion leasing deal for 25 A319s (*Wall Street Journal*, May 11, 1994).

and manufacturing. Airbus Industrie plays a coordinating role among the four member companies in constantly researching new technologies and new forms of aerodynamic design. The coordination among the four partners is on the level of strategic decisions regarding R&D and the choice of new technologies. Our main imperative is *to be better than the competition* and that means having technologies that allow us to build lighter, more fuel efficient, easier to fly and maintain airplanes; and finally having a line of products as complete as the competition (Boeing) or more complete than the competition (McDonnell-Douglas).

Another point of product differentiation is the flexibility built by design in the structure of the product line itself, to make the Airbus planes better competitive tools for the air transportation industry. Finally, the *technological superiority** per se of the Airbus planes also helps to clinch billion dollar deals. These strategic marketing features of its products allow Airbus to compete in markets previously saturated by its competitors; and once it gains a "bridgehead" in those markets, these same features ensure a continuous process of market share growth.

The A330,** the A340-200,*** and the A340-300 are built to address the needs of different market segments and equally important, were available by 1994, whereas Boeing's answer to the A330 and A340, the Triple Seven, was not introduced until 1997**** (*Airbus Today*, 1993):

> At the higher capacity end of the Airbus product line are the twin-engined A330, seating between 300 and 400 passengers, and the four-engined A340. The A340 is built in two versions, the 260-seat A340-200 which has the longest range of any airliner, and the 295-seat A340-300 for service on slightly shorter routes requiring higher capacity.... Offering three-quarters of the passenger capacity of the 747-400, the A340 enables airlines to achieve higher load factors on routes where competition is severe.

Airbus Industrie and its partners are increasing their investment in advanced research. Of particular interest is the Environmentally Friendly Aircraft research program sponsored by the Aeronautical Task Force of the European Union. Working with the CNRS government research institute of France and several major European universities, Airbus Industrie developed and introduced innovations to reduce drag, limit aircraft engine noise, and lower engine emissions.

To improve the design process, in 1995 Airbus initiated the Airbus Concurrent Engineering (ACE) team among the four major partners to enable an all-digital design capability for future aircraft. ACE's goals are to cut development costs by 30% or more, reduce time-to-market for a new product to 36 months, respond to market demand for a derivative of an existing aircraft within a year, and reduce maintenance costs by 30%. This would be accomplished by consolidating the part-

---

* "We like to say we are offering a BMW to our clients and not a Ford," says Stewart Iddles, Airbus Chief Marketing Officer (*Fortune*, June 1, 1992).

** The A330 first flew in November 1992 and entered service in late 1993.

*** The A340 first flew in October 1991 and entered service in January 1993.

**** The significance of timing was underscored by an $800 million order for six long-haul A340-330s Airbus won from Cathay Pacific Airways, previously a loyal Boeing customer, that will now most likely cancel options on 11 Boeing 777Bs (*Wall Street Journal*, December 8, 1993).

ners around a single set of design systems; previously, the four companies used 12 different design systems and 900 databases to store technical information on Airbus products. The focus of the team is on integrating existing design and business systems, not on creating new software. The four major components of ACE cover CAD/CAM, product data management, computer-aided engineering, computer workstations, and Enterprise Resource Planning software. Vendors involved in the partnership include Parametric Technology, MacNeal-Schwendler Corp., Hewlett-Packard, and SAP.

6.5.3 MAJOR CORPORATE DEVELOPMENTS AND STRATEGIC DECISION-MAKING FRAME

Airbus Industrie serves as the marketing interface between its partners and the worldwide industrial structure that supplies the parts including the engines for building the Airbus planes. This interface serves a coordinating function, while the partner companies and their associates retain their full capability in all aspects of aircraft construction.

Given the structure and size of the European market for commercial airliners, Airbus is export oriented with over 80% of firm orders coming from outside its home market of Germany, France, Britain, and Spain; and, in particular, from the areas of major economic growth in Southeast Asia.*

The success of Airbus has put in question the long-term survivability of McDonnell-Douglas, because it denied it the number two position worldwide and a certain level of profitability that is required for aerospace manufacturers to continue investing in R&D and thus maintain their "chain" of incremental and radical product innovation intact. The innovation chain has been broken for McDonnell-Douglas that is also suffering from the U.S. defense cutbacks, and its worldwide market share in the commercial aviation arena fell from 20% in the mid-1980s to 11% in 1993. The company needs at least another decade to position itself in a market-share-growth mode again, time its competitors may well deny it (*Der Spiegel*, March 15, 1993).

The Airbus success came in the face of formidable odds in bringing together very distinct cultures and philosophies of management and engineering involving the four major Airbus partners. According to Herbert Flosdorff, Airbus Industrie Chief Operating Officer (COO), in a June 1, 1992 interview:

> There are times when there seem to be massive conflicts because of the different educational backgrounds and different approaches. We Germans tend to be more fact-oriented, while the French are more intuitive. The British tend to play arbiter and get smashed from both sides.

---

* Airbus has been trying hard to win market share in Asia, currently considered the most promising aviation market in the world. In November 1993, Airbus received a $700 million order for six A340s from mainland China (Wall Street Journal, December 8, 1993).

In addition, Adam Brown, Airbus Industrie Marketing Director (June 1, 1992) says: "We British tend to sort of hint at what results we expect. I soon learned that the Germans sometimes did not actually understand that I wanted them to do anything in particular."

Moving into second place behind Boeing gave Airbus Industrie the opportunity to shift its marketing strategy to one more appropriate for this new duopoly. Marc Aubert, in his 1993/1994 interviews with the author comments:

> In the beginning of its creation and until recently, Airbus Industrie had been following a marketing strategy that focused on large accounts (major airlines) only. That approach was motivated by the strategic goal of becoming recognized in the marketplace (brand management) and ultimately win over North American airlines as customers.

> The new marketing paradigm we recently adopted after attaining major player status in the aerospace industry is one of going after all potential customers regardless of their size (even when it concerns one airplane). This new marketing strategy is motivated by a portfolio approach to managing the risk of large orders being cancelled.

> Another important dimension to the new marketing paradigm adopted is the decision to become one of the first true transnational and transcontinental corporations, in terms of both design and manufacturing of Airbus products. The reasons motivating this marketing strategy dimension were:

> *Explicit intent* to participate in the U.S. market not only as an exporter but also as a local content manufacturer to avoid protectionist criticisms and also insulate our business from excessively high currency exchange risks, by virtue of trading mostly in dollars. For example, 20% of the A-320 and 40% of the A-340 is currently manufactured in the United States.

> Many governments have signed offset agreements with them in order to buy our airplanes, which means that we must implement a certain amount of technology transfer into the buyer country (attain a level of locally manufactured content), which results in spreading production around quite a few countries worldwide. I literally could not tell you how many right now.

In 1999, Airbus finally achieved parity in aircraft orders with its arch rival Boeing. According to John Leahy, Airbus Industrie Senior Vice President Commercial, this goal was reached well in advance of expectations. There have been charges that Airbus boosted its order volumes by drastically discounting its aircraft, but the consortium claims that Boeing's discounts are even deeper. Airbus did earn a profit during 1999.

This success is clouded by the continuing controversy over incorporation of Airbus Industrie. To move forward with new design plans, and to adjust to the continuing deregulation of the global aircraft industry, Airbus must become more efficient by centralizing operations currently controlled by the partners. A major barrier to incorporation was removed in late 1999, when DASA, CASA, and Aerospatiale agreed to merge to form a pan-European defense corporation. This leaves British Aerospace as a minority partner in the new Airbus single corporate entity (SCE). However, British Aerospace is considering a merger with Marconi, which would give it a scale equal to the pan-European group. The three-way merger ensures that France will support the move by Airbus to the SCE model. The remaining challenge is how to properly value the contribution of each partner in terms of market capital. As a GIE, the Airbus partners were allowed to keep their monetary investment in the partnership's operations hidden. Now, as an SCE, the partners will need to reveal their financial data, especially in terms of cost and efficiency, which may not be favorable.

6.5.4 Evidence of Strategic Technological Learning at Airbus Industrie

Assessment of opportunities to invest in new technologies is now a strategic priority, given the need to compete head-on with Boeing in winning new customers. As Marc Aubert states in his 1993/1994 interviews with the author:

> We proceed based on what we have learned from our existing technologies and product lines and we try to improve on a continuous basis our existing products. In this context, we try to reach a compromise, namely, optimize the return on what we have already invested while keeping the planes under development (during the 20-year project development period) up to date with emerging technologies.

> However, when a partner(s) proposes introducing an entirely new technology, all four partners try to reach a consensus based on both strategic and financial criteria. In other words, we try to justify, by doing financial analyses, the viability and feasibility of the technology under review, while keeping in mind that our goal is to be always ahead in terms of technological and product innovation, for example, fly-by-wire technologies, or the use of carbon fibers in airplane fuselages, which reduces considerably maintenance costs and airplane weight, thus increasing payload and reducing usage costs.

> If all four partners through the coordination of Airbus deem that we must invest in a certain technology, we simply allocate enough funds for the project in question to take off and then gauge our commitment on the results and the promise shown by the technology as we acquire experience from developing and using it.

This same positioning places a premium on risk taking, as any advantage could enable Airbus to leapfrog its competitor (Marc Aubert interviews, 1993/1994):

> We do the appropriate *financial analyses* to determine whether and how to best utilize existing or emergent technologies. Especially in the case of programs that are already in place we make sure that our decisions are justified by the applicable benefit/cost ratios;, for example, when we were deciding on using carbon fibers for the fuselage of our airplanes, we considered such things as reduction of airplane weight and of costs of use and maintenance vs. the costs of integrating carbon fibers in our manufacturing processes.

> However, in the case of entirely new technologies where there is very little hard evidence to base our decisions on, we are driven by our strategic imperative: "to be the avant-garde of aerospace technologies."

Airbus Industrie also engages in learning from its business partners, including suppliers and customers (Marc Aubert interviews, 1993/1994):

Moreover, we provide permanent support to our customers, and remain in continuous interaction with them to keep learning from their experience of using our products and we keep a file for each individual airplane throughout its useful life. In that way we have a bank of experience with each product line and particular product that is continuously growing. This knowledge database allows us to infer meaningful patterns by means of statistical (cluster and other) analysis that can help us learn about and alter the way we build our planes, as well as the way we test and learn from using them. For this purpose we have a department of statistical analysis that deals with minor findings that simply add to our experience, as well as a design department that deals with major findings (recurring patterns) that alter the way we do business and affect the way we learn about our products' performance.

In addition, any airline customer of ours has access to any part of our production process with all four member companies of Airbus, and can inspect and give us feedback as their orders are being built.

This attests to the ability of the Airbus management structure to balance and bridge cultural barriers and to develop a true transnational organization, driven by technological learning links across borders, disciplines, and mentalities (*Fortune*, June 1, 1992):

Airbus has become something of a model of high-tech multinational cooperation. At least part of the reason is the work itself: aeronautical engineers and other related professionals tend to think beyond national boundaries. As [Airbus Industrie COO] Pierson put it: *"In this business, it is a kind of separate world, a kind of international fraternity. We have invented our 'own system.'"*

7 Process Sector Case Studies (Chemicals, Pharmaceuticals, and Materials)

7.1 INDUSTRY OVERVIEW

The process industries have a tradition of global business operations, with multinational companies operating as far back as the early 20th century. What is changing this industry is technology, in particular, the nature of technological change. With the combination of regulatory burdens, intellectual property concerns, and complexity of chemical and biomedical science, development costs for new products in this sector have risen dramatically. In pharmaceuticals, in particular, the cost of developing a new drug and bringing it to market has increased tenfold in the past 5 years, and now amounts to hundreds of millions of dollars (including costs such as marketing). Given that expense, the uncertainty of research success, and the time required to obtain approval to distribute a drug, each manufacturer needs to have hundreds of drugs in development at any given time to maintain the minimum necessary flow of new drugs onto the marketplace. Similar situations are found in the chemicals and materials industries.

Also, the technological basis of the process industries has changed dramatically. The biotechnology revolution promises to revolutionize research and product development in all three industries over the next decade. Some companies now identify themselves more as biotechnology firms than as traditional chemical or drug companies. Also, the product life cycle in each industry is being reduced by the increased pace of innovation. For example, the materials producer 3M generates the majority of its sales from products that are less than 3 years old.

In this entire sector, continuous technological learning is an absolute requirement to keep pace with competitors in the rate and scale of innovation. Therefore, learning itself is not enough. Technological learning must also be strategically targeted toward domains that show the greatest potential for returns.

7.2 BRISTOL-MYERS SQUIBB: TURBULENCE LEARNING

7.2.1 OVERVIEW OF BRISTOL-MYERS SQUIBB

Bristol-Myers Squibb (BMS) is one of the major pharmaceutical/biotechnology companies worldwide with revenue of $20.2 billion and net earnings of $4.1 million in 1999. It was among the top ten companies with the biggest dollar gains in market value from 1982 to 1992 with an increase of $30.5 billion dollars over this period to a total market value of $35.3 billion dollars (an almost 600% gain in market value) (*Wall Street Journal*, November 19, 1992). However, this "bonanza" has been under serious pressure with the institutional and competitive changes in the pharmaceuticals/biotechnology arena causing the market leaders, such as Merck & Co., to diversify vertically forward* to cope with the emerging trend toward managed health care and "a 'deflationary' pharmaceutical environment, where profits are driven by market share, rather than by margins" (*Wall Street Journal*, February 14, 1994).

What is unique about the pharmaceutical industry in general, including BMS, is that despite the intensity of competitive rivalry and external institutional pressures that in one form or another were always present, the same companies that were founded shortly after World War II continue to dominate the market (Henderson, January–February 1994). As Henderson concludes from her study of over 120 programs covering a period of up to 30 years with the ten major U.S. and European pharmaceutical companies, the capacity for *technological learning, metalearning,* and *unlearning* is what made the crucial difference (Henderson, January–February 1994):

> These companies have demonstrated an ability to learn and grow that confounds conventional wisdom. Despite their age, size, and success, the best of these companies have found ways to retain the flexibility and responsiveness of companies one-tenth their size. … the longevity of pharmaceutical companies attests to a unique managerial competency: the ability to foster a high level of specialized knowledge within an organization, while preventing that information from becoming embedded in such a way that it permanently fixes the organization in the past, unable to respond to an ever-changing competitive environment."

One could speculate that the companies in the pharmaceutical arena cannot afford not to be effective and efficient learning organizations given what are the stakes involved as part of their everyday business mainly defined by *risk, complexity,* and *uncertainty.* Moreover, as we see in the other arenas covered, intense competitive rivalry and high risk, uncertainty, and complexity inherent in conducting such a

---

* According to the *Wall Street Journal* (February 14, 1994): Merck acquired Medco Containment Services, a mail-order pharmacy and managed health care company, and merged it into a new unit, the Merck-Medco U.S. Managed Care Division in January 1994. This move aimed at changing Merck from "one of the highest margin pharmaceutical companies to one of the lowest." Specifically, as Merck's CFO put it, "Medco's 9% pretax margin will erode Merck's 35% margin" to about the same level as the other pharmaceutical companies.

business, foster the creation of formal and/or informal communities of interest (*Interessengemeinschaften*), open-system organizational and technological architectures, or dynamically evolving business relationships alternately gravitating between symbiosis and competition. Again we quote Merck's chief financial officer (CFO):

> On the business end, we also think that sharing information can be more productive than hiding it.... When we came out with our antihypertensive Vasotec, Bristol-Myers Squibb had already launched Capoten. Both drugs have roughly the same method of action. The strategy we adopted was not to cannibalize the Capoten markets. Rather, we wanted to go after the tenfold additional patients who were on older, less safe, and effective medicine....
>
> Q. How do you know when to support a rival and when to compete more aggressively ?
>
> A. *The paradox is that we perform in both modes at the same time*...the most interesting aspect of this is to think about the nature of innovation in the pharmaceutical industry ... it takes entrepreneurial spirit and scientific insight.... That *intangible* element of insight makes all the difference in our industry.

7.2.2 MAJOR RESEARCH AND DEVELOPMENT ACTIVITIES AND TECHNOLOGICAL POSITION

One can view this as a process of technological innovation and learning at varying rates, breadth, and depth, drastically affecting company life cycles, where some companies survive over the long run and some perish or become absorbed. The direction technology in the pharmaceuticals arena has been evolving toward is the area of *biopharmaceuticals*. These are the products of biotechnology with pharmaceutical use. They fall into eight major classes and can be developed through: (1) *serendipity and observation,* (2) *screening and specific bioassays,* and (3) *rational drug design* (Elander, March 2, 1991). While these new drugs are natural body substances, highly specific, and extremely potent, they are difficult to discover and produce, and in general cannot be orally ingested.

In an interview with the author, Richard Elander, Vice President, Biotechnology, Fermentation, Research and Development (R&D), BMS, says,

> We emphasize all kinds of innovation depending on whether we are trying to protect our franchises or establish a market niche (incremental innovation), whether we try to benefit from the results of our clinical R&D (generational and radical innovation), and finally whether we are dealing with a biological (product and process innovation) or microbial system (process innovation) in our R&D. In the case of a *biological system* we are working at the *molecular level* where we have to deal with inherent molecular complexities, something that allows us to make improvements in both the products we make *and* in the way we make them. Thus, product and process innovation are intertwined in this case. In the case of a *microbial system*, we are working at the *viral level* with much simpler cells where the process is independent of the product and we really have leverage for improvement only in terms of the products we make (product innovation). Moreover, biotechnology has allowed us to bypass both the microbial and biological system approaches by using, for example, yeast for fermentation purposes.

In particular, fungal biotechnology is now allowing human antibodies to be included in plants, which is a very efficient and fast way to produce human proteins. However, with the constraints currently being imposed on profit margins, *the process of technological learning* that has been the catalyst for the development of cost-effective and innovative biotechnologies will be drastically curtailed.*

The main factors that shape the nature and intensity of competitive rivalry in the biopharmaceuticals arena have to do with the technology (biotechnology is a very dynamic, competitive field); its complexity and risks (clinical studies validate experimental findings; however, toxicology, analysis, and formulation issues are unique to each product); and the way it is being regulated and protected (the Food and Drug Administration [FDA] has set up the Bureau of Biologics that establishes preclinical protocols to facilitate the drug development and testing process; however, patenting drugs is a very complex and rarely foolproof process). The development of a typical biotechnology process consists of three steps: (1) development on a laboratory scale, (2) scale-up to a pilot plant vessel closely resembling production configurations, and (3) final adjustment and run of the process on an industrial scale.

In a July 1993 interview with the author, Richard Elander, Vice President, Biotechnology, Fermentation, Research and Development, BMS, reveals:

> In pharmaceutical parlance we have *"scheduled" technological paradigm shifts* that occur whenever our R&D isolates a new line of drugs or strand of viruses, roughly every 5 to 10 years. The reason is that every new line of pharmaceuticals has its own unique characteristics in terms of possible applications, ethical issues involved, and public health safety considerations.

> We manage an overall portfolio of hundreds of drugs structured along several pipelines. Each pipeline and even each drug can be considered a different "technology." The cardiovascular drugs portfolio represents an investment of $2 billion, the anticancer drugs $1 billion, and the anti-infections drugs $1 billion. We change our portfolio profile, in terms of resource allocation, every 3 to 4 months and sometimes more frequently, depending on R&D breakthroughs or negative clinical trials results.

> We rely very much on technology but in a manner structured by a portfolio risk management approach. I refer to the way we conduct R&D coupled with frequent reviews of our product pipeline to ensure that our products attain therapeutic fit and are clinically safe. At the same time we have "technological gatekeepers" that keep us apprised of any major developments outside our own R&D efforts and thus enable us to benefit from such events as well, either through acquisitions or through "me-too" drugs.

As part of the turnover in top management in 1994, chief executive officer (CEO) Charles Heimbold hired Peter Ringrose of Pfizer as the new head of R&D at BMS. Ringrose also earned very challenging orders along with his new position, including:

---

* For every $1 dollar spent on health care, only 5 cents are spent on pharmaceuticals, whereas 25 cents are consumed by intermediaries. Specifically, there are 450 "paper pushers" for every 300 patients. Further, more than 60% of hospital expenses originate in intensive care focused on older people. Finally, as an example of "cost efficiency," an aspirin sold by BMS for 2 cents is resold by hospitals for $10 dollars to patients.

1. Introducing three new products a year over the next decade, compared with the recent average of one
2. Improving the ratio of internally discovered to in-licensed compounds from the current 1:1 to 4:1
3. Boosting research staff from 4000 to 6000 by 2002

At the same time, Ringrose was expected to transform the research operations of BMS, which had a history of licensing significant drug compounds instead of developing them internally. This required a tremendous investment in resources, because the cost to bring a new drug to market rose by nearly four times between 1976 and 1996.

In an interview with the author, David Brush, Strategic Planning Staff, BMS, states:

> The review of our product pipeline takes place at three different levels of comprehensiveness and frequency of occurrence:
>
> 1. Every 5 years, we update our company wide strategic plan setting our mission and long-term goals. Input into the plan comes from both the pharmaceutical and the R&D group trying to maximize the long-term benefits for Bristol Myers Squibb that accrue from matching present and anticipated market needs with research-created opportunities.
> 2. Every year, we have a comprehensive review of our products pipeline. Several stakeholders participate in this review process: The Strategic Management Group that consists of the senior management of our company, interacts with other companies, universities, sales groups, and R&D people and serves as both an active and a passive interface to integrate all the inputs and reassess and prune the pipeline. The results of this process are then integrated into the annual revision of the 5-year strategic plan.
> 3. Every month, the heads of the pharmaceutical, the R&D, the sales, and the strategic management groups meet to monitor the progress of developing the current drug pipeline. No major drug addition or pruning takes place unless R&D has come up with either a significant breakthrough or serious contraindications resulting from a drug's laboratory or clinical trials. In such cases, we try to preempt our competitors or the FDA, respectively, by either allocating resources for further development or interrupting further development.

7.2.3 Major Corporate Developments and Strategic Decision-Making Frame

According to Richard Elander, Vice President, Biotechnology, Fermentation, R&D, BMS,

> Bristol Myers acquired Squibb in 1989, to enter in an effective manner the biotechnology arena and compete directly with Merck, Glaxo, and Eli Lilly in all therapeutic areas. Moreover, acting along the same line of strategic positioning, we purchased

Genetic Systems and Oncogen focusing on immunology, drug factors involved with malign growths, anti-infectious factors, and cardiovascular drugs.

BMS's current portfolio of activities is about 57% focused on pharmaceutical and biotechnology applications (mostly anti-infectious and anticancer ones), with the remainder in nonprescription health care products (1%), medical devices and services (15%), and toiletries and beauty aids (11%). Oncogen, in particular, has a very good therapeutic fit with the preexisting products in our drug development pipeline. At the same time we sold Genetic Systems to Sanofi and also Surgitec (focusing on medical devices) as part of our continuous process of strategic realignment within our industry moving toward immunology and biotechnology and away from radioimaging and diagnostic equipment. Within this context lies BMS's Pharmaceutical Research Institute at Seattle.

In another interview, David Brush, Strategic Planning Staff, BMS, commented:

BMS first entered the biotechnology arena by purchasing the Genetic Systems company for $300 million in the mid-eighties. Bristol-Myers then acquired Squibb for $3 billion in 1989, to expand into the biotechnology arena and compete more directly with other leading companies in both pharmaceuticals and biotechnology. The synergies emanating from the Bristol-Myers–Squibb merger were due to the Bristol-Myers strength in oncology and the Squibb strength in cardiovascular products.

In 1994, as the company suffered from lagging stock prices and poor financial results, a new CEO was brought in to change the company. Heimbold made the daunting prediction that the company's sales and earning would double by 2000. Heimbold and his CFO, Michael Mee, instituted cost-cutting measures and boosts to productivity to increase profitability. However, the benefits of these efforts were taken not as profits, but instead reinvested into sales, marketing, and R&D. These moves helped the company to come close to achieving the goals set in 1994.

In 1995, BMS decided to reengineer its operations by implementing the R/3 Enterprise Resource Planning (ERP) package from SAP of Germany. The objective of this initiative was to move the entire company onto a single platform for tracking all business data. In addition, BMS added capabilities onto this platform in areas such as warehouse management and supply chain management. There are a number of such "bolt-on" systems that have been grafted onto the SAP system at BMS. Manugistics provides BMS with sales forecasting capability, while i2 Technologies allow the company to plan factory operations, inventory use, and management of transportation. Beckman is a laboratory equipment management tool necessary for the company to meet FDA rules. Epec allows BMS to use bar-code technology with SAP. The company has also added Internet access to give its suppliers direct electronic access to BMS for taking orders and processing invoices.

In his July 1992 interview with the author, Elander, Vice President, Biotechnology, Fermentation, R&D, BMS, states:

There has been renewed emphasis on better understanding the needs and expectations of the *real decision makers* in terms of the consumption of drugs: these have been until recently the prescribing physicians and not far behind the hospital administrators and the health insurance carriers. The role of the last two decision-making agents has been acquiring an increasing gravity due to serious budgetary problems that many hospitals and insurers are encountering today.

Moreover, since the institutional/legislative trend is currently toward managed health care, which entails the emphasis in the decision-making process is being shifted onto the health insurance carriers and the health management organizations (HMOs) and away from the prescribing physicians.

In the context of these changes, BMS has merged with a health product distributor like Merck did, in a forward integration adaptive strategic maneuver. This reflects the increasing strategic importance for pharmaceutical companies of the *formularies* (lists of prescribed drugs), namely, of more centralized purchasing through distribution channels as opposed through doctors. In the same context, me-too drugs have been depressing profit margins and most companies will soon have their in-house developed drugs competing with me-too drugs after the expiration of the patents protecting the proprietary drugs initially developed. Thus, companies such as BMS and Merck will put more emphasis on the production and distribution of generic drugs and will de-emphasize development of highly expensive, sophisticated drugs.

Concerning prescription drug pricing, BMS's CEO identified four factors that determine the prices of drug (from a speech by Richard Gelb, BMS CEO, March 18, 1992):

1. It depends upon how one prices new drugs.
2. It depends upon how one prices products to the huge, cost-sensitive managed health care market.
3. It depends upon how one prices products to the largest health care provider of all, the federal government.
4. Finally, responsible pricing depends upon how one deals with the indigent.

As cited in the *Wall Street Journal*, July 21, 1994:

Every year, a meeting of the top management of R&D and other functional areas takes place to decide on which areas should become the main thrust areas. Our strategic decision-making process is primarily guided *by therapeutic fit (or strategic and financial) considerations* for initial stage candidates for the development pipeline.

In particular, there are *three development phases* for managing our portfolio of drug pipelines (along with the four phases that apply for the development of each particular drug): In Phase I, we use both business and technical criteria for determining the initial contents of a drug pipeline, in Phase II, we use only technical criteria and we deal with a few drugs, and in Phase III, we still use technical criteria but we now deal with 200–300 drugs: "Phase I tests evaluate a drug's safety; Phase II tests give preliminary indications of the drug's benefit and initial risks; and Phase III, the final test before regulatory approval, establishes a drug's safety and effectiveness in a large scale clinical trial."

As cited by Elander, Vice President, Biotechnology, Fermentation, R&D, BMS, in an interview with the author:

Our system relies increasingly on cash flow-based assessments the more advanced development stage drugs we are dealing with. However, our clinically based experience is indispensable and crucial for the initial drug development stages. We have a general goal we try to reach, and that is a 66% ROI every 18 months on the pool of existing drugs. Our cash flow forecasting models are updated monthly using feedback of both a technical (clinical trial updates) and a marketing (externally interfacing) nature. On top of that, we have *contingency meetings* if there are breakthroughs we need to act quickly on; for example, in the case of taxol, we had four top management meetings within 2 weeks. We also try to focus on one strategic drug at a time along with managing our entire portfolio of drug pipelines. In this case, the closer we get to launch date for the drug, the more frequent feedback cycles we have, regarding both internal and external information about the drug's potential and health risks. Six months before launch date, we release information about the drug under development to the scientific community with journal papers and AMA announcements.

Comments made by David Brush, Strategic Planning Staff, BMS, in an interview with author follow:

Bristol Myers is a financially driven company where "gut feelings" carry much less weight in strategic decision making. However, we do use multiple screens and phases where we integrate the input of both R&D and planning/marketing people in determining and updating the content of our pipeline of products under development. In the early development phases of a drug (5 to 6 years), we rely more on the opinion of R&D researchers to determine the feasibility, therapeutic potential, and health risks associated with a candidate for our drug pipeline.

In this stage, the primary screen phase, therapeutic fit is the main criterion. Since we still have no real product in our hands, we have no cash flows or other financial criteria to use in our strategic decisions.

In the secondary screen phase, we start having cash flows occurring from introductory product deployment, and then we prioritize the emphasis assigned to drugs based not only on therapeutic fit but on cash flow projections as well. In this sense, one could say that we combine the learning-by-doing approach with the net present value [NPV] approach, since we start using cash flow projections for a specific drug, once we have some initial experience-based knowledge about that drug's market potential.

Again, from Elander's interview, we learn:

In essence we try to both differentiate our products based on therapeutic fit and extra features compared to competing drugs, as well as introduce me-too drugs in which case we compete on cost. This multidimensional strategy is also applied by the other leading pharmaceutical companies.

With the institutional/legislative changes under way in the health care arena (trend toward managed health care), BMS must have its drugs listed on HMO formularies as well as compete on therapeutic fit and other specific drug features. This has radically altered the competitive landscape for BMS, with cost leadership gaining preponderance over differentiation based on therapeutic fit.

Further comments by Brush, Strategic Planning Staff, BMS, include

We divide strategic investment decisions into two realms: internal and external projects.

The internal projects are driven by a 5-year strategic plan that is accompanied by an annual analysis of our portfolio products. This analysis is an NPV and [a] PRA (probabilistic risk assessment)-based evaluation, driven by the experience we have acquired over time with drug portfolio management. The result of this analysis is twofold: pruning and perhaps licensing out of no longer qualifying drugs as well as ranking of the remaining ones to update the prioritization of our resource allocation for drug development.

The external projects consist of acquisitions (like that of Squibb), and in-licensing from competitors of drugs that fit with our existing drug portfolio under development.

In terms of the four major phases of drug development, drug selection and pruning in Phase I is really driven by therapeutic fit criteria. In Phases II, III, and IV, we increasingly rely on cash flow projections that of course hinge very much on final FDA approval for our drugs, a very unpredictable and potentially long-lasting (measured in years) process. Thus, in our decision making that affects the content of and relative emphasis on parts of our drug portfolio, we must consider not only risks associated with therapeutic fit and market acceptance but also with FDA approval.

Once a drug passes onto Phase IV, then we conduct follow-up studies on results from distributing the drug and try to differentiate it from competing ones on extra qualities. That may mean differentiation based on *cost* for the case of me-too drugs or *additional marginal benefits* for new drugs. An example of the intensity of competition based on feature or cost differentiation is the case of the drug TPA-Aktivase made by Genentech that costs $2800 per dose. An equivalent drug, Streptokinase made by Beecham and introduced subsequently into the market, costs only $50 per dose, 1/56 of the TPA's cost.

From an interview with author, Elander, Vice President, Biotechnology, Fermentation, R&D, BMS, states:

Taxol has been a major recent breakthrough for our company, in terms not only of its clinical development but also its FDA approval (*Wall Street Journal*, December 30, 1992). It is presently produced out of a northwestern tree, the Enge tree, which is environmentally protected, with the result of limiting the availability of the drug in large quantities. We hope that by 1995 alternative, synthetic means of producing it will be available (thanks to biotechnology). Weyerhauser, in particular, has been developing a procedure whereby taxol will be derived from the needles and not the trunk of the Enge tree and, moreover, it has been fermenting bioreactors that will help achieve "in-cell" development of the raw material for taxol, thus completely bypassing the need for using the Enge tree or parts of it.

Taxol, like many major breakthroughs constitutes an opportunity for continuous learning and improvement for us, since after having established its unique therapeutic potential for cancer-related cases (much less toxic, less costly, and more effective, thanks to a new mode of action, than competing drugs), we are in the process of researching its potential for other areas of application.

7.2.4 EVIDENCE OF STRATEGIC TECHNOLOGICAL LEARNING AT BRISTOM-MYERS SQUIBB

Additional comments by Elander, BMS Vice President, Biotechnology, Fermentation, R&D, follow:

> In our industry, with the enormous up front investments required, the long horizons, and the high risks and uncertainties underlying every major decision, we clearly need to rely on and constantly improve our capacity to learn from the outcomes of our efforts and, in particular, to learn not only from our successes but more importantly from our failures. The benefit of learning from our experiences is very heavily relied on to have a positive influence on our cash flow models and to better understand the risks we try to manage.

> In the initial phase, we rely much more on whether the project under review promises to have good long-term therapeutic fit with our present products pipeline than on any financial criteria.

> In later phases, as we gain experience with the development of the particular project, and thus become more capable to account for the inherent uncertainties and risks in a more quantitative manner, we rely increasingly on NPV methods to prioritize and prune the different projects that are part of our development pipeline portfolio. The process that I am describing consists of several review and decision-making loops that are "activated" on several different levels within our company and at varying frequencies (depending on the strategic import of the decisions being made), and that rely on feedback from our most recent experiences with both internal and external events. By internal events I mean those related to the development of our products pipeline and by external those that originate either at our competitors, academic/hospital laboratories, and/or regulatory (FDA) and legislative bodies.

> *Structured learning*, namely, learning suited to managing a portfolio of drug pipelines that encompasses hundreds of drugs is crucial to our success. Initially (in Phase I), we rely on whether the candidate drugs hold promise for achieving a good strategic or therapeutic fit with the existing drug pipeline they will become part of and the overall portfolio of drug pipelines. Later on (in Phases II and III), financial fit criteria (evidence that allocating resources for a particular drug development will help and not hinder meeting our ROI goals) have also to be met for development to continue.

> Technological learning on all three levels is deemed crucial for our company's success and survival as well, since we operate in a very dynamic, uncertain, and risky environment. We perceive learning within our company as a structured process, that takes place on multiple levels and with varying speeds, depending on the strategic significance and context of the decisions that hinge on the particular learning process. Specifically, I refer to the "feedback loops" that are implemented as part of our management structure and process by means of the different meetings that take place with varying frequencies and involve each different levels of management.

Further comments by Brush (Strategic Planning Staff, BMS) include

Given the enormous up front investments and long lead times required for successful drug development, we put a lot of emphasis on protecting our drug franchises as well as developing franchises of me-too "cash cow" drugs, through continuous, incremental product innovation (such as in the case of AIDS inhibitors). However, once every few years we get a major breakthrough in the course of normal R&D and then of course we try to take full advantage of such radical innovations, for example, the case of the anticancer drug taxol. In those cases, where we are faced with major opportunities that entail substantial risk taking, we rely on both input from our R&D people and worst case, NPV-based scenarios to approve the go ahead.

With the advent of the new BMS president in March 1993, a process of organizational innovation began in earnest to enable BMS to cope with the emerging competitive and regulatory realities. The new president put emphasis on vision, teamwork, unleashing creativity and nurturing organizational "trailblazers" to lead the way to higher competitiveness and cost effectiveness. An effort to reduce the organizational layers at BMS from seven to four began, echoing the chairman of BMS when he commented on the findings of a comprehensive employee survey (from a March 1992 speech to stockholders by BMS CEO):

> Employees felt that there were too many required approvals to get a decision made. There were too many managers for the number of workers. And there were inefficiencies due to unnecessary paper work. ... Our first step was to benchmark ourselves against other major pharmaceutical companies. ... At other majors we found as few as 4 levels...at BMS there are on average seven.... Generally speaking, the recommendations will shorten the chain of command and widen the span of control.

7.3 MILES/BAYER CORP.: MULTINATIONAL, MULTIDISCIPLINARY LEARNING

7.3.1 Overview of Bayer Corp.

Bayer Corp.* (Bayer) is the U.S. subsidiary of Bayer AG, one of the largest chemicals and health care products company worldwide with $32 billion in sales and 148,000 employees in 150 countries in 1998. Bayer Corp. is located in Pittsburgh, Pennsylvania, and is the headquarters for the North America Group.

7.3.2 Major Research and Development Activities and Technological Position

In 1995, Bayer initiated the globalization of its R&D activities. Bayer's U.S. research center in New Haven, Connecticut, was bolstered, and a new center was opened in Japan. This change was a key component in the company's Vision 2010

---

* For nearly 80 years, the name Bayer was not directly associated with Bayer AG in the United States. The U.S. government confiscated in 1916 all the assets of Bayer AG in the U.S. and sold them to Sterling Winthrop Inc., a unit of Eastman Kodak for $5 million in 1919. Following that, Sterling defended its exclusive right to the use of the brand name Bayer in the US and Canada (The Wall Street Journal, August 26, 1992). Therefore, when Bayer AG reestablished its North American operations, it took the name Miles Inc. In 1994, Bayer AG regained control of the Bayer brand name by purchasing Sterling Winthrop, and changed the name of its North American unit to Bayer Corp.

strategy, which defined Bayer's business as a generator of advanced technology. The motivation for the new strategy was to increase the productivity of Bayer's substantial R&D operations, achieving market commercialization faster and improving return on investment (*Pharm. Executive*, October 1995). One strategy adopted was to give worldwide development responsibility for new products to management groups within each of the four regions. As a result, the regions would compete and cooperate with each other to select and fund development projects using technology acquired either from Bayer research or from external sources (*Pharm. Executive*, October 1995).

Bayer has used partnerships and alliances to enter the new genetics-based area of biotechnology. Without significant internal capabilities in this area, Bayer is dependent on cooperation with smaller biotechnology firms to acquire basic technologies:

Mark Yogman (Head of Strategic Planning, Bayer Corp.), in an interview with the author, says:

> Bayer has been involved since the early eighties in the biotechnology field, for example, through cooperation with Genentech. Specifically, 9 years ago it embarked on joint R&D with Genentech, aimed at producing genetically engineered factor VIII, the key component for blood clotting.

> Bayer received final approval from the FDA for its product, in February 1993. This is an instance of the way the company deals with emergent technological paradigms: incremental strategic positioning to acquire new (technological) means to pursue the same (strategic) end (continuity through change): excellence and leadership in markets where the company operates.

Determining maturation of current technologies and emergence of new technologies is a major effort for both strategic and technical management. Yogman of Bayer Corp. further states:

> For part of this effort, we rely on an "internal consulting" process that is mostly conducted by the strategic planning staff. This process consists of a division-based business analysis, which, for instance, determines which divisions incur losses or have below target returns for a series of reporting periods. Thus we reposition our product lines in terms of the degree of maturation of their current underlying technologies (e.g., textile dyestuffs) as well as new, emerging technologies (e.g., new paper dyestuffs, compatible with alkaline paper making).

> The more mature our product lines are, the more cost-driven they become. For example, with certain engineering plastics lines which are relatively new and technology driven, the focus is less on cost considerations and more on meeting customer specifications. Our other polymers lines rely on both, achieving better benefit/cost ratios and on lowering total costs and finally, with our dyestuffs business, a mature line, total cost is of "make-or-break" importance.

7.3.3   MAJOR CORPORATE DEVELOPMENTS AND STRATEGIC DECISION-MAKING FRAME

The main focus of Bayer's long-term strategy is to build the health care sector so that its share of group sales will rise from 22% in 1993 to 30% by the year 2000 (Yogman [Bayer Corp.] interview).

Over the last 2 years, Bayer AG has restructured radically its Diagnostics and Technical Imaging Systems Business Groups both in Europe and the United States to improve efficiency and enhance its competitive position with new product lines. Moreover, the systematic expansion of the worldwide R&D continues, including the pharmaceutical research center in West Haven, Connecticut, that will focus on discovering therapies for Alzheimer's disease, diabetes, and rheumatic disorders.

Bayer has acquired POLYSAR, a Canadian producer of synthetic rubber to complement its own worldwide production capacity of rubber (Bayer actually invented rubber in the early part of the twentieth century). As Yogman says:

> That action again reflects our company's philosophy of expansion, closely related to core areas of activity. It also puts the emphasis on the mode of strategic decision making that we employ: *decentralized*, driven by the division heads with the approval of the board of management (*Vorstand*) sought for the major decisions.

The acquisition of Sterling Winthrop from Eastman Kodak in 1994 also had strategic implications beyond regaining the U.S. rights to the Bayer trademark. The portfolio of Bayer analgesics held by Sterling strengthened Bayer's position in global over-the-counter medications. Concurrent with the acquisition, Bayer announced plans to invest $13 billion in research and capital projects through 1997. At the same time, Bayer's corporate structure was reorganized, with operations grouped by region (Europe, North America, Japan, and rest of the world) and reporting directly to headquarters in Germany. This was followed by a decision to move aggressively into new markets, such as Russia, China, and Latin America.

Another major move featured a change in the job evaluation system at Bayer. Overall, management became more flexible and autonomous after 1995, compared with the previous hierarchical and centralized management culture. Bayer's top leadership decided to emphasize process-, time-, and customer-oriented values in judging employee performance. Team contribution was also given higher significance (*Workforce*, May 1997). Overall, according to Bayer Corp., the firm has adopted a new statement of its corporate values:

Our people
- Rewarding performance with fair and competitive compensation
- Investing in employee professional development and personal growth
- Achieving management diversity by gender, race, and culture
- Encouraging and recognizing outstanding accomplishments

Our business
- Satisfying the requirements of external and internal customers
- Maintaining high ethical standards in all business actions

- Encouraging and supporting among employees' entrepreneurial attitudes, opportunities seeking, and applied creativity
- Managing for the long term

Our organization

- Assuring an organization unencumbered by bureaucracy
- Delegating decision-making authority
- Fostering teamwork and cooperation among organizational units worldwide

Our environment and communities

- Maintaining work environments in which employee health and safety are the highest priorities
- Developing only products that can be manufactured, used, and disposed of in an environmentally responsible way
- Taking an active role in the communities in which we work and live

The secret of Bayer's success lies in a strategy focused on both growth and continuity. The 131-year-old company has been among the most profitable major German companies surpassing in performance such larger giants as BASF and Daimler-Benz and has come to be regarded the star of European chemical companies. As the former chairman of Bayer AG, Hermann J. Strenger put it (*Wall Street Journal*, April 29, 1992):

Continuity is a key touchstone for Bayer's entrepreneurial philosophy…. At Bayer we talk of a contract for generations, in which each new management inherits certain mandates from the past…. To be a good chief executive, it's important to be able to think strategically, to motivate others, and to have a feel for people, trends, and tendencies, whether in business, technology, or politics.

The company's corporate structure encourages such continuity,* since the supervisory board (*Aufsichtsrat*) of Bayer that oversees the chairman's activities has three former chairmen as members. Their presence serves as a bridge to the past that can serve to usher in a less turbulent future for the company than would be the case if radical discontinuities prevailed in the top management succession process. Over the last few years, Bayer has been improving considerably its internationalization and marketing.

In an interview with the author, Yogman, the head of Strategic Planning, Miles/Bayer, says:

Although Bayer has had some international production sites since as early as 1876, a full 50% of its employees and capital investment now are outside Germany, as is 40% of its research and production (*Wall Street Journal*, April 29, 1992).

We assign a lot of importance to the length of top management tenure. For example, I have been head of strategic planning for the last 7 years and had previously another

---

* Another instance of fostering continuity is the case of Mark Yogman, who has been head of strategic planning for Miles for over 7 and with Bayer for over 22 years.

15 years diverse experience within Bayer. The corporate governance of German companies differs substantially from that of American companies. At Bayer, we worry less about quarterly earnings reports than our American counterparts do and we have a more stable shareholder base, so that we are also not concerned with corporate raiders (the corporate pest of the eighties). The board of management (*Vorstand*) consists of only internal to Bayer members and also our outside directors in the supervisory board (*Aufsichtsrat*), such as representatives of the Deutsche Bank, are much more patient and long-term-focused than their American peers. ... this emphasis has as its main objective to enhance the company's capacity to learn from its customers and across different cultures, so as to attain higher economies of scope and cross-fertilization of best practices.

Bayer employs all three modes with its diverse product lines depending on what stage of maturity each line is in: it uses mostly the *reactive* mode for its older, more mature (cash cows) lines of products, such as organic and inorganic chemicals and dyestuffs; the proactive mode for its growing mature lines, such as engineering plastics (injection molding, etc.); and the technology-driven mode for its younger, high growth lines (stars), such as its life sciences product lines (pharmaceuticals, agribusiness, biochemicals, genetic engineering).

7.3.4   EVIDENCE OF STRATEGIC TECHNOLOGICAL LEARNING AT BAYER CORP.

Bayer Corp.'s Yogman further states, in his interview with the author:

In the case of R&D projects that are considered to carry the highest uncertainty, the "seat-of-the-pants-and-faith" or learning-by-doing approach is followed.

In the case of manufacturing projects, short payback methods are used in conjunction with qualitative, experience-based decision making.

Since we have regulated use of materials, we take into account such operating and regulatory costs as well (environmental cost accounting), in all capital planning (as, for example, in the case of a $40 million incineration plant we recently built in the US).

Preliminary decisions for assessing and acquiring new technologies and utilizing technological assets are made at the division head level. Promising fields such as biotechnology, are screened systematically for emerging opportunities. The scientific researchers drive the process and, if they feel that something is a good prospect, they discuss it with the division management. If approved, and its potential is big, it then goes to the board of management for final approval.

The board of management (*Vorstand*) meets twice a month, but with a different composition. Once a month it convenes consisting of the six sector heads plus the head of Miles and the eight regular members of the board of management, and once a month it convenes consisting of the eight board of management members only.

Finally, the supervisory board (*Aufsichtsrat*), including labor representatives and outside directors meets occasionally as the need arises. The chair of the supervisory board is also the past CEO of the company.

Although there is a three-layered structure that guides the decision-making process, strategic decisions are driven by strategic and not financial imperatives. In other words, we "stick to our knitting" and expand into areas or adopt technologies that exhibit a good fit with the activities of one of our existing divisions.

We try to actively learn from our mistakes and failures concerning strategic investments (acquisitions, expansions, etc.). We have institutionalized the process of taking a step back and digesting the lessons learned from our failures, partly via the activities of the strategic planning staff in support of top management. From specific lessons we then try to draw general conclusions that on a continual basis help calibrate and improve Bayer's strategic decision-making process.

7.4   COMPAGNIE DE SAINT GOBAIN SA: GENERATIONAL LEARNING

Saint Gobain Glass Works was founded in France in 1665 by Jean-Baptiste Colbert, the "father" of modern tariff-driven protectionist policies, during the reign of Louis XIV, to provide windows to the Versailles palace. It had expanded into a European multinational by the end of the nineteenth century and is currently one of the top 100 companies in the world. The first foreign plants were established in Germany in 1857, in Italy in 1889, in Spain and Belgium in 1904, in Brazil in 1937, and in the United States in 1967.

After manufacturing under a special charter for more than 150 years in the form of a company with a share capital, Saint Gobain was transformed in 1830 into a public company whose shares were quoted on the Paris Bourse in 1907. Compagnie de Saint Gobain was nationalized in 1982 and was the first to be privatized in 1986.

7.4.1   OVERVIEW OF COMPAGNIE DE SAINT GOBAIN SA

Of the total group sales, 74% are made outside of France or are export sales from France. The company employs more than 100,000 people worldwide with only 30,000 in France. In 1998, Saint Gobain had approximately $20.8 billion in net sales and about $1.2 billion in net income. The company manufactures materials with a high-technological content, emanating from the transformation of abundant raw materials throughout the world and is the world or European leader in each of the areas in which it competes. The Saint Gobain Group is largely decentralized by activity sector and geographic area and each division of the group has its own marketing organization.

Saint Gobain is the world's premier industrial glass manufacturer; moreover, it actively pursues to be the innovation leader in each of its core businesses: flat glass, insulation, glass containers, reinforcement fibers, industrial ceramics, pipe and machinery, building materials, and paper–wood. The company is organized in nine divisions, four of which are specializing in industrial glass (Research, Saint Gobain Group, 1993):

1. *Flat Glass Division* that makes flat glass for the automobile and construction industries
2. *Insulation Division* that produces glass and rock wool insulation products
3. *Containers Division* that makes glass bottles and containers

4. *Fiber Reinforcements Division* that manufactures glass fiber reinforcements
   The other divisions are
5. *Industrial Ceramics Division* that makes industrial ceramics and performance plastics
6. *Abrasives Division* that makes bonded and coated abrasives
7. *Pipe Division* that makes ductile cast iron pipes
8. *Building Materials Division* that produces building materials
9. *Paper–Wood Division* that makes paper and cardboard for packaging as well as wood-based panels

7.4.2 MAJOR RESEARCH AND DEVELOPMENT ACTIVITIES AND TECHNOLOGICAL POSITION

Also from Research, Saint Gobain Group, 1993, the technological core competencies of Saint Gobain pivot around two main areas:

1. Development of a large range of innovative, high-technology products, from thin glass coating to synthetic diamond film or from ceramics fused at an extremely high temperature to glass fibers for reinforcing composite materials
2. Design and implementation of high-performance production tools typical of heavy industry, from the very largest continuous production glass furnaces to machinery for centrifugal casting of large diameter ductile iron pipes.

The Corporate R&D (CR&D) at Saint Gobain has a budget that exceeds 1.4 billion French Francs ($180 million) annually, and it has a staff of 2750 spread among its 34 main development centers in 12 countries: "The CR&D management is committed to the development of human resources, involving itself directly in the recruitment, training, and career paths of permanent staff" (Research, Saint Gobain Group, 1993). Its main goals are

1. *Understanding fundamental problems* means improving basic knowledge of raw materials and processes, embracing the latest scientific and technical breakthroughs, perfecting manufacturing processes to ensure that they remain competitive and reflect state-of-the-art technology, improving products and product reliability, and developing ever more efficient processes. Examples of meeting such a goal are the continuous manufacture of flat glass, manufacture of ductile iron pipes by centrifugal casting, enzyme treatment of pulp, etc.
2. *Creating new products in traditional areas of expertise* is the ongoing creation of new products for Saint Gobain's traditional markets to either meet new needs or satisfy underlying ones. These innovations often transform the market itself, in other words there is "a two-way technological learning interaction between Saint Gobain's core technologies and innovation processes and the market(s) to which the company caters"

(interview, Director of Technological Marketing, Saint Gobain, Paris, France, April 30, 1993). Examples of meeting such a goal are a new kind of glass bottle that blocks out 95% of UV rays, thus improving the storage of wines and champagnes, new cellulose cement composite materials, and heated car windshields fitted with a transparent conducting layer acting as defroster.

3. *Developing new applications and diversifying into related areas* is a means to open new markets. This goal has the highest priority, since "the future survival and success of Saint Gobain relies very much on a continual creation of new markets via the close cooperation of CR&D and marketing as traditional markets become saturated" (interview, Director of Technological Marketing, Saint Gobain, Paris, France). Once new markets are opened with well-known products or their derivatives, a second stage can follow to develop entirely new and innovative products. Examples of new applications are superabsorbent glass blankets to fight sea oil spills, ceramic fibers for reinforcing friction parts in the automobile industry, and high-resistance glass fibers to strengthen multilayer integrated circuit boards.

7.4.3   MAJOR CORPORATE DEVELOPMENTS AND STRATEGIC DECISION-MAKING FRAME

Saint Gobain's global leadership is continuously being enhanced through both focus on technological advances and on the customer: "Saint Gobain is committed to research and believes in a decentralized organization for optimum flexibility while ensuring a coherent approach to the accumulation of collective expertise" (Saint Gobain, 1993). Within this context of strategic focus, Saint Gobain has manufacturing facilities in 20 countries and major licenses in 10 more with 11 major research laboratories and 50 development units worldwide.

Corporate Training and Development (CT&D) programs receive special attention and funding at Saint Gobain. The costs of training represent about 4% of total payroll (Saint Gobain, 1991) and they include such corporate-wide training programs as "Connaissance du Groupe", "Connaissance du Verre et de la Fusion," and l'Ecole de Marketing Industriel: "All these training programs aim at diffusing the corporate culture centered on technological innovation and promote cross-functional and interdivisional technological learning at all levels" (interview with Saint Gobain Director of Technological Marketing, April 30, 1993).

Saint Gobain has begun to restructure its strategic position, developing a crossholding relationship with the utility firm Generale des Eaux. At the same time, Saint Gobain has reduced its cross-holding relationship with Suez Corp., a government-controlled corporation. This indicates that Saint Gobain is positioning itself more strategically with potential investment partners.

7.4.4 EVIDENCE OF STRATEGIC TECHNOLOGICAL LEARNING AT COMPAGNIE DE SAINT GOBAIN SA

Part of Saint Gobain Corporate R&D is dedicated to investing in Saint Gobain's technological future. A significant part of the CR&D budget is spent on new high-performance products to take advantage of emerging markets and fashion new ones. Examples of such long-term projects are holographic imaging within vehicle windshields to provide drivers with high-resolution, head-up displays; glass for high-definition television screens; electrochromic glass whose transparency and color can be adjusted electrically; diamond film used for cutting tools, semiconductor substrates, and highly infrared transmissive radomes; silicon nitride valves and turbochargers for cars, gas turbines, and ceramic bearings; and seeding a gel to produce submicron aluminum crystals for use in high-performance abrasives.

Saint Gobain thus relies on both consistent strategic focus and persistent technological leadership in the competitive arenas that lie within its continuously evolving technology envelope, driven by architectural, radical, generational, and incremental innovation (Utterback and Abernathy, 1975; von Hippel, 1982, 1988; Morone, 1989; Rogers, 1983; Teece, 1987).

8 Electric Power Generation Sector Case Studies (Nuclear Power)

8.1 INDUSTRY OVERVIEW

The current state of affairs for the nuclear power industry is summed up fairly accurately by Nathaniel Woodson, Vice President Energy Systems, Westinghouse Inc. in the following quotes:

> Supplying energy accounts for a major share of human impact on the global environment.... Ensuring a safe, adequate supply of energy without destroying the planet on which we live is a challenge to us all.... However, coal technologies are capital-intensive and contribute to environmental stresses through the release of sulfur dioxide ... if a link is ever confirmed between fossil fuel emissions and global warming or acid rain, continued or increased reliance on coal could come at great cost to society.

> According to a national poll conducted in 1989 by Cambridge Reports, 80% of those surveyed say nuclear energy is important in meeting future electricity needs and more than two-thirds believe that new domestic nuclear plants must be constructed in the years ahead. Those interest groups who oppose nuclear power generally point to what they see as nuclear's unfavorable economics, waste disposal issues, propensity to trigger rate shock from delayed projects, poor management and inadequate emergency preparedness.

8.1.1 THE PRIVATE ENTERPRISE ALTERNATIVE

The current ordeal of the privately owned utilities is not just of a technological nature as they try to find acceptable alternatives to meet the increasing energy needs of the country, but primarily of a financial nature forcing them to think on a much shorter term basis than their mission warrants; according to Woodson of Westinghouse (Marone and Woodson, 1989, p. 217):

> Unfortunately today's regulatory environment forces utilities to focus on short-term economics, influencing planners to avoid new capital expenditures for baseload power generation despite the very real long-term economic disadvantages of that approach.

The private enterprise was chosen as a matter of principle of belief from the beginning of the nuclear era. The preamble of the charter of the Atomic Energy Commission states clearly that: "The development and utilization of atomic energy shall, so far as practicable, be directed towards ... strengthening free competition in private enterprise" (*Atomic Energy Act of 1945*, Public Law No. 79–585, Chapter 724).

The victory of the proponents of private enterprise in the legislative process of setting up the institutional context for the fledgling nuclear power industry can be seen in the 1954 Congress Act: "The goal of atomic power at competitive prices will be reached more quickly if private enterprise, using private funds, is now encouraged to play a far larger role in the development of atomic power." (U.S. Congress, 1954, p. 999).

The United States has the highest nuclear power generation capacity in the world: 110 plants providing 22% of the total power generated, while there are 418 units worldwide providing 17% of the total power generated worldwide, equal to more than half the annual oil production in the Middle East (Atomic Energy Commission of Japan, 1992).

In February 1991, the Bush administration presented the "National Energy Strategy," which aims at achieving energy independence by the year 2010 by relying more on nuclear power and renewable energy resources, and prescribes: (1) the simplification of the licensing procedures concerning nuclear power, (2) promotion of the siting and licensing of high-level radioactive waste disposal facilities, and (3) promotion of the standardized design of light water reactors.

However, as we shall see, the path of reviving the nuclear power option is not an easy one to follow, from designing and constructing nuclear plants, to operating them, and especially to decommissioning of aging plants and disposing of high-level radioactive waste disposal: "Why is dismantling a plant so expensive? Engineers cite the extensive safety training required, the need to rotate workers to limit radiation exposure, and the lengthy planning of every move in contaminated areas.... Nuclear dismantling is made tougher by the plant designs." In addition, "The financial facts of nuclear decommissioning by utilities will usher in an era of lengthy regulatory battles over how much of the costs can be passed along to customers" (*Wall Street Journal*, December 25, 1993). The case of Chernobyl is an extreme case of decommissioning an entombed plant (*Wall Street Journal*, February 4, 1993):

> Even when Chernobyl is shut down completely, nobody knows the best way to dismantle it. Ukraine has announced an international contest to come up with the safest way to dismantle the concrete-entombed fourth block, where the 1986 accident occurred.

Moreover, there are multiple risks that the American private utilities face in designing, constructing, and operating a nuclear power plant. As a result of these risks and of the unexpectedly high cost of plant decommissioning, they are trying to extend the existing plant lifetimes by as much as 20 years, such as in the case of Yankee Rowe plant, which was eventually shut down in February 1992. The Nuclear Regulatory Commission (NRC) has set the lifetime span of a nuclear power plant at 40 years and "allows utilities to wait up to 60 years before they must dismantle a plant that has been taken out of service" (*Wall Street Journal*, January 25, 1993). In Yankee Rowe's case, a lightning storm, in June 1991, almost precipitated reactor flooding that could have led to a meltdown: "The issue at Yankee Rowe and other plants is whether the vessel steel has become so brittle it would crack like glass from the shock of a sudden change in temperature or pressure [such as emergency flooding with cold water]" (*Wall Street Journal*, September 12, 1991). The two following views on situations like the one at Yankee Rowe are diametrically opposed, thus hindering a meaningful dialogue and missing the challenge of moving toward the future with new technologies, according to the following two quotations from the *Wall Street Journal* (September 12, 1991): "Richard Wilson, a Harvard physics professor and member of the pronuclear Scientists and Engineers for Secure Energy, calls industry critics 'irresponsible and inflammatory' because they consider only the worst-case scenario at every turn. Also, "Mr. Randall, the retired NRC metallurgist, says '... the plant's reactor vessel is brittle as hell. You can't just say it is going to be OK if you don't know how bad it is.'"

8.1.2 Public Ownership Alternative

While the economic benefits of choosing the path of private enterprise vs. public ownership can be perhaps easily argued for, one must keep in mind that nuclear power is not just another commodity with the regular time length of horizons inherent in its decision making, but with much longer horizons. Thus, although under public ownership the system is less subject to market forces and subsidy of inefficient power may take place (Morone and Woodhouse, 1989, p. 116):

> ... such a subsidy for nuclear power, although inefficient in a narrow economic sense, might be efficient from a broader, societal perspective. Nuclear power plants do bring public good with them: a diversified base for energy security and a reduced dependence on coal, especially important in a period of growing concern about the greenhouse effect and acid rain. *Or, to state it more formally, the price of electricity generated using fossil fuel fails to reflect the entire price that society will eventually pay in coping* with the externalities [emphasis added].

What Morone and Woodhouse are referring to here is environmental cost accounting. Moreover, to the greenhouse effect one should also add the costs of conflicts such as the 1991 Persian Gulf War with its $60 billion plus price tag and the associated loss of human life, as well as the long-term damage to the environmental integrity of the Persian Gulf natural habitat due to the huge oil spills. After such accounting is instituted, one cannot be as unequivocal about which is "the least of all evils;" and the price of public passivity, namely, insufficient scrutiny and weighing of complex technological choices with long term impact, becomes unacceptably high.

We conducted studies of varying length and detail of both private and state-owned utilities in the United States, Canada, and France shown in Table 8.1. We focused on the process and content of the management of complex technologies in three different cultures and the role of technological learning (Dodgson, 1991; Carayannis, 1992a, 1993, 1994a, 1994b, 1994c) for these utilities, both internally and in their interaction with the oversight agencies (World Association of Nuclear Operators [WANO], Nuclear Regulatory Commission [NRC], Institute of Nuclear

Power Operations [INPO], Nuclear Management Research Commission [NUMARC], etc.).

The Niagara Mohawk (NIMO) study, in particular, was a three year long ethnographic study, where the company's process of transforming its culture and management style under considerable pressure, both regulatory and market driven, was studied. The regulatory pressure emanated from unsatisfactory safety performance of NIMO's nuclear power plants that led to lengthy plant closedowns with huge cost implications for the company. The market-driven pressures emanated from the Six Cents Law requiring NIMO to purchase at a preset price (higher than its own cost of energy generation) any power produced by *independent power producers* (IPs) or *nonutility generators* (NUGs), as well as cogeneration plants constructed by many of NIMO's industrial customers aimed at reducing their consumption of NIMO-generated power. Finally, an overall trend toward deregulating the power generation arena means radical and tremendous changes for the utilities, both sheltered from competition and encumbered in their efforts to transform themselves by existing regulatory oversight.

TABLE 8.1
Case Study Utilities

Utility	Nuclear Power Plant
Consolidated Edison (ConEd) Corp.	Indian Point II
Duke Power Corp.	Oconee, McGuire, and Catawba
Rochester Gas and Electric (RG&E) Corp.	GINNA
	Nine-Mile Point Unit 2
	(cotenant with Niagara Mohawk)
Tennessee Valley Authority	Various
Ontario Hydro	Various
Electricité de France	Various

8.2   CONSOLIDATED EDISON CORP.

8.2.1   OVERVIEW OF CONSOLIDATED EDISON CORP.

Consolidated Edison (ConEd) Corp. is an investor-owned utility in the New York City area. It services the smallest franchised area in New York State but it meets the energy needs of the largest customer base with 3.9 million residential, commercial, and industrial customers (2.9 million electric power and 1 million natural gas customers), covering a franchise area of only 604 sq mi. The sources for the electric generation are nuclear, oil, and natural gas. In 1999, ConEd had $15.5 billion in assets and $7.5 billion in sales of which approximately $6.0 billion came from electrical power services.

The Indian Point II nuclear power plant is the only nuclear power plant of ConEd licensed for commercial operation. It is located in the Bear Mountain region of upstate New York. The initial announcement for the construction of this nuclear power plant was made in late 1965 and the actual construction began in late 1966. The construction took 7 years and was commissioned in 1973, but was not fully operational until early 1974. The Indian Point II nuclear power plant is a medium size facility that generates 864 MW of electrical power.

ConEd also owns Indian Point I that is actually used for noncommercial purposes, such as operation and safety training.

Indian Point II accounts for 9.2% of the installed electrical capacity of ConEd. The plant has 310 employees whereas the total workforce of ConEd is about 19,000 employees. That means that 1.6% of the personnel are responsible for 9.2% of the installed capacity of ConEd.

On the other hand, during 1990, Indian Point II generated 28% of all the electricity produced by ConEd (ConEd, 1990); thus, in terms of electricity generation, 2.6% of the corporate personnel were responsible for a very large share of the principal service provided by the corporation.

8.2.2 MAJOR RESEARCH AND DEVELOPMENT ACTIVITIES AND TECHNOLOGICAL POSITION

In 1995, New York's state-owned utility and six investor-owned utilities successfully pooled their research and development (R&D) resources as members of the Empire State Electric Energy Research Corp. (Eseerco), New York, New York. The seven Eseerco members are the state-owned New York Power Authority; Consolidated Edison Co. of New York Inc.; Orange and Rockland Utilities Inc.; Central Hudson Gas & Electric Corp.; New York State Electric & Gas (NYSEG) Corp.; Rochester Gas & Electric (RG&E) Corp.; and Long Island Lighting Co. (Lilco). The collaboration enables the participants to invest in large-scale research projects and jointly share the benefits. For example, a system developed by Eseerco was used by ConEd to conduct the first full-scale chemical decontamination of an operating commercial nuclear power plant, the Indian Head 2 reactor. ConEd has conducted regular assessments of the benefits of participation in R&D consortia, such as Eseerco and the Electric Power Research Institute (EPRI), and has found that it derives significant benefits from these groups. Consortium-based approaches such as this are becoming more important, as companies cut their R&D budgets to become more cost competitive in this era of impending deregulation.

8.2.3 MAJOR CORPORATE DEVELOPMENTS AND STRATEGIC DECISION-MAKING FRAME

ConEd's mission is to "provide reliable electric service at a competitive cost, in an environmentally compatible manner, while producing a fair return for our stockholders." (ConEd, 1990, p. 4). A major step toward realizing its mission is the Enlightened Energy Program, started in 1990 with the objective of involving the public in the drive for more productive and environmentally safer power generation for New York City and Westchester County.

The Indian Point II nuclear power plant is the only operational power unit of the nuclear division of ConEd. The following general outline of the Indian Point II power plant organization was obtained in an interview conducted on the plant site with the plant management.

8.2.3.1   Organizational Structure

The parent company structure is function oriented. However, Indian Point II is organized to resemble a hybrid organizational structure. The plant is divided into three departments, and each department head reports directly to the vice president of nuclear power. They are

1. Nuclear Power Generation
2. Technical Services
3. Administrative Services

The vice president for nuclear power is responsible for the overall operation of Indian Point II, and the office for this position is located at the headquarters of ConEd in New York City. Our finding was that there is no one permanently on site responsible to manage and coordinate the activities of the three department heads at the plant site on a day-to-day basis.

In addition to the departmental structure, the organization also uses project or matrix-type structures on a temporary basis to accomplish a given project. The decision to use a matrix structure or project structure for a given project depends on its complexity and the length of time it takes to accomplish the task. In general, projects are carried out in three ways. First, if the project is small enough to be handled with plant personnel, a project team is formed in a matrix-type structure. Second, if the project is bigger and complex, a project team is created with fully dedicated personnel until the project is completed. Finally, if the project is even bigger and too complex to be managed with the plant's resources, a corporate level department of project management takes responsibility for the project and uses their own staff.

Even though departments are designed to accomplish distinct functions, there exists a great deal of interdependence among departments that management defines as "systems synergy" that they try to enhance at all levels of the organization. Therefore, the organization tries to reduce, if not eliminate, any communication barriers by encouraging both formal and informal communications vertically and horizontally. To achieve the goal of open communication, department managers meet weekly on a permanent basis; they also communicate freely two or three times a day or as many times as necessary to discuss problems or concerns. There are also monthly structured meetings among managers and supervisors. Top management tries to increase communication between personnel, and they take into consideration such factors as plant geography and even office arrangement to improve communication.

Corporate top management continuously visits the plant. The vice president for nuclear power visits the site once or twice a week, and the president of ConEd visits the plant once or twice a year.

Managers at different levels of the organization are authorized to spend up to a specified amount of money prior to receiving approval from higher authority. This amount ranges up to $2 million for the vice president for nuclear power and up to $500 million for the President and CEO. These monetary limits define the scope and level of decision-making authority of managers at different positions.

The span of control for upper and middle level managers is a narrow one ranging from 4 to 8. However, for supervisory level personnel the span of control goes as high as 19 or 20.

The goal of this corporation is to "produce electricity cleanly, efficiently and safely" (ConEd, 1988). The evolution of these goals can be observed (ConEd, 1990):

> Consolidated Edison recently reevaluated its long-range plan for the electric system. The plan has five goals: to continue to provide reliable service at reasonable cost, to earn an adequate return for stockholders, to keep Con Edison service competitive, to limit dependence on foreign oil, and to maintain flexibility to respond to changing conditions. The plan calls for continuing our power plant life-extension program and our emphasis on conservation and demand management.

In the same reference it is mentioned that even though the steam generators of Indian Point II need replacement, this upgrading will be delayed as long as possible, in spite of the fact that the new steam generators are already on site, ready to be installed. The replacement work would cost around $127 million and would take about 6 months to complete. This reflects the fact that funds for upgrading facilities are restricted.

Indian Point II is managed by objectives (MBO), set by corporate and plant top management at the beginning of each fiscal year. All managers are supposed to make their goals for the year in advance, and create a new file that contains all the goals that must be met during the year. Top management considers the plant as a product-oriented organization; however, they do not have direct contact with the consumers of their product.

8.2.3.2 Human Resource Management

All positions are filled with very skilled personnel, and there are specific job descriptions for each position. Each job description not only specifies the requirements to fill the position, but also includes the responsibility, reporting relationship and accountability involved.

MBO is used at each level of the organization. At the beginning of each fiscal year, each employee sits with his/her manager and together they establish and agree on the goals that must be achieved. Then each employee is assigned a certain goal or goals corresponding to the section or departmental goals, and progress is reviewed on a weekly basis. At the end of the year the achievement of assigned goals is used to evaluate employees' job performance. These performance evaluations are the basis for raises as well as for promotion consideration.

Personnel in the operations department enter at two different levels: on the first level are engineers and on the second level are reactor operators and plant technicians.

1. Engineers — Engineers who become certified as watch engineers must undergo an 18-month training to qualify and be certified as watch engineers by the NRC.
2. Reactor operators and plant technicians — They enter as trainees and usually are high school graduates without a formal college education. However, they must pass a written comprehensive examination to be accepted into the program. Once accepted into the program, they will undergo 7 to 12 years of training, depending on ability, to be certified as senior reactor operators. It takes less time to qualify as a plant technician or as an entry level reactor operator.

There is a well-established policy to promote from within the organization. Positions are filled from outside the organization only if there are no qualified individuals within ConEd. This policy assures employees that if a vacancy exists within the organization, they are to be given the first opportunity for assignment and they have the opportunity for growth within the organization. To ensure that employees have a wide breadth of experience the organization allows lateral moves. For example, those employees who are qualified in an operations area can move laterally to the support area as instructors in their specialty, or work in technical services in a related field. In fact, many employees have experience and training in more than one functional area.

Each year the reactor operators are evaluated by the NRC, and to retain their license they must pass a very detailed written examination of procedures and scenario testing in the plant simulator. This also means that the operators must spend about 6 weeks in training every year. At the managerial level, there is no dual managerial–technical career path, and top management positions can be filled by either operations or staff managers.

ConEd has an established employee recognition program to acknowledge deserving employees on a monthly basis. One of the ways they recognize an employee is having an employee-of-the-month parking space very close to where they work and there is a prominent sign to indicate that it is reserved for such an employee. Another way they recognize employees is by awarding from $100 to $15,000 for employee suggestions that are implemented by the organization. The amount of the award is based on an analysis of the cost efficiencies achieved or by its contribution to plant safety. Therefore, employees are encouraged to participate in improvements of operations and working conditions.

The employee turnover at Indian Point II power plant is about 5%. Management believes that it is a healthy turnover rate and allows them to get new talent at a steady rate.

8.2.3.3 Strategic Environment

Change can be initiated by a change in technology, by a change of rules and procedures by NRC, by other environmental factors, or from within the organization to improve efficiency or safety of plant operation.

The organization has a procedure to handle changes initiated internally. This program is called Consolidated Improvement Program (CIP). Any suggestion for improving procedures and for safe operation of the plant has to go through CIP. Suggestions submitted by employees have to be evaluated by systems engineers for feasibility and an estimate to be made of the probable improvements that could be achieved if the suggestions are adopted. Once the system engineer submits his/her analysis to the CIP committee, it decides if the suggestion should be implemented after coordination with all parties affected by the change. Therefore, adoption of change requires a commitment by all affected parties.

Whether the change is initiated internally or externally, it must go through the five stages of change process, and all changes that the organization makes are assessed with respect to the safety of the plant. For example, because of the 1979 Three-Mile Island accident, the organization has made several changes resulting in the expansion of the contingency planning section from one person to nine. In addition, another layer in the reporting chain was added by establishing a watch engineer position in every shift. Furthermore, they have made certain that every member of the organization has a role to play should there be a need to mobilize a contingency team.

Because of technological change and inability of the current simulator to meet their training requirements, the corporation has undertaken the construction of a new training simulator facility at a cost of $38 million. The current system is 20 years old; although it has gone through two upgrades, it still does not meet their training needs. Top management felt that it would be more effective to construct a new facility than to continue to upgrade the existing one. Westinghouse has the contract to build the new simulator. The project is being monitored by a project team of ten people. This is an example of an ad hoc structure created to deal with the specific project and to be disbanded after the project is completed.

Finally, nuclear fuel is replaced annually. This operation lasts for 3 months; and a completely new department is established to carry out that job, and any other responsibility that arises during the refueling period, with a temporary assigned fuel-change resident–manager. Coordinators are designated for each of the areas involved, who are responsible for each activity before, during, and after the work has been completed.

The management of Indian Point II perceives the environment of the corporation and especially the nuclear power station to be stable. The NRC monitors the plant continuously by using two permanent on-site inspectors that carry out prescheduled regulatory evaluation procedures. The plant is also evaluated formally once a year by different NRC inspectors. Plant managers believe that meeting the NRC requirements is only the minimum safety requirement; hence, they strive to maintain an even higher safety standard. In that sense, the regulations laid down by NRC, INPO, Environmental Protection Agency (EPA), etc. are not a serious environmental concern, because the internal corporate standards are more stringent.

There is a concerted effort to maintain good community relations because management realizes the strategic importance of public opinion as it can affect the future of ConEd. There are three different offices in charge of public relations and external relationships with governmental agencies (NRC, Department of Environmental

Conservation [DEC], EPA, Occupational Safety and Health Administration [OSHA], etc.) and other power utilities and organizations (NUMARC, INPO, environmentalists, etc.). These offices report directly to corporate headquarters. The plant management actively participates in local community activities (civic affairs, clubs, chamber of commerce, etc.).

The corporation is a member of INPO, the industry safety monitoring agency, that complements NRC's monitoring and reports its results only to the senior management of each utility. As all the other utilities in New York State, it is also a member of the New York Power Pool (NYPP).

8.2.4 EVIDENCE OF STRATEGIC TECHNOLOGICAL LEARNING AT CONSOLIDATED EDISON

ConEd is developing a clear pattern of strategic directions for its future business. One lesson learned is the importance of scale and concentration in the increasingly competitive electricity distribution industry. In 1998, the company bought Orange and Rocklands, a neighboring electricity utility. In late 1999, the company announced a merger with Northeast Utilities to create the largest electricity distribution firm in the United States.

ConEd also continues to engage in cooperative R&D with its competitors in the New York area and nationwide to gain access to new technologies. The company has developed a methodology to assess the advantage it has achieved from cooperative research, and is able to analyze which technologies have contributed to corporate performance.

Still, in its nuclear power operations, it appears that performance continues to lag behind promise. At the Indian Head 2 reactor, the NRC has found that safety problems have continued since a series of concerns were identified in 1993, and that overall safety practices have declined. In 1998, the company incurred over $400,000 in fines from the NRC for safety violations. ConEd is now pursuing a possible sale of the power plant.

8.3 DUKE POWER CORPORATION

8.3.1 OVERVIEW OF DUKE POWER CORP.

Duke Power is headquartered in Charlotte, North Carolina, and supplies electricity to more than 1.7 million residential, commercial, and industrial customers in a 20,000 sq mi service area. It was founded 90 years ago and is currently the seventh largest investor-owned electric utility in the United States. Duke Power operates 3 nuclear-generating, 8 coal-fired, and 27 hydroelectric stations; and produced 79,000 MWh of electricity in 1992. Duke Energy Corp., the parent of Duke Power, earned a total of $4.5 billion from electrical power sales in 1998, with an overall net income of $1.5 billion.

8.3.2   MAJOR RESEARCH AND DEVELOPMENT ACTIVITIES AND TECHNOLOGICAL POSITION

Duke's power generation plants are actually somewhat out of date, but supported by other technologies that more than compensate. For example, Duke Power makes extensive use of advanced communications technologies to support its operations. Duke Power uses three Windows-based desktop videoconferencing systems from Incite, a division of telecommunications equipment firm Intecom, at both McGuire and Catawba nuclear plants. One system is located in each plant's technical support center, which is responsible for evaluating potential emergencies. That system links to two other desktop systems in each plant's operations support center, which directs the actions taken to respond to the situation, based on the technical support center's evaluation.

Each system connects to Duke's fiber backbone network via an Incite Multimedia Hub that integrates voice, video, and data. To manage the desktops, there's a Windows NT server at each site — Catawba, McGuire, and the Emergency Operations Facility — loaded with Incite's Multimedia Manager server software. Duke needs only one server to operate the system; the others are failover systems. Fortunately for Duke, the videoconferencing system has been used primarily for safety drills five to six times a year.

8.3.3   MAJOR CORPORATE DEVELOPMENTS AND STRATEGIC DECISION-MAKING FRAME

Duke Power top management assigns very high importance to education and especially quality improvement training programs (1992 was named the Year of Education). These programs aim at providing all employees with a common quality language and tools that enable them to continuously improve quality, customer satisfaction, and lower costs. These achievements are of strategic importance to Duke Power, because with the passage of the Energy Policy Act in 1992, competition has been and is expected to continue intensifying greatly. Responding to this heightened degree of competitive rivalry among utilities in quest of market share, Duke Power's strategic focus pivots around the following seven points (Duke Power, 1993, pp. 5–12):

Customer satisfaction — to understand and meet our customers' expectations
Financial management — to manage the business to increase value and lower costs
Nuclear excellence — to safeguard and serve the public with our nuclear investment
Expanding business opportunities — to profitably use our strengths to serve a variety of customers and enhance developmental opportunities for employees
Environmental leadership — to provide leadership to maintain a sustainable environment
Team Excellence — to prepare the team to achieve excellent business results and reward success
Excellence management philosophy — to implement the excellence management philosophy throughout our business.

In 1994, the company was split into two primary divisions: the electricity generation and distribution unit, Duke Power; and a unit to pursue new ventures in energy project development, communications, and other related businesses. The company also downsized in preparation for impending price competition in its electricity business. Duke Power has now formed numerous partnerships to leverage its resources in new businesses, such as managing outsourced power plant on behalf of cities and private companies. One move is the acquisition of Pan-Energy to create one of the largest combined natural gas and electricity energy firms in the United States.

On the nuclear side, the three stations of Duke Power—Oconee, McGuire, and Catawba—operated at 90% of capacity in 1995, well above the U.S. industry average of just over 78%. Duke Power nuclear system is the second largest in the United States, with the seven units totaling 7054 MW of capacity, of which the firm owns 5078 MW. Duke Power runs the two, 1129 MW reactors at the Catawba station, but only owns 25% of Unit 1. The nuclear plants account for 30% of the utility's installed capacity, but because of their high capacity factor, they generated 54% of Duke Power net electricity in 1995.

For Duke Power's nuclear businesses (three nuclear stations with seven reactors), taking a new look at workforce planning has made a lot of sense in staffing for the future. A key reason why the nuclear units needed a better handle on staffing has resulted from the business downsizing over the past 5 years. In addition to downsizing its other businesses, Duke Power has reduced the number of staff in the nuclear business from 5800 to 4350 people since 1991.

At the company's McGuire nuclear plant, a new philosophy called teamwork, quality, and persistence (TQP) has helped to boost performance. TQP has propelled McGuire to its fastest and most efficient refueling ever. The T—or teamwork—part of it starts at the top, with the plant's work control organization, which is responsible for outage management. It includes daily exercises for the maintenance workers who want to participate in stretching and aerobics, to ready them for the day's activities and to let them know that the company is concerned about their well-being.

Under the Q—quality—category of TQP, Duke Power has for a few years been putting into place a total quality management process. The process has affected all levels of the company. The final letter of TQP—P for persistence—means simply staying the course to attain the desired quality of the job. The McGuire team is proud that it both scheduled and executed a recently refueling outage in 48 days.

8.3.4   Evidence of Strategic Technological Learning at Duke Power

In 1992, Duke Power created the Corporate Performance Review Committee to offer policy recommendations for improving performance and supporting the company's emphasis on *continuous quality improvement*. The committee consists of four members of the board of directors from outside the company. Duke Power aims at being within the top 25% of companies applying for the Malcolm Baldrige National Quality Award by 1996 (Duke Power, 1993, pp. 5–12).

Plant operators and technicians receive most significant input from impact of actions on plant operations. Direct and immediate feedback is reflected in change of plant operating indications as a result of control manipulations. This results in immediate training on outcomes of actions and directly reinforces training received in classrooms or on simulators. Simulators are effective in training for evolutions not encountered frequently or for severe conditions not experienced in actual plant operations.

Other means, such as review of operating experience, also provide learning opportunities but are much less effective than firsthand experiences. Frequent review of operating events and use of detailed procedures incorporating operating experience items are used to compensate for complexity of equipment and operator inability to assimilate all experiences.

Shift supervisors and plant engineers receive the majority of plant information from direct observations and results of routine equipment performance monitoring. Investigation of equipment problems is formalized so that lessons learned are widely available. Human performance issues are also captured in formal programs that can be used to capture increasingly adverse trends.

Plant and utility management personnel typically receive their information from performance reports that provide operating data and trends on a wide range of indicators ranging from plant electrical production to human performance issues. Outside organizations, such as the NRC, and liability insurance companies, as well as INPO, provide independent assessments of performance.

Deviations from targeted safety norms are documented in a variety of programs to ensure that appropriate lessons are learned, procedures are effectively modified, and training is updated to reflect the new experiences acquired. A formal computerized problem tracking and trending system, the problem investigation process (PIP), is employed to allow first-line employees to quickly identify problems to be further evaluated by professional staff.

Operators and technicians have the responsibility to promptly correct any operational problem that adversely affects safety or reliability. This is performed using input from computer monitoring of plant operations for various systems and control board indications. Shift supervisors and engineering staff also may use this direct means but may rely on PIP process for identifying longer term trends that may indicate a slowly developing problem. Plant and utility management can rely mainly on trend reporting and operating statistics to gather information about adverse trends and track completion of corrective actions that can rectify problems. From a nuclear safety standpoint, the actions of the control board operators are the first line of defense against any potential safety problem that is not immediately resolved by automatic protection systems. A great deal of emphasis is placed on training and development for plant operators so they can address effectively any safety issues occurring. Monitoring of plant operations by engineering and management can help resolve any slowly developing trends especially in reliability and economy issues.

The root cause of operational events is normally part of the review and analysis process for any operational problem, especially events that directly affect plant operations or reliability. The industry maintains an extensive database of equipment failures through the Nuclear Plant Reliability Data System (NPRDS), managed by

INPO. This system serves to encapsulate and organize in a readily usable format for utility and plant management, based on years of operational experience and equipment failure case histories, for aiding in diagnostic root cause* analysis and for learning from past experience for preventive action. The data can be sorted by equipment type, service conditions, vendors, etc. to fully evaluate past events in all U.S. plants. Plant maintenance uses this information to establish preventive maintenance schedules and equipment inspections. Human performance issues are also tracked by Duke Power as part of the PIP; in addition, operating experience reports from INPO, NRC (on a nationwide basis), and WANO (on a worldwide basis) are used to help identify human-related root causes and prevent the reoccurrence of human-triggered significant events. Thus, emphasis is put on identifying corrective actions from the national and global nuclear power operations experience that should be incorporated into routine plant procedures and training schedules to improve safety, reliability, and economy.

Analysis of equipment failure data has allowed the development of computerized monitoring systems that can detect impending failures so that operators can be alerted to take corrective actions long before a level is reached where automatic control systems would be triggered. Large rotating equipment, such as turbines, large motors, and emergency generators, all now have such monitoring systems attached, which can trend, identify problems, and in some cases even suggest corrective actions much earlier than ever before. These diagnostic-type systems have greatly enhanced the operators' ability to monitor equipment performance and learn from experience quickly enough so that corrective action can avoid the interruption of operations with its inherent very high costs in the case of nuclear power plants.

On a longer term basis, worldwide performance monitoring parameters have been accepted by the industry, and plant operating data are being supplied by virtually all nuclear operators around the world. This can greatly help in global benchmarking of best practices, as well as the worst performers from a global perspective of performance parameters preventing group think-style plant or utility management myopia. In short, it facilitates intra- and interorganizational learning from performance success and failure for utility and plant management.

Long-term deviations from targeted norms are identified through formal plant performance monitoring and industry-wide monitoring. Engineering staffs use this information to develop long-range plans for plant modifications or operational procedure changes to prevent recurrence of events. While safety and reliability issues have been the main focus of these analyses in the past, the economy dimension is currently also being emphasized, because of deregulatory trends (such as the 1992 intensifying cost- and value-driven competition among utilities). Thus, economic and cost-efficiency monitoring has increased and culminates in benchmarking against industry performance leaders that drives a continuous improvement process. One of the major means for implementing this process is a formal task-based qualifications system incorporating continually updated training and development

---

* A *root cause* is defined as a fundamental cause that, if corrected, will prevent occurrence/recurrence of an event.

requirements that ensures personnel are kept current with cutting edge technologies and operational experiences learned at all nuclear power plants.

Monitoring of plant performance on an industry-wide basis with the ten performance indicators currently defined by INPO has allowed a consistent comparison of plant operational performance. This has made possible the identification of the best performers and has enabled all plants to emulate and learn from the success of others by quantifying this success and thus facilitating its incorporation in all plant processes and procedures. Industry peer reviews, conducted by INPO, moreover, have helped identify opportunities for improvement (OFI) in a wide range of plant operational areas, thus further promoting shared learning by doing and the institutionalization of innovative best practices across the industry.

The number of equipment failures has been drastically reduced in many areas thanks to the collection and analysis of relevant data by the NPRDS program. Manufacturers have used these data to take preventive corrective action with, for instance, equipment design problems; and the nuclear operators have benefited from NPRDS insights to prevent and avoid significant events. The NPRDS thus serves as a tool for continuously improving the design of machine and human interfaces as well as the learning from experience mechanisms embedded in operating, maintenance, and monitoring procedures.

The most effective means to ensure learning at this level is through shift meetings for the operators and group meetings for the technicians. Immediate measures are recorded and exchanged from one shift to the next, but overall impacts to the station location are discussed and analyzed within these weekly meetings. The operators and technicians also are very much involved with feedback to the station engineers used to change procedures and guidelines. Both operators and technicians are encouraged to initiate draft incident reports, which are used to analyze and document nonroutine equipment operations. Operators and technicians also are encouraged to provide the input used to change the operator qualification program to reflect operational changes that ensure the qualification package remains current and reliable as a determinant of successful operator performance.

The shift supervisors coordinate with the plant engineers to upgrade operational policies and procedures to reflect current operational conditions and improvements. The shift supervisors and plant engineers work jointly on investigation reports of abnormal operational incidents. These reports are often distributed *company-wide* for review. Both of these groups of individuals are normally involved with certain major equipment user groups that review practices and analyze abnormal incidents. Changes to the operator training policies and procedures are initiated at the shift supervisor/plant engineer level. Both groups are actively involved with the station location continuous improvement team (CIT).

There is such a team resident at each station and it puts primary emphasis on such areas as incident investigation, root cause analysis, and improved operational methods and procedures. Plant engineers in conjunction with general office engineers are actively involved with industry activities/organizations through such means as the EPRINET and EEI-RISE computer networks. Both shift supervision and plant engineering personnel coordinate closely with general office engineering support organizations. This helps ensure consistent, focused approaches throughout the Duke

Power generation system. Operational information exchange between station locations is much more easily attained thanks to the PROFS electronic mail system, over which questions can be easily and quickly dispatched to all stations triggering immediate real-time feedback.

Operational information is shared at the plant management level through the use of functional area meetings (FAMs) and quality steering teams (QSTs). Information and lessons learned are distributed at each of these meetings. Continuous improvement is the primary focus of these groups, not only in operations, but also throughout the entire system including both the particular power station and the corporation itself. Plant and utility management are also involved with national user groups for major equipment design and operation.

The primary areas of focus of such groups are generic operational problems and enhancements. The EPRI and the Edison Electric Institute (EEI) committees provide invaluable information and feedback at both the plant and the utility management levels. This information is shared organization-wide to facilitate learning from the industry-wide experiences.

All employees participate in an incentive goals program to help ensure improvement in such areas as unit availability, safety, etc. All station locations have monthly performance meetings, as well as quarterly performance meetings coordinated with the general office operations and performance areas.

The general office performance area tracks and trends current performance data/indicators, and publishes quarter performance reports that are distributed organization-wide to facilitate learning from experience throughout Duke Power. Both station location and department strategic plans are dynamic and reflect current expectations and future projections.

The company's nuclear division also adopted a new approach to human resources. Instead of continuing to hire high school graduates who typically had filled nonlicensed operator positions in the past, the company decided to recruit and hire technical school graduates or ex-Navy nuclear operators instead. These were people who already had some advanced experience or affinity for nuclear operations. The plan is expected to significantly shorten the training path from nonlicensed operator to licensed senior reactor operator. By the end of 1996, Duke Power will have hired a total of 45 employees in this way since 1994. The company also is working with university engineering students prior to graduation to prepare them for careers in Duke Power nuclear operations.

At all levels, the answer is the same. Duke Power, as part of its continuous improvement quality evolution, is incorporating benchmarking as one of its primary tracking/trending/learning tools. Industry data can be used throughout the process as external indications of our process and success. Both predictive and preventive measures can also be used for continuous improvement.

8.4 ROCHESTER GAS & ELECTRIC CORP.

8.4.1 OVERVIEW OF ROCHESTER GAS & ELECTRIC CORP.

RG&E is an investor-owned utility that supplies electric and gas service wholly within the state of New York in a nine-county area centering around Rochester, New York. The RG&E franchised area has about 900,000 residents and caters to residential, commercial, and industrial customers. The energy sources for electricity generation are hydroelectric, nuclear, fossil (oil and coal), and natural gas.

In 1999, RGS Energy Group, the parent company to RG&E, had $2.5 billion in assets and $1.2 billion in sales. RG&E has given emphasis on demand side management programs as well as purchasing energy from third-party generation (independent power producers), to avoid embarking on new power plants construction.

RG&E fully owns and operates the GINNA nuclear power plant and is a cotenant with 14% participation at the Nine-Mile Unit 2 nuclear power plant operated by Niagara Mohawk. The GINNA plant is a pressurized water reactor (PWR) of 515 MW electrical installed capacity, and the ownership of Nine-Mile Unit 2 adds to 14% of the total installed capacity of 1080 MW resulting in 150 MW of additional electrical capacity. This means that 50% of the electricity installed capacity of RG&E is nuclear. For 1989, the total amount of nuclear electricity generated was 4016 GWh corresponding to 60% of the total electricity generated. The share of nuclear electricity generation could have been much higher if it where not for the low availability of Nine-Mile Point Unit 2.

By focusing only on the performance of the GINNA plant, it is possible to realize that 478 people generated approximately 3600 GWh, representing an average of 7.5 GWh per employee.

The information for RG&E was obtained from company annual reports as well as from interviewing the two top managers at the nuclear division of the firm.

8.4.2 MAJOR CORPORATE DEVELOPMENTS AND STRATEGIC DECISION-MAKING FRAME

As shown in an RG&E document (May 1989), the corporate mission is "… to be the preeminent private utility in New York State operating as an effective supplier of energy and related services by optimizing customer satisfaction, investor return, and employee achievement."

The nuclear division mission statement stresses the points of improving safety, reliability, and economy by providing employees with a challenging and safe environment that rewards high-quality performance and creativity. The 5-year goals for the nuclear division hinge on the following aspects: quality, public safety, personnel safety, regulatory compliance, reliability and economy. The results achieved up to date by following those goals are reflected in the following excerpts from RG&E (1990, p. 2): "Last year in our letter to you in our annual report we said that we entered the new decade in pretty good shape, all things considered." Furthermore, RG&E (May 1989) states:

Our GINNA power plant again had another excellent year of operation with an availability factor of 84% for 1990. ... Along with excellent production levels at our GINNA
power plant, we are very pleased that inspections and reviews at that plant by the
Federal Nuclear Regulatory Commission (NRC), in 1990 found improvement in many
areas of operation ...

In the words of one of the interviewees, RG&E has been "a quiet performer,"
which means that it has not had to deal with any crises of a nature similar to those
facing Niagara Mohawk. Their GINNA plant, which produces over half of the RG&E
customer electric requirements, has been consistently performing at excellent levels
(75.5% average availability factor for the last 10 years as compared with 59.8%
average for the state of New York for the same period) and hence management has
been taking mostly proactive measures trying to improve on their good record.

That resolve has been further enhanced by their experience with the Nine-Mile
Point Unit 2 plant, managed by Niagara Mohawk, which is under increased monitoring by the NRC. This experience has provided them with useful information
relating to moves they should avoid taking or on which they should focus more.
Starting in July 1988, RG&E developed its own strategic business plan, with the
encouragement of the new senior Vice President of nuclear operations.

RG&E has also embarked on a program of continuous improvement to prevent
most of the potential problems that might cause a regulatory intervention. Another
step taken in the direction of improving performance and safety at the GINNA plant
is a steady increase in the number of employees working at the plant since 1985,
growing from 330 to an expected steady state of 591 in 1992 — an increase of
approximately 80%.

This change in personnel size came as a result of a study conducted to match
the size of the plant with the appropriate number of staff, taking into consideration
industry information; according to the executives interviewed this increase in personnel can also improve training.

The nuclear division has undergone a relatively minor reorganization and is now
headed by a vice president, whereas the fossil and hydroelectric operations are still
under a division manager. This change reflects the increased attention given to
nuclear operations. However, this reorganization was far less drastic than the one
that took place at Niagara Mohawk, mostly because the former was of a proactive
while the latter was of a reactive nature, and also because the existing organizational
structures at RG&E were performing satisfactorily.

The poor performance of Nine-Mile Point Unit 2 has hampered the realization
of the RG&E goals to make nuclear power the main source of energy for the
corporation. This concern is expressed in the 1990 annual report (RG&E, 1990,
p. 3): "The performance of the Nine-Mile Point Unit 2 nuclear power plant has fallen
short of our expectations in 1990. The 1,080,000-kilowatt plant had an availability
factor of only 54 percent."

8.4.2.1 Organizational Structure

In the organizational structure of RG&E, it is possible to observe that there is a vice president for nuclear operations that is higher in hierarchy than the other general managers and reports directly to the senior vice president for nuclear operations.

At the GINNA nuclear plant there is a general manager on site. It is worth noting that at this plant there is a Corrective Action Coordination Department in charge of assuring that action procedures are properly implemented during the daily operations at GINNA.

During the refueling outage period, an outage manager is appointed to oversee the fuel replacement and general maintenance process. This position is temporary and reports to the general manager of the plant, who retains the overall responsibility.

The corporation supports an open-door policy and awards cash bonuses for ideas that further support corporate goals in a tangible fashion. There are no unions at RG&E and that allows for more flexibility in the communication between exempt and nonexempt employees. The nonunion status of the personnel at RG&E is consistent with the nonunionized status of the largest employer in the Rochester area (Eastman Kodak Corp.).

The emphasis assigned to enhancing the communications richness and effectiveness is expressed in the following excerpts from the 5-year goals of RG&E (May 1989):

1. Promoting public understanding of nuclear safety issues
2. Providing effective communication and training for personnel safety
3. Providing timely information concerning company operations

The decision-making process has a hierarchical structure as dictated by the nuclear technological imperative. However, the process has a team-oriented nature wherever that is possible.

Furthermore, in the outline of two of the seven 5-year goals, quality and employee achievement, it is explicitly stressed that the company should focus on (RG&E, May 1989):

- Recognizing individual achievement
- Utilizing verification processes and feedback mechanisms
- Taking advantage of opportunities for improvement
- Providing timely information concerning company operations
- Recognizing individual achievement
- Teamwork

Management practices and policies must (RG&E, May 1989):

1. Convey an attitude of trust and an approach that is supportive of teamwork at all levels.
2. Recognize and expect professionalism from all personnel.

3. Enhance communication and require teamwork among and between groups that operate, maintain, and support the plant.
4. Encourage personnel to view themselves as part of the overall team with successful operation of the plant being a common goal.

The span of control at the top management level ranges in the entire corporation between four and eight, but it is the least in the case of the nuclear division. This means that the organizational structure is more hierarchical in the nuclear division than in any of the other divisions.

8.4.2.2 Human Resource Management

The way the human resources management process is approached becomes apparent when looking at what to be an "outstanding performer" means for RG&E (May 1989): "... We must provide a vital, challenging, and safe environment for our people; one that provides opportunity and encourages and rewards high quality performance and creativity...."

The people involved in the nuclear power generation operations are the most strategic factor in ensuring the achievement of the short- and long-term goals set forth by the corporation. Hence, they are treated with the utmost attention and specifically in the case of RG&E that may be the single most important reason why the labor force is nonunionized (RG&E, May 1989, p. 3):

> ...The RG&E's staff is the company's most valuable resource.... We attribute GINNA's success to a highly skilled, capable, and professional, staff who have dedicated their careers to achieving high standards of performance.... Continue the improvement and implementation of programs to retain and develop qualified people through training, job rotation, and the enhancement of professionalism....

RG&E has implemented its version of MBO that it calls objective-based management (OBM) (RG&E, May 1989):

> ... The OBM program is a core productivity system that is designed to provide a series of integrated methods that help people work effectively. The purpose of the system is to convert organizational goals into coordinated actions with maximum utilization of resources and optimal results.

The fact that RG&E operates only one nuclear power station limits its capacity to laterally rotate people within the division. RG&E has a succession plan for 40 key top management positions with two to three candidates for each position. They use a matrix evaluation method to select the most appropriate candidate for each position.

From the interviews we conducted at RG&E we can safely conclude that the company follows a policy of almost exclusive promotion from within its ranks. While that may deprive it from outside potential talent, it also enhances employee loyalty.

Training carries a lot of weight at RG&E (as part of the nuclear technological imperative). The importance of training can be deduced from the following excerpts from RG&E (1990):

> ... The [GINNA] plant has established a good reputation by achieving many firsts and near firsts in operation, maintenance, engineering, and training. The company has developed a well-trained, technically competent, highly experienced, and motivated staff dedicated to the safe operation of the plant.

Employees can enroll in a company-sponsored, on-site training program that culminates with their graduation into bachelors of technology, or they can enroll in any of several technical or managerial programs offered by local universities (University of Rochester, Rochester Institute of Technology, and even University of Michigan). Most managers have technical backgrounds with bachelors or masters in engineering and other technical fields.

The main way of recognizing employee achievement is very direct: cash prizes for useful, productive suggestions that can be fairly substantial. Another implicit way is involving the employees in the technical management of the plant processes, not with quality circles, but with open communication channels of effective feedback to employee inquiries and ideas. Employees at the nuclear division are provided with an additional salary bonus that corresponds to a certain percentage of their base salary.

Because of its nonunion condition, when overall maintenance is performed at the GINNA plant, personnel from all the other generating plants of the corporation are assigned to work at GINNA. This has allowed RG&E to function effectively with only a low number of external contractors. The personnel that work at GINNA only on a temporary basis receive the corresponding training to be qualified to work in a nuclear environment, and according to the executives interviewed, they also receive a bonus for working at the nuclear station. This increased training and commitment by all the RG&E personnel in the performance of the nuclear plant certainly produces a very rich working environment.

One of the interviewees characterized the employee turnover as exceedingly low. The reasons given for that were employee job satisfaction and the need to nurture and grow employees for long periods of time, because longtime experience at nuclear operations is of great importance.

8.4.2.3   Strategic Environment

The main changes that RG&E has faced recently have to do mostly with the Nine-Mile Point Unit 2 plant, which because of its managerial association with Unit 1 has been kept under close supervision by the NRC. RG&E has tried to play an active advisory role under its cotenant capacity in that plant, to improve its performance record.

RG&E has more flexibility to respond to environmental changes, both planned and unexpected ones, given its impressive performance record and its emphasis on anticipating changes through effective long-term planning procedures (RG&E, 1989):

The essence of strategic planning is the systematic identification of the issues which, in combination with other pertinent facts and information, provide a basis for making decisions which will allow the company to set future directions....

8.5 TENNESSEE VALLEY AUTHORITY

8.5.1 OVERVIEW OF TENNESSEE VALLEY AUTHORITY

The Tennessee Valley Authority (TVA) is one of the nation's largest electric power producers and a regional development agency. TVA was established as a federal agency by the U.S. Congress in 1933. Its primary objectives have been: (1) to provide flood control, (2) to improve navigation, and (3) to produce electric power for the Tennessee Valley region.

The history of TVA can be traced to 1824, when Secretary of War John C. Calhoun sent a report to President Monroe recommending the improvement of the Tennessee River at Muscle Shoals, Alabama, as part of an ambitious program for developing a network of rivers and roads interconnecting the various parts of the evolving United States. Under the passage of the National Defense Act of 1916, Wilson Dam, and several plant — including two steam–electric power generation facilities — were constructed.

Currently, TVA serves about 91,000 sq mi in the southeastern United States including Tennessee and parts of six other states, Alabama, Mississippi, Kentucky, Virginia, North Carolina, and Georgia. TVA employs about 19,500 people and its power system funds its operations by selling electricity to its customers, hence using no tax dollars. Almost all TVA electric power comes from coal, water, or nuclear power. TVA had a total net electric power generation of 121,744 GWh in 1992.

TVA has 11 coal plants that produce 69% of its total electricity, 29 hydroelectric plants that produce 13% of its total electricity, and 9 nuclear power plants at four locations that produce 18% of its total electricity. The electric power produced by TVA is about 35% cheaper than the national average of 7.7 cents per kWh.

TVA operates nine nuclear power plants in four locations: Sequoyah, Browns Ferry, Watts Bar, and Bellefonte, with a total generating capacity of 11,102 MWh. In 1992, the NRC gave permission to the Watts Bar nuclear power plant to resume full construction activities and gave the Browns Ferry nuclear power facility its highest systematic assessment of licensee performance (SALP) evaluations ever and removed it from the NRC "watch list" of nuclear power plants across the United States.

8.5.2 MAJOR CORPORATE DEVELOPMENTS AND STRATEGIC DECISION-MAKING FRAME

The TVA vision is to be "the very best electric utility in North America and the most productive and effective agency in the federal government" (TVA, 1992). The TVA strategic planning for the 1992–1999 period is built around the following three themes: competitiveness, customer focus, and innovation (TVA, 1992): "We also learned that world-class quality would not come overnight. Instead, we would progress toward our goal to become world-class as we developed data, analyzed and improved processes, and empowered each other to make decisions based on fact — eliminating guesswork."

- *Competitiveness* — That means that TVA strives to "provide services at lower cost and with higher value than our competitors," while helping TVA "suppliers and customers improve their own competitive posture (TVA, 1992): ... We recognize that the competitive forces influencing our suppliers, our customers, and own businesses of energy services and regional development are not independent.... The forces of monopoly franchise that have served to protect electric utilities in the past will not be present (at least in their previous form) in the future. Our strategy in response must be competitiveness.
- *Customer Focus* — TVA has intensified its customer research efforts (TVA, 1992): "we are learning more about our customers, what it takes to help them be successful, and how to translate this knowledge into actions within our own work groups that will lead to continuously improving service. ... We are concentrating on doing the right things right."
- *Innovation* — TVA is putting special emphasis on the benchmarking of best practices across both federal agencies and other businesses leading to the invention of new, more effective, and efficient approaches to doing business: "We must all participate in the innovation process. To do this, we must create a workplace that is free from fear. Our workplace should encourage and reward responsible risk-taking if we are to become successful at innovation. ... Our strategy of innovation is two-pronged: We must innovate to create entirely new "cutting edge" solutions and practices, and we must innovate to select and combine the best ideas from the past, from benchmarking, and from the cutting edge."

The TVA Nuclear Generating Group Management System (GGMS) is based on ten policies and is complemented by a corrective action program, problem evaluation reports, finding identification reports, and the nuclear experience review program. The ten basic policies of the GGMS have been modeled after the Malcolm Baldrige National Quality Award (MBNQA) guidelines and address (TVA, October 9, 1992):

1. *Organization and leadership principle* — How management leads people and manages the business
2. *Communications* — How we communicate within the Generating Group
3. *Employee involvement* — How employees are involved in the conduct of their business
4. *Team and employee recognition* — How to recognize the contribution of employees
5. *Strategic and business planning* — How we plan our future direction and develop work plans
6. *Customer focus and satisfaction* — How we listen to our customers to ensure their satisfaction

7. *Process improvement* — Methods to improve processes and solve problems.
8. *Information resources* — Means to use and analyze information for improvement
9. *Education and training* — Education and training required for effective operations
10. *Supplier quality and partnering* — The way we do business with our suppliers.

Formal procedures are required for all levels of plant/utility management. The most emphasis is on those utilized at the operational and tactical learning level, because they have immediate impact on safety and economy (two of the three major objectives of all nuclear power plants, the other being reliability). Personnel are advised to stop work activities and revise instructions that are found to be in error.

Incident investigations are conducted for events that occur at the plant to determine root cause and extent of condition so as to prevent the reoccurrence. Similarly, industry events are evaluated in accordance with an operating experience program to prevent occurrence of events in-house. In-house events are trended to ensure that low-threshold events are monitored for common themes.

Formal means are used to trend deviations over time on a quarterly and annual frequency. Result-oriented performance indicators are trended on a monthly basis. Equipment failures are trended in accordance with a formal plant instruction to ascertain if there is a repetitive trend and if the failure rate is increasing.

8.6 ONTARIO HYDRO

8.6.1 OVERVIEW OF ONTARIO HYDRO

Canada, a country rich in uranium as well as in hydroelectric power, has 19 plants operating that provide 16% of the total power generated. The two main Canadian utilities Ontario and Quebec Hydro are studies in contrast in terms of the composition of the different sources of energy: more than 50% (50.8% in 1991) of the Ontario Hydro energy is nuclear generated, while less than 1% is nuclear and more than 95% hydroelectric in the case of Quebec Hydro, which operates only one 685 MgW nuclear power plant. Ontario Hydro's Nuclear Generation Division (NGD) has 16 CANDU units in service at three stations, with another four units planned, as well as a facility for producing the heavy water used as a moderator and primary coolant in the CANDU system. Moreover, two local training facilities and one central department support these facilities. The company recorded US$6.2 billion in revenues in 1998, with assets of US$27.4 billion.

8.6.2 MAJOR CORPORATE DEVELOPMENTS AND STRATEGIC DECISION-MAKING FRAME

The enhanced opportunity to learn that a single customer enjoys from the operation of multiple plants of the same design philosophy operating within the same technical, financial, and organizational context, is also evident in the case of Canada with the superior performance record of the CANDU reactors: "... the utility serving the province of Ontario [in Canada] owns twenty reactors and is considering four more; eight reactors are at each site" (Morone and Woodhouse, 1989, p. 114).

Indeed, both utilities have very good performance records compared with industry standards (Ontario Hydro, 1991, p. 18): "Energy production at Hydro's nuclear generating stations for 1991 totaled almost 71 million MgWh, an increase of 19% over 1990. The corporation's overall nuclear capability factor — indicating level of operating performance — for the year was 69.2% compared with 62.3% in 1990."

In addition, Ontario Hydro keeps expanding its continuous quality improvement (CQI) programs, which started in 1990 and resulted in "significant gains in productivity, performance and safety in Hydro's operations, and better management and staff relations" (Ontario Hydro, 1991, p. 21). At the core of a CQI program lies an increased emphasis on learning from experience processes, thus reinforcing our view, based on the operating success of the Canadian utilities, that such processes are the secret of success for managing complex and risky technologies. To learn from undesirable events, it is necessary to document their occurrence and follow-up with the appropriate root cause analysis and corrective action processes.

The lessons learned should be shared by all Ontario Hydro nuclear facilities and the external nuclear community by virtue of the operating experience program (OEP) for the NGD, integral parts of which are the special event reports and the follow-up processes. The objectives of the OEP are

1. To ensure regulatory and legal reporting requirements are met
2. To provide formal documentation of unplanned, undesirable events for historical process mapping
3. To ensure adequate, timely follow-up and investigation of events.
4. To ensure corrective actions adequately address root causes and are implemented in a timely manner.
5. To ensure relevant lessons are disseminated to the appropriate organizations, both internal and external to the corporation

Ontario Hydro attaches great importance to learning from its experiences and those of others, followed by dissemination of information and the implementation of appropriate corrective actions. The major means for accomplishing this process of learning and informing are the significant event reports (SERs) in conjunction with review and follow-up processes. SERs are prepared for events in the NGD that have the potential to have an undesirable impact on any of the division's key effectiveness areas (KEAs) of worker safety, public safety, environmental protection, product quality, and product cost.

Two forms of the SER are used, an "immediate" report and a "depersonalized" report. The former records the initial impressions of the personnel about the event that occurred and provides the facility management with an immediate factual summary of what happened, while the latter records the primary means of transmitting this information about significant events throughout Ontario Hydro and external organizations (regulatory agencies and other utilities management). Specifically, the immediate report must contain (Mitchell, 1990, p. 3):

1. Names of personnel involved in the event
2. Relevant conditions existing prior to the event (such as reactor power level, maintenance activities, etc.)
3. Description of the event
4. Actual or potential consequences of the event
5. Completed human performance worksheet, if inappropriate human actions were involved

The depersonalized report includes the same information as the immediate report but with the names of the people involved deleted. A pattern and trend database is under development to monitor all events for developing adverse trends and deriving insights for corrective action. Following the SER, root cause determinations (RCDs) are conducted by appropriately trained people depending on whether the event was human or equipment related. When the root causes have been identified, the corrective action process (CAP) begins and leads to recommendations for preventing recurrence of the significant event (Mitchell, 1990, p. 3).

Significant event follow-up reports (FURs) document the results emanating from the RCDs and the CAP; and include brief summaries of the conclusions, root causes identified, and lessons learned along with the follow-up activity.

The central operating experience group screens the FURs to determine what lessons learned should be disseminated throughout the organization and over to other nuclear utilities and regulatory agencies to facilitate the processes of intraorganizational and interorganizational learning from experience (Carayannis, 1992a, 1993). The only events that are restricted are related to site security.

The transfer of lessons learned is thus both internal and external. Events designated for potential lesson transfer are investigated for applicability to other facilities, and the progress of actions triggered by them is monitored via a commitment tracking database maintained by each nuclear facility. Ontario Hydro shares the lessons it learns from its operating experience with INPO and WANO through the CANDU owners' group (COG). The COG screens the lessons learned to determine which ones would be of interest to the international community so that it reports them to WANO and INPO through event notification reports (ENRs) that are followed by event analysis reports (EARs) prepared by Ontario Hydro.

8.7   ELECTRICITÉ DE FRANCE

8.7.1   OVERVIEW OF ELECTRICITÉ DE FRANCE

Electricité de France (EdF) is the only French electrical utility, whose plants are manufactured by the same company, Framatome, and the architect–engineering services are supplied by EdF itself. It has 54 PWR plants in operation, that cover 73% of the electricity produced in France and help reduce the dependence on imported energy to less than half the country's needs, while it exports 12% of the total power generated to neighboring countries. "France is second only to the United States in installed nuclear capacity" (Nuclear Eng. Int., December 1988, p. 60). The company generated revenues of $34.4 billion in 1999.

8.7.2 MAJOR CORPORATE DEVELOPMENTS AND STRATEGIC DECISION-MAKING FRAME

Currently, EdF has been increasingly emphasizing the importance of learning from experience or "experience feedback" as they call it (EdF, 1992, p. 30): "As an essential element in the improvement of quality and safety, experience feedback has played an increasingly important role in 1992 ... drawing lessons from plants in operation as well as from plants currently being constructed and those in the planning stage."

EdF has actually *institutionalized* the learning from experience process by setting up the Engineering and Construction Division's Experience Feedback Committee (COREX).

In an author interview (May 1993), a manager with the Director of Research at EdF stressed the importance assigned to understanding and capitalizing on the "experience feedback" concept corporate-wide at EdF, stating:

> External events such as Three-Mile Island and Chernobyl, influence greatly, and in a diffused corporate-wide manner, our practices of managing nuclear technology and our measures for continuously improving that management. We believe that better understanding the learning process associated with experience feedback has strategic importance for EdF.

Moreover, France, along with Germany and Britain, participates in the European fast reactor (EFR) project that aims at unifying the R&D and design efforts in these countries as well as improving the economy, reliability, and safety of the new reactors.

Morone and Woodhouse (1989, p. 113) outline very clearly why standardization and opportunity to learn from experience were hampered so much more by the U.S. private ownership of nuclear power plants approach compared with the French public ownership approach:

> Public ownership ... could have prevented the American nuclear industry from becoming the only major one in the world to have virtually every power plant practically custom-built. The reasons for this lack of standardization can be traced largely to the industry's competitive characteristics:
>
> 1. Two basic reactor concepts instead of France's one
> 2. Four manufacturers (originally five), each with different designs
> 3. Multiple sizes and periodically updated designs
> 4. Twelve architect-engineering firms

EdF also assigns strategic importance to the role of environmental policy (EdF, 1992, pp. 30–31):

The drawing up, in 1991, of an Environmental Plan, marks EdF's intention of henceforth making environmental protection an integral part of its business culture.... The control of environmental problems is indeed a key factor in the success of future programs, on which the whole credibility of the Company turns.... In 1992, *action for environmental protection* [emphasis added] was pursued in three areas: specific studies relating to existing electric power generation plants, analysis of modifications that the company must carry out due to changing regulations, and communication and training activities.

In addition, EdF and the German nuclear power industry have been pursuing the development of a nuclear island, namely, the creation of an appropriately sited area, based on clearly strategic (long-term) criteria, where many nuclear plants can be constructed away from populated areas: "In the area of nuclear power, preparation for production after the year 2000 was intensified, particularly with agreements taking place on the development of the Franco-German EPR [European pressurized water reactor] nuclear island project" (EdF, 1992, p. 40). This is also referred to as one of the benefits of standardized central control of the nuclear power industry by Morone and Woodhouse (1989).

Finally, it may be worth noting the experiments by EdF in Cadarache, France. This is concerning an experimental "induced meltdown" of a nuclear power station microreplica (1/5000 scale) to learn by actually *doing* a controlled nuclear accident (meltdown) and derive valuable insights for environmental management and safety considerations (*Der Spiegel*, June 1993).

9   Synthesis of Theory and Evidence

9.1   TOWARD AN ORGANIZATIONAL ARCHITECTURE OF TECHNOLOGICAL LEARNING

I have but one lamp by which my feet are guided, and that is *the lamp of experience*. I know of no way of judging of the future but *by the past*.

Patrick Henry, 1775

At this juncture we are challenged with the task of integrating the multitude of theoretical and empirical threads we isolated into a cohesive whole or system. This task of *conceptual integration* of interdisciplinary perspectives is certainly nontrivial (Linstone, 1984, p. 82):

Integration resembles the task of conceptualizing a three-dimensional object from a series of one-dimensional descriptions and two-dimensional drawings. Alternatively, we can think of the process *in terms of the integration of the stimuli to the left and right hemispheres in the brain*. The perspectives cross-cue each other. Most decision makers find it quite difficult to describe this process explicitly, although they execute every day. It is often just as difficult to reconstruct how a jury arrived at a decision. The fact that in both cases effective decision making does occur suggests that *the integration process* in our situation be left to the user or decision maker.

A triple-layered organizational architecture of technological learning needs two support pillars:

1. An organizational culture* of learning that fosters learning at all levels, through all functions, and by all means, creating an ambiance of total technological learning in a dynamic system approach (Senge, 1990, p. 164):

The five disciplines [systems thinking, personal mastery, mental models, building shared vision, team learning], now converging, appear to comprise a critical mass. They make building learning organizations a systematic undertaking, rather than a matter of

---

* *Culture* is the invisible force behind the tangibles and observables in any organization, a social energy that moves people to act. Culture is to the organization what personality is to the individual — a hidden, yet unifying theme that provides meaning, direction, and mobilization. (Killman, 1985)

happenstance. ... perhaps one or two developments emerging in seemingly unlikely places, will lead to a whole new discipline that we cannot even grasp today.

2. A continuous process or multilevel cycle for creating, upgrading, and destroying *tacit* technological core competencies*, which serve at a given point in time as the firm's competitive arsenal or dynamically evolving, firm-specific skill or resource reservoir (Teece et al., 1992, p. 12):

> The resource-based perspective [of strategic management] focuses on strategies for exploiting firm-specific assets. However, the resource-based perspective also invites consideration of strategies for developing new capabilities.... It is this second dimension, encompassing skill acquisition, learning, and capability accumulation that we believe lies the greatest potential for the resource-based perspective to contribute to strategy. We will refer to this as the "dynamic capabilities approach."

Teece et al. (1992, p. 12) write that learning engenders skills, capabilities, and organizational routines with "a tacit dimension that often cannot be readily articulated. Hence, the routines themselves and the ability of management to call upon the organization to perform them, represents firm's business capability."

9.2 BUILDING SUSTAINABLE COMPETITIVE ADVANTAGE BASED ON LEARNING: HYPERLEARNING AND HYPERCOMPETITION

> The new architecture of world power will depend less on traditional force than on the high quality power of knowledge.
>
> Chalmers Johnson, *Japan 2000 Report: Observations about a Firestorm*, June 20, 1991

> In an economy where the only certainty is uncertainty, *the only sure source of lasting competitive advantage is knowledge.*
>
> Nonaka, 1994, p. 96

As we approach the twenty-first century, technological paradigm shifts (Kuhn, 1970) and social challenges facing corporations and postindustrial societies alike are becoming increasingly pronounced and frequent.

At the *societal level*, the challenges are persistently high structural unemployment coupled with a declining standard of living, and acceleration of skill obsolescence due to technological innovations.

At the *corporate level*, the challenge is that competitive advantage is becoming increasingly hard to create and maintain, due to accelerating technological change, combined with continuous globalization, and mobility of corporate activities that underscore the production factor price equalization pressures exerted on high-cost producers by the low-cost ones. This has resulted in an ongoing drive for *leaner*

---

* *Tacit knowledge* is defined as "practical know-how that usually is not openly expressed or stated" (*Oxford English Dictionary*, 1933).

corporations across the board and continued "rightsizing" even in times of economic recovery in the United States.

Dynamically renewable technological skills and knowledge and, in particular, the know-how to continuously update them, have become the key for corporations to survive and succeed. In essence, a corporation's only source of sustainable competitive advantage in hypercompetitive environments (D'Aveni, 1994) seems to be its focus on building its capacity for multilevel technological learning (learning, learning how to learn, and learning to learn how to learn) to perform the necessary strategic maneuvers.

This is corroborated by the determinants of success in a hypercompetitive environment (D'Aveni, 1994, pp. 227–228):

1. Firms must destroy their competitive advantage to gain advantage....
2. Entry barriers only work if others respect them....
3. A logical approach is to be unpredictable and irrational....
4. Traditional long-term planning does not prepare for the long term.... Long-term success depends on a dynamic strategy that allows for a series of short-term advantages.
5. Attacking competitors' weaknesses can be a mistake.... Using the company's strengths against an opponent's weaknesses may work once or twice, but *not over several dynamic strategic interactions....*
6. Companies have to compete to win, but competing makes winning more difficult. *Companies have no choice but to move the level of competition up the escalation ladder [through multilevel technological learning]* or be left behind. ... Because of the difficulty of recognizing these paradoxes, companies often make mistakes by pursuing a strategy of sustaining advantage in an environment in which every advantage is eroded.

D'Aveni (1994) describes the strategic maneuvering of hypercompetitive firms as one of continuous technological discontinuities:

Hypercompetitive firms attempt to avoid or break out of perfect competition (where no one has an advantage by (1) speeding up the ladder faster than the other players or (2) restarting the cycle by building new knowledge bases that allow new products and business methods to be used Nonaka and Takeuchi, 1995, p. 109).

We believe that the *core corporate competence* that allows a firm to perform such strategic maneuvers is its capacity for multiple-level, and especially second (tactical)- and third (strategic)- order technological learning.

This core competence for technological learning must take place as individual, group-wide, organization-wide, interorganizational, and even inter-industry learning (Jelinek, 1979, pp. 162–163):

To be organizational, rather than individual, learning, knowledge must be accessible to others rather than the discoverer, subject to both their application or use, and to their change and adaptation. ... Organizational learning, to be learning rather than "mere adaptation" must be generalized. It must go beyond simple replication to application, change, refinement. It must include "rules for learning" and their change and adaptation, rather than the rote iteration of past successful actions.... Finally, if learning is to include innovation, it must encompass a system for governing the future as well as the present.

Moreover, this learning process must be endowed with an organizational memory that is both accurate and precise to build, maintain, and renew continuously the firm's reservoir of skills and competencies.

Teece et al. (1992) define learning as "a process by which repetition and experimentation enable tasks to be performed better and quicker and new production opportunities to be identified." Furthermore, they focus on the nature of learning as both an individual and an organizational process (Teece et al., 1992):

> Learning processes are intrinsically social and collective phenomena. Learning occurs not only through the imitation and emulation of individuals, as with teacher–student, or master–apprentice, but also *because of joint contributions to the understanding of complex problems.* Learning requires *common codes of communication* and coordinated search procedures.

Seen from the hypercompetition/hyperlearning perspective, learning thus becomes the tool for continually creating new technological realms of competition and "languages of strategic thought," and the higher levels or orders of technological learning (Carayannis, 1992a, 1993, 1994a, 1994b, 1994c) and especially *strategic technological learning*, serve to leapfrog onto a new competitive realm and to increase the slope of the learning curve as well as the rate by which the slope per se increases by means of enhanced and innovative organizational routines (Teece et al., 1992):

> Routines are patterns of interactions that represent successful solutions to particular problems.... Routines can be of several kinds. *Static routines* embody the capacity to replicate certain previously performed tasks.... *Dynamic routines* are directed at establishing new competences.

Thus, a technology-driven firm's sustainable competitive advantage accrues from:

1. Critical mass of strategic assets (SA)
2. Self-organizing capacity (SOC) to continuously improve its strategic assets (operational technological learning) and, being self-organizing, to improve itself through learning from experience (tactical technological learning)
3. Capability to further organize the self-organizing of its SOC

9.3   TECHNOLOGY TRANSFER AND TECHNOLOGICAL INNOVATION

Innovation is creative destruction.

Joseph Schumpeter

Experience and scientific understanding are like two legs without which we cannot walk.

Varela et al., *The Embodied Mind*, 1991, p. 14

Technology transfer and technological innovation can be viewed as instances of multilevel technological learning, especially within the hypercompetition context of strategic maneuvering (D'Aveni, 1994).

Thus, technological learning is the medium or "tool" for facilitating and managing technology transfer. The significance of the underlying link between the two processes is the potential for creating and renewing an organization's competitive advantage by means of diffusing firm-specific and proprietary technological competencies throughout the organization thus maximizing the firm's leverage on its dynamic capabilities.

In a similar context, technological innovation is defined by Tornatzky and Fleischer (1990 p. xvi) as:

... a situationally new development through which people extend their control over the environment. Essentially, technology is a tool of some kind that allows an individual to do something new. A *technological innovation* is basically information organized in a new way. So *technology transfer* amounts to the communication of information, usually from one organization to another.

Technological innovation is classified into incremental, generational, and radical by Morone, and these classes of innovation can be viewed as outcomes of each of the three levels of technological learning, operational, tactical, and strategic, respectively (Carayannis, 1992a, 1993, 1994a, 1994b, 1994c). Throughout, however, the significance of the tacit dimension of technological learning cannot be emphasized enough (Jung, 1958, p. 99–100):

But even though the first step along the road to a momentous invention may be the outcome of a conscious decision, here, as everywhere, the *spontaneous idea — the hunch or intuition* — plays an important part. In other words, the unconscious collaborates too and often makes decisive contributions. So it is not the conscious effort alone that is responsible for the result; somewhere or other the unconscious with its barely discernible goals and intentions, has its finger in the pie. ... *Reason alone does not suffice.*

In addition, the mutually reinforcing and complementing role that all three levels of learning and kinds of innovation play sometimes results in major breakthroughs (Sahal, 1982, p. xi):

> In many fields, technological advance reflects the gradual accretion over time of understanding on the part of technologists of the potential of a broadly defined technology, and the progressive exploitation of the potential. Put another way, *a progressive flow of innovation results from a cumulative learning process.*

9.4 METACOGNITIVE PARADIGM OF DECISION MAKING: THINKING ABOUT THINKING AND ABOUT LEARNING

> When I am, as it were, completely myself, entirely alone, and of good cheer ... it is on such occasions that my ideas flow best and most abundantly. Whence and how they come, I know not; nor can I force them. Those ideas that please me I retain in memory.
>
> W. A. Mozart, quoted in Brewster Ghiselin, 1952, p. 34

> The essence of ultimate decision remains impenetrable to the observer — often, indeed, to the decider himself.... There will always be the dark and tangled stretches in the decision-making process — mysterious even to those who may be most intimately involved.
>
> John F. Kennedy, 1963

The strategic incrementalism style of strategic decision making emanates from the metacognitive paradigm of strategic decision making (where metacognitive means thinking about one's thinking), a paradigm of decision making that integrates multiple levels of learning and decision making through multilevel feedback and hence focuses on their interdependence and the need for managing them simultaneously by taking a dynamically adaptive holistic approach (Figure 9.1).

The validity of the holistic approach is corroborated by Itami and Roehl (1987, pp. ix, x): "This holistic approach combines the analytical economic approach with the soft-behavioral one;" and "the new concepts ...: first, the invisible assets of a firm, which are based on information, and second, overextension as an unbalanced growth strategy that stimulates resource accumulation and organizational vitality."

The metacognitive paradigm can be defined as: ... the process of making decisions in a "new form of disaggregated specialized 'intellectual coordinating company'" (Quinn, 1992), where technology acquires an increasingly important role in redefining at an increasing frequency and through a process of multiple-loop technological learning, the concepts of functional, business, corporate, and institutional firm-specific strategy and the points on which competitive advantage *vis-a-vis* other firms is built. The metacognitive paradigm is based on multilevel, higher order self-organizing technological learning processes that, in a Popperian sense, is the synthesis of causal, instrumental, and constrained learning which underlie the analytic, cybernetic, and cognitive paradigms of strategic decision making, respectively.

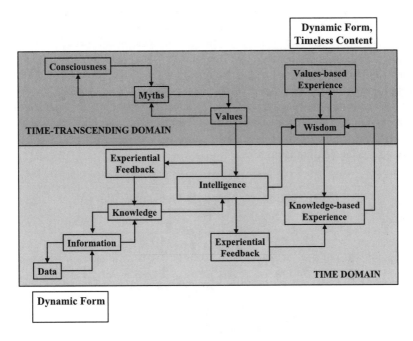

FIGURE 9.1   Experiential metacognitive map.

The metacognitive paradigm may thus be a way for better understanding the *causes*, the *nature*, and the *changes in the nature per se* of the transnational competition among companies, industries, and nations, which are frequently tantamount to technological, economic, and social paradigm shifts (Kuhn, 1970).

This new paradigm may be considered part of the experience-based school of strategic decision making under the caveat that it puts the most succinct emphasis on multiple-level, multiple-loop, higher order learning and suggests a clear-cut architecture of the strategic decision-making process that capitalizes on the comparative advantages accrued from the tacit component of multiple-loop, multiple-level learning (Nelson and Winter, 1982, p. 92):

> An experienced businessman acting in the pursuit of pecuniary gain is an individual exercising a complex skill. As with any such skill, the pursuit of gain is based on *tacit knowledge* [emphasis added] of relevant conditions and involves at most subsidiary awareness of many of the details of the procedures being followed.

In that sense, the metacognitive paradigm of decision making identifies closely with the emerging "Austrian"/experiential school of strategy making (Jacobson, Mintzberg), notwithstanding Ansoff's and Mintzberg's philosophical differences (Ansoff, 1991, pp. 90–91), which is proposed as an alternative to the design (Porter) and planning (Ansoff) schools of strategy making, and it could serve as a *kernel* for the development of a new decision-making theory inspired by the philosophical underpinnings of the Austrian school of strategy making.

We believe that the metacognitive paradigm of strategic decision making along with the style of strategic or active incrementalism, are most effective in allowing better strategic decisions to be made as fast as possible, because it focuses on minimizing the transaction costs (Williamson, 1975) associated with converting tacit knowledge to explicit or articulable knowledge by means of an integrated hierarchy of multiple learning loops.

The faster and more extensive such a conversion is within an organization, the more sustainable competitive advantages accrue to it, especially under the five pathologies of strategic decision making: uncertainty, complexity, ambiguity, uniqueness, and value conflict (Figure 9.2).

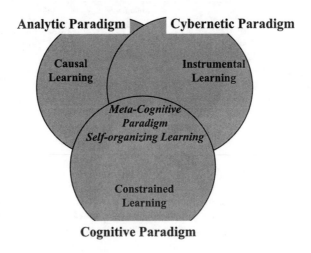

FIGURE 9.2   Four types of strategic learning.

9.5   STRATEGIC OR ACTIVE INCREMENTALISM: LANGUAGE OF TECHNOLOGICAL LEARNING AND UNLEARNING

The doctor's discursive, reflective perception and the philosopher's discursive reflexion on perception come together in a figure of exact superposition, since the world is for them the *analogue of language.*

Michel Foucault, *The Birth of the Clinic: An Archaeology of Medical Perception*

To learn one must be humble.

James Joyce, *Ulysses*

The strategic management of technological learning (SMOTL) concept motivates the decision-making model or style of strategic incrementalism (de Geus, 1991):

When people play with [mental models of the world], they are actually creating a *new language* among themselves that expresses the knowledge they have acquired. And here we come to the most important aspect of institutional learning, whether it be achieved through teaching or through play as we have defined it: *the institutional learning process is a process of language development. As the implicit knowledge of each learner becomes explicit, his or her mental model becomes a building block of the institutional model.*

The main attributes of this model are a dynamically adaptive nature and an emphasis on continuous learning and unlearning from experience, as well as a simultaneous awareness of both the short and the long term. It accounts for the weaknesses associated with incrementalism (such as short-sightedness and excessive conservatism) through its inherent dynamism and its readiness for radical change. It is inspired from the metacognitive paradigm, where technology acquires an increasingly important role in redefining at an increasing frequency the concepts of corporate strategy and the points on which competitive advantage is built.

It has thus become the cause for changes in the nature of the competition per se among companies, industries, and nations, that are more and more frequently tantamount to a paradigm shift (Kuhn, 1970). These changes in the nature of competition among firms is dealt with by D'Aveni (1994) who introduced the concept of hypercompetition and which leads to the concept of hyperlearning or higher order self-organizing learning and unlearning (see Figures 9.3 and 9.4).

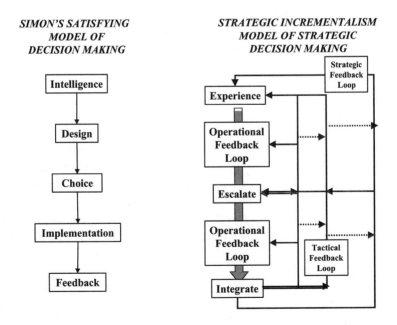

FIGURE 9.3 Decision-making models.

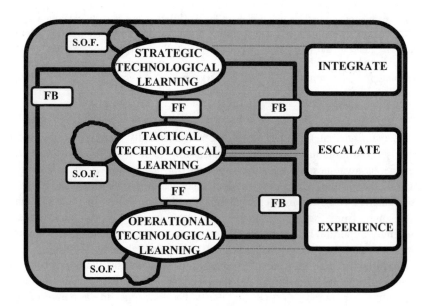

FIGURE 9.4 Strategic management of technological learning topology.

We propose to define the concept of strategic or active incrementalism as:

… an incremental/radical (evolutionary/revolutionary), dynamically adaptive (responsive over time, feedback driven), and multiple (triple) loop self-organizing technological learning (first, second, and third order learning and unlearning, that is, a hyperlearning-driven strategic decision-making process, which manifests itself on three consecutive levels of increasing conceptual breadth and depth of the decisions involved (see Figure 9.3).

Strategic incrementalism focuses heavily, albeit implicitly, on continuous feedback and learning and unlearning* from experience not on one but on three levels:

1. Operational, single-loop or first-order technological learning level — on the first level we have accumulating experience and learning by doing (*we learn new things*).
2. Tactical, double-loop, self-organizing or second-order technological learning or learning how-to-learn level — on the second level we have learning

---

* Miner stressed that learning, especially what is effectively tacit learning (although he does not use the word tacit, he in essence describes tacit learning), can have adverse effects by creating beliefs, or conceptual constraints (paradigms), that impede clairvoyance when making strategic decisions: "A primary point is that *organizational learning is not necessarily adaptive or a source of wisdom and improved performance under conditions of ambiguity. This is because it is not always obvious what happened, or why it happened, or whether what happened is a good thing* [emphasis added]. Given this ambiguity, learning can get far removed from what rationality would indicate" (Miner, 1983).

of new tactics about applying the accumulating experience and the learning process (redefinition of the fundamentals [rules and contingencies] of our short-term operating universe): we build new contingency models of decision making by changing the rules for making decisions and/or adding new ones.

3. Strategic, triple-loop, self-organizing metalearning or third-order technological learning or learning to learn-how-to-learn level — on the third level we have development and learning (internalization and institutionalization) of new views of our operating universe or *Weltanschauungen* (Hedberg, 1981),* hence we learn new strategies of learning (Cole, 1989). Thus, we redefine our fundamentals (our rules and contingencies) for our decision making; or, in other words, we redefine the fundamentals of our operating universe not only in the short term but primarily in the long term.

Strategic incrementalism is validated by Hedberg's (1981, pp. 3–27) *tripartite classification of learning types*: *"adjustment learning*: applicable when a worldview remains the same and temporary changes can be handled inside the existing behavior repertoire, *turnover learning*: that involves restructuring of ... the metasystems that handle stimuli responses, and *turnaround learning* that involves major restructuring of the firm's cognitive processes," and by Argyris and Schoen's (1978, pp. 18, 24, 26).

Strategic incrementalism is thus an *overarching framework*, combining elements of the other forms of incrementalism in decision making suggested by Lindblom (1959) as disjointed incrementalism, Quinn (1980) as logical incrementalism, and Joyce as functional incrementalism.

The strategic or active incrementalism style or framework emanates from the metacognitive paradigm, which is akin to the logical incrementalism, the critical decision making, and the bounded emotionality perspectives, but moreover, it incorporates a whole new dimension, the concept of multiple (triple)-level or loop technological learning as the driver of the decision-making process.

The concept of strategic learning was explored in a limited fashion by Ansoff, who prescribes it as the appropriate mode of strategic management behavior under conditions of high complexity, low predictability, and high novelty. These form a subset of the five pathologies of strategic decision making (uncertainty, complexity, ambiguity, uniqueness, and value conflict), which we singled out as defining the operating realm of the SMOTL (Ansoff, 1984, p. 93):

> Complex and discontinuous reality and speed of change make it necessary to anticipate and to plan as far as possible, but the unpredictability also makes it necessary to make up for the shortcomings of planning by continually testing and learning from reality. *Thus a synthesis of the opportunistic and planned approaches is necessary.* This

---

* A *Weltanschauung* is a definition of the situation: it influences what problems are perceived, how these problems are interpreted, and *what learning ultimately results* [emphasis added].

synthesis must combine the advantages of rational analysis with a sensitivity and responsiveness to the unpredictable environment.

The self-organizing learning (see Figures 9.2 and 9.3) takes place on four levels (Tables 4.1, 4.2A to 4.2C):

1. Individual
2. Intraorganizational (functional/business strategy at the firm level)
3. Interorganizational (corporate/institutional strategy at the industry level)
4. Supraorganizational (metastrategy or strategy-about-strategies level)

We found numerous instances of the three levels of technological learning (learning from experience, learning how to learn from experience, and learning to learn how to learn from experience) throughout the empirical study of 13 companies from four different industries outlined in detail in Chapters 6 through 8. Next we compiled selective key instances of the three kinds of technological learning we identified with our field research case studies.

9.6 EMPIRICALLY IDENTIFIED INSTANCES OF TECHNOLOGICAL LEARNING, METALEARNING, AND UNLEARNING IN ORGANIZATIONS STUDIED

9.6.1 LEARNING FROM EXPERIENCE

Learning from experience involves heavy initial and requalification training and moderate sharing of industry/in-house information. For a shift supervisor, heavy initial and requalification training and moderate sharing of industry/in-house information are needed. For plant engineering, sharing of industry/in-house information; and a fair amount of industry/in-house information sharing are included.

From a July 20, 1993 interview with the author, a BMS Strategic Planning Senior Staff Member states:

> *Every year*, we have a comprehensive review of our products pipeline. Several stakeholders participate in this review process: The strategic management group that consists of the senior management of our company, interacts with other companies, universities, sales groups, and R&D people and serves as both *an active and a passive interface* to integrate all the inputs and reassess and prune the pipeline. The results of this process are then integrated into the annual revision of the 5-year strategic plan.

9.6.2 LEARNING TO LEARN HOW TO LEARN FROM EXPERIENCE

The central operating experience group screens the FURs to determine what lessons learned should be disseminated throughout the organization and over to other nuclear utilities and regulatory agencies to facilitate the processes of intraorganizational and interorganizational learning from experience (Carayannis, 1992a, 1993). The only restricted events are related to site security.

The transfer of lessons learned is thus both internal and external. Events designated for potential lesson transfer are investigated for applicability to other facilities, and the progress of actions triggered by them is monitored via a commitment tracking database maintained by each nuclear facility. Ontario Hydro shares the lessons it learns from its operating experience with INPO and the WANO through the CANDU Owners' Group (COG). The COG screens the lessons learned to determine which ones would be of interest to the international community so that it reports them to WANO and INPO through Event Notification Reports (ENRs) that are followed by event analysis reports (EARs) prepared by Ontario Hydro.

In a July 1993 interview with the author, a BMS strategic planning senior staff member says:

> *Every five years*, we update our companywide strategic plan setting our mission and long term goals. Input into the plan comes from both the pharmaceutical and the R&D group trying to maximize the long-term benefits for Bristol-Myers Squibb that accrue from matching present and anticipated market needs with research created opportunities.

10 Conclusions and Recommendations

Imagination is more important than knowledge. To raise new questions, new possibilities, to regard old problems from a new angle, requires creative imagination and marks real advance in science.

Albert Einstein

You can do anything if you have enthusiasm. *Enthusiasm* is the yeast that makes your hopes rise to the stars. Enthusiasm is the sparkle in your eyes, the swing in your gait, the grip of your hand, the *irresistible surge of will and energy to execute your ideas.* Enthusiasts are fighters. They have fortitude. They have staying qualities. Enthusiasm is at the bottom of all progress. With it, there is accomplishment. Without it, there are only alibis.

Henry Ford

In conclusion, the essence of the motivation — founded on both theoretical and empirical evidence — for proposing the metacognitive paradigm and the *strategic* or *active incrementalism style* of strategic decision making as most appropriate for technologically driven, hypercompetitive (D'Aveni, 1994) and very dynamic environments, is encapsulated in the following five propositions:

1. A technology-driven firm's sustainable competitive advantage (SCA) is contingent on the inimitability of its dynamically evolving strategic assets (SA) (Amit and Shoemaker, 1993).
2. A technology-driven firm's capacity to create strategic assets is commensurate to its ability to manage strategically its processes of technological learning at the operational, tactical, and strategic levels (Carayannis, 1992a, 1993, 1994a, 1994b, 1994c), in order of increasing significance.
3. A technology-driven firm's capacity to learn, to learn to how to learn (self-organizing learning), and to learn to learn how to learn (self-organizing metalearning) (Carayannis, 1992a, 1993, 1994a, 1994b, 1994c), in order of increasing strategic leverage, is considerably more instrumental in creating and enhancing SCA than the firm's existing stock of SA at any given time.
4. The higher in the strategic management of technological learning (SMOTL) cone (Figure 10.1), the bigger the magnitude and the smaller the speed of change in strategic assets, because of the increasing tacitness

of both the process and the content (see Tables 4.1 and 4.2A to 4.2C) of the SMOTL.

5. The higher in the SMOTL cone and the strategic incrementalism (SI) feedback architecture (Carayannis, 1993), the more tacit become the process of technological learning as well as the nature of organizational rent and the larger becomes the rent-earning potential (Grant, 1991). This is due primarily to the increasingly high durability, the imperfect transparency, and the low transferability and replicability (Grant, 1991) as we move up the SMOTL cone (Figure 10.1).

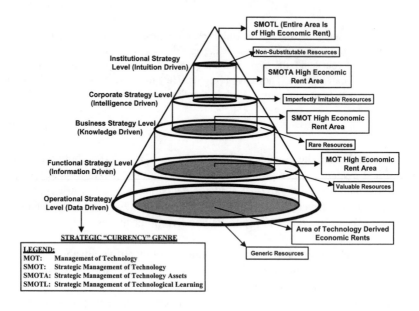

FIGURE 10.1 Cone of strategic technological learning.

10.1 FURTHER RESEARCH ON TECHNOLOGICAL LEARNING

10.1.1 TECHNOLOGICAL LEARNING AND CATASTROPHE THEORY

History does not repeat itself, it forms new combinations.

John Lukacs

Mathematical theories that include and emphasize system nonlinearities instead of ignoring them have been emerging as conceptual "tools" for understanding, explaining, and predicting the behavior of organizational systems. The motivation lies in the fact that such systems, made up of people, are highly nonlinear and apparently unpredictable in many cases.

The concepts of the strategic management of technological learning and strategic incrementalism introduced earlier, are inherently dynamically nonlinear inspired by natural and artificial systems with such a nature. For that reason, they have considerable conceptual affinities with catastrophe theory and chaos theory (Gleick, 1987).

Catastrophe theory, conceived by Thom in 1972, is one of the two major theories of system nonlinearities (the other one being chaos theory), that have been increasingly employed in the social and business disciplines, often being misunderstood and misapplied in the process. Catastrophe theory is a *static* method for studying and modeling unstable discontinuous processes (with two to six continuously changing external variables acting on the system) that shift from one steady state to another until a certain barrier or threshold is exceeded and then they move on to the next steady state. Such processes are ubiquitous in organizations, especially where technological learning continuously modifies and shifts people's worldviews

Catastrophe theory has not so far provided us with an effective means to predict unstable, highly nonlinear processes such as those involved in strategic decision making. Moreover, catastrophe theory applies only to dissipative systems, dynamic systems that taper off to an equilibrium state, and that can certainly not apply to growth-oriented, technology-driven businesses.

However, there are benefits to be accrued from studying catastrophe theory, especially in the case of high-level decision makers and business programs students. The reason is that they thus can be exposed to useful metaphors and paradigms that can enhance both the content and the process of their practice of management, making them "more reflective as practitioners," to paraphrase Schoen (1991), when dealing with the five pathologies of strategic decision making: *uncertainty, complexity, ambiguity, uniqueness,* and *value conflict.*

10.1.2 Technological Learning and Chaos Theory

Die Energie der Welt ist Constant. Die Entropie der Welt zu einem Maximum strebt.

Clausius

... twentieth century science will be remembered for three things: relativity, quantum mechanics, and chaos. Chaos has become the century's third great revolution in the physical sciences.

James Gleick, *Chaos: Making a New Science*, 1987

Chaos theory is a close relative of catastrophe theory, but has shown more potential in both explaining and predicting unstable nonlinearities, thanks to the concepts of *self-similarity* or *fractals* [*patterns within patterns*] and the *chaotic behavior of attractors* (Mandelbrot), as well as the significance assigned to the role that *initial conditions* play as determinants of the future evolution of a nonlinear system (Gleick, 1987).

There is a strong affinity with strategic incrementalism, viewed as a third-order (triple-layered), feedback-driven system that can exhibit instability in any given state as a result of the operational, tactical, and strategic technological learning

(Carayannis, 1992a, 1993, 1994a, 1994b, 1994c) *that takes place* within the organization in question.

It is interesting that giants of science from very diverse fields, such as Maxwell, Poincare, and Clausewitz, very early diagnosed the existence and significance of chaotic systems, each in their own language (Maxwell, 1882):

> There are certain classes of phenomena ... in which a small error in the data only introduces a small error in the result.... The course of events in these cases is stable. There are other classes of phenomena which are more complicated, and in which cases of instability may occur, the number of such cases increasing, in an extremely rapid manner, as the number of variables increases.

The nineteenth-century mathematician, Poincare, argued that the connection between chance and uncertainty can serve to better understand both. Poincare argued that chance comes in three guises: a statistically random phenomenon; the amplification of a microcause; or a function of our analytic blindness:

> A very slight cause which escapes us, determines a considerable effect which we cannot help seeing, and then we say this effect is due to chance. If we could know exactly the laws of nature and the situation of the universe at the initial instant, we should be able to predict exactly the situation of this same universe at a subsequent instant. ... But this is not always the case; it may happen that slight differences in the initial conditions produce very great differences in the final phenomenon; ... Prediction becomes impossible and we have the fortuitous phenomenon (Poincare, in Halsted, 1913).

War was conceptualized as "a remarkable trinity" (eine wunderliche Dreifaltigkeit) composed of "a) the blind natural force of violence, hatred, and enmity among the masses of people; b) chance and probability, faced or generated by the commander and his army; and c) war's rational subordination to the policy of the government" (Poincare, in Halsted, 1913). One could see there a parallel to the structure inherent in strategic incrementalism, where the three dimensions of the remarkable trinity of war correspond to *operational, tactical,* and *strategic learning,* respectively. As with strategic incrementalism, where the pivotal role is played by the *interaction (feedback)* between the three levels of technological learning along with the self-organizing that occurs at each level (see Figure 9.4), Clausewitz (1832, p. 213) emphasized the importance of the interactions between the three points in his remarkable trinity:

> Die Aufgabe ist also, dass sich die Theorie zwischen diesen drei Tendenzen wie zwischen drei Anziehungspunkten schwebend erhalte. [The task is therefore that the theory would maintain itself floating among these three tendencies as among three points of attraction.]

Thus, these three points act as *attractors* (potentially *chaotic attractors*) in the same fashion that the three levels of technological learning are active in a continuum of dynamic imbalances pulling the learning organization in their direction (to focus more on operational vs. tactical vs. strategic learning) at any given point in time and forming complex interactions with each other:

> A paradox seems to pose itself here: Living near boundaries of a stable domain (i.e., in sufficient nonequilibrium) is a precondition for a system's capability of evolving, of changing to another, qualitatively different stable domain (Prigogine, 1980); but at the same time, apparently through more effective flexible coupling of the subsystems (Prigogine, 1989) it enhances that system's resilience, or capability for persistence in the original domain (Holling, 1988), which in turn, tends to increase the fluctuations until they are big enough to drive the system to a new regime (Prigogine, 1989). *Does life with high fluctuations enhance both structural persistence and transformability?* And at what point and by what mechanism is structural persistence relinquished in favor of process persistence, or long-term viability through qualitative transformation of the space–time structure? *This crucial question has not yet found an answer for complex sociobiological and sociocultural systems* and *this question could well be expanded to cover complex sociotechnical systems and the strategic management of technology*]. *But it would not come as a surprise if the capabilities of resisting well and transforming well turned out to be just complementary aspects of that same system's flexibility which we keep encountering in so many manifestations. After all, is this not what is implied by a life lived to the fullest extent?* [emphasis added] (Jantsch and Waddington, 1976, p. 66–67].

10.1.3 FUTURE RESEARCH DIRECTIONS: TOWARD A NEW THEORY OF THE GROWTH OF THE FIRM?

> You believe in the God who plays dice and I in complete law and order in a world which objectively exists, and which I, in a wildly speculative way am trying to capture.
>
> Einstein: Letter to Niels Bohr, 1944

> Comforted by idols, we can lose the urge to question and thus we can willingly arrest our growth as persons: "One must invoke tremendous counter-forces in order to cross this natural, all too natural progresses in simile, the continual development of man toward the similar, average, herdlike common!"
>
> Nietzsche, *Thus Spoke Zarathustra*, p. 58

One of the earliest authors on leadership, the ancient Greek philosopher Plato, emphasized the significance of the capacity to learn and isolated it as perhaps the most important factor in leadership (Plato, *The Republic*):

> We should prefer the steadiest and bravest and, so far as possible, the best looking. But we shall also look not only for moral integrity and toughness, but for natural aptitude for this kind of education.... They need intellectual eagerness, and must learn easily. For the mind shirks mental hardship more than physical.... They must have good memories, determination, and a fondness for hard work.... If we pick those who are sound in limb and mind and then put them through our long course of instruction and training, Justice herself can't blame us and we shall preserve the constitution of our society.

Thus, we see that *knowledge generation, acquisition,* and *renewal* were singled out very early on as "a source of competitive advantage" to use modern terminology. Similarly, Penrose (1959, pp. 2, 53) in her treatise on the nature and the reasons behind the growth of firms focuses on knowledge both, objective and empirical:

> What I have done is to attempt to build a consistent, self-contained theory of the growth of firms, synthesizing my own ideas and those of others, moulding both into a reasonably formal whole which I hope provides a way of looking at the growth of firms that will be useful for both theoretical and "practical" purposes. ... Knowledge comes to people in two different ways. One kind can be formally taught, can be learned from other people or from the written word, and can, if necessary, be formally expressed and transmitted to others. The other kind is also the result of *learning, but learning in the form of personal experience....* The first form is what might be called *objective* knowledge. It is knowledge about things which is, conceptually at least, independent of any particular individual or group of individuals. ... *If the processes for the transmission of knowledge are not perfect, different groups of individuals may possess this knowledge in different degrees.* ... In this it differs from the second form in which knowledge appears — the form I have called *experience. Here emphasis is placed on the change in the services human resources can supply which arises from their own activity.* Experience produces increased knowledge about things and contributes to objective knowledge.... *But experience itself can never be transmitted; it produces a change — frequently a subtle change in individuals — and cannot be separated from them.*

In a sense, the concepts developed throughout this work, focusing on the ways that organizations and the people therein generate, process, and alter their explicit knowledge and tacit skills, as well as the paths of change that such styles of organizational cognition can follow, expand on the conceptual foundations laid by Penrose (1959) in her classic work and create questions and motives for further research on the dynamics of the creation and evolution of firm core competencies.

Appendix:
Field Research Questionnaires

OVERVIEW RESEARCH QUESTIONS ON LEARNING*

1. What promotes technological learning in your organization and how (at the strategic, tactical, and operational level)?
2. What hinders technological learning in your organization and how (at the strategic, tactical, and operational level)?
3. What formal and informal means are in place to enhance the factors that promote learning and suppress the factors that hinder learning in your organization at each level (see 1.)?
4. What formal and informal means could be, or are in the process of being, instituted to further optimize/reinforce the means referred to in 3. and at the strategic, tactical, and operational levels?

DECISION-MAKING AND LEARNING PROCESSES IN PRODUCT DEVELOPMENT AND MARKETING

PRODUCT DEVELOPMENT STAGES

I. Initial idea
  A. Formulation phase
    • What are the questions that are actually asked?
    In terms of:
    Strategic imperatives
    • What is the definition of the targeted market?
    • What is the targeted market size?
    Financial imperatives
    • What is expected Return on Investment (ROI)?
    • What is expected breakeven period?
  B. Implementation phase
    • What lessons were learned from implementing the initial idea phase?
    (Single-loop learning)

---

* Note: Technological learning: learning driven by technological change and innovation; strategic level of technological learning: learning accruing from company/market interaction affecting strategic decisions; tactical level of technological learning: learning accruing from company/specific product interaction affecting product development decisions; operational level of technological learning: learning accruing from specific product/market interaction affecting product development and marketing decisions.

- How was learning concerning future product decisions affected? (Double-loop learning)
- How was learning about learning per se (and within the context of future product decisions) affected? (Triple-loop learning)

II. Decision to commercialize
   A. Formulation phase (similar to phase I)
   B. Implementation phase (similar to phase I)

III. Commercialization process
   A. Formulation phase (similar to phase I)
   B. Implementation phase (similar to phase I)

IV. Feedback from commercialization
(Success/failure/question mark)
   A. Formulation phase (similar to phase I)
   B. Implementation phase (similar to phase I)

V. Integration of commercialization feedback into future product decisions via strategic, tactical, and operational learning
   A. Strategic learning
      (Company–market interaction)
- What lessons were learned?
- How was learning about future decisions affected?
- How was learning about learning per se affected?

   B. Tactical learning
      (Company–product interaction)
- What lessons were learned?
- How was learning about future decisions affected?
- How was learning about learning per se affected?

   C. Operational learning
      (Product–market interaction)
- What lessons were learned?
- How was learning about future decisions affected?
- How was learning about learning per se affected?

   D. Tacit learning
      (Tacit knowledge: To know more than you can tell)
- Did any tacit learning take place?
- Were your project evaluation and decision-making criteria affected in a nonquantifiable (nonarticulable but nonetheless clearly present and influential) manner?
- Where was tacit learning more pronounced: at strategic, tactical, or operational level?

Case Study Questions

RESEARCH QUESTIONS FOR NUCLEAR POWER UTILITIES

1. What are the formal and informal means employed as well as the relative emphasis assigned to each one of them, to ensure that effective learning from positive and negative outcomes of plant operations takes place on each of three levels in the plant/utility management hierarchy :
    a. Plant operators and technicians (operational level)
    b. Shift supervisors and plant engineers (tactical level)
    c. Plant and utility management (strategic level)
2. What are the formal and informal procedures followed on each of the three levels of the plant/utility management hierarchy (operational, tactical, strategic), as well as the relativue emphasis assigned to each one of them, to ensure that deviations (of varying severity) from a targeted safety, economy, and reliability norm:
    a. Are rectified
    b. Trigger effective learning from such events not only in the plant in question but also in other similar plants, that leads to:
        (1) A better understanding of the root causes of each deviation from the targeted norm so as to prevent similar reoccurences
        (2) Based on (1), modification of performance measures and other performance monitoring meaning to ensure an even faster and more sensitive problem detection system
3. What formal and informal means are in place on all three levels of the plant/utility management hierarchy (operational, tactical, strategic), as well as the relative emphasis assigned to each one of them, to assist [by assessing their effectiveness over time (3 to 5 years)], in further fine-tuning the means (such as performance indicators) used to enhance the learning about the learning and from the experience, accrued across several similar plants and concerning:
    a. Deviations over time (3 to 5 years) from a targeted safety, economy, and reliability norm, and the causes behind them,
    b. Improved performance over time (3 to 5 years) and the reasons behind it
    c. Outright equipment failures over time (3 to 5 years) and the causes behind them.

RESEARCH QUESTIONS FOR FOUR UNREGULATED INDUSTRIES

I. Industry focus
   A. New technological paradigms adopted over the last 5 years within industry to which your company belongs
   B. Strategic alliances/acquisitions/expansions in new markets as part of the strategic management of technology process in your company
   C. New marketing paradigms adopted within industry to which your company belongs
II. Company focus/generic issues
   A. Which strategic management of technology (SMOT) planning mode is prevalent
      1. Reactive (to opportunities/threats)
      2. Proactive (capitalize on technology-based competitive advantage)
      3. Technology driven (Japanese bonzai tree concept)
   B. Net Present Value (NPV) or the learning-by-doing (LBD) approach used more in practice to approve investments in projects of high technological and market uncertainty
   C. What emphasis is placed on discounted cash flow analysis (DCF) in the decision making involving strategic investments
   D. What weight is assigned to NPV analysis results in the decision making concerning strategic investments
   E. How formal (NPV dependent) the system is for assessing new technologies, deciding to acquire technologies, and utilizing technological assets; what are the main parameters used in such decision making
   F. How optimum amount of investment in technology is determined (relative emphasis on NPV or learning-by-doing approach)
   G. Criteria for determining maturation of current technologies and emergence of new technologies
   H. Technology as basis for competitive advantage: primary focus being on improving customer's benefit/cost ratio or on lowering total cost
   I. Where more emphasis is placed on radical, generational, or incremental and product or process innovation
   J. What strategic significance is assigned to learning (on an individual, group, and organizational level) within your company and for what reasons
   K. What strategic significance is assigned to the length of top management tenure and the specific corporate governance structure prevailing in your company

References

Aaker, D. A., Managing assets and skills: the key to sustainable competitive advantage, *Calif. Manage. Rev.*, 31:2, 91, Winter 1989.

Adler, P. (Ed.), *Technology and the Future of Work*, Oxford University Press, Oxford, U.K., 1992.

Allison, G., *The Essence of Decision*, Little, Brown, New York, 1971.

Amit, R. and Shoemaker, P., Strategic assets and organizational rent, *Strategic Manage. J.*, 14, 33, 1993.

Andrews, K., *The Concept of Corporate Strategy*, Irwin, Homewood, IL, 1965.

Ansoff, I., *Corporate Strategy*, McGraw-Hill, New York, 1965.

Ansoff, I., *Concept of Strategic Management*, McGraw-Hill, New York, Summer 1972.

Ansoff, I., *Implanting Strategic Management*, John Wiley & Sons, New York, 1984.

Ansoff, I., *The New Corporate Strategy*, John Wiley & Sons, New York, 1988.

Ansoff, I., Critique of Henry Minztberg's "The Design School": reconsidering the basic premises of strategic management, *Strategic Manage. J.*, 12, 449, 1991.

Argyris, C., *Strategy, Change, and Defensive Routines*, Pitman, New York, 1985.

Argyris, C., *Overcoming Organizational Defenses: Facilitating Organizational Learning*, Allyn & Bacon, New York, 1990.

Argyris, C. and Schoen, D., *Organizational Learning: A Theory of Action Perspective*, Addison-Wesley, New York, 1978.

Arthur, W. B., Increasing returns and the new world of business, *Harv. Bus. Rev.*, July–August, 100, 1996.

Atomic Energy Commission of Japan, White Paper on Nuclear Energy, 1992 (unofficial translation).

Atomic Energy Act of 1959, Public Law No. 79–585, Chapter 724.

Bahrami, H. and Evans, S., Strategy making in high technology firms: the empiricist mode, *Calif. Manage. Rev.*, 31: 2, 107, Winter 1989.

Barnard, C., *The Functions of the Executive*, Harvard University Press, Cambridge, MA, 1938.

Barney, J., Strategic factor markets: expectations, luck and business strategy, *Manage. Sci.*, 32, 1231, 1986.

Barney, J., Firm resources and sustained competitive advantage, *J. Manage.*, 1, 99, 1991.

Baron, J., *Thinking and Deciding*, Cambridge University Press, Cambridge, MA, 1988.

Bartunek, J., First-order, second-order, and third-order change and organization development interventions: a cognitive approach, *J. Appl. Behav. Sci.*, 23, 4, 1987.

Bateson, G., *Steps to an Ecology of Mind: A Revolutionary Approach to Man's Understanding of Himself*, Ballantine Books, New York, 1972.

Bierly, P. and Chakrabarty, A., Technological learning and financial performance, in Hantula, D. A., Ed., *Virtual Proceedings of the 1996 Meeting of the Eastern Academy of Management*, Crystal City, VA, 1996.

Bode, E., *Control Theory*, McGraw-Hill, New York, 1960.

Boeing Annual Report, Washington State, 1992.

Bourgeois, F. and Brodwin, S., *Five Steps to Strategic Action*, Free Press, New York, 1984.

Brandenburger, A. M. and Nalebuff, B. J., *Co-opetition*, Doubleday, New York, 1996.

Braybrook, D. and Lindblom, C., *A Strategy of Decision: Policy Evaluation as a Social Process*, Free Press, New York, 1963.

Brown, G., *On Cognition*, McGraw-Hill, New York, 1948.

Burgelman, R. and Rosenbloom, R., Technology strategy: an evolutionary process perspective, in *Research on Technological Innovation, Management and Policy*, Vol. 4, JAI Press, Greenwich, CT, 1989, 1.

Campbell, J., *The Power of Myth*, Doubleday, New York, 1988.

Carayannis, E. and Maldifassi, J., Improving the quality of the management of nuclear technology: technical, financial, and organizational measures for assessing the performance of nuclear utilities. *Working Paper No. 128*, School of Management, Rensselaer Polytechnic Institute, Troy, New York, 1991.

Carayannis, E. and Maldifassi, J., Improving nuclear technology management: technical, financial, and organizational measures for assessing the performance of nuclear utilities, *Int. J. Global Energy Issues*, 4(3), 1992.

Carayannis, E., An Integrative Framework of Strategic Decision Making Paradigms and their Empirical Validity: The Case for Strategic or Active Incrementalism and the Import of Tacit Technological Learning, *Working Paper Series No. 131*, School of Management Rensselaer Polytechnic Institute, Troy, New York, 1992a.

Carayannis, E., Incrementalisme strategique, *Le Progres Tech.* (Paris), 1993.

Carayannis, E., The strategic management of technological learning from dynamically adaptive high tech marketing perspective: sustainable competitive advantage through effective supplier–customer interfacing, in UIC/AMA Research Symp. Marketing and Entrepreneurship, Paris, France, June 29–30, 1994.

Carayannis, E., A multi-national, resource-based view of training and development and the strategic management of technological learning: keys for social and corporate survival and success, in 39th ICSB Annual World Conf., Strasbourg, France, June 27–29, 1994a.

Carayannis, E., The Strategic Management of Technological Learning: Transnational Decision-Making Frameworks and Their Empirical, Ph.D. dissertation, School of Management, Rensselaer Polytechnic Institute, Troy, New York, 1994b.

Carayannis, E., La gestion strategique de l'acquisition des savoirs-faire, *Le Progres Tech. (Paris)*, No. 1, 1994c.

Carayannis, E. and Kassicieh, S., The relationship between market performance and higher order technological learning in high technology industries, 5th Int. Conf. on Management of Technology, Miami, FL, February 27–March 1, 1996.

Carayannis E., Re-engineering high risk, high complexity industries through multiple level technological learning: a case study of the world nuclear power industry, *J. Eng. Tech. Manage.*, 12, 301, 1996a.

Carayannis, E. and Stokes, R., A historical analysis of management of technology at Badische Anilin und Soda Fabrik (BASF) AG, 1865 to 1993: a case study, *J. Eng. Tech. Manage.*, 14, 175, 1997.

Carayannis, E., Higher order technological learning as determinant of market success in the multimedia arena; a success story, a failure, and a question mark: Agfa/Bayer AG, Enable Software, and Sun Microsystems, *Technovation*, 18(10), 639, 1998.

Carayannis, E., The strategic management of technological learning in project/program management: the role of extranets, intranets and intelligent agents in knowledge generation, diffusion, and leveraging, *Technovation*, 18(11), 697, 1998a.

Carayannis, E. and Alexander, J., The wealth of knowledge: converting intellectual property to intellectual capital in co-opetitive research and technology management settings, *Int. J. Tech. Manage.*, 17(3/4), 1998b.

Carayannis, E. and Alexander, J., Secrets of success and failure in commercializing U.S. government R&D laboratories technologies: a structured case studies approach, *Int. J. Tech. Manage.*, 17(3/4), 1998c.

Carayannis, E. and Jorge, J., Bridging government-university-industry technological learning disconnects: a comparative study of training and development policies and practices in the U.S., Japan, Germany, and France, *Technovation*, 1(6/7), 383, 1998d.

Carayannis, E. and Rogers, E., High-technology spin-offs from government r&d laboratories and research universities, *Technovation*, 18(1), 1, 1998e.

Carayannis, E. and Rogers, E., Cooperative research and development agreements (CRADAS) as technology transfer mechanisms, *R&D Manage.*, Spring 1998f.

Carayannis, E. and Hazlett, J., Business–university virtual teaming for strategic planning, *Tech. Forecasting Soc. Change*, 57(3), 261, 1998g.

Carayannis, E., Higher order technological learning as determinant of market success in the multimedia arena; a success story, a failure, and a question mark: AGFA/Bayer AG, Enable Software, and Sun Microsystems, *Technovation*, 18(10), 639, 1998h.

Carayannis, E., Fostering synergies between information technology and managerial and organizational cognition: the role of knowledge management, *Technovation*, 12, 1999.

Carayannis, E., Organizational transformation and strategic learning in high risk, high complexity environments, *Technovation*, 13, 1999a.

Carayannis, E., Knowledge transfer through technological hyperlearning in five industries, *Technovation*, 19(3), 141, 1999b.

Carayannis, E. and Alexander, J., Winning by competing in knowledge-driven, complex environments: the formation of strategic technology government–university–industry (GUI) partnerships, *J. Technol. Transfer.*, 24(2/3), 197, August 1999c.

Carayannis, E. and Egorov, I., Transforming the post-soviet research system through technological entrepreneurship, *J. Technol. Transfer.*, 24(2/3), 159, August 1999d.

Carayannis E., Re-engineering rehabilitative health care delivery in the nineties and beyond: a systems approach to medical technology, quality, and cost management, *Int. J. Healthcare Technol. Manage.* (Special Issue on the Advances in the Management of Technology in Health Care), 1(1/2), 180, 1999e.

Carayannis, E. and Forbes, J., An interpretive formulation of systems engineering: lessons learned from success and failure in the U.S. Department of Defense procurement and logistics systems, *Technovation*, in press.

Carayannis, E., Learning more, better, and faster: a multi-industry, longitudinal, empirical validation of technological learning as the key source of sustainable competitive advantage in high-technology firms, *Technovation*, in press.

Carayannis, E. and Samanta, R., Davids vs. Goliaths in the small satellite industry: the role of technological innovation dynamics in firm competitiveness, *Technovation*, in press.

Carayannis, E., Kassicieh, S., and Radosevich, R., Strategic alliances as a source of early-stage seed capital in technology-based, entrepreneurial firms, *Technovation*, in press.

Carayannis, E., Alexander, J., and Ioannidis, I., Leveraging knowledge, learning, and innovation in forming strategic government-university-industry (GUI) R&D partnerships in the U.S., Germany, and France, *Technovation*, in press.

Chandler, A., *Strategy and Structure: Chapters in the History of the Industrial Enterprise*, MIT Press, Cambridge, MA, 1962.

Christensen, C., *Innovation and the General Manager*, Irwin-McGraw-Hill, New York, 1999.

Ciborra, C. U. and Schneider, L. S., Transforming the routines and contexts of management, work and technology, in *Technology and the Future of Work*, Adler, P. S., Ed., MIT Press, Cambridge, MA, 1992.

Clausewitz, K., *On War*, Penguin, New York, 1832.

Cohen, W. and Leventhal, D., Absorptive capacity: a new perspective on learning and innovation. *Adm. Sci. Q.*, 35(1), 128, 1990.

Cole, R., *Strategies for Learning: Small Group Activities in American, Japanese, and Swedish Industry*, Berkeley University Press, Berkeley, CA, 1989.

Collingridge, D., *Critical Decision Making: A New Theory of Social Choice*, St. Martin's Press, New York, 1982.

Consolidated Edison (ConEd), New York State, Annual Report, 1988.

Consolidated Edison (ConEd), New York State, Annual Report, 1990.

Cyert, R. M. and March, J. G., *A Behavioral Theory of the Firm*, Prentice-Hall, Englewood Cliffs, NJ, 1963.

Daimler-Benz High Tech Report, Stuttgart, Germany, February 1994.

D'Aveni, R., *Hyper-competition: Managing the Dynamics of Strategic Maneuvering*, Free Press, New York, 1994.

Davis, E., *Strategy of Decision*, Wiley, New York, 1984.

Day, M., The learning organization, *Plant Eng. Maint.*, 16:6, 21, October/November, 1993.

De Geus, A., Planning as learning, *Harv. Bus. Rev.*, 66:2, 70, Winter 1988.

de Mey, M., *The Cognitive Paradigm*, Reidel, New York, 1982.

Dewey, J., *The Need for a Recovery Philosophy*, Southern Illinois University Press, Carbondale, IL, 1917.

DiBella, A. J., Nevis, E. C., and Gould, J. M., Organizational learning style as a core capability, in Moingeon, B. and Edmondson, A., Eds., *Organizational Learning and Competitive Advantage*, SAGE, London, 1996.

Dodgson, M., *The Management of Technological Learning: Lessons from a Biotechnology Company*, de Gruyter, Berlin, 1991.

Drucker, P., *The New Realities*, Harper & Row, New York, 1989.

Duke Power Corp., North Carolina, Annual Report, 1993.

Dussauge, P., *Technology and Strategic Management*, HEC, Paris, 1988.

Edmondson, A. and Moingeon, B., When to learn how and when to learn why: appropriate organizational learning processes as a source of competitive advantage in Moingeon, B. and Edmondson, A., Eds., *Organizational Learning and Competitive Advantage*, SAGE Publications, London, 1996.

Eisenhardt, K. and Burgeois, Politics of strategic decision-making in high-velocity environments, *J. Acad. Manage.*, Dec., 31-4, 737, 1988.

Eisenhardt, K., Building theories from Can. study research, *Acad. Mgt. Rev.*, Oct. 14: 4, 532, 1989.

Eisenhardt, K., Speed and strategic choice: how managers accelerate decision making, *Calif. Manage. Rev.*, Winter 1990.

Emery, J. and Trist, I., *Organizational Transformation*, Wiley, New York, 1965.

Etzioni A., Mixed scanning revisited, *Public Adm. Rev.*, 46:1, 8, January–February 1986.

Etzioni, A., Humble decision making, *Harv. Bus. Rev.*, 67:4, 122, July–August 1989.

Flesher, C., BMW R&D, *Roundel*, June 1992.

Fodor, J., *The Language of Thought*, Harvard University Press, Cambridge, MA, 1980.

Follett, M., *The Creative Experience*, Harvard University Press, Cambridge, MA, 1924.

Ford, D., Develop your technology strategy, *Long Range Plann.*, 21: 85, 1988.

Forrester, J., *The Impact of Feedback Control Concepts on the Management Sciences*, John Wiley & Sons, New York, 1960.

Frederickson, J., *Human Resource Accounting*, CEDEFOP, Lanham, MD, 1998.

Fredrickson, J., *Perspectives on Strategic Management*, Harper Business, New York, 1990.

Fredrickson, J. and Iaquinto, A., Bounded rationality and the politics of muddling through, *Publ. Admin. Rev.*, 44: 23-31, 1989.

Fredrickson, J. and Mitchell, T., Strategic decision process, *Acad. Mgmt. J.*, 27, 399–423, 1994.

Freud, S. *Future of An Illusion*, Norton, New York, 1973.

Frost, R., *Alternating Currents: Nationalized Power in France, 1946–1970*, Cornell University Press, Ithaca, New York, 1991.

Gioia, D. and Sims, H., *The Thinking Organization*, Jossey Bass, San Francisco, 1986.

Gleick, J., *Chaos: Making a New Science*, Viking Penguin, New York, 1987.

Goodwin, A., *Conflict in Europe, 1783–1915*, Carendon Press, Oxford, U.K., 1951.

Granstand, O., Towards a theory of the technology-based firm, *Res. Policy*, 27, 465, 1998.

Grant, R., The resource-based theory of competitive advantage: implications for strategy formulation, *Calif. Manage. Rev.*, Spring 1991.

Griliches, Z., Patent statistics as economic indicators, *J. Econ. Lit.*, 28, 1661, 1990.

Hagedoorn, J. and Schakenraad, J., The effect of strategic technology alliances on company performance, *Strategic Manage. J.*, 15, 291, 1994.

Halsted, M., *Henri Poincare*, Editions Larousse, Paris, 1913.

Hammermesh, R., *Making Strategy Work: How Senior Managers Produce Results*, John Wiley & Sons, New York, 1985.

Hedberg, B., How organizations learn and unlearn, in Nystrom, M. and Starbuck, M., Eds., *Handbook of Organizational Design*, Oxford University Press, New York, 1981.

Hegel, F., *Philosophy of History*, Penguin, New York, 1948.

Henderson, R., Managing Information in the innovation age, *Harv. Bus. Rev.*, 100–106, January–February, 1994.

Hollings, C.S., *Resilience of Ecosystems: Local Surprise and Global Change*, Cambridge University Press, Cambridge, U.K., 1986.

Huber, G. P., Organizational learning: the contributing processes and the literature, *Organ. Sci.*, 2(1), 88, 1991.

Hughes, T.P., *Networks of Power: Electrification in Western Society, 1880 to 1930*, Johns Hopkins University Press, Baltimore, MD, 1983.

Hurwitz, D., *Control Theory*, Penguin, New York, 1895.

Iansiti, M., Technology integration: managing technological evolution in a complex environment, *Res. Policy*, 24, 521, 1995.

Itami, H. and Roehl, T., *Mobilizing Invisible Assets*, Harvard University Press, Cambridge, MA, 1987.

Jacobson, R., The "Austrian" school of strategy, *Acad. Manage. Rev.*, 4, 782, 1992.

Jaggar, G., *Feminist Philosophy*, Penguin, New York, 1983.

James, W., *The Principles of Psychology*, Dover, New York, 1950.

Jantsch, E. and Waddington, C., *Evolution and Consciousness: Human Systems in Transition*, Addison-Wesley, New York, 1976.

Jelinek, M., *Institutionalizing Innovation: A Study of Organizational Learning Systems*, Praeger, New York, 1979.

Johnson, C., Japan 2000 Report: Observations about a Firestorm, June 20, 1991.

Jung, C., *On Schizophrenia*, Penguin, New York, 1958.

Khanna, T., Gulati, R., and Nohria, N., The dynamics of learning alliances: competition, cooperation and relative scope, *Strategic Manage. J.*, 19, 193, 1998.

Killman, R., *Gaining Control of the Corporate Culture*, McGraw-Hill, New York, 1985.

Kochan, T. and Useem, M., *Transforming Organizations*, Oxford University Press, Oxford, U.K., 1992.

Krogh von, G. and Vicari, S., An autopoiesis approach to experimental strategic learning, in *Implanting Strategic Processes: Change, Learning, and Co-operation*, Lorange, P. et al., Eds., Basil Blackwell, London, 1993.

Kuhn, T., *The Structure of Scientific Revolutions*, University of Chicago Press, Chicago, 1970.

Leonard-Barton, D. A., Core capabilities and core rigidities: a paradox in managing new product development, *Strategic Manage. J.*, 13, 111, 1992.

Levitt, B. and March, J. G., Organizational learning, *Annu. Rev. Sociol.*, 14, 319, 1988.

Lindblom, C., *The Science of Muddling Through*, Oxford University Press, New York, 1959.

Lindblom, C., *The Intelligence of Democracy*, Free Press, New York, 1965.

Lindblom, C. *Disjointed Incrementalism*, Oxford University Press, New York, 1980.

Linstone, H., *Multiple Perspectives for Decision Making: Bridging the Gap between Analysis and Action*, North-Holland, New York, 1984.

Lotka, A., *Elements of Control Theory*, Addison Wesley, Reading, MA, 1925.

Louis, J., *Organizational Cultures*, Penguin, New York, 1985.

Lukacs, J., *Der Junge Hegel*, Springer-Vertlag, Vienna, Austria, 1948.

Lyapunov, T., *Control Theory*, Penguin, New York, 1892.

Machlup, F., Marginal analysis and empirical research, *Am. Econ. Rev.*, 36, 519, 1946.

March, J. and Simon, H., *Organizations*, John Wiley & Sons, New York, 1958.

Martin, J., *Cultures in Organizations: Three Perspectives*, Oxford University Press, Oxford, U.K., 1992.

Matra Annual Report, Paris, 1992.

Maxwell, J., *On Electromagnetism*, Penguin, New York, 1882.

Mayr, D., *A Taxonomy of Species Definitions*, McGraw-Hill, New York, 1970.

McCann, J.E. and Selsky, J., Hyperturbulence and the emergence of type 5 environments, *Acad. Mgmt. Rev.*, 9, 3, 1984.

Miner, J., Type of entrepreneur, type of firm, and managerial motivation: implications for organizational life-cycle theory, *J. Strat. Mgt.*, Oct./Dec. 4:4, 325, 1983.

Mintzberg, H., *The Nature of the Managerial Work*, McGraw-Hill, New York, 1971.

Mintzberg, H., Patterns in strategy formation, *Manage. Sci.*, 24(9), 934, 1978.

Mintzberg, H., *Mintzberg on Management*, Free Press, New York, 1989.

Mintzberg, H., The design school: reconsidering the basic premises of strategic management, *Strategic Manage. J.*, 11, 171, 1990.

Mintzberg H., *Perspectives on Strategic Management*, Fredrickson, J., Ed., Ballinger Press, New York, 1990.

Mintzberg, H., Brief case: strategy and intuition — a conversation with Henry Mintzberg, *Long Range Plann.*, 2, 108, 1991a.

Mintzberg, H., Learning 1 planning 0: reply to Igor Ansoff, *Strategic Manage. J.*, 12, 463, 1991b.

Mitchell, J., *Shared Decision Making: The Benefits and the Pitfalls*, Wiley, New York, 1990.

Moore, J., *The Death of Competition*, Harper Collins, New York, 1996.

Morone, J., Strategic use of technology, *Calif. Manage. Rev.*, 31:4, 91, Summer 1989.

Morone, J. and Woodhouse, E., *Averting Catastrophe: Strategies for Regulating Risky Technologies*, University of California Press, Berkeley, CA, 1986.

Morone, J. and Woodhouse, E., *The Demise of Nuclear Energy? Lessons for a Democratic Control of Technology*, Yale University Press, New Haven, CT, 1989.

Morone, J., *Winning in High Technology Industries*, Harvard Business School Press, Cambridge, 1993.

Morrow, W., *The Human Zero*, Penguin, New York, 1981.

Mumby, D. and Putnam, L., The politics of emotion: a feminist reading of bounded rationality, *Acad. Manage. Rev.*, 7, 478, 1992.

Nanda, A., Resources, capabilities, and competencies, in Moingeon, B. and Edmondson, A., Eds., *Organizational Learning and Competitive Advantage*, SAGE, London, 1996.

National Academy of Engineering, *Management of Technology: The Hidden Advantage*, National Academy Press, Washington, D.C., 1987.

Nelson, R., How do firms differ, and why does it matter?, *Strategic Manage. J.*, 12, 61, 1991.

Nelson, R. and Winter, S., *An Evolutionary Theory of Economic Change*, John Wiley & Sons, New York, 1982.

Nickerson, J., Strategic objectives supported by licensing, in Parr, R. and Sullivan, P., Eds., *Technology Licensing: Corporate Strategies for Maximizing Value*, John Wiley & Sons, New York, 1996.

Nielsen, R., Woolman's "I am we" triple-loop action-learning: origin and application in organization ethics, *J. Appl. Behav. Sci.*, March, 1993.

Nonaka, I., Toward middle up-down management: accelerating information creation, *Sloan Mgmt. Rev.*, Spring, 9, 1988.

Nonaka, I., Creating organizational order out of chaos: self-renewal in Japanese firms, *Calif. Manage. Rev.*, 30:3, 57, Spring 1988.

Nonaka, I., A dynamic theory of organizational knowledge creation, *Organ. Sci.*, 5:1, 14 February 1994.

Nonaka, I. and Takeuchi, H., *The Knowledge-Creating Company*, Oxford University Press, Oxford, U.K., 1995.

Nuclear Operations Strategy (NOSI), May 1989.

Ontario Hydro, Annual Report, Ontario, Canada, 1991.

Pascale, R. T., *Perspectives on Strategy; the Real Story behind Honda's Success*, Simon and Schuster, New York, 1984.

Penrose, E., *Theory of Growth of the Firm*, John Wiley & Sons, New York, 1959.

Peteraf, M. A., The cornerstones of competitive advantage: a resource-based view, *Strategic Manage. J.*, 14, 179, 1993.

Plato, On leadership, in *The Republic*, Cambridge University Press, Cambridge, 1957.

Polanyi, M., *Personal Knowledge*, University of Chicago Press, Chicago, 1958.

Polanyi, M., *The Tacit Dimension*, Doubleday, New York, 1966.

Polanyi, M., *Knowing and Being*, University of Chicago Press, Chicago, 1969.

Porter, M., *Competitive Strategy: Techniques for Analyzing Industries and Competitors*, Free Press, New York, 1980.

Porter, M., *Competitive Advantage: Creating and Sustaining Superior Performance*, Free Press, New York, 1985.

Porter, M., *The Competitive Advantage of Nations*, Free Press, New York, 1990.

Porter, M., Towards a dynamic theory of strategy, *Strategic Manage. J.*, 12, 95, 1991.

Prahalad, C. K. and Hamel, G., The core competence of the corporation, *Har. Bus. Rev.*, 68:3, 79, May–June, 1990.

Prigogine, I., *From Being to Becoming: Time and Complexity in the Physical Sciences*, Freeman, New York, 1980.

Prigogine, I. and Nicolic, G., *Exploring Complexity*, Freeman, New York, 1989.

Quinn, J. B., *Strategies for Change: Logical Incrementalism*, Irwin, Chicago, 1980.

Quinn, J. B., *Managing Strategies Incrementally*, Irwin, New York, 1982.

Quinn, J. B., *The Intelligent Enterprise: A New Paradigm*, Free Press, New York, 1992.

Reitman, W., *Decision Making*, Wiley, New York, 1976.

Richardson, G., *Feedback Thought in Social Sciences and Systems*, Wiley, New York, 1991.

Rochester Gas and Electric (RG&E), Annual Report, 1990.

Rochester Gas and Electric (RG&E), Nuclear Operations Strategy Implementation (NOSI), Rochester, New York, May 1989.

Rogers, E., *The Diffusion of Innovations*, Free Press, New York, 1983.

Romanelli, E., New venture strategies in the minicomputer industry, *Calif. Mgmt. Rev.*, 30:1, 160, 1987.

Rosenbloom, R., *Engines of Innovation*, Harvard University Press, Cambridge, MA, 1996.

Rosenblueth, R., Wiener, N., and Bigelow, C., *Control Theory*, Wiley, New York, 1943.

Routh, E., *On Feedback Control*, Penguin, New York, 1877.

Sahal, D., *Patterns of Technological Innovation*, Addison-Wesley, New York, 1982.

Saint Gobain, A Commitment to Excellence in Materials, Paris, France, 1993.

Saint Gobain, Annual Report, Paris, France, 1991.

Sanchez, R., Strategic flexibility, firm organization, and managerial work in dynamic markets: a strategic-options perspective, in *Advances in Strategic Management*, Shirvastava, P., Huff, A. S., and Dutton, J., Eds., Vol. 9, JAI Press, Greenwich, CT, 1993.

Saridis, G., Analytic Formulation of the Principle of Increasing Precision with Decreasing Intelligence, CIRSSE, Report No. 5, 1987.

Schein, E., *Organizational Culture and Leadership*, Jossey Bass, New York, 1992.

Schoen, D., *The Reflective Practitioner: How Professionals Think in Action*, Basic Books, New York, 1983.

Schoen, D., *The Reflective Turn*, Teachers' College Press, New York, 1991.

Selznick, P., *Leadership in Administration: A Sociological Interpretation*, Row, Peterson, New York, 1957.

Senge, P., *The Fifth Discipline: The Art and Practice of the Learning Organization*, Doubleday, New York, 1990.

Simon, H. A., On the application of servomechanism theory in the study of production control, *Econometrica*, 20, 247, 1952.

Simon, H., *The Architecture of Complexity*, MIT Press, Cambridge, MA, 1957.

Simon, H., Programs as factors of production, Proceeding of the Industrial Relations Research Assoc., 1967.

Simon, H., *The Sciences of the Artificial*, MIT Press, Cambridge, MA, 1969.

Simon, H., Managerial decision making: the role of intuition and emotion, in intuition in organizations: leading and managing productively, Weston, A., Ed., SAGE, New York, 1987.

Simon, H. and March, J., *Organizations*, Wiley, New York, 1958.

Sims, R., *An Experiential Learning Approach to Employee Training Systems*, Quorum Books, New York, 1990.

Spender, J.-C., Making knowledge the basis of a dynamic theory of the firm, *Strategic Manage. J.*, 17, 45, 1996.

Steinbruner, J., *The Cybernetic Theory of Decision*, Princeton University Press, Princeton, NJ, 1974.

Sternberg, R. and Frensch, P., *Complex Problem Solving: Principles and Mechanisms*, Lawrence Erlbaum, New York, 1991.

Teece, D. J., Profiting from technological innovation: implications for integration, collaboration, licensing, and public policy, *Res. Policy*, 15:6, 285, 1986.

Teece, D. J., Ed., *The Competitive Challenge: Strategies for Industrial Innovation and Renewal*, Bollinger, New York, 1987.

Teece, D., Pisano, G., and Shuen, A., Dynamic Capabilities and the Concept of Strategy, *University of California at Berkeley Working Paper*, 1992.

Teece, D., Pisano, G., and Shuen, A., Dynamic capabilities and strategic management, *Strategic Manage. J.*, 18, 509, 1997.

Tennessee Valley Authority (TVA), Strategic Plan, Knoxville, TN, 1992.

Tennessee Valley Authority (TVA), Generating Group Management System, Knoxville, TN, October 9, 1992.

Tornatzky, L. and Fleischer, M., *The Processes of Technological Innovation*, Lexington Books, New York, 1990.

Tustin, A., *The Shape of the Curve*, McGraw-Hill, New York, 1953.

U.S. Congress. House. *Legislative History*, 1954.

Utterback, J. and Abernathy, W., A dynamic model of process and product innovation, *Omega*, 3(6), 639, 1975.

Varela, F., *The Embodied Mind: Cognitive Science and Human Experience*, MIT Press, Cambridge, MA, 1991.

Veblen, T., *The Higher Learning in America*, Hill & Wang, New York, 1924.

Verhulst, P., *The Logistic Equation*, Penguin, London, 1838.

Volterra, N., *Volterra Equations*, Addison Wesley, Reading, MA, 1931.

von Hippel, E., Appropriability of innovation benefit as a predictor of the source of innovation, *Research Policy*, 11:2, 95, 1982.

von Hippel, E., *The Sources of Innovation*, Oxford University Press, Oxford, U.K., 1988.

Weiss, G., GE Report on the History of Technology, 1998.

Wiener, N., *Cybernetics: Control and Communication in the Animal and the Machine*, Prentice Hall, Princeton, NJ, 1948.

Wiener, N., *Cybernetics*, MIT Press, Cambridge, MA, 1961.

Williamson, O., *Markets and Hierarchies: Analysis and Antitrust Implications*, Free Press, New York, 1975.

Womack, J., Jones, D., and Roos, D., *The Machine that Changed the World: The Story of Lean Production*, Harper Collins, New York, 1989.

Review of models, *Airbus Today*, 1993.
Creativity in education: interview with NEW director, *Albany Times Union*, April 3, 1994.
Review of top ten models: BMW, Mercedes, Lexus and others, *Automob. Mag.*, Fall 1993.
Review of current best practices and models in author industry, *Automot. Eng. Int.*, May 1, 1999.
Benchmarking excellence: BMW vs. others, *Automot. News*, September 27, 1993.
Best practices review, *Assembly*, June 1998.
Bangle, C., The new three series, *BMW Mag.*, January 1994.
BMW model line-up review, *BMW Today*, 1993.
Daimler-Benz (DB) High Tech Report, Review of long term research at DB, February 1994.
Die konkurrenz in der auto industrie, Die Welt, March 30, 1994.
Gespraech mit Edzard Reuter, DB Chef, *Der Spiegel*, April 6, 1992.
Gespraech mit Edzard Reuter, DB Chef, *Der Spiegel*, March 1993.
Gespraech mit Edzard Reuter, DB Chef, *Der Spiegel*, March 15, 1993.
Gespraech mit Ebernhard von Kuenheim, BMW Chef, *Der Spiegel*, June 1993.
Boeing Corp., Report to stockholders, Annual Report, 1992.
Auto industry review, *Edge*, November 1, 1993.
Survey of the European industries, *Eur. Ind. Relations Rev.*, August 1996.
Report on the auto industry, *Forbes*, September 8, 1997.
Analysis of the aerospace industry: winners and losers, *Fortune*, June 15, 1991.
Report on the auto industry: emerging trends, *Fortune*, June 1, 1992.
Survey of the US auto industry, *Fortune*, May 15, 1994.
Die Deutsche auto industrie, standort und konkurrenz, *Frankfurter Allgemeine Zeitung*, April 15, 1994.
The US auto industry, *Investor's Business Daily*, May 27, 1993.
Analysis of high tech R&D at Mercedes, Mercedes, 1992/1993.
Mercedes, April 1993.
The state of the US nuclear industry, *Nuclear Eng. Int.*, 60, December 1998.
L'Airbus industrie: analyse et perspectives, *Paris-Match*, May 1992.
Bristol Myers-Squibb: secrets of success, *Pharm. Executive*, October 1995.
Europe vs. US: an industry review, *Prism*, 2Q98, 1984.
Owner report, Roundel, June 1992.
Head bolts fail, *Roundel*, November 1992.
One lap of America, *Roundel*, September 1993.
The US auto industry: a survey, *U.S. News World Rep.*, July 30, 1997.
Airbus vs. Boeing: a look ahead, *USA Today*, September 23, 1993.
Wall Street Journal (New York), September 12, 1991.
Wall Street Journal (New York), March 30, 1992.
Wall Street Journal (New York), August 26, 1992.
Wall Street Journal (New York), November 19, 1992.
Wall Street Journal (New York), December 30, 1992.
Wall Street Journal (New York), January 25, 1993.
Wall Street Journal (New York), January 28, 1993.
Wall Street Journal (New York), February 4, 1993.
Wall Street Journal (New York), May 14, 1993.
Wall Street Journal (New York), May 15, 1993.
Wall Street Journal (New York), May 27, 1993.
Wall Street Journal (New York), June 15, 1993.
Wall Street Journal (New York), September 23, 1993.
Wall Street Journal (New York), October 10, 1993.

Wall Street Journal (New York), December 8, 1993.
Wall Street Journal (New York), December 1993.
Wall Street Journal (New York), December 16, 1993.
Wall Street Journal (New York), December 25, 1993.
Wall Street Journal (New York), February 1, 1994.
Wall Street Journal (New York), February 11, 1994.
Wall Street Journal (New York), February 14, 1994.
Wall Street Journal (New York), February 23, 1994.
Wall Street Journal (New York), March 4, 1994.
Wall Street Journal (New York), March 10, 1994.
Wall Street Journal (New York), April 13, 1994.
Wall Street Journal (New York), April 14, 1994.
Wall Street Journal (New York), May 4, 1994.
Wall Street Journal (New York), May 11, 1994.
Wall Street Journal (New York), June 13, 1994.
Wall Street Journal (New York), July 21, 1994.
Wall Street Journal (New York), March 17, 2000.
Ward's Automot. Int., July 1993.
Washington Post, March 28, 2000.
Workforce, May 1997.

Index